ECONOGUIDE® DISNEYLAND® RESORT, UNIVERSAL STUDIOS HOLLYWOOD®

ECONOGUIDE® SERIES

ECONOGUIDE® DISNEYLAND® RESORT, UNIVERSAL STUDIOS® HOLLYWOOD

And Other Major Southern California Attractions Including Disney's California Adventure®

Fourth Edition

COREY SANDLER

INSIDERS' GUIDE®

GUILFORD, CONNECTICUT
AN IMPRINT OF THE GLOBE PEQUOT PRESS

The prices and rates listed in this guidebook were confirmed at press time. We recommend, however, that you call establishments to obtain current information before traveling.

To buy books in quantity for corporate use or incentives, call **(800) 962–0973, ext. 4551,** or e-mail **premiums@GlobePequot.com.**

INSIDERS' GUIDE®

Text design by Lesley Weissman-Cook
Maps created by Stefanie Ward © Morris Book Publishing, LLC.

ISSN 1540-6121
ISBN 0-7627-3872-3

Manufactured in the United States of America
Fourth Globe Pequot Press Edition/First Printing

To Willie and Tessa,
May their lives always be a magic theme park

CONTENTS

Acknowledgments

As always, dozens of hard-working and creative people helped move my words from the keyboard to the book you hold in your hands.

Among the many to thank are Mary Luders Norris of Globe Pequot Press; we look forward to many years of partnership. Thanks, too, to the editorial and production staff at Globe Pequot, including Elizabeth Taylor, Amy Paradysz, Melissa Evarts, and Joanna Beyer.

Gene Brissie has been a believer for more than a decade, and the feeling is mutual. Ed Claflin has signed on for the next chapter.

My appreciation extends to the public relations staffs who helped me with my research.

As always, thanks to Janice Keefe for running the office and putting up with me, a pair of major assignments.

And thanks to you for buying this book. We all hope you find it of value; please let us know how we can improve the book in future editions. (Please enclose a stamped envelope if you'd like a reply; no phone calls, please.)

Corey Sandler
Econoguide Travel Books
P.O. Box 2779
Nantucket, MA 02584

To send electronic mail, use the following address:
info@econoguide.com.
You can also consult our Web page at:
www.econoguide.com.

I hope you'll also consider the other books in the Econoguide series. You can find them at bookstores, or ask your bookseller to order them. All are written by Corey Sandler.
Econoguide Walt Disney World, Universal Orlando
Econoguide Las Vegas
Econoguide to Buying or Leasing a Car
Econoguide to Buying and Selling a Home
Econoguide Cruises

Also by Corey Sandler:
Fix Your Own PC, Seventh Edition
Watching Baseball by Jerry Remy with Corey Sandler

INTRODUCTION TO THE FOURTH EDITION

Disneyland occupies a critical piece of our global cultural DNA. There's not a place on the planet where Mickey Mouse and the fantasy theme parks that celebrate his creator's vision are not known.

And somewhat to the amazement of children of all ages, the park built on Mickey's broad shoulders celebrated its fiftieth birthday in 2005 with a party that will continue all the way through to the end of 2006. The hoopla includes new and improved attractions, parades, and a spectacular nighttime fireworks show.

Party favors include:

- **Buzz Lightyear Astro Blasters** at Tomorrowland, a high-tech intergalactic shoot-'em-up, including a new feature that allows people at home to play along with guests on the ride.
- *Disneyland: The First 50 Magical Years* on Main Street, a humorous historical trip through Walt Disney's dreams . . . as seen through the eyes of two of the park's most famous alums, Steve Martin and Donald Duck.
- **Walt Disney's Parade of Dreams** on Main Street, the latest in a long string of great moving celebrations.
- **Remember . . . Dreams Come True** fireworks, which is by most judgments the most spectacular regularly scheduled air show in the world.
- **Space Mountain,** reopened after an earth-to-cosmos reconstruction.

If you've never been to Disneyland, you need to make a pilgrimage. If you haven't been there in years, you'll hardly recognize the place; the Disneyland Resort now comprises two parks: Disneyland and Disney's California Adventure.

At California Adventure, the **Twilight Zone Tower of Terror** is up and running . . . and regularly falling to earth.

And plans are under way for new attractions at both parks:

- An underwater ride based on *Finding Nemo* to fill the void left behind at Disneyland's Submarine Voyage (*Twenty Thousand Leagues Under the Sea*).
- **Mike & Sully to the Rescue,** a dark ride based on *Monsters, Inc.,* at Disney's California Adventure.
- A new soundtrack to better transmit squawks and puns of the Enchanted Tiki Room, a longtime favorite for many visitors.

THE GOLDEN STATE

We love L.A.—from the historic city itself to the make-believe world of Hollywood to the very real world of the mountains and canyons of Southern California, from the spectacular museums and fabulous new concert hall of Los Angeles to the pounding surf. I don't know of many other places with so much to do, so many interesting places to visit . . . and so many ways to spend your hard-earned dollars.

This book is not a guide to California on $5.00 a day; that's not a realistic goal, and it's not the way we look at the world. Rather, our goal is to help readers get the most for their time and money at whatever level they travel, ultraluxury to superbudget. If there's a way to get more and pay less, we'll help you find it; if an attraction is not worth a visit, you won't find it here.

We cover familiar—and rapidly changing—places, including Disneyland, Disney's California Adventure, Universal Studios Hollywood, Universal Studios CityWalk, Knott's Berry Farm, Six Flags Magic Mountain, the big-city appeals of Los Angeles, and the tinsel dreams of Hollywood. We also journey farther afield in Southern California, from Palm Springs, Santa Barbara, and Malibu down to San Juan Capistrano and SeaWorld in San Diego.

You'll find our selection shows the best places to visit and the best ways to do so. We've included Web addresses, telephone numbers, and price ranges for hundreds of attractions, museums, and hotels.

That other book about Disneyland, the one with "The Official Guide" on its cover, is an interesting collection of material. But in our humble opinion it suffers from a fatal closeness to its subject: It is prepared by the Walt Disney Company. We suspect this explains why it finds very little that is anything less than wonderful within the boundaries of the Disneyland Resort, and why it almost ignores the world outside.

Another feature of this book is the exclusive section of special offers to travelers. A savvy consumer can easily save hundreds of dollars on a trip by using some of the discount coupons we publish. An important note: The author and publisher of this book have no connection or financial interest in any of the coupons or companies presented.

The Econoguide Best of Los Angeles and Southern California

▶ Disneyland

▶ Disney's California Adventure

▶ Downtown Disney

▶ Universal Studios Hollywood

▶ Universal CityWalk

▶ Knott's Berry Farm

▶ Six Flags Magic Mountain

▶ SeaWorld California

▶ TV Show Tapings

▶ Warner Bros. Studio VIP Tours

▶ The *Queen Mary*

▶ Downtown Los Angeles Museums

THEME-PARK ATTENDANCE CHAMPS

The Walt Disney Company continued to own the top five spots in theme-park attendance in 2004, and six of the top eight parks, according to the trade magazine *Amusement Business*. In Orlando Walt Disney World was the big guy in town, followed by Universal's two parks and SeaWorld Orlando.

Overall attendance at North American amusement parks increased by about

4 percent in 2004, ending a two-year slump. The magazine estimates that 169.1 million guests passed through the turnstiles at the top fifty parks.

Here are the magazine's estimates:

1. **The Magic Kingdom,** Walt Disney World, Orlando: 15.17 million visitors, up 8 percent from 2003.

2. **Disneyland,** Anaheim: 13.36 million, up 5 percent.

3. **Epcot,** Walt Disney World: 9.4 million, up 9 percent.

4. **Disney–MGM Studios,** Walt Disney World: 8.26 million, up 7 percent.

5. **Disney's Animal Kingdom,** Walt Disney World: 7.82 million, up 7 percent.

6. **Universal Studios Florida,** Orlando: 6.7 million, up 14 percent.

7. **Universal's Islands of Adventure,** Orlando: 6.3 million, up 13 percent.

8. **Disney's California Adventure,** Anaheim: 5.6 million, up 6 percent.

9. **SeaWorld Orlando:** 5.6 million, up 4 percent.

10. **Universal Studios Hollywood:** 5 million, up 8 percent.

11. **Adventuredome,** Las Vegas: 4.4 million, up 2 percent.

12. **Busch Gardens,** Tampa Bay: 4.1 million, down 5 percent.

13. **SeaWorld California,** San Diego: 4 million, unchanged.

14. **Knott's Berry Farm,** Buena Park, California: 3.6 million, up 3 percent.

Other California parks:

21. **Six Flags Magic Mountain,** California: 2.7 million, down 2 percent.

PART I

SOUTHERN CALIFORNIA–BOUND

CHAPTER ONE

PLANES, TRAINS, AND AUTOMOBILES

I LOVE TO TRAVEL, but I hate to waste time and money. It all but kills me to know that I spent $200 more than I should have for an airline ticket, or that the next guy over has a nicer hotel room at a better price. Put another way, my goal is to take more vacations and spend more time in wondrous places than most people, and to have a better time while I'm at it.

Let's get something straight here, though: This book is not a guide for the cheapskate who wants a $10-a-night tour of dreadful dives and uninspiring-but-free sights. I'm perfectly willing to spend a reasonable amount of money for good value. In this book, I'll help you make the same sort of good use of your own money and time.

AIR TRAVEL

The way I figure it, one major airline is pretty much like another. Sure, one company may offer a larger bag of peanuts while the other promises its flight attendants have more accommodating smiles. Me, I'm much more interested in other things:

1. Safety
2. The most convenient schedule
3. The lowest price

Though I'm sometimes willing to trade price for convenience, I'll never risk my neck for a few dollars. But that doesn't mean I don't try my hardest to get the very best price on airline tickets. I watch the newspapers for seasonal sales and price wars, clip coupons from the usual and not-so-usual sources, consult the burgeoning world of Internet travel agencies, and happily play one airline against the other.

LOS ANGELES AREA

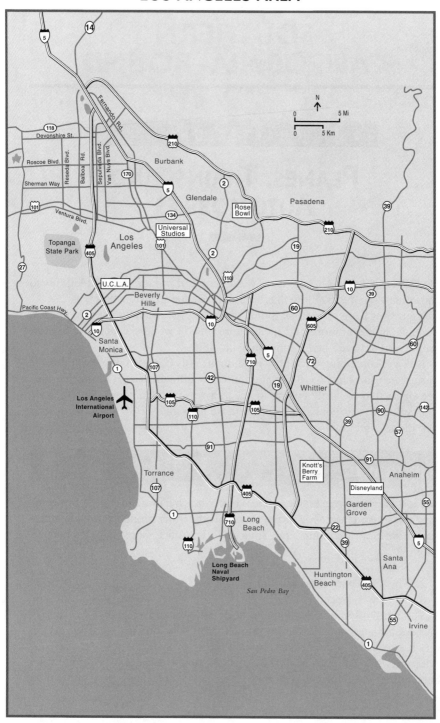

Let's start with a real-life scenario: It's September 2005 and I'm flying from Boston to Los Angeles. Available tickets, purchased in advance as a bargain special on a Web site, were quoted at $266. If I had called the airline directly, the best standard fare for the same flights would have been $258; if I had gone to a travel agent, I might have been asked to pay a service charge of as much as $25 for the privilege of buying the ticket. Or I could have taken a chance on a blind-bidding Web site where I could choose the days and airports but not the times and airlines, and paid about $250.

The least expensive flight left very early in the morning, which would have required a 5:00 A.M. commute, or left well past dinner and would have arrived after 1:00 A.M. Neither works wells for most travelers, especially vacationers who will suffer jet lag the next morning. A mid-day departure would have cost about $50 more.

Now, on that same day, there's a businesswoman making a last-minute flight to California, and she paid $649 for her ticket because the airline had raised prices as the number of available seats dwindled. She will suffer through the same plastic baggie of fried something-or-other, watch the same crummy movie, and arrive in Los Angeles hours later than me after a change of planes in Minneapolis, which is not somewhere she wanted to visit that day. And on another plane someone paid an astounding $1,328.48 for a slightly wider, plusher seat and a relatively better meal in the first class section. (I'd rather spend just some of that money on a better place to sleep and a meal at a restaurant where half the food doesn't end up in your lap.)

And depending on seasons and the variable marketing plans of the airlines, I could have saved a bit more by flying out of Providence, Rhode Island, or Manchester, New Hampshire, to California airports in Long Beach, Orange County, or Burbank that are all within an hour of Disneyland once I'm on the ground.

All of those prices are real, as I write these words. Now, consider a few more positive examples.

Somewhere else on this same plane is a couple who was bumped off a previous flight because of overbooking. They are happily discussing where to use the two free round-trip tickets they received in compensation. Up front in first class, a family of four is traveling on free tickets earned through Mom's frequent flier plan.

Me, I'm perfectly happy with that cut-rate ticket. I use some of the money I saved to buy a bag lunch to eat on the plane, and I'm daydreaming about where to use the frequent flier miles I'm earning on the airfare, hotel, and car rental. And on my trip home, depending on how busy the season and the security climate, I might try to get on the flight I really wanted to take instead of the less-convenient reservation I was forced to sign up for when I bought that cut-rate ticket.

▇ ALICE IN AIRLINELAND

In today's strange world of air travel, there is a lot of room for the dollarwise and clever traveler to wiggle. You can pay an inflated full price, you can take advantage

Double Indemnity

Your homeowner's or renter's insurance policy may include coverage for theft of your possessions while you travel, making it unnecessary to purchase a special policy. Check with your insurance agent.

of the lowest fares, or you can play the ultimate game and parlay tickets into free travel.

There are three golden rules when it comes to saving hundreds of dollars on travel—be flexible, be flexible, and be flexible. Here's how to translate that flexibility into extra dollars in your pocket:

■ Be flexible about when you choose to travel. Go during the off-season or low-season when airfares, hotel rooms, cruises, and attractions are offered at substantial discounts. Try to avoid school vacations, spring break, and the prime summer travel months of July and August, unless you enjoy a lot of company.

■ Be flexible about the day of the week you travel. In many cases you can save hundreds of dollars by bumping your departure date one or two days in either direction. Ask your travel agent or airline ticket agent for current fare rules and restrictions. If this puts you into your destination a day or two ahead of your intended arrival, use the time to become acclimated to a new time zone and to explore.

The days of lightest air travel are generally midweek, Saturday afternoon, and Sunday morning. The busiest days are Sunday evening, Monday morning, and Friday afternoon and evening. Most airlines have ended the "excursion fare," a scheme which gave the lowest fares to travelers whose stay included a Saturday; they used this as a way to exclude business travelers from the cheapest fares, assuming that businesspeople will want to be home by Friday night. Although this class of ticket may have disappeared, keep your eyes open for price differentials around the weekends.

■ Be flexible about the hour of your departure. Generally there is lower demand— and therefore lower prices—for flights that leave in the middle of the day or very late at night. The highest rates are usually assigned to breakfast-time (7:00–11:00 A.M.) and cocktail-hour (4:00–7:00 P.M.) departures.

■ Be flexible on the route you will take, and be willing to put up with a change of plane or stopover. Once again, you are putting the law of supply and demand in your favor. For example, a nonstop flight from Boston to Los Angeles for a family of four may cost hundreds more than a flight from Boston that includes a plane change in Chicago before proceeding on to California.

You should understand that in airline terminology, a "direct" flight does not mean a "nonstop" flight. Nonstop means the plane goes from Point A to Point B without stopping anywhere else. A direct flight may go from Point A to Point B, but may include a stopover at Point C or more than one airport along the way. A connecting flight means you must get off the plane at an airport en route and change to another plane. And just to add one more level of confusion, some airlines have "direct" flights that involve a change of plane along the way—the flight number stays the same but passengers have to get off at an intermediate stop, dragging all their carry-on luggage to another gate and aircraft. Go figure.

Consider flying on one of the newer, deep-discount airlines, but don't let economy cloud your judgment. Some carriers are simply better run than others. Read the newspapers, check with a trusted travel agent, and use common sense. Two of the best newer airlines also generally deliver very good service: JetBlue and Southwest. (One way they keep prices down is to operate their own online and telephone booking services; you won't find them listed on multiairline Web sites, and travel agents may not offer them as alternatives.)

Delta has a discount offshoot, Song, and United has a mini airline-within-an-airline named Ted. Even if you don't fly one of the professed cheapo airlines, they put pressure on the established carriers to lower prices or even to match fares on certain flights. Look for the cheapest fare you can find, and then call your favorite big-name airline to see if it will sell you a ticket at the same price—it just might work.

■ Don't overlook the possibility of flying out of a different airport either. For example, metropolitan New Yorkers can find domestic flights from LaGuardia, Newark, White Plains, and a developing discount mecca at Islip. Suburbanites of Boston might want to consider flights from Providence as possibly cheaper alternatives to Logan Airport. Chicago has O'Hare and Midway. From Southern California there are major airports at Los Angeles, Orange County, Burbank, Long Beach, and San Diego.

■ Plan way ahead of time and purchase the most deeply discounted advance tickets, which usually are nonrefundable. Most carriers limit the number of discount tickets on any particular flight. Although there may be plenty of seats left on the day you want to travel, they may be offered at higher rates.

■ Understand the difference between nonrefundable and noncancelable. Most airlines interpret nonrefundable to mean that they can keep all of your money if you cancel a reservation or fail to show up for a flight. You can, though, apply the value of the ticket (minus a fee of as much as $150) toward the purchase of another ticket. A noncancelable fare means that you have bought a specific seat on a specific flight. If your plans change or you are forced to cancel your trip, you lose the value of the ticket. (Think of it as missing a concert performance. You can't use the ticket another day.) Of course, if the airline cancels your flight or makes a schedule or routing change that doesn't meet your needs, you are entitled to a refund of your fare.

■ If you're feeling adventurous, you can take a big chance and wait for the last possible moment, keeping in contact with charter tour operators and accepting a bargain price on a leftover seat and hotel reservation. You may also find that some airlines will reduce the prices on leftover seats within a few weeks of your departure date; don't be afraid to check with the airline regularly or ask your travel agent to do it for you. In fact, some travel agencies have computer programs that keep a constant electronic eagle eye on available seats and fares.

■ Take advantage of special discount programs such as senior citizens' clubs, military discounts, or offerings from other organizations to which you belong. If you are in the broadly defined "senior" category, you may not even have to belong to a group such as AARP; simply ask the airline ticket agent if there is a

Mileage to/from Disneyland and Los Angeles

MILEAGE TO/FROM DISNEYLAND	Miles	Driving Time
San Juan Capistrano	27	0:31
Los Angeles	28	0:42
Hollywood	34	0:53
San Diego	93	1:49
Palm Springs	96	1:47
Santa Barbara	129	2:39
Las Vegas	271	4:56
San Francisco	407	7:54
South Lake Tahoe	498	9:48
Disney World, Florida	2,512	46:14

MILEAGE TO/FROM LOS ANGELES	Miles	Driving Time
Hollywood	6	0:11
Disneyland	28	0:42
San Juan Capistrano	54	1:13
Santa Barbara	102	1:57
Palm Springs	105	2:06
San Diego	121	2:31
Las Vegas	271	5:04
San Francisco	380	7:14
South Lake Tahoe	471	9:08
Disney World, Florida	2,521	46:33

discount available. You may have to prove your age or show a membership card when you pick up your ticket or boarding pass.

■ Consider doing business with discounters, known in the industry as consolidators or, less flatteringly, as bucket shops. These companies buy the airlines' slow-to-sell tickets in volume and resell them to consumers at rock-bottom prices. Look for their ads in the classified listings of many Sunday newspaper travel sections. Be sure to study and understand the restrictions; if they fit your needs and wants, this is a good way to fly.

You can also find ticket broker and bucket shop ads online and in classified ads in USA Today, the "Mart" section of the Wall Street Journal, the back pages of The Village Voice, or in specialty magazines aimed at frequent fliers.

Some travel agencies can also offer you consolidator tickets. Just be sure to weigh the savings on the ticket price against any restrictions attached to the tickets; for example, they may not be changeable, and they usually don't accrue frequent flier mileage.

■ Shop online through one of the Internet travel sites or the Web sites of individual airlines. You can expect to receive the lowest possible airfares—usually a few percent below the best prices offered if you call the airline directly—but little assistance in choosing among the offerings. Be sure to pay close attention to details such as the number of connections required between origin and destination. Note, too, that tickets sold in this way may have severe restrictions on changes and cancellations.

I list some of the best Internet travel booking sites and direct links to airlines later in this chapter.

■ Consider, very carefully, buying tickets from an online travel auction site such as www.priceline.com or www.hotwire.com. These sites promise to match your travel plans with available seats on major airlines at deep-discount prices; you will not be able to choose departure or arrival times or a particular airline. The way to use these sites is to do your research beforehand on one of the regular Web sites to find the best price you can; compare that with the "blind" offerings from the auction sites. Although the auction sites can often deliver the best prices, the tickets come with some detractions: You cannot time your arrival to meet a particular schedule and may have to build in an extra hotel stay at each end of the trip; it may be impossible to make changes or obtain a refund if your plans change; and you may not be permitted to stand by for another flight with your limited ticket. And read the fine print carefully: Prices may not include taxes and fees, and the sites may tack on a service charge. Be sure to compare the true bottom line with the price quoted on other Web sites or from a travel agent.

These auction sites have also begun offering a more traditional form of ticket booking, displaying the airline and flight times before you make your purchase. Be sure to check the price against another Web travel site to make sure you are receiving a real discount from the regular fare.

■ The day of the week on which you buy your tickets may also make a price difference. Airlines often test higher fares over the relatively quiet weekends. They're looking to see if their competitors will match their higher rates; if the other carriers don't bite, the fares often float back down by Monday morning. Know the prevailing rates and look for up-and-down fluctuations.

■ Use an electronic ticket when necessary. Most major airlines have dispensed with their former practice of producing a customized ticket for your travel and mailing it to you; instead you'll be given a confirmation number (sometimes called a record locator) and asked to show up at the airport with proper identification to receive your ticket and boarding pass. If you absolutely insist on receiving an actual ticket in advance of your flight, some airlines charge as much as $50 per ticket for their trouble.

In general, electronic ticketing works well. At many major airports, airlines have begun installing automated check-in machines, similar in operation to a bank's ATM. You'll be asked to insert a credit card or a frequent flier ID card just for the purposes of identification, and then the device will print out your ticket and boarding pass. A nearby attendant will take your bags and attach luggage tags.

■ OTHER MONEY-SAVING STRATEGIES

Airlines are forever weeping and gnashing their teeth about huge losses due to cutthroat competition. And then they regularly turn around and drop their prices radically with major sales. I don't waste time worrying about the bottom line of the airlines; it's my own wallet I want to keep full. Therefore, the savvy traveler keeps an eye out for airline fare wars all the time. Read the ads in newspapers and keep an ear open for news broadcasts that often cover the rash of price drops. If you have a good relationship with a travel agent, you can ask to be notified of any fare sales.

The most common times for airfare wars are in the weeks leading up to the quietest seasons for carriers, including the period from mid-May to mid-June (except the Memorial Day weekend), between Labor Day and Thanksgiving, and again in the winter with the exception of Christmas, New Year's, and Presidents' Day holiday periods.

Don't be afraid to ask for a refund on previously purchased tickets if fares go down for the period of your travel. The airline may refund the difference, or you may be able to reticket your itinerary at the new fare, paying a penalty of about $100 for cashing in the old tickets. Be persistent: If the difference in fare is significant, it may be worth making a visit to the airport to meet with a supervisor at the ticket counter.

Study the fine print on discount coupons distributed by the airlines or third parties such as supermarkets, catalog companies, and direct marketers. In my experience, these coupons are often less valuable than they seem. Read the fine print carefully, and be sure to ask the reservationist if the price quoted with the coupon is higher than another fare for which you qualify.

■ YOUR RIGHTS AS A CONSUMER

The era of airline deregulation has been a mixed blessing for the industry and the consumer. After an era of wild competition based mostly on price, we now are left with fewer but larger airlines and a dizzying array of confusing rules. The U.S. Department of Transportation and its Federal Aviation Administration (FAA) still regulate safety issues. Almost everything else is between you and the airline.

Policies on fares, cancellations, reconfirmation, check-in requirements, and compensation for lost or damaged baggage or for delays all vary by airline. Your rights are limited and defined by the terms of the contract you make with an airline when you buy your ticket. You may find the contract included with the ticket you purchase, or the airlines may "incorporate terms by reference" to a separate document that you will have to request to see.

Whether you are buying your ticket through a travel agent or dealing directly with the airline, here are some important questions to ask:
■ Is the price guaranteed, or can it change from the time of the reservation until you actually purchase the ticket?
■ Can the price change between the time you buy the ticket and the date of departure?
■ Is there a penalty for cancellation of the ticket?

■ Can the reservation be changed without penalty or for a reasonable fee? Be sure you understand the sort of service you are buying.

■ Is this a nonstop flight, a direct flight, or a flight that requires you to change planes one or more times?

■ What seat has been issued? Do you really want the center seat in a three-seat row, between two strangers?

You might also want to ask your travel agent:

■ Is there anything I should know about the financial health of this airline?

■ Are you aware of any threats of work stoppages or legal actions that could ruin my trip?

■ BEATING THE AIRLINES AT THEIR OWN GAME

In my opinion, the airlines deserve all the headaches we travelers can give them because of the costly pricing schemes they throw at us—deals such as take-it-or-leave-it fares of $350 to fly 90 miles between two cities where they hold a monopoly, and $198 bargain fares to travel 3,000 miles across the nation. Or round-trip fares of $300 if you leave on a Thursday and return on a Monday, but $1,200 if you leave on a Monday and return the next Thursday.

But a creative traveler can find ways to work around most of these roadblocks. Nothing I'm going to suggest here is against the law; some of the tips, though, are against the rules of some airlines. Here are a couple of strategies.

Nested Tickets. This scheme generally works in either of two situations: when regular fares are more than twice as high as excursion fares that include a Saturday night stayover, or in situations where you plan to fly between two locations twice in less than a year.

Let's say you want to fly from Boston to Los Angeles. Buy two sets of tickets in your name. The first is from Boston to Los Angeles and back. This set has the return date for when you want to come back from your second trip. The other set of tickets is from Los Angeles to Boston and back to Los Angeles, this time making the first leg of the ticket for the date you want to come back from the first trip, and the second leg of the trip the date you want to depart for the second trip.

If this sounds complicated, that's because it is. It will be up to you to keep your tickets straight when you travel. Some airlines have threatened to crack down on such practices by searching their computer databases for multiple reservations. That doesn't mean you can't buy such tickets. Check with a travel agent for advice. One solution: Buy one set of tickets on one airline and the other set on another carrier.

Split Tickets. Fare wars sometimes result in super-cheap fares through a connecting city. For example, an airline seeking to boost traffic through a hub in Cincinnati creates a situation in which it is less expensive to get from New York to Los Angeles by buying a round-trip ticket from New York to Cincinnati, and then a separate round-trip ticket from Cincinnati to Los Angeles.

Be sure to book a schedule that allows enough time between flights; if you miss your connection you could end up losing time and money.

The Best Policy

Consider buying trip cancellation insurance from a travel agency, tour operator, or directly from an insurance company (ask your insurance agent for advice). The policies are intended to reimburse you for any lost deposits or prepayments if you must cancel a trip because you or certain members of your family become ill. Read the policy carefully to understand the circumstances under which the company will pay.

Take care not to purchase more coverage than you need; if your tour package costs $5,000 but you would lose only $1,000 in the event of a cancellation, then the amount of insurance required is just $1,000. Some policies will cover you for health and accident benefits while on vacation, excluding any preexisting conditions.

Be sure you understand your contract with your airline; you may be able to reschedule a flight or even receive a refund after payment of a service charge. Some airlines give full refunds or free rescheduling if you can prove a medical reason for the change.

■ STANDING UP FOR STANDING BY

One of the little-known secrets of air travel on most airlines and most types of tickets is the fact that travelers with valid tickets may be allowed to stand by for flights other than the ones for which they have reservations; if there are empty seats on the flight, standby ticket holders are permitted to board.

Some airlines are very liberal in their acceptance of standbys within a few days of the reserved flight, while others will charge a fee for changes in itinerary. And some airline personnel are stricter about regulations than others.

Here's what I do know: If I can't get the exact flight I want for a trip, I make the closest acceptable reservations available after that flight and then show up early at the airport and head for the check-in counter for the flight I really want to take. Unless you are seeking to travel during an impossibly overbooked holiday period or arrive on a bad weather day when flights have been canceled or buy a budget ticket, your chances of successfully standing by for a flight are usually pretty good.

One trick is to call the airline the day before the flight and check on the availability of seats for the flight you want. Some reservation clerks are very forthcoming with information; many times I have been told something like, "There are seventy seats open on that flight." Be careful with standby maneuvers if your itinerary requires a change of plane en route; you'll need to check the availability of seats on all of the legs of your journey. Some deep-discount fares may include prohibitions against standing by for other flights; read the fine print, especially if you are booking your own flight over the Internet.

The fly in the ointment in today's strict security environment is this: Airlines are required to match bags to passengers before a flight takes off. It is difficult, if not impossible, to stand by for a flight other than the one you hold a ticket for if you have checked a bag. Your chances are much better if you limit yourself to carry-on bags. And, security screeners may not let you into the concourse for flights more than two hours before scheduled departure. Consult with the ticket agents at check-in counters outside of the security barriers for advice.

Some airlines have clamped down on standby travel recently, making it available only to holders of unrestricted tickets; be sure to check with the carrier to learn the rights that go with your particular class of service.

And a final note: Be especially careful about standing by for the very last flight of the day. If you somehow are unable to get on that flight, you're stuck for the night.

■ OVERBOOKING

Overbooking is a polite industry term for the legal business practice of selling more than an airline can deliver. It all stems, alas, from the rudeness of many travelers who neglect to cancel flight reservations that will not be used. Airlines study the patterns on various flights and city pairs and apply a formula that allows them to sell more tickets than there are seats on the plane in the expectation that a certain percentage of ticket holders will not show up.

But what happens if all passengers holding a reservation do show up? Obviously, the result will be more passengers than seats, and some will have to be left behind. The involuntary bump list will begin with passengers who check in late. Airlines must ask for volunteers before bumping any passengers who have followed the rules on check-in. Assuming that no one is willing to give up a seat just for the fun of it, the airline will offer some sort of compensation— either a free ticket or cash, or both. It is up to the passenger and the airline to negotiate a deal.

Some air travelers, including this author, look forward to an overbooked flight when their schedules are flexible. My most profitable score: $4,000 in vouchers on a set of four $450 international tickets. The airline was desperate to clear a large block of seats, and it didn't matter to us if we arrived home a few hours late. We received the equivalent of three tickets for the price of one, and we went on to earn some more free travel on future tickets purchased with those vouchers.

The U.S. Department of Transportation's consumer protection regulations set some minimum levels of compensation for passengers who are bumped from a flight due to overbooking. If you are bumped involuntarily, the airline must provide a ticket on its next available flight. Unfortunately, there is no guarantee it will arrive at your destination at a convenient time.

If the airline can get you on another flight that will get you to your destination within one hour of the original arrival time, no compensation need be paid. If you are scheduled to get to your destination more than one hour but less than two hours late, you're entitled to receive an amount equal to the one-way fare of the oversold flight, up to $200. If the delay is more than two hours, the bumpee will receive an amount equal to twice the one-way fare of the original flight, up to $400.

It is not considered bumping if a flight is canceled because of weather, equipment problems, or the lack of a flight crew. You are also not eligible for compensation if the airline substitutes a smaller aircraft for operational or safety reasons, or if the flight involves an aircraft with sixty or fewer seats.

■ HOW TO GET BUMPED

Why in the world would you want to be bumped? Well, perhaps you'd like to look at missing your plane as an opportunity to earn a little money for your time instead of an annoyance. Is a two-hour delay worth $100 an hour to you? For the inconvenience of waiting a few hours on the way home, a family of four might receive a voucher for $800—that could pay for a week's hotel plus a heck of a meal at the airport.

If you're not in a rush to get to your destination—or to get back home—you might want to volunteer to be bumped. We wouldn't recommend doing this on the busiest travel days of the year or if you are booked on the last flight of the day, unless you are also looking forward to a free night in an airport motel.

■ BAD WEATHER, BAD PLANES, STRIKES, AND OTHER HEADACHES

You don't want pilots to fly into weather they consider unsafe. You also don't want them to take up a plane with a mechanical problem. No matter how you feel about unions, you probably don't want to cross a picket line to board a plane piloted by strikebreakers. And so, you should accept an airline's cancellation of a flight for any of these legitimate reasons.

Here's the bad news, though: If a flight is canceled for an "act of God" such as bad weather, an earthquake, or a plague of locusts, or because of a strike or labor dispute, the airline isn't required to do anything for you except refund your money. In practice, carriers will usually make a good effort to find another way to get you to your destination more or less on time, which could mean rebooking on another flight on the same airline or on a different carrier. But you could be facing a delay of a day or more in the worst situations, such as a major snowstorm.

Here is a summary of your rather limited rights as an air passenger:

■ An airline is required to compensate you above the cost of your ticket only if you're bumped from an oversold flight against your will.

■ If you volunteer to be bumped, you can negotiate for the best deal with the ticket agent or a supervisor; for your inconvenience, you can generally expect to be offered a free round-trip ticket on the airline.

■ If your scheduled flight is unable to deliver you directly to the destination on your ticket, and alternate transportation such as a bus or limousine is provided, the airline is required to pay you twice the amount of your one-way fare if your arrival on the alternate transportation will be more than two hours later than the original airline ticket promised.

■ If you purchased your ticket with a credit card, the airline must credit your account within seven days of receiving an application for a refund.

All that said, in many cases you will be able to convince an agent or a supervisor to go beyond the letter of the law. I've found that the best strategy is to politely but firmly stand your ground. Ask the ticket clerk for another flight, for a free night in a hotel and a flight in the morning, or for any other reasonable accommodation. Don't take no for an answer, but remain polite and ask for a supervisor, if necessary. Sooner or later, they'll do something to get you out of the way.

And then there are labor problems such as those that have faced airlines including American Airlines and US Airways in recent years. Your best defense against a strike is to anticipate it before it happens; keep your ears open for labor problems when you make a reservation. Then keep in touch with your travel agent or the airline itself in the days leading up to any strike deadline. It is often easier to make alternate plans or seek a refund in the days immediately before a strike; wait until a strike is under way and you're going to be joining a very long line of upset people.

In the face of a strike, a major airline will attempt to reroute you to another airline if possible; if you buy your own ticket on another carrier, you're unlikely to be reimbursed. If your flight is canceled, you'll certainly be able to claim a full refund of your fare or obtain a voucher in its value without paying any penalties.

■ AIRLINE SAFETY

There are no guarantees in life, but in general, flying on an airplane is considerably safer than the drive to the airport. All the major air carriers have very good safety records; some are better than others. I pay attention to news reports about FAA inspections and rulings, and then make adjustments. And although I love to squeeze George Washington until he yelps, I avoid start-up and cut-rate airlines because I have my doubts about how much money they can afford to devote to maintenance.

Among major airlines, the fatal accident rate during the last twenty-five years stands somewhere between .3 and .74 incidents per million flights. Not included in these listings are small commuter airlines (except those affiliated with major carriers). Put another way, if you were to take one flight a day—randomly selected—chances are it would be about 22,000 years before you end up as a statistic in a fatal crash.

The very low numbers over such a long period of time, experts say, make them poor predictors of future incidents. Instead, you should pay more attention to reports of FAA or National Transportation Safety Board (NTSB) rulings on maintenance and training problems.

■ THE NEW WORLD OF AIRPORT SECURITY

Travel has become all the more complicated and less convenient in the wake of the terrorist attacks of 2001. The bottom line for well-meaning, nonviolent business and pleasure travelers is this: You'll need to add an hour or more to the check-in process, and your options to stand by for a different flight or make other changes to your itinerary are severely limited.

Here are some things you can do to lessen the pain:

■ Consult with the airline or your travel agent about current policies regarding check-in times.

■ Be sure to carry at least one form of identification that includes a photo. A driver's license or a passport will work well; if you have neither, check with the airline ahead of time to find out about acceptable alternatives.

■ Consider your departure time; lines for check-in and security clearance are longest during peak travel times—early morning and late afternoon.

■ Check out an alternate airport. It may have shorter lines. Some major hubs may, by necessity, be more efficient at processing huge crowds; at the same time, smaller airports with fewer passengers may be easier to navigate.

■ Try to avoid carrying unnecessary metallic items on your person. Choose a belt with a small buckle rather than the one with the three-pound world-championship steer wrestling medallion. Put your cell phone, keys, coins, and wristwatch into a plastic bag and place it in your carry-on bag as you approach the magnetometer; this will speed your passage and reduce the chances of losing items.

■ Travel in a pair of sneakers instead of heavy boots or high heels; it's less likely you'll have to remove your shoes.

■ Be cooperative and remember that the screening is intended to keep you safe, and hope that the guards do their job well.

Don't Wait to Make a Call

If you have booked a trip through a travel agent or tour operator, keep in touch. In many cases they can anticipate major changes before departure time and will let you know. And many operators will try hard to keep you from demanding a refund if you find a major change unacceptable. They may offer a discount or upgrade on a substitute trip or adjust the price of the changed tour.

If you have booked a flight directly through an airline, make sure it has your phone number in case of a change in the schedule. Call the airline a few days before your first flight to confirm your reservation and check for any changes.

ABOUT TRAVEL AGENCIES

Here's my advice in a nutshell about travel agents: Get a good one, or go it alone. Good travel agents are those who remember who they work for: you. Of course there is a built-in major conflict of interest here, because the agent is in most cases paid by someone else. Agents receive a commission on airline tickets, hotel reservations, car rentals, and many other services they sell you. The more they sell (or the higher the price), the more they earn.

I would recommend you start the planning for any trip by calling airlines and a few hotels to determine the best package you can put together for yourself. Then call your travel agent and ask him or her to do better. If your agent contributes knowledge or experience, comes up with dollar-saving alternatives to your own package, or offers some other kind of convenience, then go ahead and book your trip through the agency. If, as I often find, you know a lot more about your destination and are willing to spend a lot more time to save money than is the agent, do it yourself.

A number of large agencies offer rebates on part of their commissions to travelers. Some of these companies cater only to frequent fliers who will bring in a lot of business; other rebate agencies offer only limited services to clients.

You can find discount travel agencies through many major credit card companies (Citibank and American Express among them) or through associations and clubs. Some warehouse shopping clubs have rebate travel agencies. If you establish a regular relationship with your travel agency and bring it enough business to make it glad to hear from you, don't be afraid to ask for a discount equal to a few percentage points.

Internet travel agencies offer airline, hotel, car, cruise, and package reservations. You won't receive personalized assistance, but you will be able to make as many price checks and itinerary routings as you'd like without apology. Several of the services feature special deals, including companion fares and rebates you won't find elsewhere.

Some of the best Internet agencies are:

- Microsoft Expedia, www.expedia.com
- Orbitz.com, www.orbitz.com
- Travelocity, www.travelocity.com

You can link directly to Travelocity from the Econoguide Web site, at www.econoguide.com.

You can also book directly with a number of major airlines, sometimes taking advantage of special Internet prices or bonus frequent flier mileage. Among the airlines that offer online booking are:

- American Airlines, www.aa.com
- Continental Airlines, www.continental.com
- Delta Airlines, www.delta.com
- JetBlue, www.jetblue.com
- Northwest Airlines, www.nwa.com
- Southwest, www.southwest.com
- United Airlines, www.united.com
- US Airways, www.usairways.com

■ TOUR PACKAGES AND CHARTER FLIGHTS

Tour packages and flights sold by tour operators or travel agents may look similar, but the consumer may end up with significantly different rights. What you end up with is greatly dependent on whether the flight is a scheduled or nonscheduled flight. A scheduled flight is one that is published in the *Official Airline Guide* and available to the general public through a travel agent or from the airline. This doesn't mean that a scheduled flight will necessarily be on a major carrier or that you'll be flying on a 747 jumbo jet; it could just as easily be the propeller-driven pride of Hayseed Airlines. In any case, a scheduled flight does have to meet stringent federal government certification requirements.

A nonscheduled flight is also known as a "charter flight." The term also sometimes is applied to a complete package that includes a nonscheduled flight, hotel accommodations, ground transportation, and other elements. Charter flights are generally a creation of a tour operator who will purchase all the

Second Chance

Most tour operators, if forced to cancel, will offer another package or other incentives as a goodwill gesture. If a charter flight or charter tour is canceled, the tour operator must refund your money within fourteen days.

seats on a specific flight to a specific destination or who will rent an airplane and crew from an air carrier.

Charter flights and charter tours are regulated by the federal government, but your rights as a consumer are much more limited than those afforded to scheduled flight customers. You wouldn't buy a hamburger without knowing the price and specifications (two all-beef patties on a sesame seed bun, etc.). Why, then, would you spend hundreds or even thousands of dollars on a tour and not understand the contract that underlies the transaction?

When you purchase a charter flight or a tour package, you should review and sign a contract that spells out your rights. This contract is sometimes referred to as the "Operator Participant Contract" or the "Terms and Conditions." Look for this contract in the booklet or brochure that describes the package; ask for it if one is not offered.

Remember that the contract is designed mostly to benefit the tour operator, and each contract may be different from others you have agreed to in the past. The basic rule here is this: If you don't understand it, don't sign it.

■ HOW TO BOOK A PACKAGE OR CHARTER FLIGHT

For charter flights and packages, consider using a travel agent, preferably one you know and trust. The tour operator usually pays the agent's commission. Some tour packages, however, are available only from the operator who organized the tour; in certain cases, you may be able to negotiate a better price by dealing directly with the operator, although you are giving up one layer of protection of your rights.

Pay for your ticket with a credit card; I consider this a cardinal rule for almost any situation in which you're paying in advance for a service or product. If you end up in a dispute with the travel provider or a travel agency, you should be able to enlist the assistance of the credit card issuer on your behalf.

Keep in mind that charter airlines don't have fleets of planes available as substitutes in the event of a mechanical problem or an extensive weather delay. They may not be able to arrange for a substitute plane from another carrier.

If you're still willing to try a charter after all of these warnings, make one more check of the bottom line before you sign the contract.

■ First of all, is the air travel significantly less expensive than the lowest nonrefundable fare available from a scheduled carrier? (Remember that you are, in effect, buying a nonrefundable fare with most charter flight contracts.)

■ Have you included taxes, service charges, baggage transfer fees, or other charges the tour operator may put into the contract?

■ Are the savings significantly more than the 10 percent the charter operator may (typically) boost the price without your permission? Do any savings come at a cost of time? Put a value on your time.

■ Finally, don't buy a complete package until you have compared it with the a la carte cost of such a trip. Call the hotels offered by the tour operator or similar ones in the same area, and ask them a simple question: "What is your best price for a room?" Be sure to mention any discount programs that are applicable, including the American Automobile Association (AAA) or other organizations.

Do the same for car rental agencies, and place a call to any attractions you plan to visit to get current prices.

LOS ANGELES INTERNATIONAL AIRPORT (LAX)

Information: (310) 646–5252. www.lawa.org.

LAX is located in Westchester, at the intersections of Century and Sepulveda Boulevards. The airport is near the Inglewood/Century Boulevard exit of Interstate 405, and is about 34 miles from Disneyland.

An MTA bus stop is located between the passenger terminals. Call (213) 626–4455 for schedules.

Terminal 1: America West, Southwest, US Airways, Mesa Airlines

Terminal 2: Air Canada, Air China, Air New Zealand, Aviacsa, Champion, Hawaiian Airlines, KLM, Northwest, Virgin Atlantic, World Airways, Miami Air, TACA International Airlines, Jetgo, LACSA Airlines

Terminal 3: Alaska, AirTran Airways, American Trans Air (ATA), Midwest Express Airlines, West Jet, Frontier, Horizon

Bradley International Terminal: Aero California, Aeroflot, Aer Lingus, Air India, Air Pacific, Air Tahiti Nui, Alaska Airlines ANA (All Nippon), Asiana, British Airways, Cathay Pacific, China Airlines, China Eastern, Copa Airlines, El Al, Eva Air, Japan Airlines, Korean Airlines, Lan Chile, Lan Peru, LTU, Lufthansa, Malaysia, Mexicana, Philippine Airlines, Qantas, Singapore, Swiss International Air Lines, Thai, Varig

Terminal 4: American, American Eagle, Qantas

Terminal 5: Aeroliteral, Aeromexico, Air Jamaica, China Southern, Delta, Spirit, SunCountry, Air France, Omni Air International, Song Airlines, Spirit Airlines

Terminal 6: Continental, Copa Airlines, United (International) Airlines, United Express

Terminal 7: United (Domestic), United Express

Terminal 8: Ted Airlines

OTHER AREA AIRPORTS

Although LAX has by far the broadest selection of airlines and flights, you may be able to save time and sometimes a bit of money by flying through one of several smaller regional airports.

The nearest airport to Disneyland is John Wayne

Lug it Yourself

If you are using a scheduled airline to connect with a charter flight, or the other way around, your baggage will not be automatically transferred. You must make the transfer yourself.

Charter and tour flights operate independently of other flights. If you are on a trip that combines scheduled and nonscheduled flights or two unrelated charter flights, you may end up losing your money and flight because of delays. It may make sense to avoid such combinations for that reason or to leave extra hours or even days between connections. Some tour operators offer travel-delay insurance that pays for accommodations or alternative travel arrangements necessitated by certain types of delays.

AIRPORTS NEAR LOS ANGELES

Airport in Orange County near Santa Ana, about 13 miles away. Long Beach Airport is about 19 miles from Disneyland. Ontario Airport is about 35 miles from Disneyland. The Bob Hope Airport in Burbank, formerly the Burbank–Glendale Pasadena Airport, is 40 miles from Disneyland, and only about 6 miles from Universal Studios Hollywood.

■ JOHN WAYNE AIRPORT/ORANGE COUNTY AIRPORT

Information: (949) 252–5200. www.ocair.com.

The airport is located at I–405 and MacArthur Boulevard in Santa Ana. Bus service is available from points in Orange County by OCTA; call (714) 636–7433 for information.

Airlines serving John Wayne Airport include Alaska, Aloha, America West, American, Continental, Delta, Northwest, Southwest, United, and US Airways.

■ BOB HOPE AIRPORT/BURBANK AIRPORT

Information: (818) 840–8840. www.burbankairport.com.

Metrolink information: (800) 371–5465.

The airport is located in Burbank, 1 mile south of the Golden State Freeway (Interstate 5). The main entrance is at Thornton Avenue and Hollywood Way. An MTA bus stop is located at the airport entrance and a CalTrain station is just outside the gates.

Airlines serving Burbank include Alaska, Aloha, American, America West, Southwest, United, Delta, and JetBlue.

■ LONG BEACH AIRPORT

Information: (562) 570–2640. www.lgb.org.

The airport is located at 4100 Donald Douglas Boulevard, near the intersection of Lakewood Boulevard and Spring Street in Long Beach. From I–405, take the Lakewood Boulevard exit. This small airport is much easier than LAX and even John Wayne/Orange County Airport to deal with; it is located about forty-five minutes from Anaheim or thirty minutes from Los Angeles.

Airlines serving Long Beach include Alaska, American, America West, and JetBlue.

■ ONTARIO INTERNATIONAL AIRPORT

Information: (909) 937–2700. www.lawa.org.

The airport is located 2 miles east of Ontario, on Airport Drive at Vineyard Avenue, near the Vineyard Avenue exit of Interstate 10.

Airlines serving Ontario include AeroMexico, Alaska, America West, American, Continental, Delta, JetBlue, Lineas Areas Azteca, Northwest, Southwest, United, and United Express.

Omnitrans offers regularly scheduled bus service to Ontario International Airport. For routes and schedules, call (800) 966–6428.

LOS ANGELES REGION BUS AND TRAIN SERVICE

Here is a list of a few of the larger transportation services that connect LAX and other airports to the Greater Los Angeles area. Be aware that you may have to take some side trips en route if you share a van with others. For direct service, use a taxi or limousine service.

Airport Bus. Between LAX and Disneyland-area hotels (adult round-trip about $25), between John Wayne/Orange County Airport and Disneyland-area hotels (adult round-trip, about $18). (800) 772–5299. www.airportbus.com.

FlyAway. Bus service between LAX and Van Nuys Airport Bus Terminal. (818) 994–5554.

Metropolitan Express. Vans to airports, Amtrak, harbors. (310) 417–5050.

Prime Time Airport Shuttle. Vans in Los Angeles and Orange County. (800) 262–7433.

Super Shuttle. Door-to-door service to LAX and area airports. (800) 258–3826 or (714) 517–6600.

■ LOS ANGELES COUNTY METROPOLITAN TRANSPORTATION AUTHORITY (MTA)

Information: (213) 626–4455. www.mta.net.

The MTA serves the Greater Los Angeles area from the San Fernando Valley to northern Orange County with bus, rail, and light-rail service on more than 200 routes.

Free shuttle service is provided to and from the Metro Green Line Light Rail's Aviation Station. Passenger pickup is on the Lower/Arrival Level under the LAX Shuttle sign.

Metropolitan Transit Authority (Los Angeles area) city bus information is available by telephone on the Information Display Board in the baggage claim area in each terminal. Board city buses adjacent to Parking Lot C by taking the C Shuttle.

MTA buses connect to all Metro Blue Line and Red Line stations, Union Station, and Metrolink stations in Los Angeles County.

Buses run twenty-four hours a day, with limited service during late-night hours, weekends, and holidays.

■ PUBLIC BUS FROM LAX TO DISNEYLAND

If you've got a bit of time and patience, you can travel by Metro Rail and Metro Bus from Los Angeles International Airport to Disneyland in three steps and about two hours for a fare (in mid-2005) of $2.35.

At the airport make your way to Terminal 4 and World Way South. Take the free G Shuttle East to the Metro Green Line Light Rail's Aviation Station. Take the Metro Green Line East toward Norwalk. Purchase a ticket for $1.35 and obtain a transfer coupon. Get off at Norwalk/I–105/I–605 Green Line station.

Transfer to the Metro Bus 460 South toward Disneyland; use the transfer coupon and pay an additional $1.00. Get off at Disneyland.

■ METRO RAIL

In car-clogged Los Angeles, the idea of an underground subway system would make a lot of sense (notwithstanding the fact that the tunnels run through a pretty active earthquake zone; that's something that Angelenos seem able to live with in everything they do).

The $4.5 billion project to Hollywood was completed in 2000. The next challenge is to convince more than a few Angelenos to get out of their cars and into the underground. Operators hope for about 125,000 passengers a day during the week, which should leave plenty of room on the trains. (New York's sprawling system draws more than three million users daily.)

Actually, the system may be of most use to tourists who can take the train to travel from downtown to Hollywood and Universal Studios in about fifteen minutes. The modern rubber-tired trains glide almost silently between clean and attractive stations. The base fare is $1.35 for adults for the Red and Green Lines, plus 25 cents for each transfer to bus service. Self-service ticket vending machines can be found at each station.

The train stations themselves are worth seeing. The stop at Hollywood and Vine, in the heart of Hollywood, pays homage to the movies. A yellow brick road rises out of the red floor, leading upstairs to the street. The Vermont and Sunset station, near a hospital district, is decorated with medical symbols; the elevator to the street echoes the design of the Griffith Park Observatory's dome in the Hollywood Hills above it.

The Union Station end of the line has connections to Metrolink commuter rail trains and the Amtrak terminal, and it is near to Chinatown, Olvera Street, and Little Tokyo. A station at the Tom Bradley Civic Center Station (First and Hill Streets) is near the Music Center; City Hall; Times Mirror Square; and several city, county, and government buildings. Travelers can transfer to the Metro Blue Line at the Pershing Square Station (Fifth and Hill Streets).

The Blue Line is a light-rail system of about 40 miles, with service from Los Angeles to Long Beach, from 5:00 A.M. to 11:00 P.M. daily.

Fares vary by distance traveled, and exact change is required. All buses and trains are wheelchair-accessible. Special family and tourist passes are available, usually limited to off-peak times. You can purchase a Metro Day Pass—priced at $3.00 in 2005—that allows unlimited use of any Metro bus or rail line in Los Angeles. The passes are sold on board any Metro bus or at any Metro rail station. (Additional charges may be assessed on freeway bus routes.)

For a timetable and route map, call MTA Information or write to: MTA Customer Relations, 425 South Main Street, Los Angeles, CA 90013–1393. For information, call (800) 266–6883. www.mta.net or www.metro.net.

The newest extension, the Gold Line, runs from downtown to Pasadena. The tracks begin at Union Station and Gateway Transit Station with stops in Los Angelos's Chinatown, Highland Park, Mission–South Pasadena, Fillmore, and Del Mar.

METRO RAIL SYSTEM

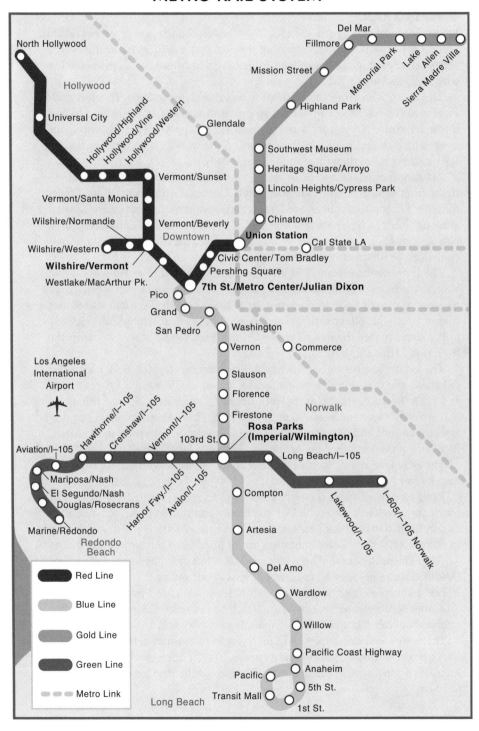

North Hollywood

Hollywood

Universal City

Hollywood/Highland
Hollywood/Vine
Hollywood/Western

Glendale

Del Mar
Fillmore
Mission Street
Memorial Park
Lake
Allen
Sierra Madre Villa

Highland Park

Southwest Museum
Heritage Square/Arroyo
Lincoln Heights/Cypress Park

Vermont/Sunset

Vermont/Santa Monica

Wilshire/Normandie

Vermont/Beverly

Downtown

Chinatown

Union Station

Cal State LA

Wilshire/Western

Wilshire/Vermont

Civic Center/Tom Bradley

Pershing Square

Westlake/MacArthur Pk.

7th St./Metro Center/Julian Dixon

Pico
Grand
San Pedro

Washington

Vernon

Commerce

Los Angeles
International
Airport

Slauson

Florence

Firestone

Norwalk

Hawthorne/I–105
Crenshaw/I–105
Vermont/I–105
103rd St.

**Rosa Parks
(Imperial/Wilmington)**

Aviation/I–105

Long Beach/I–105

Mariposa/Nash
El Segundo/Nash
Douglas/Rosecrans

Harbor Fwy./I–105
Avalon/I–105

Compton

I–605/I–105 Norwalk

Marine/Redondo

Redondo
Beach

Lakewood/I–105

Artesia

Del Amo

Wardlow

Willow

Pacific Coast Highway

Anaheim

Pacific

5th St.

Transit Mall

Long Beach

1st St.

Red Line

Blue Line

Gold Line

Green Line

Metro Link

■ METRO RAIL STATIONS

Red Line (Downtown Los Angeles, Wilshire Center, Hollywood)

North Hollywood. Lankershim and Chandler Boulevards. Academy of TV Arts and Sciences, El Portal Center for the Performing Arts.

Universal City. Lankershim Boulevard and Universal Terrace Parkway. Universal Studios Hollywood, Universal CityWalk. Shuttle bus to theme park.

Hollywood/Highland. Hollywood Boulevard and Highland Avenue. Egyptian Theater, El Capitan Theater, Hollywood Bowl, Mann's Chinese Theater.

Hollywood/Vine. 6250 Hollywood Boulevard. Hollywood Walk of Fame, Pantages Theater, The Palace.

Hollywood/Western. 5450 Hollywood Boulevard.

Vermont/Sunset. 1500 North Vermont Avenue.

Vermont/Santa Monica. 1015 North Vermont Avenue.

Vermont/Beverly. 301 North Vermont Avenue.

Wilshire/Western. 3775 Wilshire Boulevard.

Wilshire/Normandie. 3510 Wilshire Boulevard. Koreatown and Korean-American Museum.

Wilshire/Vermont. 3191 Wilshire Boulevard.

Westlake/MacArthur Park. 660 South Alvarado Street.

Seventh Street/Metro Center. 660 South Figueroa Street. (Red and Blue Line connection.) Los Angeles Visitor Center, downtown hotels.

Pershing Square. 500 South Hill Street.

Civic Center/Tom Bradley. 101 South Hill Street. Ahmanson Theater, Dorothy Chandler Pavilion, Los Angeles Children's Museum.

Union Station. 801 Vignes Street. Chinatown, Olvera Street, Little Tokyo.

Gold Line (Downtown to Pasadena)

Union Station/Gateway Transit Station. 801 Vignes Street. Chinatown, Olvera Street, Little Tokyo.

Chinatown. 901 North Spring Street.

Lincoln Heights/Cypress Park. 370 West Avenue 26.

Heritage Square/Arroyo. 3545 Pasadena Avenue.

Southwest Museum. 4600 Marmion Way.

Highland Park. 151 North Avenue 57.

Mission-South Pasadena. 901 Meridian Avenue.

Fillmore. 95 Fillmore Street.

Del Mar. 230 South Raymond Avenue.

Memorial Park. 125 East Holly Street.

Lake. 340 North Lake Avenue.

Allen. 395 North Allen Avenue.

Sierra Madre Villa. 149 North Halstead.

The Metro Blue Line's Pico station. *Photo by Jeff Hyman, © Corel Corporation*

Blue Line (Downtown Los Angeles to Long Beach)

Seventh Street/Metro Center. 660 South Figueroa Street. (Red and Blue Line connection.) Los Angeles Visitor Center, downtown hotels.

Pico. 1236 South Flower Street. Los Angeles Convention Center, Staples Center.

Grand. 331 West Washington Boulevard.

San Pedro. 767 East Washington Boulevard.

Washington. 1945 Long Beach Avenue.

Vernon. 4421 Long Beach Avenue.

Slauson. 5855 Randolph Street.

Florence. 7225 Graham Avenue.

Firestone. 8615 Graham Avenue.

103rd Street. 10100 Grandee Avenue. Watts Towers.

Rosa Parks. 11611 Willowbrook Avenue. (Blue and Green Line connection.)

Compton. 275 Willowbrook Avenue.

Artesia. 1920 Acacia Avenue.

Del Amo. 20220 Santa Fe Avenue.

Wardlow. 2420 North Pacific Avenue.

Willow. 2750 American Way.

Pacific Coast Highway. 1798 North Long Beach Boulevard.

Anaheim. 1290 North Long Beach Boulevard.

Fifth Street. 598 North Long Beach Boulevard.

First Street. 108 North Long Beach Boulevard.

Transit Mall. 128 West First Street. Long Beach Aquarium of the Pacific, *Queen Mary*, Long Beach Convention and Entertainment Center.

Pacific. 498 Pacific Avenue.

Green Line (Norwalk to Redondo Beach)

Marine/Redondo. 2406 Marine Avenue, 5301 Marine Avenue.

Douglas/Rosecrans. 700 South Douglas Street.

El Segundo/Nash. 2226 East El Segundo Boulevard.

Mariposa/Nash. 555 North Nash Street.

Aviation/I–105. 11500 Aviation Boulevard. Los Angeles International Airport via free shuttle.

Hawthorne/I–105. 11230 South Acacia Street.

Crenshaw/I–105. 11901 South Crenshaw Boulevard.

Vermont/I–105. 11603 South Vermont Avenue.

Harbor Freeway/I–105. 11500 South Figueroa Street.

Avalon/I–105. 11667 South Avalon Boulevard.

Rosa Parks. 11611 Willowbrook Avenue. (Blue and Green Line connection.)

Long Beach/I–105. 11508 Long Beach Boulevard.

Lakewood/I–105. 12801 Lakewood Avenue.

I–605/I–105 Norwalk. 12901 Hoxie Avenue.

■ METROLINK

Information: (800) 371–5465. www.metrolinktrains.com.

Metrolink is a long-distance commuter train system that serves Los Angeles and area communities, including Burbank, Glendale, Riverside, and San Bernardino. There is also service to a station near Anaheim Stadium. Trains run about 4:00 A.M. to 9:00 P.M. weekdays. Fares are based on distance traveled; free transfers to MTA lines are available.

■ AMTRAK

Information: (800) 872–7245. www.amtrak.com.

Amtrak connects Union Station (800 North Alameda Street) in downtown Los Angeles to points in California, including Orange County and San Diego, as well as limited cross-country service; some destinations are served by a combination of trains and buses. There are Amtrak stations near Anaheim Stadium in Orange County as well as in Santa Ana, Fullerton, San Juan Capistrano, Irvine, Oceanside, Del Mar, and San Diego.

Union Station in Los Angeles, the terminal for long-distance Amtrak service. *Photo by Jeff Hyman, © Corel Corporation*

■ INTERCITY BUSES

Greyhound Bus Lines. The company has a terminal in downtown Los Angeles, and one in Anaheim at 100 West Winston Street. Information: (800) 231–2222. www.greyhound.com.

Orange County Transportation Authority (OCTA). (714) 636–7433. www.octa.net. You'll find a description of major bus routes in the county on the Web site.

Metropolitan Transit Authority. Greater Los Angeles area, downtown, and airport service. Information: (213) 626–4455 or (800) 266–6883 in California. www.mta.net.

SHOULD YOU RENT A CAR?

Do you need to rent a car? In a word, probably. If you can arrange to stay at a hotel that offers shuttle bus service to and from one of the Los Angeles area airports (Los Angeles International, John Wayne/Orange County, or Ontario) and a shuttle to and from Disneyland, you may be able to do without a car. You'll be limited, though, in your ability to visit other attractions such as Knott's Berry Farm, Universal Studios, or Six Flags California.

An alternative is to hire a car service from your hotel to attractions and back; expect hourly rates of $40 to $80.

■ CAR RENTAL STRATEGIES

All the major car rental agencies, and a selection of smaller ones, have offices in Southern California. Most of the companies operate from the major airports, but a few also have pickup and drop-off sites in big cities and at some large hotels.

As this edition went to press, prices for rental cars from Los Angeles International Airport began at about $25 per day for an economy car and about $35 for a full-size vehicle; the best deal is for weeklong contracts, which usually work out to be about the cost of five days. Rates tend to increase in high-season. To put it into perspective, think of the deal as borrowing $25,000 for a $25 fee per day.

In general, you'll get the best deals on car rentals by booking in advance. Rental companies, like airlines and hotels, usually publish a limited number of deep-discount rates that they use to lure customers, and when these are gone you may end up paying a higher rate than the guy next to you at the counter for the same class of car.

However, as you fly across the country, read the airline's magazine in the seatback pocket. There are often special car rental rates advertised for destinations served by the airline. It may be worthwhile to take the ad with you to the rental counter and ask for a better rate than the one you've reserved.

Fast Food

One advantage to bringing a car to a theme park is the chance to save a bit of money and get a more relaxed, better meal by ducking out at lunch or dinner and visiting a decent buffet or menu restaurant; come back to the park for some evening rides and the fireworks. (Be sure to get your hand stamped when you leave the park and hold on to your ticket stub—both are needed for readmission the same day. Your parking receipt also is valid for reentry to any of the parking lots for the day.)

Your travel agent may be of assistance in finding the best rates; make a few phone calls by yourself, too. Sometimes you'll find significant variations in prices from one agency to another. Be sure to check online as well; Web sites such as www.expedia.com and www.travelocity.com allow you to compare rates from several rental agencies for the dates and locations you specify. You may also find lower rental rates on the Web sites of the rental car companies themselves. Join the agencies' priority clubs—usually free—to receive special offers.

If you fly into a large city like Los Angeles, be aware that the least-expensive car rental agencies usually don't have stations at the airport itself. You'll have to wait for a shuttle bus to take you from the terminal to their lots, and you must return the car to the outlying area at the end of your trip. This may add about twenty to thirty minutes to your arrival and departure schedule but the savings may be worth the inconvenience.

Car rental companies will try—with varying levels of pressure—to convince you to purchase special insurance coverage. They'll tell you it's "only" $7.00 or $9.00 per day. What a deal! That works out to about $2,500 or $3,330 per year for a set of rental wheels. Of course the coverage is intended primarily to protect the rental company, not you.

Before you travel, check with your insurance agent to determine how well your personal automobile policy will cover a rental car and its contents. I strongly recommend you use a credit card that offers rental car insurance; such insurance usually covers the deductible below your personal policy. The extra auto insurance by itself is usually worth an upgrade to a gold card or other extra-service credit card.

The only sticky area comes for those visitors who have a driver's license but no car, and therefore no insurance. Again, consult your credit card company and your insurance agent to see what kind of coverage you have or what kind you need.

Pay attention, too, when the rental agent explains the gas policy. The most common plan says you must return the car with a full tank; if the agency must re-fill the tank, you will usually be billed a very high per-gallon rate and sometimes a service charge as well. Other optional plans include one where the rental agency sells you a full tank when you first drive away and takes no note of how much gas remains when you return the car. Unless you somehow manage to return the car with the engine running on fumes, you are in effect making a gift to the agency with every gallon you bring back. I prefer the first option, which requires making it a point to refill the tank on the way to the airport on getaway day.

Although it is theoretically possible to rent a car without a credit card, you will find it to be an inconvenient process. If the rental agency cannot hold your credit card account hostage, it will most often require a large cash deposit—perhaps as much as several thousand dollars—before it will give you the keys.

And finally, check with the rental company about its policies on taking the car out of the state. Some companies will charge you extra if you're planning to take the car across a state line.

FROM HERE TO THERE IN LOS ANGELES AND ORANGE COUNTY

Getting from here to there in Los Angeles and Orange County mostly involves driving, and mostly on one of the famed California freeways. These free expressways are among the wonders of the world—broad four- or even six-lane ribbons of concrete winding through valleys or arching over canyons.

The most important roads for readers of this book are the north–south freeways, including Interstates 5 and 405, which run between Los Angeles and Orange County, and U.S. Highway 101, which connects Pasadena to Hollywood. The busy I–5 also serves visitors traveling between Disneyland, Knott's Berry Farm, Universal Studios, and Six Flags California.

There are two idiosyncrasies about California driving that may be confusing to out-of-towners. First is the fact that most of the highways have names as well as numbers, and some have more than one name for different sections. Second, many of the exit signs do not emphasize north or south but instead indicate a major destination point of the road.

You can find a guide to Southern California freeways on the Web site of the Orange County Transportation Authority, www.octa.net. And you can consult a toll-free help line for information on delays and detours, (800) 724–0353.

Your rental car will come with a small map, which probably should be relegated to the glove compartment; pick up a Los Angeles map from AAA or a bookstore and give it a few minutes of study before you set out on a trip.

There are some times when you can drive at or near the speed limit, but from early morning through early evening, the roads choke with traffic. The drive from Disneyland to Six Flags California, for example, is about 63 miles, which should take just a bit more than an hour, which is probably possible at midnight. At 8:00 A.M. or 5:00 P.M., you will be in and among commuters, and the drive could easily take two hours. At midday, the drive should be somewhere between one and two hours.

Keep your radio on as you drive. Nearly every Los Angeles area station offers regular traffic reports, which may help you avoid traffic jams by taking detours. Major roadways also have electronic displays to alert drivers to delays.

■ TRIPTIKS

Los Angeles International Airport to the Disneyland Resort

Freeway route: Take Interstate 105 east/Imperial Highway west ramp toward Imperial Terminal, and merge onto I–105 east. Travel 17 miles to the Interstate 605 north exit. Continue about 2 miles to the I–5/Santa Ana Freeway exit, and proceed on I–5 south toward Santa Ana for about 13 miles. Take the Disneyland Drive exit toward Ball Road and merge onto Disneyland Drive. About 34 miles, thirty-eight minutes without traffic.

Alternate route: From the airport, take State Highway 42 (Manchester Avenue) about 24 miles east through Inglewood, Huntington Park, Bell Gardens, and Downey to I–5. Head south on I–5, 11 miles to the Harbor Boulevard exit, which leads into Disneyland. About 35 miles, one hour and six minutes.

Disneyland to Knott's Berry Farm

Take I–5 north about 5 miles to State Highway 91 (Artesia Freeway) west. Exit on State Highway 39 (Beach Boulevard) south to entrance. About 7 miles, ten minutes.

Disneyland to Los Angeles

Take I–5 north 23 miles through Buena Park, Norwalk, Santa Fe Springs, and Pico Rivera. At East Los Angeles, turn off onto US 101 north into Los Angeles. About 27 miles, forty-two minutes.

L.A. Freeways

Directions refer to the path of the freeway through the Los Angeles area.

NORTH–SOUTH ROUTES

5	Golden State/ Santa Ana
101	Hollywood
110	Harbor/Pasadena
170	Hollywood
405	San Diego
605	San Gabriel River
710	Long Beach

EAST–WEST ROUTES

2	Glendale
10	Santa Monica/ San Bernardino
60	Pomona
91	Artesia/Redondo
134	Ventura
210	Foothill

Disneyland to Universal Studios

Take I–5 north 23 miles through Buena Park, Norwalk, Santa Fe Springs, and Pico Rivera. At East Los Angeles, turn off onto US 101 north into Los Angeles. Continue on US 101 about 12 miles to Universal Studios exit. About 40 miles, sixty minutes.

Disneyland to Six Flags California

Take I–5 north 60 miles through Buena Park, Norwalk, Santa Fe Springs, Pico Rivera, East Los Angeles, and Newhall. Exit at Magic Mountain Parkway in Valencia. About 63 miles, ninety minutes.

Disneyland to Long Beach and *Queen Mary*

Take I–5 south 3 miles toward Santa Ana. At Orange, turn off onto Highway 22 west toward Garden Grove, and drive 8 miles. Turn right onto I–405 north toward Long Beach. About 25 miles, forty minutes.

■ BUS SERVICE

Airport Bus. From LAX to Disneyland, with shuttles from Disneyland to Knott's Berry Farm and Universal Studios Hollywood. (714) 938–8900 or (800) 938–8933. www.airportbus.com.

Best Shuttle. On-call, to and from LAX and points in Orange County. (800) 606–7433 within Orange County.

LAXpress Airport Shuttle. (310) 216–3336 or (800) 427–7483. www.xpress shuttle.com.

Prime Time Shuttle International. LAX, Orange County, Ontario, Burbank Airport, San Pedro Harbor. (800) 262–7533. www.primetimeshuttle.com.

SuperShuttle. To Anaheim and Orange County from LAX. (714) 517–6600 or (800) 258–3826. www.supershuttle.com.

■ TAXI SERVICES

Yellow Cab of Orange County. Fixed-rate service to and from Anaheim for up to five passengers per cab. (714) 535–2211. www.californiayellowcab.com.

■ SHOPPING SHUTTLES

Anaheim Indoor Marketplace. Complimentary shuttle service from Disneyland-area hotels to this indoor swap meet. (714) 999–0888. www.anaheim marketplace.com.

Anaheim Visitor Center. Transportation to the Block at Orange. (714) 239–1340 or (877) 991–4636.

South Coast Plaza. Transportation to mall in Costa Mesa. (714) 435–8571. www.southcoastplaza.com.

Westfield Shoppingtown MainPace. Transportation from major Anaheim-area hotels to mall in Santa Ana. (714) 547–7000. www.westfield.com.

PART II

THE DISNEYLAND RESORT

CHAPTER TWO

ONCE UPON A MOUSE

ONCE UPON A MOUSE, Walter Elias Disney sat down at the drawing board. The year was 1928, and the star of the cartoon short he created was named Steamboat Willie. His more familiar name, Mickey Mouse, came a bit later.

Everything else has been built upon the shoulders of this cute little rodent, along with his gal, Minnie, buddies Donald, Daisy, Goofy, Pluto, Snow White, and a cast of thousands of other cartoon and movie favorites. (When Disneyland celebrated its fiftieth anniversary in 2005, the mouse himself was a spry seventy-seven years old.)

Flushed with his early success in cartooning, Disney planned to set up a little park alongside his first movie studios in Burbank to entertain his employees and their families; part of the entertainment was to include an expansion of Disney's hobby, a small train system. World War II interfered with the plans for the humble park; when the postwar boom arrived, Disney was ready with a much more ambitious scheme.

Beginning in 1953 Disney conducted a search for a site of about one hundred acres somewhere in the Los Angeles area. He was looking for enough space to build a fantasy world with rivers, mountains, flying elephants, and a fairy-tale castle.

The land that Disney found was a 160-acre orange grove in rural Anaheim, near the new Interstate 5, a freeway that would eventually become the spine of California and the West Coast, reaching from San Diego to Vancouver.

He called the place **Disneyland,** and he put his company into debt to commit every available dollar to the purchase of the land and construction of the park. The bottom line was about $17 million, a huge amount of money for an unproven entertainment concept at the time.

When Walt Disney opened his park on July 17, 1955, Anaheim was surrounded by orange groves. As the popularity of Disneyland grew, so did the city of Anaheim, to the point where the park was landlocked by a sea of motels and restaurants within a few years.

As Timur Galen, Walt Disney Imagineering General Manager of the Disneyland Resort, subsequently noted, "If Disneyland had started as the only development in a sea of green, it was now the only green in a sea of asphalt."

Although a great deal has changed in the half-century since the first plans for Disneyland were drawn, the basic structure of the park, and all that has followed, is the same.

DISNEYLAND TODAY

Today, breathes there a man, woman, girl, boy, or mouse who has not dreamed of making a pilgrimage to Disneyland? The entertainment vision of Walt Disney—along with the incredible marketing skills of the company he left behind—has made Disney's parks and characters among the world's best-known popular icons.

You can see Mickey Mouse T-shirts on the streets of Moscow, Epcot towels on the beaches of the Caribbean, Minnie dresses on the boulevards of Paris, and Roger Rabbit hats in the alleys of Tokyo.

But if you haven't been to Disneyland since early 2001, you may not recognize the place, at least not until you are strolling up Main Street toward Sleeping Beauty Castle.

The Disneyland park itself is little changed, but everything around it has: Almost magically, Disneyland has become the **Disneyland Resort.** The neon jungle of motels and restaurants around the park has been legislated into a buffer of greenery and palm trees.

The **Downtown Disney** shopping and entertainment district is now the sparkling gateway to the resort, an avenue of attractive restaurants and shops and entertainment for the grown-ups that jumps until late into the night.

And most important, the gateway leads to not one but two theme parks: **Disneyland** and **Disney's California Adventure.**

BEHIND THE SCENES AT DISNEY'S CALIFORNIA ADVENTURE

For 500 years, California has been considered one of the world's great golden lands of opportunity. People came there from all over the world for gold, oil, oranges, and railroads. In more modern times, they came for freedom of expression and adventure.

California is the capital of the global motion picture industry, music, and television industries. It was also the birthplace of Mickey Mouse and Disneyland, the theme park that became the model for all others.

Walt Disney had been unable to buy enough land around his park to prevent the encroachment of outsiders or to allow enough space to expand his park; he took these lessons with him to Florida when he planned the massive Walt Disney World, which spreads across some 40 square miles. According to the company, Michael Eisner began looking for a way to expand Disneyland soon after he became chairman of the company in 1984.

The goal was to expand Disneyland from a one-park, one-day attraction to a destination resort. At one point it appeared that a second park would be built in Long Beach or other nearby communities, but the plans were never finalized. Instead, Disney Imagineers came up with a scheme to build a second park in the parking lot of Disneyland.

Disney worked with the City of Anaheim to improve the appearance of the resort area and to create a whole new infrastructure to support expansion. The plan began by putting the Anaheim Mighty Ducks, an NHL hockey team, onto the ice at city-owned Arrowhead Pond in Anaheim. Disney next acquired the California Angels baseball team, renaming them the Anaheim Angels and improving and transforming Anaheim Stadium into an attractive modern field. (The Angels were sold in 2003, a season after the team won the World Series.)

In 1990 Disney and the City of Anaheim began work on master plans for the Disneyland Resort and the Anaheim Resort Area, including expansion of the Anaheim Convention Center. A not-insignificant element of the plans was the creation of a new tourist district that encompassed the neighborhood surrounding Disneyland. The city enacted regulations that required the removal of large signs and advertising billboards, replaced with a standardized set of tasteful informational signs. The Disney Corporation was not immune, taking down the venerable Disneyland marquee that had stood outside the original theme park for decades as well as the big blue neon tube letters from atop its own hotels. Disney bought several hotels and other businesses that were adjacent to its property and bought other land to be used for new parking lots and a massive parking structure. Disney also owns a large piece of land several blocks away, most recently used as a strawberry field. Disney has already conducted preliminary negotiations with Anaheim city officials for zoning and planning approvals for a third park at the resort, which could be located there.

■ DESIGNING DISNEY'S CALIFORNIA ADVENTURE

The concept behind Disney's California Adventure was born in 1995. A Disney Imagineering team added new concepts to elements from other Disney parks around the world as well as pieces that had been developed for the company's unsuccessful attempt to build Disney's America in Virginia near Washington, D.C., and for an earlier concept for a new park in California, called Westcot.

"Disney's America in Virginia was a great idea and would have been a great park with a lot of great content," Eisner said in a meeting with reporters in 2001. "When it came time to find a more friendly place than Washington, a place that would embrace freedom of speech, we came back to California."

"First thing, we threw out the rule book," said Barry Braverman, Walt Disney Imagineering executive producer for Disney's California Adventure park. "This

Cutting the Lines

With great fanfare and much appreciation by guests weary of waiting in lines, Disney introduced the Fastpass system at all of its parks.

Here's how it works: You insert your ticket into a reader at special booths near attractions and receive a Fastpass ticket with an assigned time period. When you return, you'll enter into a special gateway to the attraction with a promise of no more than a fifteen-minute wait. On all but the busiest days of the year, you're allowed to hold only one Fastpass ticket at a time; when waiting time for a reservation extends to several hours, Disney allows ticket holders to make reservations at two different attractions.

is a park that is very open in its views. You can stand at the park's entry plaza and see the gateway to Golden State; you can see the California Grizzly Bear icon high atop Grizzly Peak; you can see the gates to Hollywood; and you can see Paradise Pier's massive roller coaster, along with so much more. Here we have a park that embraces 'visual intrusion' and turns it into an attribute that draws guests into the environment and the excitement happening throughout.

"Usually we're working in a completely green field situation and we locate a site to fit the idea, much like what was done for Disney's Animal Kingdom at Walt Disney World in Florida," continued Braverman. "In this case, we knew where we were going to build it, and the space clearly has constraints such as size, configuration, and the fact that it was completely surrounded by an urban environment. We had to work our ideas inside that framework."

Construction commenced in 1997. By the time of its opening, Anaheim, Orange County, the State of California, various federal agencies, and the Walt Disney Company had invested nearly $4 billion to revitalize the Anaheim resort area and to expand the Disneyland Resort. In addition to Disney's California Adventure, Downtown Disney, and Disney's Grand Californian Hotel, the overall project included an expansion of the Anaheim Convention Center. Revitalization of the surrounding region brought new palm tree–lined streets, repaved walkways, colorful boulevard banners, and lush landscaping throughout.

A parking structure, the largest in North America, now serves the new resort. Disney theme park guests heading north on the I–5 freeway can exit directly into the structure where parking for 10,250 cars is available. A pedestrian walkway leads from the parking structure to an escalator that goes directly to the tram loading areas. Convention Center and Downtown Disney guests travel on a separate roadway system. In addition, surface parking is available for 16,500 more vehicles.

Disney's California Adventure officially opened to the public on February 8, 2001. With the addition of Disney's Grand Californian Hotel, the Disneyland Resort has a total of 2,243 guest rooms, including the existing Disneyland Hotel and Disney's Paradise Pier Hotel.

CHAPTER THREE

FROM YOUR LAND TO THE DISNEYLAND RESORT

WHEN AND HOW—WE ALREADY KNOW WHERE AND WHY

Here are two hypothetical days spent at the Disneyland Resort:

July 4. It wasn't exactly the flight you wanted. However, you're grateful for the privilege of forking over $840 for a coach seat in the jammed cabin of the wide-body jet. All the rooms at the three Disney hotels—at $300 per night—are sold out, but you were lucky enough to pay just $100 for an extremely ordinary hotel room that's a twenty-minute, bumper-to-bumper drive from the parking lots.

You're directed to the very last space in what looks like the world's largest parking structure (it is). According to the driver of the tram that takes you on a journey to the entrance plaza, you are in the same county as the Matterhorn and Grizzly Peak, although you're not really sure.

When you get to the entrance, there's a thirty-minute wait just to buy your ticket. And as you get close to the counter, you see a sign posted by the window: "Disney reserves the right to halt the sale of tickets when Disneyland or Disney's California Adventure reaches full capacity."

If you make it through the gates of Disneyland, you sprint to Tomorrowland to find that the line for the Indiana Jones Adventure includes what seems like the entire population of Boston. That's the good news; the bad news is that the first Fastpass tickets to skip the line at Space Mountain are for 6:00 P.M.

You might as well go out to lunch. You'd better plan on showing up at 10:45 A.M. to get the food and then make plans for a 4:30 P.M. dinner if you hope to find a table at even the lowliest overpriced burger stop.

If instead you've chosen to visit Disney's California Adventure, you may want to bring a good book to read while you wait for your spin on the Sun Wheel.

DISNEYLAND RESORT AND SURROUNDING AREA

March 20. It seems like it's just your family and a crew of flight attendants stretched out across the empty seats in the warm sun at 30,000 feet. Even nicer, you were able to grab a deep-discount cross-country ticket for $198. Your hotel room cost you $39.95 (you could have rented one next to the park for just a bit more), and the highway to the park is empty.

At Disneyland, your leisurely walk to the Indiana Jones Adventure puts you into a ten-minute queue; later in the day you hop onto a rocket car at Space Mountain without breaking stride.

Over at Disney's California Adventure, the attendant asks if you want to ride the Sun Wheel by yourself or if you'd like to share the car with Mickey and Minnie. The ghoul at the gate of the Twilight Zone Tower of Terror offers you an elevator of your own.

Take your pick of restaurants, and feel free to take a break in the afternoon and run over to the hotel pool.

Do I have to point out which trip is likely to be more enjoyable?

◼ OUR GUIDING RULE

The basic *Econoguide* strategy to getting the most out of your trip to the Disneyland Resort and Los Angeles is this:

Go when most people don't; stay home when everyone else is standing in line.

Specifically, try to visit California when school is in session and in the weeks between holidays. Come between Labor Day and Thanksgiving, between Thanksgiving and Christmas, between New Year's Day and Presidents' week, between Presidents' week and spring break/Easter, and after spring break until Memorial Day.

I'm not just talking about ways to avoid the crowds at the Disneyland Resort, Universal Studios Hollywood, Knott's Berry Farm, Six Flags California, and elsewhere in Southern California. I'm also talking about the availability of discount airline tickets, off-season motel rates, and restaurant specials.

You'll find the lower prices when your business is needed, not when the "No Vacancy" lamp is lit. The best deals can be found in low-season, or during the shoulder-season midway between the least-crowded and busiest periods.

This doesn't mean you can't have a good time if your schedule (or your children's) requires you to visit at high-season. I'll show you ways to save money and time, any month of the year.

A DISNEYLAND RESORT VACATION CALENDAR

The number of theme parks at the Disneyland Resort doubled in 2001 with the opening of Disney's California Adventure. So did the potential crowds.

The maximum capacity of the Disneyland park is about seventy thousand, a level often approached or achieved during the Easter period, around Memorial Day, the Fourth of July, and from Christmas through New Year's Day.

At Disney's California Adventure (DCA), the maximum capacity is about thirty-five thousand with a similar attendance pattern—the park rarely reaches

Key to Calendar

👤 = Semiprivate

👤 👤 = Moderate crowds

👤 👤 👤 = Heavy crowds

👤 👤 👤 👤 = Elbow-to-elbow

👤 👤 👤 👤 👤 = Too much

full capacity. Although attendance levels have begun to grow, DCA continues to attract much smaller crowds than the numbers at Disneyland. The introduction of the Twilight Zone Tower of Terror in 2004 is expected to boost numbers at the park.

According to industry estimates, in 2004 Disneyland attracted about 13.4 million visitors, an increase of about 5 percent over the previous year; DCA drew about 5.6 million guests, an increase of about 6 percent.

The eighteen-month-long celebration of Disneyland's fiftieth anniversary is expected to boost attendance at both parks, especially during the numerous special events planned during that period.

■ JANUARY TO MARCH

👤 👤 👤 👤 New Year's Day

👤 Second week of January through mid-March

👤 👤 👤 👤 Presidents' Weekend in February and days surrounding

Headaches on New Year's Day and too much company for the weekend of Presidents' Day. January through mid-March is a semiprivate experience.

New Year's Day and a day or two afterward mark the end of the Christmas rush. But a day or two into January, the kids go back to school and most of the adults return to work, and attendance drops off sharply. A great day to visit is Super Bowl Sunday, when couch potatoes take up positions in front of the television screen for the day.

The period from the beginning of January through mid-March is usually among the least crowded times of the year, with weekday attendance at the Disneyland Resort of about ten to twenty thousand daily at each park; on weekends, the crowds usually double to a moderate to heavy level of twenty to forty thousand per day. Hotel room rates are generally at low-season levels.

Note that Disneyland generally closes early and does not offer nighttime parades or fireworks except during holiday periods.

■ MID-MARCH TO PRE-EASTER

👤 👤 Moderate crowds on weekdays

👤 👤 👤 Lots of company on weekends

From mid-March until the first week of April, attendance begins to grow slowly.

Disneyland generally stays open until 9:00 or 10:00 P.M. during the week and until midnight on weekends, with *Fantasmic!* and fireworks offered only on weekends. Disney's California Adventure follows a similar schedule.

Weekday room rates are below peak rates.

■ EASTER

👤 👤 👤 👤 Week leading up to Easter Sunday

👤 👤 👤 Week after Easter Sunday

The Easter Parade can get very thick.

The second and third weeks before Easter are among the most crowded times of the year, with holiday visitors and spring break students clogging the turnstiles to near-capacity levels.

Disneyland may be open as late as midnight, with *Fantasmic!* and fireworks shows offered most nights. Disney's California Adventure will usually offer some late hours as well.

Room rates are at high-season levels.

■ END OF APRIL TO PRE-MEMORIAL DAY

👤 👤 Weekdays in early spring

👤 👤 👤 👤 Weekends in early spring

A lovely time, with moderate attendance during the week and growing crowds on the weekends.

As the summer approaches, both parks begin with a schedule that calls for closing at 8:00 or 9:00 P.M., moving toward midnight later in May.

Room rates are between low- and high-season rates (called "shoulder" rates by travel agents), creeping into high-season rates near the end of May.

■ MEMORIAL DAY HOLIDAY PERIOD

👤 👤 👤 Weekdays leading up to Memorial Day

👤 👤 👤 👤 Memorial Day weekend

👤 👤 👤 👤 👤 Memorial Day

Lots of company for the holidays.

Memorial Day marks the unofficial start of the summer holiday season, and by the time it arrives, the Disneyland Resort is ready to meet the public with operating hours running until midnight on the weekends. *Fantasmic!* and fireworks are presented most nights.

Room rates are at high-season levels.

■ JUNE, JULY, AND AUGUST TO PRE-LABOR DAY

👤 👤 👤 👤 Weekdays in summer

👤 👤 👤 👤 👤 Weekends in summer

The crazy days of summer.

Just after Memorial Day the throngs come. They stick around from the first week of June through the third week of August. Both parks are open late into the night, with nighttime parades and fireworks scheduled.

Room rates are at high-season levels for the entire summer.

▓ LABOR DAY

👤 👤 👤 Labor Day week

👤 👤 👤 👤 Labor Day weekend

The last gasp of summer.

As Labor Day approaches, many visitors from elsewhere in the country head back home. At the same time, many Californians come to the park for one last fling before school and other obligations take hold.

Room rates are discounted from peak levels.

▓ SEPTEMBER TO MID-OCTOBER

👤 Weekdays in early fall

👤 👤 Weekends in early fall

Where have all the tourists gone?

On the day after Labor Day, the turnstiles slow to a relative crawl. The locals return on the weekends.

The parks generally close about 9:00 P.M.; there are some late hours on weekends, with parades or fireworks.

Room rates are at low-season levels.

▓ COLUMBUS DAY TO PRE-THANKSGIVING

👤 👤 Weekdays

👤 👤 👤 Weekends

The holidays arrive early.

The holiday season begins in mid-October with a Disneyfied observance of Halloween. In recent years, the Haunted Mansion received a mock-creepy Nightmare Before Christmas makeover.

The run-up to Christmas begins early November with special events and decorations. If the weather cooperates this can be a very pleasant time to visit, with small crowds during the week and moderate levels on the weekend.

The parks generally close about 9:00 P.M.; there are some late hours on weekends, with fireworks.

Room rates are at high-season levels.

▓ THANKSGIVING WEEKEND

👤 👤 👤 👤 Turkey time

Merchants give thanks for huge crowds.

Crowds build to near-peak levels, especially on the Friday through Sunday after Thanksgiving. Both parks are open until late in the night, with fireworks and shows.

Room rates reach high-season levels.

■ POST-THANKSGIVING TO PRE-CHRISTMAS

🚶 Weekdays in late November and early December

🚶 🚶 Weekends in late November and early December

This is it: the secret season.

Mickey can get lonely at times like these, especially during the week. From after Thanksgiving until the day Christmas vacation starts is the quietest time of the year for a visit.

The parks generally close at 8:00 or 9:00 P.M., and there are no nighttime parades or fireworks, except for weekends.

Room rates are at rock-bottom levels during the week, slightly higher on weekends.

🚶 🚶 Weekdays in mid-December

🚶 🚶 🚶 Weekends in mid-December

'Tis the weeks before Christmas.

■ CHRISTMAS THROUGH NEW YEAR'S DAY

🚶 🚶 🚶 🚶 🚶 Every day is a holiday

Your sisters and cousins and aunts will all be in line—in front of you.

The Christmas–New Year's holiday is the most crowded, least time-efficient time to visit the Disneyland Resorts. You can expect the park to be open late and to offer one or more nighttime parades, and fireworks.

Christmas is a special place at the Disneyland Resort, with holiday decorations, celebrity appearances, and a Christmas parade usually scheduled to run from just before Thanksgiving until New Year's Day. You may even get a chance to be a part of the nationally televised festivities on Christmas Day—West Coast activities are usually taped a day or two ahead of time. The bad news is that if you visit Disneyland at this time of year, you will not be alone. If you must go, be sure to arrive at the parks early and follow the Power Trip plan for your best chance.

Hotel rooms are at or above high-season levels.

THE BEST DAY TO GO TO THE PARKS

At least half the typical crowd at the Disneyland Resort comes from local residents making a day trip. The proportion of out-of-town visitors goes up during school vacation periods. Disneyland helps regulate the flow a bit by excluding some classes of season-pass holders from both of the parks at the busiest times of the year.

Overall, Saturday is usually the busiest day of the week; Tuesday through Thursday are usually the least crowded days to visit. Here are the days of the week, from least crowded to most crowded.

👤 **Tuesday, Wednesday, Thursday**

👤 👤 Monday, Friday

👤 👤 👤 Sunday

👤 👤 👤 👤 Saturday and holidays

If you're planning a multiday visit to Disneyland Resort, consider visiting Disneyland on a weekday and crossing over to Disney's California Adventure on the weekend.

■ WEATHER OR NOT

Temperatures can go through a fairly broad range, from cool mornings to hot afternoons and back to chilly evenings. And you can get a bit moist on Splash Mountain in Disneyland or soaked at Grizzly River Run at Disney's California Adventure. If the wind is blowing from the north, the mist from *Fantasmic!* can also dampen the crowd at Disneyland.

Think about bringing along sweatshirts and jackets and stowing them in a locker in the park; some visitors bring backpacks for the family. If there is a hint of rain in the forecast, you may want to bring along your own lightweight raincoat. With the first drop of rain, Disney stores and pushcarts will quickly uncrate cases of throwaway plastic covers, which may or may not match your ensemble or please your pocketbook.

Anaheim Weather

	Average High	Average Low
January	65	47
February	67	49
March	68	50
April	70	53
May	72	56
June	77	60
July	82	64
August	83	65
September	81	63
October	77	59
November	73	52
December	67	48

(temperatures in degrees Fahrenheit)

■ WHAT TIME DO THE PARKS OPEN?

It depends. On the busiest holiday weekends of the year, the parks may open to the public as early as 7:30 A.M. In the summer and certain holidays, the parks open early and stay open very late, often until midnight. In slow periods, the parks may open as late as 10:00 A.M. and close as early as 6:00 or 8:00 P.M.

Guests at one of the three Disneyland Resort hotels may be offered early admission to certain sections of either park; at peak times, gates for guests with special passes open as much as ninety minutes before regular time.

Be sure to check with the Disneyland Resort the day before your visit to confirm operating hours. Call (714) 781–7290. The Disneyland Resort Web site, at www.disneyland.com, includes a complete list of hours of operation and show schedules. You will also find listings of attractions closed for refurbishing.

For information about special events and entertainment at Downtown Disney, consult the Upcoming Events page in the Downtown Disney section of www.disneyland.com.

YOU'VE GOT TO HAVE A TICKET

Ticket prices for Disneyland were in effect in 2005 and are subject to change. Prices are often adjusted (almost always upward) in early spring.

Note that in recent years Disney's definition (you may have your own) of a child declined a bit to ages three through nine.

From time to time Disney also sells other tickets, including **Ultimate Park Hopper** tickets available for extended periods to guests at Disney-owned hotels, and **Flex** tickets available at some nearby independent hotels. Visitors to major conventions in Anaheim can usually purchase special tickets, including an after-4:00 P.M. pass.

Lines at the ticket booths can grow to unhappy lengths at the start of the day and stay that way on very busy days. Arrive early to buy the tickets, or get them ahead of time to save the aggravation.

You can purchase multiday tickets, usually at a slight discount, by advance order through www.disneyland.com.

Tickets can be purchased by mail from Disneyland Ticket Mail Order, P.O. Box 61061, Anaheim, CA 92803–6161. Call (714) 781–4043 to confirm current prices and handling charge; the same number can also be used to purchase by credit card.

Disney Stores around the country also sell daily tickets.

■ A PRIVATE TOUR

Guests can rent a Guest Relations host or hostess for a private Premiere Tour of Disneyland. A group of as many as ten guests can walk with the guide; larger groups require an additional guide. In 2005, the tour cost $75 per hour, booked for a minimum of four hours. The cost is $95 per hour if booked fewer than

Disneyland and Disney's California Adventure Tickets

	ADULT	CHILD (ages 3 to 9)**
ONE-DAY PASS	$53	$43
Tickets are valid in one park on one day.		
ONE-DAY PARK HOPPER ♦	$73	$63
TWO-DAY PARK HOPPER ♦	$105	$85
THREE-DAY PARK HOPPER ♦*	$159	$129
FOUR-DAY PARK HOPPER ♦ ●*	$189	$159
FIVE-DAY PARK HOPPER ♦ ●*	$209	$179

♦ Park Hopper passes allow entrance to either or both parks every day; pass must be used within fourteen days of first visit.

● Bonus pass includes $10 ESPN Zone Arena Game card.

* Special discount pricing on three-, four-, and five-day passes available with packages and through advance purchase at www.disney.com.

** Child younger than age 3 admitted free.

forty-eight hours in advance. It requires a separate admission ticket. For information and necessary advance reservations, call (714) 300–7710.

■ WALK IN WALT'S FOOTSTEPS GUIDED TOUR

This three-hour tour includes a guided ride on the Disneyland Railroad, a visit to an attraction like the Enchanted Tiki Room, a glimpse of the lobby of the exclusive Club 33, and lunch on the patio of the Disney Gallery. It requires an admission ticket. $49 per person. For information and reservations call (714) 781–4400.

■ WELCOME TO DISNEYLAND TOUR

A two-and-a-half hour walking tour introduces new visitors to the Disneyland Resort. The visit to Downtown Disney, Disneyland hotels, Disneyland, and Disney's California Adventure includes VIP seating for *Disney's Aladdin*, Fastpass to Pirates of the Caribbean, and other goodies. It requires an admission ticket. $25 per person. For information and reservations call (714) 781–4400.

■ MILITARY DISCOUNTS

Active members of the U.S. military and the Department of Defense can obtain discounted tickets through the Morale, Welfare and Recreation (MWR) offices. For information call (714) 781–4565.

■ ANNUAL PASSPORTS

Disney offers several types of annual passports including a premium pass valid every day and a deluxe pass with as many as forty-five excluded days. In years past annual passes were a great deal for visitors who come to the park for five or more days per year.

In past years Disneyland has offered substantial discounts to local residents for daily admission at slow times of the year, as much as one-third off regular ticket prices. Visitors must show a driver's license or utility bill. These tickets are available only at Disneyland ticket booths and only for the day of purchase. In years past, Californians were permitted to bring along a few friends; perhaps you can meet one in line.

Y'all Come Back

If you want to leave the park during the day and return, be sure to have your hand stamped at the exit, and hold on to your passport; you'll need to show both the stamp and passport to get back in.

MORE DISNEY DETAILS

Parking. Autos: $8.00. Trailers, campers, and recreational vehicles: $10.00.

Guests with Disabilities. For specific information, obtain a copy of the *Guidebook for Guests with Disabilities* from Disneyland. An audiotape tour and *Disneyland Braille Guidebook* are available at City Hall in the Disneyland park and at Guest Services in Golden Gateway at Disney's California Adventure.

Wheelchairs and electric convenience vehicles are available for rent just inside the main entrance of each park, for a fee of $7.00 for wheelchairs and $30.00 for ECVs. Both require a refundable deposit of $20.00.

Strollers. Strollers are available for rent for $8.00 per day at Disneyland inside the main entrance and at Star Trader in Tomorrowland. At Disney's California Adventure strollers can be rented inside the main entrance in Golden Gateway and in Condor Flats at Fly 'n' Buy.

Baby Care Centers. You'll find a bit of privacy for baby matters in Disneyland at the end of Main Street across from Central Plaza next to First Aid. At Disney's California Adventure the Baby Center is located next to the Mission Tortilla Factory in Pacific Wharf. Facilities are available for preparing formulas, warming bottles, and nursing and changing infants. The centers also offer diapers, formulas, bottles, and pacifiers for sale. Diaper machines and changing tables are available in most restrooms throughout the parks.

First Aid. Medical assistance is available in Disneyland at the end of Main Street, across from Central Plaza next to the Baby Center. At Disney's California Adventure, help is available next to the Mission Tortilla Factory in Pacific Wharf next to the Baby Center. At Downtown Disney, First Aid is located between Ralph Brennan's Jazz Kitchen and Island Charters.

Suspended Animation

A recurring rumor about dear old Walt Disney is that he chose to be cryogenically frozen when he died of lung cancer in 1966, in hopes of a defrost in another day and age. Actually, according to the company, he went to the other extreme and was cremated before burial at the famous Forest Lawn Memorial Park in California.

Kennel Club. Pets can be boarded for the day for about $15 at kennels, located to the right of the main entrance of the Disneyland park. No overnight accommodations are offered.

Money Matters. The Disneyland Resort will be happy to accept just about any form of payment for tickets including cash, checks, and most credit cards.

At Disneyland, ATMs are located at the main entrance, on Main Street, in Frontierland, in Fantasyland, and in Tomorrowland. At Disney's California Adventure, ATMs can be found at the main entrance, in the Bay Area, at Pacific Wharf, and in the Hollywood Pictures Backlot. At Downtown Disney, ATMs are located across from the Häagen-Dazs store and next to the Lego Imagination Center. With appropriate identification, checks can be used to pay for purchases in shops within either park at the Disneyland Resort.

Lockers. At Disneyland, lockers are available outside the main entrance and within the park on Main Street and at Fantasyland. At Disney's California Adventure, lockers are outside the main entrance and within the park at Golden Gateway. Locker prices range from $4.00 to $6.00 per day, depending on size. Availability can change based on security concerns.

Lost and Found. The central repository for hats, sunglasses, wallets, and just about anything else you can possibly leave behind at a theme park is located outside the main entrance to Disney's California Adventure park.

Captioning. Special devices to provide captions to shows for visitors with hearing difficulties are available in both parks. At Disneyland, reflective captioning is offered at the *Walt Disney Story,* featuring *Great Moments with Mr. Lincoln,* Country Bear Playhouse, and *Honey, I Shrunk the Audience.* Video captioning is available in preshow portions of Indiana Jones Adventure, *Honey, I Shrunk the Audience*, Innoventions, Space Mountain, and Star Tours. At Disney's California Adventure, reflective captioning is offered at Golden Dreams, Golden Vine Winery, Disney Animation, Jim Henson's Muppet✳Vision 3D, and *It's Tough to Be a Bug!* Video captioning is available in preshow portions of Soarin' Over California, Disney Animation, and Jim Henson's Muppet✳Vision 3D.

To use the reflective captioning systems, seek the assistance of a cast member at the locations; for use of the video captioning system, visit City Hall in Disneyland or Guest Relations Lobby at Disney's California Adventure to obtain remote controls.

Restaurant Reservations. Reservations at many sit-down restaurants at Disneyland, Disney's California Adventure, and Downtown Disney can be made by calling (714) 781–3463.

A DISNEYLAND RESORT PHONE AND ADDRESS DIRECTORY

Disneyland Resort recorded information line: (714) 781–4565. You'll hear a menu of options. From the first menu, press 1 for Disneyland, 2 for Disney's California Adventure, 3 for Disney hotels, 4 for Downtown Disney, and 5 for annual pass information.

Once you select one of the two theme parks, press 1 for hours, 2 for ticket prices, 3 for entertainment schedules, 4 for dining reservations, 5 for attraction refurbishment information, and 6 for directions to the park.

To speak to a human being during business hours, call (714) 781–7290.

Disneyland operator: (714) 999–4560. Available Monday through Friday 7:00 A.M. to 7:00 P.M., Saturday and Sunday 7:00 A.M. to 10:00 P.M.

Disneyland Resort Web site: www.disneyland.com.

Disneyland Hotel, Disneyland Grand Californian Hotel, Disney's Paradise Pier Hotel: (714) 956–6400.

Character Meal reservations at hotel restaurants: (714) 956–6406.

Disneyland Guest Relations, City Hall, Disneyland: (714) 781–4565.

The Walt Disney Travel Company: For information on travel packages call (800) 225–2057.

Information is also available via mail by writing to: Walt Disney Travel Company, Inc., Travel Port Boulevard, 1441 South West Street, Anaheim, CA 92803.

You may also write for information on the park (at least three weeks in advance): Disneyland Guest Relations, 1313 Harbor Boulevard, P.O. Box 3232, Anaheim, CA 92803-6161.

THE DISNEYLAND RESORT WITH CHILDREN

Doesn't the title of this section sound ridiculously obvious? Well, yes and no: The fact is that for many kids a visit to the Disneyland Resort is the biggest thing that has ever happened to them—and although it almost always will be the most wonderful vacation they've ever had, there are special concerns for youngsters and their parents.

Here are ten suggestions to make the trip go well.

1. Involve the children in the planning of the trip. Obtain maps and brochures and study them at the dinner table; read sections of this book together. Work together to come up with a schedule for the places you want to go each day.

2. Draw up the "rules" for the visit and make sure each child understands and agrees with them. The basic rule in our family was that our young children always had to be within an arm's length of Mom or Dad.

Mom and Dad, I Promise . . .

One of the best things about going to Disneyland or Universal Studios with kids is that a resourceful parent should be able to milk a few weeks of "If you don't behave right now, I'm not taking you to Disneyland" threats. My ever-resourceful son, Willie, came up with his own contract:

THE TEN THEME PARK COMMANDMENTS
I.   Thou shalt not leave thy parents' sight.
II. Thou shalt not go on twister rides after a meal.
III. Thou shalt not complain about the lines.
IV. Thou shalt not fight with thy sister or brother.
V.   Thou shalt not ask to buy something at the shops that costs more than the admission ticket.
VI. Thou shalt enjoy any of the boring things that Mom and Dad want to see.
VII. Thou shalt stand still so Dad can take at least one picture.
VIII. Thou shalt not pester the characters to talk.
IX. Thou shalt not sing "It's a Small World After All" more than sixteen times in a row.
X.   Thou shalt go on at least one educational ride, even if it has a long line.

3. Study and understand the height and age minimums for some of the more active rides at the parks. Don't build up expectations of your 41-inch-tall child for a ride that requires you to be 42 inches in height. (Did we hear someone say something about lift pads in shoes? Just remember that the rules are there to protect children from injury.) And, alas, there have been more than a few accidents at Disneyland over the years, many of them related to youngsters wriggling out of harnesses or purposely breaking the rules. The following lists show the height requirements for rides in each park.

Disneyland has begun experimenting with a system that adds a bit of fun—and takes away a bit of imprecision—when it comes to measuring the heights of youngsters.

The Disney system, tested at Disneyland at the top of Main Street, uses an ultrasonic beam to measure height. The beam bounces from a post to a paddle held over the guest's head and the system flashes a colored light. Wristbands are color coded with Disney characters, and matching signs at each attraction make it simple for short guests to determine if they can ride that attraction.

Disneyland

Autopia: Riders must be at least 52 inches to drive. Young children may ride with an adult at the wheel.

Big Thunder Mountain Railroad: 40 inches minimum

Chip 'n' Dale's Treehouse and Acorn Crawl: 49 inches maximum

Gadget's Go-Coaster: 35 inches minimum
Goofy Bounce House: 52 inches maximum
Indiana Jones Adventure: 46 inches minimum
Matterhorn Bobsled: 35 inches minimum
Space Mountain: 40 inches minimum
Splash Mountain: 40 inches minimum
Star Tours: 40 inches minimum. Riders must be at least seven years old to ride alone or three years old to ride with an adult.

Disney's California Adventure
Jumpin' Jellyfish: 40 inches minimum
Grizzly River Run: 42 inches minimum
Mulholland Madness: 42 inches minimum
Redwood Creek Challenge Trail: 42 inches minimum
Soarin' Over California: 42 inches minimum
California Screamin': 48 inches minimum
Orange Stinger: 48 inches minimum
Maliboomer: 52 inches minimum
Tuck 'n' Roll's Drive 'Em Buggies: 47 inches minimum for passenger, 48 inches for driver
Twilight Zone Tower of Terror: 42 inches minimum

4. Come to a family agreement on financial matters. Few parents can afford to buy everything a child demands; even if you could, you probably would not want to. Consider giving your children a special allowance they can spend at the park. Encourage them to wait a day or two into the trip so they don't hit bottom before they find the souvenir they really want to take home.

5. When you arrive, and as you move through various areas, pick a place to meet if you are separated from your children. You should also have a backup plan—instruct your children to find a uniformed park attendant if they become lost, and check with attendants and security personnel yourself if you have misplaced a child.

You might want to attach a name tag to youngsters (available at Guest Services in the parks if you don't have your own) or put a piece of paper with your name and hotel in your child's pocket. Some parents even issue their kids walkie-talkies and keep the other one with them!

6. In summer and most any other time, keep your kids (and yourself) under hats and behind sunscreen, especially at midday. You may want to bring bottles of water for the entire family—it's a lot cheaper than soda at the snack bars, and much better for you.

7. You are not supposed to bring food into the park. You'll probably be stopped if you arrive with a picnic basket, but we've never seen a paying guest searched for sandwiches less obviously stored in pockets or small backpacks.

8. A good strategy with youngsters, especially if you are staying at a Disneyland Resort hotel or nearby, is to arrive early and leave at lunchtime for a quick nap or a swim in the pool; return at dusk to enjoy the evening at the park. You'll miss the hottest, most crowded part of the day and probably enjoy yourself much more. Be sure to have your hands stamped when you leave the park, and hold on to your tickets (including your parking pass if you leave the lot) if you intend to return.

9. Although you can bring your own stroller, it is also easy to rent one for the day at the park. Park the stroller near the exit to the attraction so that it is waiting for you when you come out. Don't leave any valuables with the stroller.

10. Most restrooms (male and female) in the park include changing tables. You can also purchase diapers and even formula at baby services stations. There are also places set aside for nursing mothers.

■ A KID'S-EYE VIEW OF THE BEST OF DISNEYLAND

What are the best attractions for youngsters three to ten years old? Some youngsters find Haunted Mansion a real hoot, while others will have nightmares for weeks. You know your particular child's interests and fears better than anyone else, but here are some favorites and a few warnings.

Disneyland for Youngest Visitors

Autopia (Tomorrowland)*
Dumbo the Flying Elephant (Fantasyland)
Enchanted Tiki Room (Adventureland)
Gadget's Go-Coaster (Mickey's Toontown)**
It's a Small World (Fantasyland)
Jungle Cruise (Adventureland)***
King Arthur Carrousel (Fantasyland)
Mad Tea Party (Fantasyland)**
Many Adventures of Winnie the Pooh (Critter Country)
Mickey's House, Minnie's House (Mickey's Toontown)
Peter Pan's Flight (Fantasyland)
Pirates of the Caribbean (New Orleans Square)***
Roger Rabbit's Car Toon Spin (Mickey's Toontown)
Snow White's Scary Adventures (Fantasyland)***
Storybook Land Canal Boats (Fantasyland)
Tom Sawyer Island (Frontierland)

Disney's California Adventure for Youngest Visitors

Bountiful Valley Farm
Disney Animation
Golden Dreams
Golden Zephyr**
Grizzly River Run*
Hyperion Theater***
It's Tough to Be a Bug!***
Jim Henson's Muppet✳Vision 3D

Jumpin' Jellyfish
King Triton's Carousel
Mulholland Madness**
Orange Stinger**
Redwood Creek Challenge Trail
Soarin' Over California**
S.S. *rustworthy*
Sun Wheel**
Superstar Limo

NOTES: *Adult must accompany small children.
　　　　**Can make some children dizzy.
　　　　***Loud noises and special effects (pirates, skeletons, beasts) may startle.

CHAPTER FOUR

THE WORLD OF DISNEYLAND

THE HAPPIEST CELEBRATION ON EARTH—the fiftieth birthday of Disneyland—began on May 5, 2005 (for numerologists, that's 05/05/05), and will continue through the end of 2006. But as Walt Disney promised when he opened the park, the place will never be completed.

The latest and greatest at the park includes:

- **Buzz Lightyear Astro Blasters** in Tomorrowland
- **Space Mountain,** also in Tomorrowland, rebuilt, renewed, and recharged for blastoff
- **Walt Disney's Parade of Dreams** on Main Street

Also part of the celebration is a spectacular new film commemorating the history of the park: *Disneyland: The First 50 Magical Years.* And at night there is the beyond-spectacular *Remember . . . Dreams Come True* fireworks show.

The heart of Disneyland—Main Street, Sleeping Beauty Castle, Pirates of the Caribbean, the Matterhorn Bobsleds, Space Mountain, Haunted Mansion, and more—has been a comforting constant for fifty years. Since it opened on July 17, 1955, more than 500 million people have made their pilgrimage to the park.

The celebration extends to all of the other Disney theme parks around the world, with the premiere of new shows and attractions at Walt Disney World Resort in Florida, Tokyo Disney Resort in Japan, Disneyland Resort Paris in France, and the new Hong Kong Disneyland.

Within its gates the original Disneyland is pretty much just as you remember it, and just as your children imagine it. For the big party, though, **Sleeping Beauty Castle** has been transformed into a breathtaking focal point for "The Happiest Homecoming on Earth." Through the end of 2006, the castle is swathed in richly colored royal banners, trimmed in gold and jewels, and topped by five glowing regal turret "crowns."

One thing that has changed: Today Disneyland is the centerpiece of a sprawling resort. Most guests enter through the lively Downtown Disney entertainment district, with restaurants, theaters, and shops open late into the night.

When they reach the entrance plaza, visitors can turn left into Disneyland or right into Disney's California Adventure.

■ A SENSE OF PLACE

There are eight lands and districts at the park:

Main Street, U.S.A. Frozen in time in early twentieth-century America with the Disneyland Railroad at one end and the Central Plaza and Sleeping Beauty Castle at the other.

Adventureland. Home to Indiana Jones, Tarzan, and the impossibly corny Jungle Cruise and Enchanted Tiki Room.

New Orleans Square. Two of Disneyland's most cherished dark rides are the lure here: Pirates of the Caribbean and Haunted Mansion.

Frontierland. The slightly wild Big Thunder Mountain Railroad stands across the river from Tom Sawyer Island.

Critter Country. Splash Mountain, a raft ride with the Disney touch, is the big draw here for thrill-seekers. You'll also find the charming dark ride, Many Adventures of Winnie the Pooh.

Mickey's Toontown. Disney's classic cartoon characters have their homes here, and they welcome millions of visitors.

Fantasyland. This is Disneyland in a kid's mind's eye: Dumbo, Alice in Wonderland, Peter Pan, Snow White, and King Arthur Carrousel. Looking over it all is Disney's first mountain and still a classic ride: Matterhorn Bobsleds. And new in 2004 was a Broadway-style production of "Snow White—An Enchanting Musical," at Fantasyland Theatre.

Tomorrowland. You can blast off on Space Mountain (which returned in the summer of 2005 after a complete retooling), soar above a Jules Verne streetscape in an Astro Orbitor, or visit the moons of Endor in Star Tours. And there's also the intergalactic shoot-'em-up of Buzz Lightyear Astro Blasters.

MAIN STREET, U.S.A.

Walt Disney's memory of small-town America lives forever here. Main Street, U.S.A. is a place of friendly shopkeepers, mom-and-pop soda fountains, and

MUST-SEES

Indiana Jones Adventure
(Adventureland)

Jungle Cruise
(Adventureland)

Many Adventures of Winnie the Pooh
(Critter Country)

Splash Mountain
(Critter Country)

Pirates of the Caribbean
(New Orleans Square)

Haunted Mansion
(New Orleans Square)

Big Thunder Mountain Railroad
(Frontierland)

Fantasmic!
(Frontierland)

It's a Small World
(Fantasyland)

Matterhorn Bobsleds
(Fantasyland)

Roger Rabbit's Car Toon Spin
(Mickey's Toontown)

Space Mountain
(Tomorrowland)

Star Tours
(Tomorrowland)

Autopia
(Tomorrowland)

Buzz Lightyear Astro Blasters
(Tomorrowland)

DISNEYLAND

Mickey's Toontown

Fantasyland

Frontierland

Critter Country

Tomorrowland

New Orleans Square

Main Street U.S.A.

Adventureland

1. Tickets
2. Disneyland Railroad
3. Main Street Cinema
4. Enchanted Tiki Room
5. Jungle Cruise
6. Indiana Jones Adventure
7. Tarzan's Treehouse
8. Pirates of the Caribbean
9. Haunted Mansion
10. *Fantasmic!*
11. Golden Horseshoe Stage
12. *Mark Twain* Riverboat
13. Rafts to Island
14. Splash Mountain
15. Many Adventures of Winnie the Pooh
16. Tom Sawyer Island
17. Big Thunder Mountain Railroad
18. Special Events
19. Gadget's Go-Coaster
20. Mickey's House/Minnie's House
21. Roger Rabbit's Car Toon Spin
22. Jolly Trolley
23. It's a Small World
24. Sleeping Beauty Castle
25. Snow White's Scary Adventures
26. Pinocchio's Daring Journey
27. King Arthur Carrousel
28. Dumbo the Flying Elephant
29. Storybook Land Canal Boats
30. Mad Tea Party
31. Mr. Toad's Wild Ride
32. Alice in Wonderland
33. Peter Pan's Flight
34. Autopia
35. Matterhorn Bobsleds
36. Cosmic Waves
37. Monorail Station
38. Starcade
39. *Honey, I Shrunk the Audience*
40. Astro Orbitor
41. Star Tours
42. Innoventions
43. Space Mountain
44. Buzz Lightyear Astro Blasters

Disneyland Park's famous Main Street, U.S.A. *Photo by Corey Sandler. Used by permission from Disney Enterprises, Inc.*

horse-drawn trolleys. The streets are clean, the landscape neat, and litter never lingers on the ground.

For most visitors at the start of the day Main Street, U.S.A. is a place to rush through on the way to somewhere else. That's fine: If you are following our advice, you will have arrived early at the park with a specific destination in mind. But be sure to come back later to browse, shop, or eat. When you do, marvel at the attention to detail of the storefronts and interior decor of the shops.

Take a ride on a horse-drawn streetcar, a horseless carriage motorcar, an antique omnibus, or a vintage fire engine. Just before you pass through the tunnels under the railroad to enter Main Street, glance up to read the famous words of greeting: "Here you leave today and enter the world of yesterday, tomorrow, and fantasy."

A bit farther on, the 1955 dedication plaque on a flag pole reads, "To all that come to this happy place, welcome. Disneyland is your land. Here, age relives fond memories of the past, and here youth may savor the challenge and promise of the future. Disneyland is dedicated to the ideals, the dreams, and the hard facts that have created America . . . with the hope that

Baby Biz

Walt Disney's baby picture adorns the wall at the Baby Care Center, where you can change diapers, nurse a baby, warm a bottle, and do all those other baby things.

The center is located next to the First Aid Station at the top of Main Street. Next door is the Lost Children Center. If you misplace a kid, contact the nearest cast member, who will spread the word throughout the park by radio and contact the center to arrange a proper reunion.

Power Trip: A Fastpass Plan

For years, a big crowd at Disneyland guaranteed big lines and long waits at the most popular attractions. There are few things less appealing to four-year-olds waiting in the sun for a ride on Roger Rabbit's Car Toon Spin, a teenager chilling out in the line for Space Mountain, or an adult revisiting the ineffable charms of Pirates of the Caribbean.

In years past, we have offered detailed battle plans to our readers to help beat the waiting lines. We're happy to report that for the most part, Disney has come to the rescue with the introduction of Fastpass, a system that allows visitors to obtain a reserved time for a popular ride. Fastpass is not perfect, but it's a whole lot better than life without it.

In 2005 Fastpass was offered at Autopia, Big Thunder Mountain, Buzz Lightyear Astro Blasters, Indiana Jones Adventure, Roger Rabbit's Car Toon Spin, Space Mountain, Star Tours, and Splash Mountain. It is also offered at Haunted Mansion during the holiday season. In this book, look for the ≡*FAST* icon to spot Fastpass opportunities. (Among the popular rides not part of the Fastpass system: all of the kiddie rides in Fantasyland, plus Matterhorn Bobsleds, Astro Orbitor, and It's a Small World.) So, our recommended Power Trip for Disneyland works like this: (1) start by coming up with a list of the attractions you most want to see; (2) divide the list into Fastpass attractions and waiting-line attractions; (3) get to the park as early as you can; and (4) begin your day by making a beeline to the first Fastpass attraction on your list and grabbing a ticket.

On busy days, weekends, and holidays the gates open about thirty minutes before the park itself; you will be able to stroll to a rope barrier at the top of Main Street. On extremely busy days, the park may open earlier than the officially announced time.

At busy times of the year, your first Fastpass reservation will tell you to come back in an hour or two; later in the day, the gap may extend to several hours. Going back to our Power Trip strategy: Put the Fastpass in your pocket and head for the first stop on your non-Fastpass list. With a bit of luck, you can bounce back and forth between ride reservations and waiting lines.

Waiting times for the major rides are listed on a board near the Plaza Restaurant, which is just outside the entrance to Frontierland and Adventureland. Cast an eye on the waiting times as you enter to help adjust your Power Trip, and check the lines any time you're in the neighborhood. Your goal: Go where the crowds are not.

Moving beyond Fastpass, it's also important to understand the ebb-and-flow of traffic at the park. I've already suggested you arrive at the park early. You should also plan to eat lunch and dinner early to avoid lines and to take advantage of a break in the crowds when the rest of the world is chowing down. Another reduction in crowds at attractions comes during the daily parades, major shows, and fireworks.

Depending on how crowded the park is, you may want to repeat a few of the rides in the dark. My favorite after-dark excursions are on the Matterhorn and Big Thunder Mountain. You can also catch some of the story rides at Fantasyland, including Peter Pan, Mr. Toad's Wild Ride, and (for the hopelessly romantic or the hopelessly child-directed) It's a Small World.

In peak season and holidays, you can catch the late performance of the *Fantasmic!* show to end your day with a bang.

it will be a source of joy and inspiration to all the world."

As you proceed up Main Street, stop from time to time and look up: Most of the names on the second-story windows are those of former and present Disney employees responsible for creation or maintenance of the park.

And then grab a piece of sidewalk. Main Street is one of the best places to be if you are a serious parade fan. The entertainment moves toward or ends near the railroad station just inside the gates. (Other good spots include the Central Plaza at the top of Main Street near Sleeping Beauty Castle and on the streets of Frontierland, both of which are nearer the major attractions of the park.)

◼ DISNEYLAND RAILROAD

A pleasant way to tour the park, these real steam engines take passengers on a 1.5 mile, twenty-minute circuit of the park. A trip on the train is a great way to end up the day or to take a midday break.

Walt Disney was a railroad nut who ran a small-scale system in his own backyard. His first plans for a small amusement park for the employees of his studio were based around the trains.

The Disneyland line includes four engines, each one of them named for former executives of the Santa Fe Railroad. The oldest engine is the *Fred G. Gurley,* originally built in 1894 and used to haul sugarcane from plantations to the docks in New Orleans; it was rebuilt for Disney using original parts. The *Ernest S. Marsh* dates from 1925, originally built for a lumber mill in New England. The first engines at the park, the *C. K. Holiday* and the *E. P. Riley,* were designed and assembled by the Walt Disney Studios.

Each of the engines has a slightly different design. Pay attention to the number of wheels on each side of the engines and whether there are wheels beneath the tender (coal car). The locomotives no longer burn coal, by the way; all of the boilers have been converted to burn oil.

Lockers

You'll find a set of coin-operated lockers outside the gates of Disneyland all the way to the left, near a picnic area.

Inside the park, you'll find a bank of lockers on the right side of Main Street about midway between the Main Street Train Station and the Hub. Spots in this prime location often fill up on busy days. Another group of lockers can be found deeper within the park near the Fantasyland Theatre.

Disney Choo-choo

The fabulous theme-park empire that bears Walt Disney's name can trace its roots back to Disney's personal train set.

Train fanciers and Disneyphiles will want to visit the waiting room of the Main Street Train Station. There is an interesting display of photographs of Disney's private line, the Carolwood-Pacific Railroad, which he operated in the backyard of his Holmby Hills home. Disney was fond of taking his daughters, employees, family, and friends for a ride on the miniature line, which later served as a ⅛-scale model for the full-size *C. K. Holiday* that has circled Disneyland since 1955. You will also see old pictures of Disney with his railroad system in his backyard seated on the little steam train.

A wooden display case exhibits a caboose from the Carolwood-Pacific Railroad built by Walt Disney himself. He handcrafted all of its interior appointments, including bunk beds, clothes lockers, a magazine rack that has miniature newspapers, a desk, washstands, and a potbellied stove.

The trains run in a clockwise circle from Main Street to Adventureland, New Orleans Square, Frontierland, Fantasyland, Tomorrowland, and back to Main Street. They pass through the Zip-a-Dee Lady scene inside Splash Mountain, through the loading area for It's a Small World, and into the mass transportation corridor of Tomorrowland where the tracks for the steam train, the monorail, and Autopia cars come close together.

The train offers some views of areas that can be seen only from the rails. After clearing the station in Tomorrowland, the train enters a tunnel that holds two of Disneyland's less well-known attractions: the Grand Canyon Diorama and the Primeval World.

The Grand Canyon display re-creates a tiny bit of the South Rim of the canyon with a football-field-long painting and stuffed animals. Some of the original trees and plants were harvested from the canyon itself.

Primeval World, originally created for the Ford Motor Pavilion at the New York World's Fair in 1964–1965, was in part inspired by Disney's animated classic *Fantasia*. The fair exhibit in turn helped set the tone for the considerably more detailed and realistic world of the dinosaurs installed at the Universe of Energy at Walt Disney World's Epcot.

If you ask nicely, you may be permitted to ride on the seat directly behind the engineer at the front of the train, although security concerns may block your access. When available, first priority is usually given to visitors with special needs.

■ THE MAIN STREET OPERA HOUSE

Within the ornate opera house, the birthday party is celebrated with a new film, **Disneyland: The First 50 Magical Years,** which showcases fifty years of memories through never-before-seen artwork, models, and designs. Comedian Steve Martin, who worked at Disneyland as a youngster, narrates the film, which features some rediscovered footage that has not been seen in more than forty years.

Martin shares the screen with another famed comedian who has spent a lot of time at Disneyland: Donald Duck. At the grand opening of the film on May 5, 2005, there was a bit of one-duckmanship: Martin showed up late because Donald gave him the wrong time to be there. ("Well, ex-cu-use me," said Donald.) But when it came time to unveil the theater's revised marquee, Martin pulled the string to show a temporary sign reading "Great Moments with Steve Martin."

Martin, who first worked at Disneyland at the age of ten selling guidebooks, later worked his way up to the Fantasyland Magic Shop and the Main Street Magic Shop. ("This place is called the Magic Kingdom," Martin told us. "Coincidence? I think not.")

The film celebrates the history of Disneyland as a national treasure, including rare footage of Walt Disney pacing off the property lines in the orange grove at the end of a dirt road in Anaheim that fifty years later would be one of the most famous places in the world.

The difficulties of opening day are not overlooked, either: It was in the vicinity of one hundred degrees, 11,000 guests were invited and about twice as many showed, and the asphalt on Main Street was soft and sticky.

The former occupant of the opera house, the Audio-Animatronic Abraham Lincoln, has been given some time off to rest during the party.

The Unhappy Kingdom

Look up at the store windows on Main Street for some neat surprises. Above the Cone Shop you'll see a dentist's office; listen carefully and you can hear some poor soul having a tooth extracted.

And speaking of pain, listen beneath the piano teacher's window for the sounds of a not particularly talented child receiving a piano lesson.

Main Street Cinema

What else would you expect to be playing in the movie house on Disneyland's main drag but continuous Disney cartoons? Among the biggest treats are those that reach back to the dawn of Disney, such as *Steamboat Willie*, the first Mickey Mouse cartoon, released in 1928.

The small theater has six small screens and no seats; it's rarely busy and is a great place to cool off on a hot day or dry off on a rare wet day. It's also a great meeting place if you and your party become separated.

Penny Arcade

Disneyland's marvelous collection of antique games and amusements includes penny hand-crank movies and some modern video games. The old nickelodeons in the front work on a penny, probably the only thing in all of Orange County available at that price; the new machines eat quarters and dollars.

Antiques include the Love Tester, a hand-squeeze meter that claims to measure your sex appeal. Some of the nickelodeon movies I've seen include Snitz

Sounds Like

More sounds on Main Street: There are some strange goings-on at the Hotel Marceline. (The hotel gets its name from Walt Disney's childhood home in Marceline, Missouri.) Listen in at the Detective's Office for the sounds of a snoring sergeant.

Edwards in *Small Town Sheik* and Ben Turpin in *Home Sweet Home*. Esmeralda, the Card-Reading Gypsy, stands in the position of honor right on Main Street.

Main Street Vehicles

Old-fashioned cars, a horse-drawn trolley, and fire engines move slowly down one end of Main Street to the other. (Following not far behind the horses are uniformed sanitation engineers with shovels.) You can jump right on board one of the vehicles, but it will usually be faster to walk the length of Main Street; at the end of a long day, though, a seated ride is mighty appealing.

The vehicles don't run during parade periods.

ADVENTURELAND

This is one of the quirkiest corners of Disneyland, home to the indescribably bizarre charm of the Enchanted Tiki Birds, the robotic alligators and the awful puns of the Jungle Cruise, the cement branches of Tarzan's Treehouse (the former Swiss Family Treehouse), and the wild Indiana Jones Adventure, one of the most impressive theme-park rides anywhere.

MUST-SEE INDIANA JONES ADVENTURE ≡FAST

Whatever you do, don't look at the Forbidden Eye. You know, the one that's right ahead of you, the one that's pulsing brightly in front of your car full of explorers, the one that will make the walls of the temple crash down all around you if you sneak a peek. Oh no!

The Indiana Jones Adventure is a spectacular combination of a (slow) roller coaster and a simulator with some of the best special effects anywhere in Disneyland or most anywhere else. The ride is based on the famous (and always exciting) explorations of Indiana Jones.

The Indiana Jones Adventure became one of the most popular attractions at the park when it opened in 1995. On a busy day, you definitely want a Fastpass for this attraction.

Private Digs

Proprietor Walt Disney built a private apartment over the Fire House on Main Street for special occasions when he stayed overnight at Disneyland. The lamp in the window is kept burning in his memory.

It seems that intrepid archaeologist Indiana Jones has made yet another fabulous find deep within a densely overgrown jungle. According to legend, the god Mara offers to all visitors one of three magical gifts: restoration from the Fountain of Eternal Youth, fabulous wealth from the Hall of Riches where all of the great treasures of history have been collected, or knowledge of all that is to come with the aid of a mystical amulet from the Observatory of the Future.

In fact, says the legend, Mara is so powerful that she can peer into your soul to choose the one gift that is best for you. But the legend also tells of a terrible curse for any visitor who is so foolish as to look directly into Mara's eye.

Unfortunately, funding for continued excavation is running out. To raise cash, Dr. Jones and his assistant Sallah have agreed to conduct tours. That's you, folks. Step right up!

As you approach the entrance to the temple, you'll pass through a reconstructed pre–World War II universe including trucks, generators, phones, typewriters, books, and more. You'll also see a loading dock stacked with treasures waiting to be picked up by one of the Jungle Cruise boats that pass nearby.

You'll make your way into the temple through an appropriately creepy torch-lit waiting area that includes caverns, an old well, and a makeshift movie theater where you'll learn details of the discovery of Mara's temple.

This is not a ride for the timid. If the waiting line doesn't scare you, consider that the ride includes skulls and skeletons, bugs, snakes, a crumbling bridge, explosions, fire, and a car that will give you the shakes. And the waiting line is not for the claustrophobic; some of the areas are very narrow and cave-like.

On the busiest days the waiting line extends outside to the plaza near the Jungle Cruise. When you enter the building itself, if the queue ahead of you is full, you can expect a forty-five-minute wait.

About halfway through the wait you will come to the Rotunda Room with a maze that circles a well—this point is about fifteen minutes from the end of the line. The sign warns against pulling the rope, but of course that is exactly what you are expected to do.

"Leave off the rope, old fella!" comes a yell from below; every once in a while the words are more extreme.

Another waiting area takes you through a screening room where you can watch a portion of the "Eye on the Globe" newsreel flashed up on the screen by a rickety old projector. You'll learn how celebrities have been flocking to visit Professor Jones's latest discovery; one of the segments of the newsreel tells of a celebrated but aging actress who visited the temple of Mara and received the gift of eternal youth. "No more matronly roles for her," the breathless announcer reports. If you listen very carefully, you will also hear how not all of the visitors seem to have escaped.

Finally, you're boarded onto a twelve-seater military transport. There are three rows of four narrow seats in the vehicle. The left-most passenger in the front row gets to hold on to the steering wheel—it does not steer the car, though.

In my experience, it seems that the wildest ride is given to the passengers sitting in the back row and the mildest to those sitting in the center row of the car. Then again, the front seat gives the best view, and that rider gets to spin and hold on to the (nonfunctional) steering wheel.

There are a total of sixteen transports, each nicely

Free?

Here's the best bargain in the park. You can obtain a free pair of aspirin or Tylenol to cure a headache at the First Aid Station at the top of Main Street. The cup of water costs $10, though. Just kidding. There's a nurse on duty at the station, and arrangements can be made to store medication there. Over-the-counter medications can also be purchased at the Emporium on Main Street.

Going to the Dogs

You can't bring the family pet into the park—it might scare the mice, you know. And please don't be so cruel as to leave Bowser or Kitty in the car; temperatures in a glass and metal box in the sun can kill.

Disney offers a day kennel to the right of the main gate. The exercise area for dogs offers canines their own private fire hydrant.

decorated to look dirty and beaten up. Vehicles are dispatched every eighteen seconds, and the ride can carry as many as 2,400 people per hour.

The ride handlers are very strict about enforcing the 46-inch minimum height requirement; adults shouldn't take the ride if they have back problems or other health issues, including pregnancy and heart conditions. Pay attention to the medical warnings: The ride is as wild as anything else at Disneyland, and severe enough that Disney has had to face a number of medical claims from visitors over the years. Be sure to buckle your seat belt and grab hold of the handlebar in front of you.

Beneath the shell of the transport is some of the highest technology of any ride at any theme park. Each vehicle has its own ride computer for sound and control. The troop transports use a Disney-developed technology known as Enhanced Motion Vehicle, which controls the movement of the transport forward and backward, up and down, and side to side, as well as the sounds and some of the special effects of the ride. Each vehicle can stop, back up, slow down, or go faster based on computer decisions. (The mechanism was adapted for use at Disney's Animal Kingdom at Walt Disney World in Orlando, where the vehicles run through Dinosaur!)

The ride is accompanied by John Williams's music from the Indiana Jones films, specially adapted and rerecorded by a ninety-piece orchestra. To tell you the truth, we can't remember hearing it, though; we were very busy holding on for dear life and watching the wild goings-on all around.

According to Disney there are something like 160,000 possible combinations of sounds, motion, and events on any particular journey through the temple, and no two rides will be identical. In reality, the difference from one ride to another is actually rather minor, but it is interesting to remember that you are in the electronic hands of a computer throughout.

Carved over the door to the temple is a warning in a strange language: It translates as "Beware of the eyes of Mara." (The characters are not that difficult to read once you realize they are like our standard alphabet with a few missing parts here and there.)

As your transport enters the temple, you arrive at the Chamber of Destiny where you find three doors—one for each of the possible "good" gifts of Mara. Remember the warning against looking Mara in the eye, though.

You'll be offered the chance to decide together on the route you wish to take: The left door is labeled Knowledge, the center is Riches, the right is Youth. (We don't want to spoil the illusion by pointing out that the computer will ultimately make the decision for you, so we won't.)

Of course somebody in your transport just has to look in Mara's eye and things go wrong. As you turn the corner from the Chamber of Destiny, you'll meet Indy himself. "We've got a problem here," he might tell you. Or, crankily, "Tourists! You had to look."

The transport careens into and out of a series of caves, across a shaking suspension bridge, through clouds of smoke and sixty-mile-per-hour winds, alongside bubbling lava pits, steam vents, and more. The best effect of the ride is the final one when your vehicle comes face to face with a huge rolling ball; at the last moment the jeep ducks under and out of the way. And then Indiana Jones himself congratulates you on surviving the trip. Sometimes he's in a foul mood: "Next time you're on your own," he told us once. On another visit he was in a more congratulatory mood: "Not bad for tourists."

And then it's over . . . and if you've got the nerve you can get back in line.

In addition to the Indiana Jones Adventure, George Lucas has several other links to Disney, including Indiana Jones et le Temple du Péril, a roller-coaster adventure at Disneyland Paris; the Indiana Jones Epic Stunt Spectacular and Star Tours at Disney–MGM Studios in Florida; Star Tours at Disneyland and Disneyland Paris; Captain EO, formerly at Disneyland; and the ExtraTERRORestrial Alien Encounter formerly at the Magic Kingdom of Walt Disney World.

Some of the original renderings for the Indiana Jones Adventure are on display from time to time at the Disney Gallery, located over the Pirates of the Caribbean in New Orleans Square. In addition to drawings that were eventually adapted for the ride as it now exists, you can also learn about some concepts that were not used, including a walk-through adventure and a high-speed mine-car adventure within a temple. At one point, Imagineers considered using Jungle Cruise launches to shuttle guests to the new ride.

■ TARZAN'S TREEHOUSE

This "climb-through" experience begins with a climb up a wooden staircase made of salvaged items from a shipwreck. On the other side of a suspension bridge is the moss-and-vine-covered tree that is the home of Tarzan's human parents and his ape foster mother Kala. Sketches by Tarzan's faithful companion Jane help explain the story of Tarzan's survival in the jungle.

On the other side of the bridge is a small hut that was once the heart of the family but is now obviously the scene of a terrible event. A canvas wall, ripped and shredded, testifies to an attack by Sabor, a vicious leopard; listen carefully and you may hear him growling nearby.

Size Matters

In California, Disneyland occupies just eighty acres and Disney's California Adventure fifty-five acres. In Florida, the Magic Kingdom takes up 107 acres, the Disney-MGM Studios is spread over 135 acres, and Epcot covers 260 acres (including a forty-acre lake). The sprawling Walt Disney World resort includes 28,000 acres or some 43 square miles of land, making it about the size of San Francisco or twice the size of Manhattan.

In the next room is a tiny overturned cradle that once belonged to the infant Tarzan. Jane's sketchbook shows how the baby was saved from the attack by an ape named Kala, who then raised the boy as if he were her own.

At the base of the tree is an interactive play area where Jane has turned salvaged belongings into playthings and musical instruments. At times cast members bring live animals to the area to introduce them to young visitors.

The treehouse was the home of another shipwrecked clan, the Swiss Family Robinson, from 1962 until 1999. For the conversion, the tree was extended by 10 feet and nearly six thousand artificial leaves were applied to its 450 branches. If you listen very carefully you can hear "Swissapolka" playing from the old gramophone—a salute to the original attraction.

MUST-SEE JUNGLE CRUISE

Another Disneyland classic, an escorted boat tour along the rivers of a wild kingdom that somehow stretches from the African veldt to the Amazon rain forest to the Nile valley and the jungles of southeast Asia. The cruise is one of the original entertainments from Disneyland's opening in 1955.

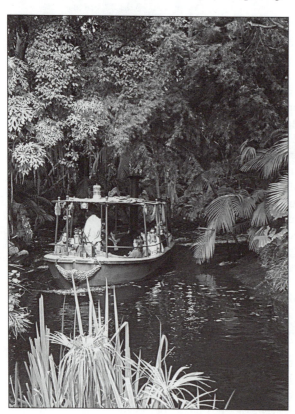

A Jungle Cruise boat rounds a bend. *Photo by Corey Sandler. Used by permission from Disney Enterprises, Inc.*

You are a somewhat willing participant in a trip with the Jungle Cruise Trading Company. The journey begins in the mist-filled rain forests of the Irrawaddy in Burma and continues up the Mekong River in Vietnam to Egypt's fabled Nile.

You'll see some of Disney's most famous special effects, such as the automated hippos lurking just below the water and the cavorting elephants that spray water from their trunks. The shores are lined with robotic zebras, lions, and giraffes.

The best part of the ride is the hokey, but still entertaining, patter of the tour guides in pith helmets. ("Be sure to tell your friends about Jungle Cruise," our guide told us on one trip. "It cuts down the lines." He also sincerely apologized to passengers for some of the worst [or best] one-liners in the patter: "I'd tell funnier jokes, but they have to be approved by Disney.")

You want more? "Welcome aboard," my deadpan host began. "If you're here for fun and excitement, we got rid of that three years ago."

As we passed a slightly gruesome scene of wild animals feasting on a carcass, he cast a glance at some of the younger passengers on the boat. "Oh, look," he said, "a pride of lions protecting a sleeping zebra."

Some guides encourage riders to laugh at the line of people waiting their turn to enter the nearby Indiana Jones Adventure.

Amateur gardeners may be most thrilled by the amazing collection of unusual plants, flowers, and trees Disney's crew of groundskeepers keep alive. "On the right we have plants," the guide told us, pausing a beat for effect. "On the left we have more plants.

"Check out the gigantic bamboo plants. That's something you don't see every day. You don't, but I do."

The ride is just short of ten minutes; the line to get on board, alas, can sometimes wind around and around the corral for more than an hour. Go early or late on busy days.

◾ ENCHANTED TIKI ROOM

In the Tiki, Tiki, Tiki, Tiki, Tiki Room (you'll understand the reference after you sit through this exceedingly strange squawking show) you'll find a collection of more than 200 wisecracking, flapping, automated winged creatures, along with a collection of chanting and singing flowers, totem poles, and statues in a somewhat interesting place decorated with wood carvings and a bamboo lattice roof. This is among the strangest attractions in the Disney realm, and you've got to be in exactly the right frame of mind to enjoy the show. Try tired and giddy, not wired-up and antsy.

The birds were among Disney's first attempts at Audio-Animatronics and represented the state of the art as it existed around 1963. We know some young children who have been absolutely enchanted by the birds; the very young and the very cynical need not apply. Adults might want to bring a Walkman.

Like it or not, the show received a major technological upgrade in 2005. The birds, the songs, and the wisecracks remain the same, but all of the mechanisms—from animatronics to feathers—have been rebuilt, and Imagineers have also delivered a vastly improved sound system.

CRITTER COUNTRY

You can take a gentle ride in a real Davy Crockett canoe, or make a wet and wild splashdown in the most enchanting log ride anywhere.

One thing you can no longer do is groan through the puns at the Country Bear Playhouse, the place that answered the question of what bears do on their vacations; here's Disney's answer: "A loaf of bread, a jug of wine, and seven thousand ants." The playhouse closed at the end of 2001, and was replaced by the giddily entertaining dark ride the **Many Adventures of Winnie the Pooh.**

▮MUST-SEE▮ THE MANY ADVENTURES OF WINNIE THE POOH

Oh, bother! It's a blustery day, and the pages of one of our favorite books are blowing out of the building and into Critter Country. Welcome to a lovingly detailed step into the pages of one of the best-known children's books. Giant honey-pot vehicles carry up to six people into the pages of the book, and we begin in Chapter 1, in which Pooh begins his search for honey in a very enchanted place.

The ride begins outdoors, in the Hundred-Acre Wood, in the back corner of Critter Country near Splash Mountain.

"Happy Winds-day," says Gopher. "Maybe for you," replies Piglet. Pooh announces, "I'm in the mood for food," but Eeyore doubts the bear will reach the tree.

We move on to Rabbit's Garden, where Kanga holds onto Roo, flying like a kite in the wind and into Owl's House. Then we enter the dramatic darkness of the Blustery Night, where we meet Tigger for the first time. "Come bounce with me," he invites, and so we do. Ever sat in a bouncing giant honey pot before?

One of the more dramatic scenes is Pooh's Dream, a view into his nightmare. What could he possibly fear? Why Heffalump and Woozle honey thieves, of course. Watch for the jack-in-the-boxes. Pooh wakes up in the Floody Place, and here Disney Imagineers pull out all the stops. There's water all about, and we seem to float through the room. The only one who isn't upset about the flooding is Pooh, happy to find that the rising water allows him to float to a honey bonanza high up in a tree.

All in all, this is one honey of a ride: a bit too sweet, too slow, and not all that exciting for adults, but youngsters will be attracted like bears. Pooh takes about three-and-a-half minutes, and sixteen to eighteen cars are on the track at any one time.

By the way, the catchy music for the Pooh ride is by the composer of the score for *Mary Poppins* and the It's a Small World attraction.

▮MUST-SEE▮ SPLASH MOUNTAIN ═*FAST*

This favorite, especially on hot days, is a log flume ride that splashes together bits of Pirates of the Caribbean, It's a Small World, and Brer Rabbit.

Splash Mountain has several false drops—including one with a little hump in the middle—before the big one that plunges about 50 feet at a forty-five-degree angle and a top speed of about forty miles per hour. The big drop, visible to the crowds outside, makes it appear as if the log car has fallen into a pond. For the riders, though, the anticipation is much more intense than the experience itself—the drop is over in a few seconds.

Some of the best special effects take place within the mountain with a story based on Disney's classic *Song of the South* cartoon, made in 1946. The ride follows Brer Rabbit as he tries to outwit Brer Fox and Brer Bear on a wild journey to the Laughin' Place.

When you enter the Splash Mountain building itself, there are a few interesting exhibits, including a series of placards that tell the Brer Fox story: "Some critters ain't never gonna learn" and "You can't run away from trouble. Ain't no place that far" among them.

More? "It was one of those zip-a-dee-doo days, the kind of day where you can't open your mouth without a song jumping right out." And, "Everybody's got a laughing place—the trouble is most folks won't take the time to go look for it. And where it is for one, mightn't be for another."

The interior waiting line for Splash Mountain is not a place for claustrophobics; it's tight and dark in places, and on busy days it seems to last forever. You'll start by loading into your eight-passenger "log"; you may find the seats slightly damp. Be sure to protect cameras and other valuables from water; traveling with a plastic bag to cover them is a good idea.

The logs climb up into the mountain—you'll see the bottom of the big drop, and first-time riders will certainly be expecting a sudden sharp drop over the precipice they've seen from the ground. These are just teases. Instead of the great fall, your log will move gently through a beautiful, tuneful, and peaceful water world filled with more than a hundred Audio-Animatronic characters and lots of delightful details and insistently bouncy music. At the end of the first room there's a drop, but again it's not the big one. Eventually you'll come to the big one, the spectacular waterfall you've seen from the walkway below. You're over . . . and down in about four seconds.

There is one final surprise at the very end: a visit to a "Welcome Home Brer Rabbit" party. The Zip-a-Dee Lady paddleboat chugs alongside. This is the scene you can also spy from the Disneyland Railroad as it passes through a portion of the Splash Mountain building.

All told, Splash Mountain is one of the longer rides at Disneyland at nearly eleven minutes. Despite the brevity of the final drop, it does give you a lot more for your waiting time than Thunder Mountain or Space Mountain. If you can convince the kids (or the adults) to look past the short drop, they are sure to love the rest of the ride, which is pure Disney. Try the ride during the day and at night; the view of the park from near the top is worth the wait.

Splash Mountain is a watery place, and the log car makes a huge wave as it lands at the bottom of the big drop, but you really won't get very wet on the ride. The two wettest places seem to be the very first row of seats and the last—the wave flies over the car. The front row has the best view of the drop; the last row has the most suspense.

When It Rains . . .

. . . you will get wet. Most of Disneyland is outdoors and many of the waiting lines are open to the skies. When the rains come, vendors magically appear selling bright yellow plastic ponchos decorated with Disney characters; they are usually good for a few wearings before they tear. If you fear the weather, you might want to shop before you travel or stop at one of the discount stores near Disneyland and purchase raingear there; you may save a few dollars, end up with something a bit more durable, and make a non-Disney fashion statement.

Disabled Guests

Disneyland is pretty accommodating to visitors who have special needs; a list of attractions with wheelchair access is available at Guest Relations. Wheelchairs can be brought into the park or can be rented. Disabled visitors, along with a limited number of family members, can avoid waiting lines and enter certain rides directly.

On a busy day, you should use a Fastpass to avoid lines of ninety minutes or more.

Imagineers tell us that many of the Audio-Animatronic characters within the ride are recycled from "America Sings," a show that ran at Disneyland in Tomorrowland through 1988.

There are Splash Mountains at Walt Disney World and at Tokyo Disneyland; in California, guests sit one behind another while in Japan and Florida guests sit side-by-side. We think the Walt Disney World version is the most spectacular.

■ DAVY CROCKETT'S EXPLORER CANOES

Do you remember Davy Crockett, or at least the television show that celebrated him? If you do, you're probably well over the average age around here.

The canoes are among the most realistic things in the park. These large vessels circle the Rivers of America around Tom Sawyer Island; in and among the river traffic of the *Mark Twain* Riverboat, the Mike Fink keelboats, and the sailing ship; and across the path of the rafts to the island. The canoes, alas, are not operated every day and have been rumored to be headed for permanent dry dock for a number of years.

NEW ORLEANS SQUARE

A favorite spot for the hearty of heart, New Orleans Square is home of rollicking pirates and one of the world's largest collections of grim-grinning ghosts.

⋯ MUST-SEE ⋯ PIRATES OF THE CARIBBEAN

Yo, ho, yo, ho . . . one of Disney's very best, a cruise into the middle of a pirate raid on a Caribbean island town.

The ride begins with a calm journey across a dark bayou that is among the most realistic settings in all of the park, right down to the robotic fireflies and recorded crickets. As you move deeper into the Caribbean Sea, hidden underneath the park, you'll meet a rollicking crew of pirates. "Thar be no place like home," one declares, but then he warns: "Keep a weather eye! Thar be squalls ahead."

The best of those squalls is the moonlit battle between a pirate ship and a government fortress across the harbor; cannonballs seem to land all around you in the cool water as your boat passes through the mist. Pay attention to the jail scene where a group of pirates tries to entice a mangy dog to bring them the key.

Everywhere you look you'll see members of the wondrous collection of more than 120 Audio-Animatronic humans and animals including robotic chickens and pigs.

The famous "auction" of women in chains to the pirates occupies another central scene of the ride. The sign still reads, TAKE A WENCH FOR A BRIDE. But a politically correct update removed the pirate who once held a piece of stolen lace and a woman hiding in the bushes in fear of the drunken pirates. In the central scene, a woman is still chased in circles by a pirate, but now she carries a big tray of food. A bit farther along, a woman brandishes a rolling pin at a pirate who has stolen a ham.

Even with the changes, the ride still paints a picture of some rather unpleasant pirates, an image that scholars say is relatively accurate. Some very young children may be scared by the simulated cannon fire and the skulls and bones that are liberally strewn about in some of the cave scenes.

The famed "Yo Ho" song is perhaps the second most recognizable ride song at Disneyland after "It's a Small World After All." The words here are a bit more threatening: "We kidnap and ravage and don't give a hoot. Drink up me 'earties, yo ho."

Lines can be quite long throughout the day, especially in the afternoon after serious thrill-seekers have finished with Indiana Jones, Splash Mountain, and Space Mountain. Make your visit early or at the end of the day. The ride itself takes just short of fifteen minutes.

■ THE DISNEY GALLERY

A quiet and cool respite where you can duck out of the madding crowds to absorb a bit of Disney culture and memorabilia. The entrance to the gallery is by a stairway above the Pirates of the Caribbean.

On recent visits the gallery has displayed models and sketches for Disneyland Paris, the Indiana Jones ride, and some of the original drawings for Disneyland itself showing places that had names such as the Mickey Mouse Club, Holiday Land, Frontier Country, the Hub, Fantasyland, Lilliputian Land, the World of Tomorrow, True Life Adventure Land, and Main Street. A scale model of the Disneyland Castle has a tiny mannequin of Walt Disney walking in.

The suite of rooms that is now the Disney Gallery was originally planned as a private apartment and reception room where brothers Walt and Roy Disney could entertain business associates and visiting dignitaries. Although the apartment was never completed as originally intended, certain touches remain, including the stylized initials WD and RD worked into the wrought ironwork of the balcony.

One of a Kind

The following attractions are found only at Disneyland and not at Walt Disney World:

▶ **Alice in Wonderland** (Fantasyland)

▶ **Casey Jr. Circus Train** (Fantasyland)

▶ *Disneyland: The First 50 Magical Years* (Main Street)

▶ **Indiana Jones Adventure** (Adventureland)

▶ **Matterhorn Bobsleds** (Fantasyland)

▶ **Mickey's Toontown**

▶ **Pinocchio's Daring Journey** (Fantasyland)

▶ **Sailing Ship** *Columbia* (Frontierland)

▶ **Sleeping Beauty** (Fantasyland)

▶ **Storybook Land Canal Boats** (Fantasyland)

The telegraph operator working in the train station at New Orleans Square is clicking away in Morse code: The text is drawn from Walt Disney's speech on opening day at Disneyland.

The Disney Gallery is also the site of the most elegant place to view the nightly *Fantasmic!* show. For about $30 per person, you can rent one of fifteen seats on the balcony of the gallery for the Fantasmic Dessert Buffet.

MUST-SEE HAUNTED MANSION

Scare yourself silly in this masterpiece of an attraction that hosts some of the most sophisticated special effects at Disneyland. The experience begins in the graveyard waiting line; before the tombstones make you feel too creepy, stop and read some of the inscriptions. They're a howl!

Disney Imagineers continue to have fun with this venerable attraction; they have added an old horse-drawn hearse parked out front. There's also a sign in front of the mansion that reads: RESERVATIONS ACCEPTED. GHOST RELATIONS DISNEYLAND. PLEASE DO NOT APPLY IN PERSON!

When you are admitted to the mansion itself, you are ushered into a strange room that features an interesting visual trick: Is the ceiling going up or the floor going down? Either way, the portraits on the wall will give you a laugh. (Don't read this if you don't want to know. Okay, you have been warned: At Disneyland, the floor moves down and the walls are stationary; at Walt Disney World, the ceiling moves up and the floor stays put. The stretching room was put into place in California as a way to get visitors to the loading level, which is on the other side of the railroad tracks. When the Florida house was built, there was no need to go down a level, but Imagineers wanted to keep the same illusion, even if it was accomplished in a different way.)

The attendants, dressed as morticians, are among the best actors in the park, almost always staying in character. They may tell you to "fill in the dead space" in the line. When the elevator at the start of the ride fills up they may announce, "No more bodies." They play their roles well—we've tried our best over the years to make them crack a smile, without much success.

You'll enter onto a moving set of chairs and settle in for a tour through a house that is in the control of the largest collection of spooks this side of the CIA. We've ridden the ride many times and see something different each time. Among the best effects are the dancing ghouls at the dinner party, the moving door knockers, and the face within the crystal ball.

This ride is probably the single best combination of Disney Animatronics, moviemaking, and scene setting. There are all sorts of dreadful details, enough to make it worth several rides if you have the time. Here are a few you might want to look for: the framed needlepoint that reads TOMB SWEET TOMB, the legs sticking out from under the banquet table in the ghostly wedding reception, and the skull-shaped notes rising out of the top of the organ. Some very young children may become a bit scared, although most kids of all ages can see the humor among the horrors. To break the ice stop to read the inscriptions on the tombs at the exit.

Lines for this show vary greatly; the best times to visit are early or late in the day. The ride lasts about nine minutes, including a two-minute preshow.

Disney has been subtly raising the scare level of the ride over the years, perhaps in reaction to the overall explicitness of our society. The skeletons are now just a bit more real, the ghosts are just a bit more ghoulish. A vastly improved sound system now lets guests hear the lyrics more clearly and some of the background chatter. For example, in the ghostly wedding scene, you can hear a chorus chanting "I don't."

Actually, though, the first plans for the Haunted Mansion were more gruesome than what was actually built. Because it was to be built near the New Orleans area of Frontierland, the idea was to make it look like an early 1800s southern mansion: The final design for the building was based on Evergreen House, a large mansion on North Charles Street in Baltimore built in 1857. The house still exists and is open to visitors as a museum operated by Johns Hopkins University.

Walt Disney himself vetoed a design that made the house appear to be derelict (Disney's first falling-down house would come some thirty years later with the construction of the Twilight Zone Tower of Terror at Walt Disney World).

The original plans also called for the tour to be a walk-through, with groups of about forty visitors escorted through the house by a butler or maid who would tell the story. The first story line was quite different, too, and not at all sugarcoated: It told of a wealthy sea merchant who built a fabulous mansion for his new bride but then killed her in a rage after she learned he was really a bloody pirate. Her ghost came back to haunt him and tormented him so much that he finally hung himself from the rafters, giving the mansion two unhappy spirits. About all that is left of that gruesome story is the weather vane in the shape of a sailing ship on top of the cupola of the mansion, some paintings with a seafaring theme, and a quick glimpse of a hanging body when the lights flash on in the "stretching room" in the preshow area of the ride.

For Better or Verse

The tombstones and pet cemetery are located in the upper waiting area at the Haunted Mansion. If the lines are not long you may not even pass in front of them, but they're worth a side trip. Here is a selection of some of the very worst of the verse.

"Here lies Good Old Fred. Great big rocks fell on his head."

"Rest in Peace Old Cousin Hewitt. We all know you didn't do it."

Some of the named tombstones include those of M. T. Tomb, I. L. Beback, U. R. Gone, and Rustin Pece.

And then there are the heartbreaking stories behind some of the gravestones in the pet cemetery:

"Here lies long-legged Jeb, he got tangled up in his very own web."

"Rosie was a poor little pig, but she bought the farm."

And there is the last resting place of Old Flybait the frog, who croaked in 1859.

The building was completed in 1963 but stood empty for nearly six years. The delay was in part caused by Disney's involvement in four major pavilions at the 1964–1965 New York World's Fair, including Pepsi's It's a Small World—A Salute to UNICEF ride, General Electric's Carousel of Progress, the Illinois pavilion's *Great Moments with Mr. Lincoln,* and Ford's Magic Skyway ride.

Extra Admission

Got a spare $20,000 or so for a ticket to Disneyland? That's about the price of admission to the very private and little-known Club 33, located upstairs at 33 Rue Royale in New Orleans Square. Look for the green door with the number 33 just past the Blue Bayou restaurant; there is also an entrance between the pirate shop and the One of a Kind shop. What's inside? Well, there's a bar (the only place in the park serving alcohol) and some real nice chairs.

Club 33 was originally built as a private club for Walt Disney's guests; Disney was involved in its New Orleans design but died a few months before it was completed. In case you're interested, there is usually a several-year waiting list for the right to plunk down about $20,000 for a corporate membership, $10,000 for an executive membership, or a mere $5,000 for an individual pass. Then you get to pay about $1,800 per year in annual dues.

Beyond the door is an ornate grillwork elevator to the second floor. Upstairs are some equally impressive old-style appointments, including an oak telephone booth with leaded-glass panels adapted from the one used in the Disney film, *The Happiest Millionaire*. The Lounge Alley is used for a buffet and sports a harpsichord decorated with a scene of a New Orleans harbor during the nineteenth century. The Main Dining Room is decorated in Napoleonic style, including three spectacular chandeliers.

The Trophy Room is the second dining room, a more informal place that has cypress-plank walls. Hidden within the chandeliers are microphones installed at Walt Disney's suggestion; according to Disney historians, the intent was to allow a vulture in the room to converse with guests during dinner.

French doors on the upper level open out onto a spectacular view of the Rivers of America, and it's a marvelous place to watch the *Fantasmic!* show . . . if you don't mind paying a bit extra for the privilege.

If you'd like to sign up, call Disney at (714) 781–4709.

The first three World's Fair exhibits were later recycled at Disney parks: It's a Small World came to Disneyland and became the model for similar and very popular rides at Walt Disney World, Tokyo Disneyland, and Disneyland Paris. The GE Carousel was moved to Walt Disney World; it was updated a bit in 1994 but remains essentially unchanged. *Great Moments with Mr. Lincoln* was Disney's first big success with his new Audio-Animatronic technology and was brought to Disneyland's Main Street.

The Haunted Mansion experience is accompanied by a decidedly strange soundtrack that is among the more literate writings anywhere at Disneyland. Here's part of the introduction from the stretching room:

> *When hinges creak in doorless chambers and strange and frightening*
> *sounds echo through the halls, whenever candlelights flicker where the*

air is deathly still, that is the time when ghosts are present, practicing their terror with ghoulish delight.

Your cadaverous pallor betrays an aura of foreboding, almost as though you sense a disquieting metamorphosis. Is this haunted room actually stretching? Or is it your imagination? And consider this dismaying observation: This chamber has no windows, and no doors.

Which offers you this chilling challenge: to find a way out! Of course, there's always my way.

Says your ghost host: "We find it delightfully unlivable here in this ghostly retreat. Every room has wall-to-wall creeps and hot and cold running chills."

You'll meet Madame Leota, a disembodied guide who will help you attempt to make contact with the spirits within the mansion.

Rap on a table, it's time to respond, send us a message from somewhere beyond. Goblins and ghoulies from last Halloween, awaken the spirits with your tambourine. Wizards and witches wherever you dwell, give us a hint by ringing a bell.

The best special effect of the ride is the wedding party scene, as guests move from mortal coil to diaphanous spirit and back. The setting uses an old theatrical trick called "Pepper's Ghost," named after John Henry Pepper who created the illusion for the London theater in 1862. You're looking through an angled glass that allows you to see objects on the set as well as the reflections of other objects and Audio-Animatronics in a room below you.

The organ in the Grand Hall scene at Disneyland is the actual one used by Captain Nemo in the Disney film, *20,000 Leagues Under the Sea.*

After the party, you'll meet the famous grim-grinning ghosts, captured within luminous globes. Through dozens of rides at Walt Disney World's Magic Kingdom, Disneyland, and Disneyland Paris we were unable to figure out what the ghosts were saying until recently. Here's part of their song:

When the crypt doors creak and the tombstones quake, spooks come out for a swinging wake. Happy haunts materialize and begin to vocalize; grim-grinning ghosts come out to socialize.

Now don't close your eyes and don't try to hide, or a silly spook may sit by your side. Shrouded in a daft disguise, they pretend to terrorize; grim-grinning ghosts come out to socialize.

As the ride comes to an end, you'll be welcomed to hurry back; be sure to bring your death certificate.

FRONTIERLAND

The world of the Old West includes a nineteenth-century runaway mine train, the *Mark Twain* paddle wheeler, and rafts to the kids' fantasies of Tom Sawyer Island. Check out the quirky entertainment of the Golden Horseshoe Stage and stick around or come back later for the fantastic *Fantasmic!* show presented on a watery curtain in the Rivers of America.

🔆 MUST-SEE 🔆 BIG THUNDER MOUNTAIN RAILROAD ≡*FAST*

One of the best rides at the park is at the same time much more than and much less than it appears.

Big Thunder is a Disneyfied roller coaster, one of only four "thrill" rides in Disneyland (along with Space Mountain, Splash Mountain, and the Indiana Jones Adventure).

As far as roller coasters go, it is fairly tame: It has about a half mile of track and a three-and-a-half-minute ride, with a few short drops and some interesting twists and turns. But in the Disney tradition, it is the setting and the attention to detail that make this one of the most popular places to be.

You will ride in a runaway mining train up through a quaking tunnel, across a flooding village, and back down, around, and through an artificial steel-and-cement mountain.

The mountain is bedecked with real mining antiques that come from real old mines out West. Look, too, at the Audio-Animatronic animals, birds, and an old coot of a miner in a bathtub as you zoom by. The walls of the loading area are lined with actual gold-bearing rock.

The trains have been given adventuresome names. Look for *U. B. Bold, U. R. Courageous, I. M. Fearless, I. M. Brave,* and *U. R. Daring.* As they slow down to enter the loading station they pass through a small western town, including the Big Thunder Saloon, an assay office, and the local newspaper, the *Big Thunder Epitaph.*

Picking the right time to visit the railroad can make a real difference at this very popular attraction; waits of more than an hour are common at midday in peak season. The shortest lines can be found early in the day or just before dinnertime. If you can, pick up a Fastpass on busy days.

Coaster fans say the best ride (meaning the wildest) can be had in the last row of seats. We also like the very front of any coaster ride because it gives you a view of the perils ahead, over the top of the engine in front. Thunder Mountain by night is another ride altogether. Like Space Mountain, the fun is increased because the darkness hides the track ahead of you.

Children younger than seven must be accompanied by an adult; no one shorter than 40 inches is allowed to ride. Warn young children about the loud noises they will hear as their railway car is pulled up the first lift on the ride.

When you finish the ride, listen to the talk coming from the bar in the little western town, located above the ride next to the Mexican food place. At the Big Thunder Saloon: "Do you know your toupee's on crooked?" "No, but if you hum a few bars I'll try to fake it."

The ride was closed for months after a September 2003 accident in which a passenger was killed. Engineers tested the system and upgraded some of the components before it was reopened. A second accident, in April 2004, damaged some equipment, but the ride is up and running.

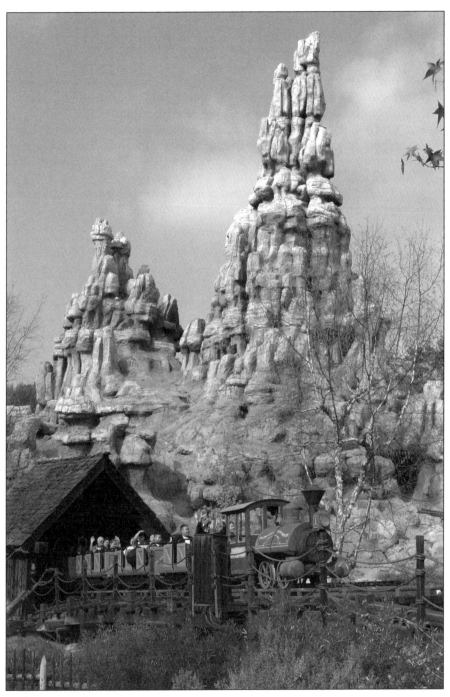

Big Thunder Mountain Railroad. *Photo by Corey Sandler. Used by permission from Disney Enterprises, Inc.*

■ THE GOLDEN HORSESHOE STAGE

A longtime favorite, this is Disney's squeaky-clean version of a western dance hall revue. The show includes pretty cancan girls, corny comics, and strolling musicians to entertain visitors of all ages.

Each performance is about thirty minutes in length. You'll need to arrive thirty to forty-five minutes before showtime to make your way to your seat and place orders for drinks or snacks, including chili, ice cream, and pickles (the food is strictly optional, although it is more than likely your kids will badger you for something at the table). In years past, admission to the show required a reservation made at the door, although in recent years the doors were thrown open on a first-come, first-seated basis.

The Golden Horseshoe can eat up as much as two hours of your busy day; it may not make sense to visit if you are pressed for time.

▦ MUST-SEE ▦ FANTASMIC!

The *Fantasmic!* show is like every other fabulous Disney entertainment, only more so. This is the highest-tech singing, dancing, and pyrotechnical show we've ever experienced. A visit to Disneyland is not complete without a glimpse.

The twenty-five-minute show is performed at the south end of Tom Sawyer Island on the Rivers of America from Frontierland to New Orleans Square. Shows are usually presented twice nightly on weekends and every night during the summer and in holiday periods. During the winter and other off-season periods when the park closes early on many days, no show is presented. The show includes fog, fireworks, soaring flames, a trio of giant, 30-foot-tall by 50-foot-wide mist screens, and an audio system that engulfs listeners.

Like much of Disneyland, the story of *Fantasmic!* is a celebration of the power of imagination. Mickey Mouse appears on a stage at the end of Tom Sawyer Island and summons forth a series of fabulous visions of fantasy creatures, including Dumbo's pink elephants and beauties of nature. But his reverie is interrupted by a band of Disney villains with such antifavorites as Maleficent from *Sleeping Beauty,* Ursula from *The Little Mermaid,* Monstro the Whale from *Pinocchio,* and the demon Chernabog from the "Night on Bald Mountain" segment of *Fantasia.*

It's up to Mickey to escape from his nightmare. Shortly before the happy conclusion (you figured that, right?) Maleficent transforms before your eyes into a 45-foot-tall, fire-breathing dragon that sets the Rivers of America aflame.

The stunning finale includes a pirate ship (the specially decorated *Columbia* sailing ship) commandeered by Peter Pan, and the *Mark Twain* riverboat packed with happy Disney characters.

There are many places to watch, including the waterfront near Splash Mountain, the bridge near the entrance to the Pirates of the Caribbean, the patios of the Cafe Orleans or the French Market Restaurant, and a tiered viewing area at the promenade at New Orleans Square.

The most elegant way to view the show is at the dessert and coffee buffet at the Disney Gallery near the Pirates of the Caribbean. Seats on the balcony sell for about $30 each. You can save a seat by registering at the Reservations Center on Main Street before noon or at the Gallery in the afternoon.

Crowds for *Fantasmic!* can be large, especially for the first (or only) show; later shows are usually more approachable. Sometimes parades are scheduled at the same time, splitting the crowd. If you beat a quick retreat from the *Fantasmic!* show and move quickly back toward the Hub and toward Main Street, you should be able to catch the tail end of the parade as it heads toward the Disneyland Railroad Station.

If you are heading for a late show, here's the insider's plan: Approach the viewing area from the Splash Mountain side as the previous show is coming to an end. This way you won't have to fight the thousands of departing guests clearing out through Frontierland.

In my opinion the best ground-level view of the show is along the river across from the entry to the Pirates of the Caribbean and facing the shack on Tom Sawyer Island. There's a KODAK PHOTO SPOT sign along the river, just to the left of the prime spot.

Disney designers hide as much of the high-tech equipment as possible by lowering it into underground pits during the day. The elaborate multitrack audio system includes speakers located in front of and behind the audience; some of the speakers are disguised as lampposts, and two large boats in the lagoon carry additional speakers. Natural gas jets feed a wall of flame that erupts from the water around the island.

Disney gives credit to an outdoor history pageant in Vendée, France, for the development of the mist screen technology. Warning: Some of the mist from the fountains in the show drifts back into the faces of the closest viewers. This can become a bit uncomfortable on a cool evening. The show will be canceled in very inclement weather or high winds.

■ TOM SAWYER ISLAND

Another essential, at least for the youngsters, is the raft ride over to this little island in the middle of the Rivers of America, based a bit on Mark Twain's classic book. You'll find dark caves, a waterwheel, a dungeon, a barrel bridge, and a bouncy rope bridge. At the western end of the island is Fort Wilderness, where kids can scramble around the parapets and fire air guns at passing riverboats, canoes, and rafts.

Parents will appreciate the space to let children burn off a bit of energy after standing in lines all day. Be advised that it is fairly easy to misplace a youngster in one of the simulated caves or on a trail. Choose a meeting place with your children in case you become separated.

Woodn't you?

The petrified tree in Frontierland along the Rivers of America in front of the Golden Horseshoe was a gift from Walt Disney to his wife, Lillian. Mrs. Disney gave it back to the park in 1957. It was taken from the Pike Petrified Forest in Colorado. According to the inscription, the section weighs five tons and measures 7.5 feet in diameter. The original tree, a redwood or sequoia, is estimated to have been 200 feet tall and was part of a subtropical forest fifty-five million to seventy million years ago in what is now Colorado.

Closed!

Let's get this straight: We flew all the way across the country with two screaming kids, paid all that money, and ran all the way across the park, and Dumbo the Flying Elephant is closed for repairs? Yeah . . .

Because Disneyland is open every day, repairs and refurbishing have to be done while the park is in operation. Some minor jobs are done at night when the park is closed, but nearly every ride is closed for days, weeks, or even months every once in a while. Most of the closings take place during quieter times of the year; in other words, you can generally count on Indiana Jones Adventure, Space Mountain, Splash Mountain, and the Matterhorn Bobsleds being open around Christmastime and in the heart of the summer.

You can call (714) 999-4565 for information on refurbishing of rides before you travel.

You can go out on the front deck of Harper's Cider Mill to see some of the mechanisms for the *Fantasmic!* show. You can see spray heads in the water and underground lighting and projection platforms.

Around the bend is a working water-powered mill. Across from the pontoon bridge is the back side of Big Thunder Mountain Railroad. Here you'll find an abandoned mining train. Look closely at the cargo strewn about—robotic chipmunks poke up their heads every once in a while.

Lines for the raft rarely require more than ten minutes of waiting. The island closes at dusk and may not be open at all during the off-season or in bad weather.

■ *MARK TWAIN* RIVERBOAT

Reaching back to the birth of the Disneyland park, the original ⅝-scale paddle wheeler was built for the park. It has traveled uncounted thousands of miles without ever leaving the Rivers of America and without once deviating from its underwater track.

The ride is no great shakes, but it is a pleasant reprieve on a hot day. Depending on the season and the crowd level, the Mike Fink keelboats, Davy Crockett explorer canoes, and the sailing ship *Columbia* make the same circle and pass the same simulated Old West sights.

The ride takes about fifteen minutes plus about ten minutes for unloading and loading. Lines rarely extend beyond a full boatload, so your waiting time should be no more than twenty minutes.

Sailing Ship *Columbia*

A full-scale replica (110 feet long, with an 84-foot main mast) of the three-masted merchant ship of the eighteenth century; the *Columbia*'s crew discovered and named the Columbia River in Oregon. The real vessel was launched in Plymouth, Massachusetts, in 1787 and made many trips around Cape Horn to the northwest. It disappeared on a voyage in the Orient.

The *Columbia* is definitely the classiest way to take a fifteen-minute tour of the Rivers of America. Below deck is a museum that depicts lifestyles of the sailors.

The vessel operates only during daylight hours and only on the busiest days.

Columbia under way. *Photo by Corey Sandler. Used by permission from Disney Enterprises, Inc.*

Mike Fink Keelboats

Small riverboats follow the same circuit as the *Mark Twain,* the canoes, and the *Columbia;* they're a bit faster and a bit more personal with your own guide. Mike Fink, by the way, was a riverboat captain of legend who had an adventure with Davy Crockett. The small boats here, the *Bertha Mae* and the *Gullywhumper,* make a complete circuit in about ten minutes.

Because of the small capacity of the boats, I'd advise you to avoid joining a long line if there is one; we'd also suggest against duplicating a trip on the keelboats and one on the riverboat.

The keelboats run only during the day and may not operate at all during slow times of the year.

Frontierland Shootin' Exposition

A durn-fancy shootin' gallery, sort of a live video game, and not like any other shootin' gallery you have seen at a county fair. For 50 cents, players aim huge buffalo rifles at a Disney replica of Boot Hill, a frontier town from the 1850s. The rifles fire infrared beams at targets on tombstones, clouds, banks, jails, and other objects; direct hits make the targets spin, explode, or otherwise respond. Some of the signs tell a story: "Old Tom Hubbard died with a frown, but a grave can't keep a good man down." If you hit the skeleton of a steer, his horns will spin around.

More? "One last drink was in his hand, died a reachin', Red Eye Dan." Or: "Six-gun Tex lies in this grave, used his gun for a closer shave."

FANTASYLAND

This is the stuff of young dreams: Dumbo, Peter Pan, Alice in Wonderland, Snow White, and the toy riot of It's a Small World. Fantasyland is a bright and cheerful place that's decorated in splashes of color and sprinkled with snippets of song. Looming over it all is Sleeping Beauty Castle.

■ SLEEPING BEAUTY CASTLE

One of the emblems of Disneyland, more famous than most any real castle in the world, Sleeping Beauty Castle towers over the center of the park; well, it towers about 75 feet, but in true Disney fashion, the forced perspective design of the building makes it look taller than it really is.

Imagineers based their original design on the famed Neuschwandstein Castle in Bavaria, tempered by Walt Disney's more whimsical touch. For the fiftieth anniversary of Disneyland, the castle was swathed in fabric and jewels.

The Sleeping Beauty Walk Through is a somewhat obscure corner of the park, located within the castle between the Castle Christmas Shop and Tinkerbell's Toy Shop. Climb the stairs to see animated dioramas of scenes from Sleeping Beauty. This display has been closed from time to time.

■ PETER PAN'S FLIGHT

A mellow excursion into some of the scenes from Disney's version of the story of the little boy who doesn't want to grow up. Riders sit in a small pirate ship that suspends them a foot or so off the floor. Everyone's favorite scene is the overhead view of London by night, which does a pretty good job of simulating Peter's flight. Strictly for kids.

Stop and listen beneath the window between the entrance and exit to the ride. You'll hear Peter Pan and Wendy discussing a trip to Never Land.

At Disneyland Paris, a jazzed-up version is one of the more popular attractions; not so at Disneyland, although lines can still reach to forty-five minutes or more on busy days for a two-minute ride.

■ MR. TOAD'S WILD RIDE

Not all that wild, but an entertaining ride based on one of Disney's more obscure films, *The Adventures of Ichabod and Mr. Toad,* which was in turn loosely based on the book *The Wind in the Willows.*

You will ride in an antique car on the road to Nowhere in Particular, crashing through fireplaces, into a chicken coop, and on a railroad track headed straight for an oncoming locomotive. It's light enough fare for most children, although the very young might become a bit scared by the Day-Glo devils and the somewhat loud sound effects. Adults will find this two-minute ride among the more ordinary at Disneyland; we'd recommend against joining a midday line unless a youngster is in charge.

■ KING ARTHUR CARROUSEL

One of the few mostly "real" things in this world of fantasy and probably the oldest antique in use in the park, the carousel was originally built in 1875. Disney reconstructed the ride with carved horses from Germany; no two are identical.

When Disneyland opened in 1955 there were more than 4,000 carousels in the United States; today there are fewer than 200. Disney located this vintage ride in Toronto, and it was relocated to Anaheim. The original cast of animals on the ride included giraffes, deer, and other creatures; at Walt Disney's request, the menagerie was changed over to all horses. Murals from Walt Disney's *Sleeping Beauty* were added. The original color scheme included tan, brown, gray, and red steeds; all seventy-two horses were repainted white in 1975. The ride underwent major refurbishing in 2003.

As one of the original rides at the park, the merry-go-round was honored with the installation of a gold-painted horse during the fiftieth anniversary celebration. Actress Julie Andrews officiated at the ceremony.

The lines for the two-minute ride ebb and flow; we'd suggest you wait for the times when you can walk right on board. And parents take note: The exit to the merry-go-round is in a different place than the entrance.

■ PINOCCHIO'S DARING JOURNEY

A trip to the scary side of Tobacco Road, the place where Pinocchio is sent when he disobeys Geppetto.

(Have you realized by now how many of our favorite fairy tales have a dark side? Are you beginning to get the idea that many of the attractions at Fantasyland emphasize the scary elements of the story?)

Later you'll enter Pleasure Island, which is a riot of Day-Glo colors, calliope music, and amusement-park rides. Eventually, we are rescued by Jiminy Cricket and reunited with Geppetto. At long last, we are reminded that "When you wish upon a star, your dreams come true."

The experience is very pretty, but doesn't do a very good job of telling the story. You might want to go over the details of the fairy tale with young children before they go on the ride.

The three-minute ride includes some of the more advanced technologies for the younger set, including fiber-optic fireworks and holograms. Lines are often slightly shorter than at other surrounding attractions in Fantasyland.

■ DUMBO THE FLYING ELEPHANT

Disney has taken an ordinary amusement-park ride and made it something special, at least for little visitors. Riders sit inside fiberglass flying elephants that they can move up and down as they circle around a mirrored ball and a statue of Timothy Mouse, the little guy who becomes Dumbo's manager in the classic Disney movie.

Snow White Is Watching

Lean into the wishing well in Snow White's Grotto to the right of the castle at the entrance to Fantasyland to hear Snow White singing "I'm Wishing" from the Disney movie. The song was rerecorded for the fiftieth anniversary of the classic cartoon by the original Snow White, Adriana Caselotti. You'll also find statues of Snow White, the seven dwarfs, and various woodland creatures.

The evil queen is watching too. Keep your eye on the windows above the entrance to Snow White's Scary Adventures. Every once in a while the curtains will part and the evil queen will glare out at the visitors below.

This ride has always held a tremendous draw for young children, with lines of up to an hour for the ninety-second ride. If your kids insist on an elephant-back ride, head for Dumbo early or late in the day.

One of the Disney rites of passage, we suspect, is the day youngsters tell you they're willing to skip the lines for Dumbo in favor of a second pass at Space Mountain.

■ ALICE IN WONDERLAND

A bit of this and a bit of that in a Disneyland version of the classic story: You'll climb into a four-seat caterpillar vehicle for a four-minute journey down the rabbit hole in a chase after the White Rabbit. A merry time is had by most; get there early or late to avoid lines during busy times. There's not a lot to the ride; it's like a roller coaster without the roll.

■ SNOW WHITE'S SCARY ADVENTURES

Read the sign over the door: see SCARY? Now understand this ride can't hold a fading candle to the spooks in the Haunted Mansion across the way in New Orleans Square, but there are a lot more skeletons and witches than very young children might expect.

This ride emphasizes the grimmer parts of the Brothers Grimm fairy tale, as presented in Disney's 1937 animated movie.

Says the wicked witch: "One taste and the victim's eyes are closed forever." There's no real resolution to the threats presented in the ride except for a completely unexplained sign that reads: AND THEY LIVED HAPPILY EVER AFTER.

All that said, it's an interesting but short ride for children who can handle the dark side of the fairy tale; if your youngster is the sort who gets nightmares from Casper the Friendly Ghost, I'd suggest you go for two rides on Dumbo instead of one with Snow White.

■ FANTASYLAND THEATRE: *SNOW WHITE—AN ENCHANTING MUSICAL*

The most elaborate stage show ever presented at the Fantasyland Theatre brings to life the characters, the songs, and the story of one of the most beloved of all of Walt Disney's animated features, *Snow White*. The live twenty-eight-minute adaptation of the classic 1937 film is presented several times daily.

Snow White is one of the earliest and most well-known American musicals to combine its score and choreography into the telling of the story and the characters, predating such classics as *The Wizard of Oz, Oklahoma!, Meet Me in St. Louis,* and *Annie Get Your Gun.*

The show features classic songs and characters, including Doc, Grumpy, Happy, Sleepy, Sneezy, Bashful, and Dopey. The score, with music and lyrics by Frank Churchill and Larry Morey, is one of the best known of any musical. "Whistle While You Work," "I'm Wishing," "One Song," "Heigh Ho," "The Washing Song (Bluddle-Uddle-Um-Dum)," "The Silly Song," and "Some Day My Prince Will Come" are all parts of the show. Award-winning actor Patrick Stewart, best known for his roles in *Star Trek, the Next Generation* TV show and films, and on the stage, is the voice of the magic mirror.

The director, choreographer, and costume designers for the show all have extensive experience on Broadway. Eric Schaeffer, who directed musical productions on Broadway and in London's West End, is artistic director of the Signature Theatre in Washington, D.C., one of the country's leading musical theaters. Scenic designer Tom Butsch also created the appearance for *Fantasmic!* and "The Hunchback of Notre Dame Festival of Fools" at Disneyland. Butsch based the look of *Snow White* on the visual art of painter Maxfield Parrish (1870–1966), whose work was very popular at the time of the release of the original film. Parrish's work helped define the visual style of the early half of the twentieth century.

`MUST-SEE` IT'S A SMALL WORLD

Every little girl's wildest dream: a land of beautiful dancing dolls from all over the world. There is nothing to get your heart beating here, but even the most cynical—including little boys and adults—will probably find something to smile about in this upbeat boat ride; teenagers are hereby excused from a mandatory visit. This eleven-minute ride was first presented at the 1964–1965 World's Fair in New York City.

We especially enjoy the Audio-Animatronic can-can dancers. We only wish we could get the sugary theme song out of our heads.

The boats are large and the lines move pretty quickly, but we'd advise coming to this attraction early or late in the day. Be

It's a Small World. *Photo by Corey Sandler. Used by permission from Disney Enterprises, Inc.*

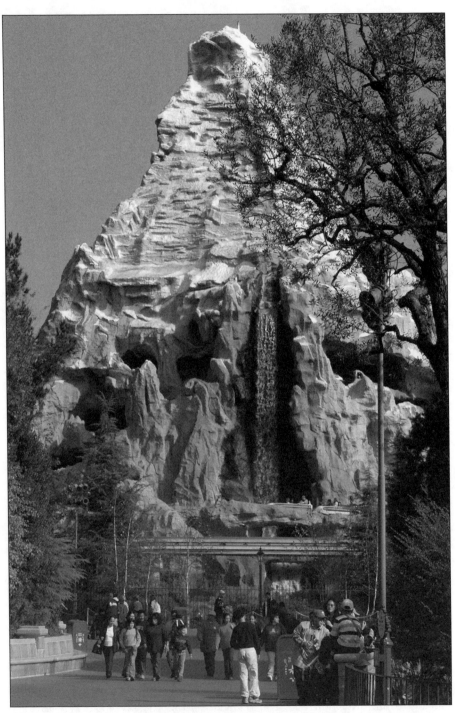

A bobsled passes through the Matterhorn. *Photo by Corey Sandler. Used by permission from Disney Enterprises, Inc.*

sure to check out the mechanical-doll parade every quarter hour on the clock outside the building. The ride features an improved digital sound system and a rerecorded soundtrack with more instrumentals, originally produced for Disneyland Paris.

MUST-SEE MATTERHORN BOBSLEDS

The Matterhorn is one of the reasons Disneyland is a magic kingdom. The Matterhorn Bobsleds is just a rather small and not-all-that-fast roller coaster that was one of the earliest attractions at Disneyland, but, like Space Mountain, which followed some two decades later, the Disney designers made it into something very special.

Here's the magic: These aren't roller-coaster cars. They're bobsleds about to make a sharp ascent up the interior of the famous pointed Swiss peak. Almost 150 feet into the air, the bobsleds start their rapid descent within the mountain and out onto exposed tracks that—if you look quickly—present some spectacular views of the park. (This is one of those rides worth riding in the daylight and again at night to experience the different views.) And do keep your eyes open for a quick glimpse of the Abominable Snowman.

The left (east) track, the one nearest the mountain at the turnstiles, has more turns and better views of the park, while the right (west) track has sharper drops.

Within the mountain, near the large ice crystals, look for a box marked WELLS EXPEDITION. This is a tribute to Frank Wells, president of the Walt Disney Company, a renowned mountaineer who died in a 1993 helicopter crash.

Lines for the bobsleds can become quite long, although the Matterhorn is no longer the number-one draw at Disneyland; that honor goes to the Indiana Jones ride, Splash Mountain, or Space Mountain. In any case, get to Matterhorn early or late to avoid lines.

Speaking of lines, Matterhorn Bobsleds is somewhat unique at Disneyland in that the twin waiting areas can be seen from the walkway; it should be fairly easy to gauge how long the wait will be. By the way, the line that heads toward Fantasyland holds fewer people than the one that heads toward Tomorrowland; if the two lines are about the same length, choose the queue toward Fantasyland.

Like Space Mountain, the Matterhorn is considerably tamer than a basic roller coaster at an amusement park; it's all in the setting. The best time to ride the Matterhorn (other than at the very start of the day) is during one of the parades. When crowds build, they usually set up two lines, one for each of the twin bobsled runs.

During parades the two lines are often combined into a single queue and routed away from the parade area. The single line looks long but moves twice as fast. When you are inside the final waiting area, turn to your right instead of the left for a slightly shorter wait.

If you're lucky, you'll see Mickey Mouse and Goofy climb up the mountain to join Minnie, who waits for them with a picnic lunch.

■ MAD TEA PARTY

A Disneyfied version of a basic amusement-park ride; circular cars move around a track and also spin around on platforms.

If it sounds dizzying, that's because it is: The very young and those with sensitive stomachs might prefer the carousel across the way. However, the riders do have some control over how fast the cups spin; to cut down on spin, grab hold of the wheel in the center of the cup and don't let go.

The ride is set in a scene from Disney's 1951 classic film, *Alice in Wonderland*. The ride itself takes only about ninety seconds; the wait can be much more than that, especially at midday. I'd recommend a spin only if lines are short.

■ STORYBOOK LAND CANAL BOATS

A kinder, gentler, smaller jungle cruise in and among some lovely miniatures taken from great fairy tales and Disney films, this is another of the early entertainments of Disneyland and a supposed favorite of Walt himself. Your journey begins with a trip into the mouth of Monstro the Whale, the giant beast of Disney's *Pinocchio*.

Guides point out some of the tiny scenes on a ten-minute tour, which has something for most everyone. The very young will enjoy spotting scenes from *Alice in Wonderland*, the Seven Dwarfs Mine, and more; adults will revel in the details, including tiny bonsai forests. As with the Jungle Cruise in Adventureland, some of the guides are about as lively as the bonsai while others put a bit of acting into their spiels.

Storybook Land has received some overdue attention in recent years, adding models of scenes from some of Disney's animated films, including *Aladdin, Beauty and the Beast,* and *The Little Mermaid*. A waterfall was added over the cave to Never Land. The improvements were derived from the Storybook area at Disneyland Paris.

■ CASEY JR. CIRCUS TRAIN

Climb into a circus animal cage or the caboose to circle Storybook Land on a three-minute train trip that your very daring youngsters may want to ride all by themselves. Adults can squeeze in, too, or can view the same displays from the Storybook Land Canal Boats.

MICKEY'S TOONTOWN

Disneyland, Walt Disney World, Disneyland Paris, Tokyo Disneyland, and the entire Disney empire were built upon the ears of the most famous rodent of all, but until recently Mickey Mouse didn't have a place of his own. At Walt Disney World, he got his own land (first a Birthday Party and then Mickey's Starland). At Disneyland, the Mickster shares the spotlight as emcee of Mickey's Toontown, a village based on some of the characters and locations of the Disney animated film *Who Framed Roger Rabbit?*

As you enter Mickey's Toontown, check out the civic signs on the railroad overpass: There's a chapter of the DAR (the Daughters of the Animated Reel), the Loyal Knights of the Inkwell, the Optimists In Toon National, and the Benevolent and Protective Order of Mouse. Take a close look at the manholes in the street: They are labeled with the more politically correct name, "toon holes."

This section of the park is definitely for the youngest visitors; it's like Fantasyland but without the crossover rides like Matterhorn and It's a Small World. If you're not traveling with kids, you're excused.

Note that this is a rather small area and can become very crowded, leading to lines that will please neither you nor your youngsters. Get there early or late in the day to avoid the lines.

This is one place where you are almost certain to find one or more Disney characters walking about. Listen for bells, horns, and whistles from Toontown City Hall for the changing of the guard.

Other funny touches include the sign outside Goofy's Gas that asks, DID WE GOOF UP YOUR CAR TODAY? Goofy also offers: IF WE CAN'T FIX IT, WE WON'T. The gas pump has fish floating around in the dispenser. Around the side of Daisy's Diner you will find the Third Little Piggy's Bank.

:::MUST-SEE::: ROGER RABBIT'S CAR TOON SPIN ≡FAST

Training wheels for the up-and-coming thrill rider. Not for the easily dizzied, this ride is based on the wild taxicabs in Roger Rabbit's Toontown. Your cab goes out of control when one of the Weasels throws a barrel of Judge Doom's toon-dissolving solution on the road. You're then off on a wild, spinning trip through special effects and Audio-Animatronic characters. Like the Mad Tea Party, you can control the speed of your spins by grabbing the wheel.

The lines for this three-minute ride can become quite long in midday; come early or late. The line you may see outside is only a hint at the interior queue that takes you through the back alleys of Toontown to your waiting cab. Figure on about thirty minutes from the entrance to the building until you are seated in a cab; if the line reaches to near the railroad underpass at the entrance to Toontown, the wait is at least one hour. Even better, pick up a Fastpass and come back later.

The waiting area, though, offers some entertainment of its own, as visitors can peek through holes in a fence to see the spinning cabs. You'll walk past Baby Herman's apartment, catch a glimpse backstage at the Ink and Paint Club, and learn about the insidious plot to literally wipe out the population of Toontown with a deadly concoction of paint solvents known as dip.

Along the way, you can even learn the formula for dip: one part acetone, one part benzene, and one part turpentine, mixed well. That actually is a real recipe for a solution that dissolves ink used by cartoon artists.

There are lots of other interesting details to be learned as you wait in line. Check out some of the license plates right inside the entrance: I M LATE, CAP 10 HK, 3 LIL PIGS, 1D N PTR, and 1DRLND among them. Whatever; all of the cars on the ride are called Lenny.

When you come to the door of the Ink and Paint Club, a hideous face will appear with one of several menacing messages, including "Beat it before I call a cop on you," or "Hey, who do you think you are, Mickey Mouse?"

You can also see Jessica Rabbit's very round shape passing by in silhouette on the window. There is a casting bulletin board outside of her dressing room announcing an audition for an upcoming Disney pic. They're looking for men, women, and animals; no giants, please.

Another sign: LOST ONE MAGIC FEATHER. IF FOUND, PLEASE CONTACT DUMBO C/O TIMOTHY MOUSE, WALT DISNEY STUDIO, HOLLYWOOD, CA.

More threatening is a "wanted" poster: WISE GUY WEASEL WANTED IN THIRTEEN STATES FOR TOON NAPPING, ASSAULT WITH A SILLY WEAPON, PETTY LARCENY, GRAND LARCENY, AND REALLY GRAND LARCENY.

When you finally board your two-person taxi, you'll follow behind Roger Rabbit as he tears through town, pursued by Weasels who dump dip in the path of vehicles. You'll spin through Ferdinand's China Shop and an electrical storm in the power plant, and eventually you'll crash through the roof of the Gag Warehouse for a showdown with the Weasels.

The concept of the ride is supposed to allow drivers to control the spin of their cars as they move through the ride. We found the steering wheel a bit stiff and difficult to control and suspect that some young children will need the assistance of an adult in driving. You can spin the cars wildly or devote all of your energy to preventing the spin.

Mickey's House and Meet Mickey

If you have kids, or ever were one, there's not a whole lot of doubt about this: You've got to pay a personal visit to Mickey Mouse. What we've got here is a series of displays within the mouse's house (including some interesting memorabilia and lots of touch-me stuff) and a waiting area where you can see old MM cartoons. It all leads up to the big enchilada: an audience with the mouse himself. Groups of one or two families are ushered into the dressing room where Mickey will pose for photos, sign autographs, and stand still while he is hugged, poked, prodded, and otherwise inspected.

One thing he won't do is talk. That's not in his job description.

Minnie's House

Next door is the home of Mickey's mouse-girlfriend; check out the strange stuff in her kitchen. Minnie herself, though, is not often in her own house; you'll more likely find her out walking the streets of Toontown visiting with guests.

Jolly Trolley

A slow trip around Toontown. Walking is faster, if less fun.

Gadget's Go-Coaster

A very short and not-very-fast kiddie coaster. In Disney fashion, though, it's been made very attractive; the bad news is that lines can become unreasonable for a ride that lasts less than a minute.

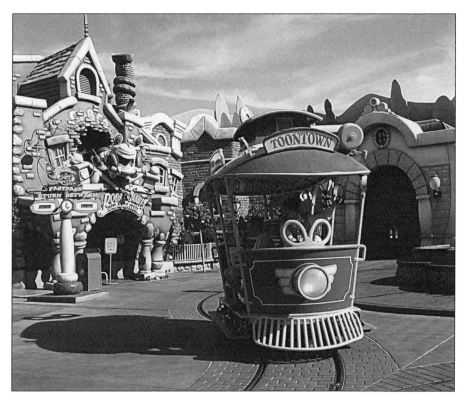

The Jolly Trolley in Toontown. *Photo by Corey Sandler. Used by permission from Disney Enterprises, Inc. and Amblin Entertainment, Inc.*

If the line is more than a hundred kids long, I'd suggest you bribe the kids with an ice cream and skip any line longer than your kid's attention span or your willingness to stand around and do nothing.

Disneyland Railroad
The vintage railroad that circles Disneyland has a station near the entrance to Mickey's Toontown, a good way to deliver kiddies at the start of the day or extricate them at the end.

Chip 'n' Dale Treehouse
A Disneyfied climbing tree and slide and playground and a great place to let the kids burn off energy while Mom and Dad collapse on a bench.

Goofy's Bounce House
Just like it says, a place to take off your shoes and bounce. A basic amusement-park play area that has a Goofy theme. Kids must be older than three years and no taller than 52 inches; keep an eye on the shoes they must leave behind. Lines can become quite long and move slowly at midday.

TOMORROWLAND

Every Disney visitor with a bit of spunk—and his or her mom and dad—has got to visit Tomorrowland at least once to catch a lift on the DL-200 Intergalactic Probe, also known as **Space Mountain.** And then there's the rare chance to journey into deep space with a rookie pilot in *Star Tours.* Other modes of transportation at Tomorrowland include submarines, monorails, and an old-fashioned steam train.

If you think about it, though, tomorrow is a place where we never arrive—it's always in the offing. So it seems appropriate that Tomorrowland should always be under construction.

Now Tomorrowland looks forward and backward at the same time: The setting is a Disneyesque salute to futuristic novelist Jules Verne, a concept first tried at Disneyland Paris and fine-tuned at Walt Disney World. You'll also see nods toward Leonardo da Vinci and H. G. Wells.

Tomorrowland's most recent update added an interesting retro-future mix. At the gateway near the Astro Orbitor, the pathway consists of colored cobblestones; Imagineers replaced the cold chrome with warm brass, and white walls with greens and golds and rich velvets.

The Astro Orbitor updated the old Rocket Jets to a phantasmagorical flight through moving planets and moons, based in part on sketches by da Vinci. (The old mechanism for the Rocket Jets was given a new life as a "kinetic sculpture," featuring satellite dishes.)

In one big step backward, Disneyland shut down the *Rocket Rods* system in 2001; the ride had been introduced with much fanfare just a few years before as the zippy replacement for the PeopleMover ride above Tomorrowland. Disney acknowledged the obvious, that the $25 million ride was subject to repeated mechanical problems and was shut down for extended periods of time. There are no announced plans for a replacement attraction.

In the earliest plans for Disneyland, the area was dubbed "The World of Tomorrow." On opening day in 1955, there were three attractions: Autopia, Space Station X-1 (featuring a "satellite" view of America), and Circarama (the predecessor of CircleVision theater).

The TWA Moonliner stood outside the Rocket to the Moon attraction when it opened a bit later in the year; the ride was updated to become Flight to the Moon, and later Mission to Mars. Now, Tomorrowland includes a rebuilt version of the Moonliner atop a soda stand near Space Mountain.

MUST-SEE **SPACE MOUNTAIN** ≡*FAST*

Everything old is new again; Space Mountain returned to action in the summer of 2005, completely reengineered. Visitors can now ride rockets by day and rock by night when the lights pulse and the cars zoom along to a thumping rock 'n' roll soundtrack.

Space Mountain is a masterpiece of Disney Imagineering, merging a relatively small and slow (top speed of about twenty-eight miles per hour) roller coaster with an outer space theme. The small cars zoom around indoors in near-total darkness, the only light coming from projected images of stars and planets on the ceiling.

The ride was shut down in 2003 when it began showing its age; the entire ride mechanism was removed and replaced with new track and cars, following essentially the same path as the original ride. Guests now board through a wondrous new Space Port. The roof of the landmark building has been restored to its former soft white color.

The initial idea for Space Mountain came from Walt Disney himself, first called Space Port. The ride opened in 1977 after more than a decade of planning and two years after a similar version opened at Walt Disney World in Orlando.

The cars feel as though they are moving much faster than they are because you have no point of reference in the dark. And no, the cars don't turn upside down.

Professional Space Mountain riders—and there are tens of thousands of them—will argue about which seat affords the best ride. The last row of seats seems to benefit from a "whip" effect as the cars make sharp turns; I prefer the very front row. You don't have the back of someone's head marring the illusion of space travel, and there is a terrific blast of rushing air as you move on the track. At busy times, you probably will not be able to cajole an attendant into allowing you to select the seat of your choice; your chances are better late at night or on the occasional slow day.

Space Mountain is one of the most popular attractions at other Disney parks. The Walt Disney World ride is similar but not identical; at Disneyland Paris a version named Discovery Mountain and based on Jules Verne's book *From the*

Space Mountain. *Photo by Corey Sandler. Used by permission from Disney Enterprises, Inc.*

Battle the evil Emperor Zurg at the Buzz Lightyear Astro Blasters. *Photo by Corey Sandler. Used by permission from Disney Enterprises, Inc.*

Earth to the Moon is a bit wilder, including a catapult launch to the top of the track and a 360-degree loop in the dark. Yet another version takes off from Tokyo Disneyland.

MUST-SEE BUZZ LIGHTYEAR ASTRO BLASTERS

It's *Toy Story* live, in a ride that combines a zippy dark ride with a shooting gallery. You'll be teamed with astro-superhero Buzz Lightyear on a daring mission to rescue the universe's crystollic fusion cell supply (better known as batteries) from the clutches of the evil Emperor Zurg.

The ride, a favorite at Walt Disney World in Orlando—where it is called Buzz Lightyear's Space Ranger Spin—was installed in Disneyland's former Circlevision Theatre as part of the celebration of the park's fiftieth anniversary.

You'll be assigned to your personal two-seater XP-37 Space Cruiser, spinning through ten scenes of toys, asteroids and meteors, and strange and wondrous aliens in the Gamma Quadrant. Each car includes a joystick to spin the car and a pair of infrared laser guns to knock down all manner of threats by Zurg—basically shoot any and all of the orange Emperor Zurg insignias scattered throughout the ride. When your laser hits a target, it triggers animation, sound, and light effects. Your score, which varies according to the complexity of the shot, is tallied on an LED screen on the cruiser's dashboard. The final scene takes you through a tunnel of energy and back out into Tomorrowland.

As cruisers complete the mission, guests compare their score with the mission profile chart to determine their space ranger rank. There is also a connection to an online game for virtual visitors on the Internet.

MUST-SEE STAR TOURS ≡FAST

Whenever your plans call for intergalactic travel, say the Disney travel posters, consider flying Star Tours to the vacation moon of Endor.

Disney builds the atmosphere and excitement beautifully from the moment you walk beneath the huge space machine outside and continues building as you walk through the indoor waiting area that simulates a gritty space garage. Our favorite flaky robots, R2D2 and C3PO, are the mechanics.

Listen carefully to the announcements on the public address system. You'll hear a call for Egroeg Sacul (Star Wars creator George Lucas, spelled backward) and a summons to the owner of landspeeder THX-1138, which has been illegally parked in a "No-Hover" zone.

When your time comes, you will enter into a forty-passenger simulator cabin and meet your pilot, Captain Rex. The doors will be closed and your seat belts tightly cinched before he informs you that this is his first trip. Too late—you're off. You'll make an uneasy takeoff and then blast (accidentally) into and then through a frozen meteor, stumble into an active intergalactic battle zone, and finally make a wild landing at your goal, the vacation moon of Endor.

This is quite a wild ride, even in a simulator; it's a bit rough for the very young; pregnant women and those with health problems are advised to sit this one out. The trip takes about seven minutes.

Much of the queue area is indoors, with waiting riders walking among artifacts from Endor. If the interior is filled to the doorway, you can expect as much as an hour's wait. Remember the rule: Go early or late to the most popular attractions.

Children must be at least 40 inches to ride; tall youngsters younger than seven years old must be accompanied by an adult.

■ ASTRO ORBITOR

Astro Orbitor is a basic amusement-park ride that has rotating rockets and an up and down lever, but in typical Disney fashion it seems like much more. The colorful five-passenger rockets (three single seats and one double) revolve in and around a fantastic, animated astronomical model of planets and constellations. (Think of Astro Orbitor as a slightly faster and somewhat higher version of Dumbo the Flying Elephant.)

Nowhere near as threatening (to some) as Space Mountain and offering a nice view of Tomorrowland, Astro Orbitor nevertheless is not for people who have a fear of heights. Originally named Rocket Jets, this ride was renovated as part of the makeover of Tomorrowland. It is especially impressive at night.

┇MUST-SEE┇ AUTOPIA ≡*FAST*

Everything old is new again, including Autopia, one of the original attractions of Disneyland that dates back to 1955.

The popular miniature car track was revamped in 2000, combining the old Fantasyland Autopia and Tomorrowland Autopia tracks into a single course. Three car models are available: Cute Car, a cute VW-bug-like vehicle; Sportscar, low-slung with air intakes; and Off-Road, with big knobby tires. Cars are painted so they seem to be encased in an ever-changing palette of colors, a Disney creation called "ChromaLusion." Each can seat up to two adults or three children.

The experience begins before drivers reach the roadway, which is a good thing because this attraction has always had some of the longest lines in the park. The entrance to Autopia is through a central tower shaped like a giant piston. Guests cross an elevated walkway to "The Grandstand" where they can view the track

Glug, Glug, Glug

The Disney classic Submarine Voyage was scuttled after millions of loops around a rather unimpressive artificial lagoon. The attraction was loosely based on the Jules Verne book *Twenty Thousand Leagues Under the Sea,* and in particular the 1954 Disney movie.

Disney insiders hint of a rejuvenated submarine ride with a *Finding Nemo* theme, perhaps for 2006. A similar reworking may appear at the also-dormant Walt Disney World sub pond in Orlando.

and the passing cars; a stadium-size video screen plays humorous animated interviews with vehicles.

As guests drive along the extended roadway, they experience the world through a car's perspective. Humorous billboards along the highway advertise directly to the vehicle. The track layout includes curves, bridges, a "car park," and an "off-road" driving experience.

Successful drivers are given a commemorative Autopia driver's license, a recollection of the 1950s version of the attraction.

The best way to avoid the lines is to pick up a Fastpass.

■ *HONEY, I SHRUNK THE AUDIENCE*

A clever 3-D thriller that picks up where the shape-altering Disney films (*Honey, I Shrunk the Kids* and *Honey, I Blew Up the Baby*) left off. In this case, the kids are all right; it's the audience that shrinks.

This is a theatrical performance that is simply not to be missed. We find ourselves as honored guests at the presentation of the Inventor of the Year award to Wayne Szalinski, played by actor Rick Moranis. Other members of the original film also appear in the Disneyland feature; they're joined by funnyman Eric Idle of *Monty Python's Flying Circus.*

As far as what happens next, we don't want to spoil the fun or play a cat-and-mouse game with you; oops, disregard that last hint.

The wild conclusion of the show comes when one of the machines goes berserk and ends up shrinking the entire audience down to toy size. "Stay in your seats and we will blow you up as soon as possible," says Wayne.

The auditorium conspires with the 3-D images to complete the illusion with moving seats, special lighting, and unusual effects that will tickle your fancy and sprinkle you with laughter.

■ INNOVENTIONS

The two-floor pavilion of technology uses the former Carousel Theatre's rotating theater base as a transport vehicle to various exhibits and showcases. Innoventions is divided into five major technology areas: Home, Entertainment, Workplace/Education, Recreation/Health, and Transportation.

Innoventions is like a permanent World's Fair, showcasing the latest in consumer and high-tech products from companies around the world; it debuted at Walt Disney World's Epcot Center. Recent exhibits included Compaq's Space Training Center, which offered an electronic labyrinth, and interactive encounters that allow visitors to pilot their own ship, explore the stars, and discover their weight on distant planets. Pioneer Electronics' futuristic Virtual Resort showcases the latest in high-definition plasma displays, recordable DVDs, and mobile and home entertainment, including an interactive aquarium. AT&T presented an exploration about interactive broadband television, personal computer, and phone technologies.

Guests board the slowly rotating building at various locations to receive introductions to a variety of show spaces. Audio-Animatronic Tom Morrow, voiced by comic actor Nathan Lane, reprises the "Great Big Beautiful Tomorrow" song that was the theme of the old *Carousel of Progress* show. Tom is a real cutup, promising a glimpse of "information you never knew you never knew you need to know, you know?"

From there it's on to the upper level of the building, home to interactive presentations and hands-on displays, showcasing creative uses of tomorrow's technology. You'll meet Tom Morrow once more, this time dressed in a see-through plastic lab coat. In his breast pocket is a reminder note: "Get 10W40." That's oil. Black gold. Texas tea. Or in this case, lubrication.

There are, by the way, no restrooms in the future. Make your plans accordingly.

■ DISNEYLAND MONORAIL

Yet another mode of transportation, but unlike all the others in this corner of the park, the monorail has a purpose: It is a quick and easy way to leave the park and zip over to a station at the head of Downtown Disney, across the road from the Disneyland Hotel and Disney's Paradise Pier Hotel and a short walk from Disney's Grand Californian Hotel. This is a great way to duck out of the park for lunch or dinner.

When the monorail was first built in 1959 it was quite a novelty: the first full-time monorail transit authority in the country. (Walt Disney World has a much more extensive system with several tracks.)

The 2.5-mile trip gives some interesting views of Tomorrowland and Fantasyland as it crosses over the Golden Gate Bridge near the entrance to Disney's California Adventure. There are only two stations, though: at Tomorrowland in Disneyland and at Downtown Disney.

On an average day there are two monorail trains running; on an especially busy day controllers might add a third set of cars to the line, but the short track won't permit more than that. The trains are capable of going seventy miles per hour, but stay at thirty-five

Mouse Mouths

Walt Disney himself performed the voices of Mickey and Minnie in the earliest cartoons, including *Steamboat Willie,* which was the first Mickey Mouse cartoon with sound—but not the first movie starring the rascally rodent. That honor went to *Plane Crazy.* The current voice of the Mickster is Wayne Allwine, the third mouse mouthpiece.

Gummed Up

You cannot buy chewing gum at any store in Disneyland. The idea of sticky rubber underfoot was too much for Walt Disney to bear, and it has always been banned. Cleaning crews regularly search the walkways for contraband.

The Disneyland monorail leaves the Tomorrowland station. *Photo by Corey Sandler. Used by permission from Disney Enterprises, Inc.*

miles per hour or slower. In recent years, the futuristic monorail has seemed . . . old. Various rumors have suggested both a revamp and a shutdown of the system.

If you leave the train at Downtown Disney, be sure to have your hand stamped and take your Disneyland day's passport with you so you can return to the park. You can also start your day by boarding the monorail at Downtown Disney if you have your passport.

For a minor thrill, you may be able to maneuver yourself into one of the five seats in the front of the monorail with the driver; tell the attendant loading the monorail you want to sit up front and move to the first gate to wait your turn.

Cosmic Waves. Outside the entrance to Space Mountain is a lively fountain where guests can interact with "waves" and "mazes" of water shooting up from the ground in synchronized patterns. You can get as wet as you'd like. (There are bathrooms nearby at Space Mountain if you need to change into dry clothing.)

Starcade. It's a bit of a concession to the outside world, but then again Disney is not known for leaving too many nickels on the table; actually, we're talking half dollars, dollars, and more at this high-tech video-game arcade located on the lower level of Space Mountain. Every successful rocket rider has to pass the enticements of the machines.

You'll find just about every major arcade game here, but to Disney's credit, you won't find any first-person shooting arcade games here or elsewhere in the park.

PARADES AND FIREWORKS

Throughout its history Disneyland has celebrated the end of the day with a fireworks display. The show is presented on nights when the park is open late.

Walt Disney's Parade of Dreams debuted at the start of the fiftieth-anniversary party. The all-new parade features one of the largest casts of Disney characters and performers ever assembled.

And at night, the **Remember . . . Dreams Come True** fireworks spectacular is the most elaborate in the history of Disneyland. The show includes a special musical score, dramatic close-proximity pyrotechnics, a whole new generation of never-before-seen fireworks, and special lighting effects.

Be sure to check with the park during off-season periods; parades, fireworks, *Fantasmic!* and other shows are sometimes presented only on weekends when attendance is low or when the park closes before dark during the week.

When a parade is under way, there are only a few marked places where you can cross the traffic; crossing zones north of the Matterhorn are usually less congested than those near Main Street. With the closure of the Skyway, the only alternative is to take the Disneyland Railroad, which circles the park in a clockwise direction.

The best advice on getting a prime spot to see a parade is to get in place early, as much as thirty minutes or more before the start. One of the best spots is from the central plaza near the railroad station above Main Street; it's no secret, though, and this is usually one of the first places to fill up.

There's good and bad news about this. For the first parade of the day, the beginning of Main Street marks the end of the parade route, and it can take fifteen to twenty minutes for the entertainment to arrive; the second parade begins at Main Street and moves toward Fantasyland. Check the parade schedule listed in the *Disneyland Today* flyer you will receive as you enter the park.

DISNEY CHARACTERS

Face it: The real reason you flew a thousand miles and spent a thousand dollars and endured twenty thousand people in line was to get a picture of yourself with your arm around Mickey or Minnie, with Goofy's mouth engulfing your head, or with Roger Rabbit standing on your feet.

There are three ways to obtain the precious mementos: by chance, by investigation, or by plan.

The characters stroll about the park throughout the day, usually accompanied by handlers who help them navigate or help them escape from the occasional attacking hordes of children of all ages.

If you are willing to take things by chance, you can often find one or another character on Main Street near the railroad station and Main Street Opera House, regular visits at the Hub near the castle, and strolling characters in Toontown.

What a Bunch of Characters

If you've ever wanted to see a child's eyes pop open like a cartoon character, watch carefully the first time a youngster comes face-to-face with a walking Mickey or Minnie Mouse.

The characters are scattered throughout Disneyland; if you or your child has a particular favorite, you can inquire at City Hall to check the day's schedule. You'll usually find them near the railroad overpass on Main Street, in and around the Castle, and in Toontown.

Don't be surprised if some very young children become frightened when their time in the spotlight arrives; the characters are large and usually surrounded by crowds. Cast members inside the suits (sorry to destroy the illusion) are pretty good at playing around with little ones, though.

Mickey, Minnie, Goofy, and most of the characters won't talk; they will, however, sign autographs if that is something you've always hoped for.

If you're lucky, you may find yourself in the middle of what Disney calls a **Character Flood,** a sudden deluge of characters. On busy days, you can expect a double-decker bus full of characters to flood the Hub near the castle, often around noon.

If you're a planner, you can count on finding Mickey and friends in Mickey's House at Toontown, where His Mouseness meets his adoring public in small groups. One of Mickey's assistants is usually available to use your camera to take your picture, if you'd like.

On busy days there are (sorry to destroy any illusions) four Mickeys in Mickey's House, in different "movie sets": *Fantasia, The Band Concert, Steamboat Willie,* and *Through the Mirror.* You're not supposed to have a choice, although you may be able to sweet-talk one of the cast members into steering you to the particular room and the Mickey of your dreams.

Finally, you may be able to enlist the assistance of a cast member who has a walkie-talkie or a representative at City Hall who can tell you where some of the characters are scheduled to be that day. The daily map you receive at the entrance gates includes a Mickey's hand icon to show the location of characters.

EATING YOUR WAY THROUGH DISNEYLAND

It's my opinion that there are three types of restaurants at Disneyland: overpriced and bad, overpriced and barely acceptable, and overpriced and almost good. Well, okay, there are a few meals that are overpriced and good. In any case, I'd recommend that you not consider meals to be an important part of your experience at the park.

You do have to eat though. Disney has a rule against bringing your own sandwiches or other food into the park. The park provides lockers and a picnic area outside the gates, to the left of the entrance.

In years past, I used to say that I had never seen an attendant search a backpack or shoulder bag for tuna fish on rye; alas, in today's security environment, your small backpacks, shoulder bags, and purses will be searched for more dangerous items. I'd still expect that the guards are not likely to confiscate sandwiches, and you certainly can bring baby formula and a few candy bars for the kids.

If you don't pack your own, it is possible to pick and choose among the offerings at the park. Disneyland does offer a few more healthful choices, such as pasta salads, turkey burgers, and smoked turkey legs, at some of its stands. You'll also find fruit stands at several locations around the park, offering oranges, apples, bananas, and other real food. In Adventureland you'll find dill pickles. The stands sell plastic bottles of soda, which can be sealed up and stowed between rides.

Another very valuable strategy is to take an afternoon break and leave the park to go to a real restaurant for lunch and then return for a second visit in the evening. Your parking ticket allows you to exit and re-enter on the same day, as does your park pass (with a hand stamp).

With the opening of Downtown Disney, lunch options are greatly improved. If the lines are not too long, consider jumping on the monorail and choosing from the impressive offerings at the new entertainment district. You can also walk to Downtown Disney from the front gate of Disneyland.

If you do eat in the park, you should try to avoid lines by eating early; arriving for lunch at 11:30 A.M. instead of noon can save an hour of your time.

Many restaurants offer a children's menu for about $4.00.

Money Matters

The Main Street Bank is a bank on, uh, Main Street and it provides basic, uh, banking services to visitors on Main Street. You can also buy stamps, upgrade tickets, and buy "Disney Dollars" or gift certificates. There are also ATMs outside the park to the left of the entrance, on Main Street near the Penny Arcade, and in Tomorrowland and Frontierland.

■ MAIN STREET

Blue Ribbon Bakery. Through the windows of a show kitchen, you'll be able to watch all sorts of goodies in the making.

Carnation Cafe. You'll enter through a gazebo into an attractive shaded Victorian dining area for a breakfast of waffles, French toast, pastries, and more. Lunch and dinner include soups, salads, and sandwiches, with meals priced around $8.00 to $15.00.

The eatery has gone a bit upscale in recent years. Specialties for lunch and dinner include shepherd's pie and chicken Caesar, both priced at about $9.00.

Gibson Girl Ice Cream Parlor. Eight flavors of ice cream and six varieties of soft-serve frozen yogurt are available.

Plaza Inn. This longtime favorite on Main Street has been redone in recent years as a large food court. Specialties include fried chicken, pot roast, pasta, and salads. Open for breakfast, lunch, and dinner; meals tend to run about $8.00 to $15.00.

■ ADVENTURELAND

Bengal Barbecue. Beef, chicken, and vegetable kabobs.

■ NEW ORLEANS SQUARE

Blue Bayou Restaurant. One of the prettiest spots in the park, this restaurant is set within the dark bayou scene at the opening of Pirates of the Caribbean. Dinner entrees, priced from $24 to $37, include offerings such as prime rib, grilled shrimp brochettes, and Cajun tri-tip. Lunch entrees range from $12 to $18, including Monte Cristo sandwiches, blackened chicken Caesar salad, and jambalaya. Lunch is served from 11:00 A.M. to 4:00 P.M. and dinner from 4:00 to 9:00 P.M. By the way, the Blue Bayou is one of two restaurants in the park, along with the Plaza Inn, to offer kosher food; inquire when making reservations.

Cafe Orleans. An informal eatery with lunch and dinner offerings priced from about $5.00 to $15.00 including prime rib and Cajun boule (spiced chicken in a bread bowl). The menu also includes soup and salad choices. Open seasonally.

French Market Restaurant. An attractive outdoor patio that has a view of the river and railroad and a simple buffeteria menu.

La Petite Pâtisserie. A somewhat hidden gem on Royal Street, this walk-up window serves decent turkey and ham sandwiches, pastries, and sweets and is usually not very crowded. Open seasonally.

Mint Julep Bar. A little bit of New Orleans located next to the French Market

A Mexican band performs in Frontierland. *Photo by Corey Sandler. Used by permission from Disney Enterprises, Inc.*

patio. It offers just about everything except bourbon: Libations include nonal-coholic mint juleps as well as espresso, cappuccino, fritters, lemonade, and ice cream novelties. Open seasonally.

Royal Street Veranda. Counter service for clam chowder and snacks.

■ FANTASYLAND

Village Haus Restaurant. Pizza, pasta, burgers, and salads.

■ CRITTER COUNTRY

Harbour Galley. In the shadow of the Haunted Mansion at the entrance to Critter Country, serving McDonald's french fries and drinks.

■ FRONTIERLAND

Golden Horseshoe Stage. Snacks, ice cream, and drinks, with regular enter-tainment by singing cowboys and dancing bar girls.

Rancho del Zocalo Restaurante. An attractive buffeteria serving tacos, en-chiladas, and more.

River Belle Terrace. Near Tarzan's Treehouse and Pirates of the Caribbean. Complete breakfasts of scrambled eggs, bacon or sausage, and potatoes for about $6.00; Mickey Mouse pancakes with bacon or sausage for about $4.55. Luncheon fare, priced from about $4.00 to $7.00, includes Huck Finn's chicken meal, Mississippi vegetable stew, the Showboat ham sandwich, and Aunt Polly's turkey sandwich.

Stage Door Cafe. Burgers, hot dogs, and chicken-breast sandwiches. Open seasonally.

■ MICKEY'S TOONTOWN

Clarabelle's Frozen Yogurt. As advertised. Open seasonally.

Daisy's Diner. Counter snacks, including pizza and salad. Open seasonally.

Pluto's Dog House. Hot dogs and snacks. Open seasonally.

■ TOMORROWLAND

Club Buzz—Lightyears Above the Rest. Fast food and fun. While you eat, you can enjoy "Calling All Space Scouts: A Buzz Lightyear Adventure," hosted by the space-age hero, Buzz Lightyear, along with his costars Space Cadet Starla, the Little Green Men from outer space, and the nefarious Emperor Zurg. Open sea-sonally.

Redd Rockett's Pizza Port. Quick pies.

DISNEY CHARACTER MEALS

Wanna chow down with Minnie Mouse, Chip 'n' Dale, or Goofy? How about dining "Under the Sea" with Ariel the mermaid? Then perhaps you should make plans for a character meal.

Prices range from $12.99 to $26.95 for adults, and $7.99 to $10.75 for kids.

For information and reservations (necessary most days), call Disneyland Resort Dining Reservations at (714) 781–3463.

Breakfast with Chip 'n' Dale. Storyteller's Cafe, Disney's Grand Californian Hotel. Daily, year-round, from 6:30 to 11:30 A.M. All-you-can-eat buffet, including scrambled eggs, breakfast meats, potatoes, French toast sticks, waffles, cereals, and fruit. Adults $18.95, children (3–11 years old) $9.95, infants (3 and younger) free. Various characters, but not Mickey. Parking validation available. Reservations suggested.

Character Breakfast in the Park. Plaza Inn, Disneyland. Offered every morning, year-round, from park opening through 10:45 A.M. Adults $19.30, children (3–11 years old) $10.75. The only character dining experience inside Disneyland park. Various characters visit for an all-you-can-eat breakfast buffet.

Goofy's Kitchen. Goofy's Kitchen, Disneyland Hotel. Brunch served daily year-round from 7:00 A.M. to 1:00 P.M.; till 2:00 P.M. on weekends. Dinner served daily from 5:00 to 9:00 P.M. Brunch: adults $18.95, children $9.95. Dinner: adults $26.95, children $9.95. Pasta, salads, breakfast items, and a build-your-own-sandwich and sundae bar. Goofy and friends attend.

Miss Minnie and Friends Breakfast. Disney's PCH Grill, Disney's Paradise Pier Hotel. Daily. All-you-can-eat buffet with hot dishes, waffles, pastries, fruits, and a selection of Japanese offerings. Adults $18.95, children (3–11 years old) $9.95. Minnie and other characters are regulars. Reservations suggested.

Ariel's Grotto. Disney's California Adventure. Hours and offerings vary by season. Call for details. Lunch: adults $12.99, children $7.99. Dinner: adults $17.99, children $10.99. An "Under the Sea" setting where Ariel and her beach-combing Disney friends, food, and views of Paradise Pier combine to create a memorable family dining experience. Selections of home-style family favorites, including a starter soup or salad, entrees, and tempting desserts. Reservations suggested.

CHAPTER FIVE

DISNEY'S CALIFORNIA ADVENTURE

DISNEY'S CALIFORNIA ADVENTURE is where they took down a parking lot and unpaved a paradise.

Visitors to the Disneyland Resort now have a choice between two wondrous Disney dreams. When you reach the ticket booths at the end of the Downtown Disney entertainment district, you can turn left to the world-famous original Disneyland park or head to the right and pass beneath a version of the Golden Gate Bridge and into the newest theme park in town.

Disney's California Adventure is not Disneyland. It's a fabulous park filled with some of the most advanced simulators and thrill rides anywhere in the world, but it is meant to supplement and not compete with the classic original across the way.

At Disneyland you'll find fairy castles, slow boats through a small world of dolls, animatronic pirates, burgers and nuggets, and Mickey Mouse.

At Disney's California Adventure you'll roll your way into a 360-degree loop on a coaster, zoom 180 feet into the air on a space shot, hang glide over Yosemite, meet the multicultural founders of the Golden State, sip on fine wine, and munch on sourdough bread baked in the park.

That doesn't mean you won't find Mickey Mouse at the new park; he's still the main guy around Anaheim. And it also doesn't mean that youngsters won't enjoy a visit to Disney's California Adventure, either; there are more than enough Disney-quality kiddie attractions and shows to make this place a must-see, including **Flik's Fun Fair,** a play area based on *A Bug's Life.*

And in 2004, the park took on a new dimension with the opening of **The Twilight Zone Tower of Terror** in the Hollywood Pictures Backlot; it is a California version of the thrilling elevator ride that is one of the most popular attractions at Disney–MGM Studios at Walt Disney World in Orlando.

MUST-SEES

Golden Dreams
(Golden State)

Grizzly River Run
(Golden State)

Soarin' Over California
(Golden State)

California Screamin'
(Paradise Pier)

Maliboomer
(Paradise Pier)

Sun Wheel
(Paradise Pier)

***Disney's Aladdin,
Hyperion Theater***
(Hollywood Pictures
Backlot)

**Jim Henson's
Muppet*Vision 3D**
(Hollywood Pictures
Backlot)

**Twilight Zone Tower
of Terror**
(Hollywood Pictures
Backlot)

It's Tough to Be a Bug!
(A Bug's Land)

As part of the celebration of the fiftieth anniversary of Disneyland next door, look for **Block Party Bash** at Disney's California Adventure. Guests will suddenly find themselves surrounded by the music, excitement, and fun from one of five instant celebrations starring Mickey, Minnie, the Muppets, the crew from *Monsters, Inc.,* Lilo and Stitch, and Flik and Princess Atta from *A Bug's Life.*

And sometime in early 2006, look for the opening of **Mike & Sully to the Rescue,** a modern version of a classic Disney dark ride based on the film *Monsters, Inc.* featuring at least forty Audio-Animatronic figures.

The ride is based on a scene in the film where a young girl named Boo is discovered on the loose in Monstropolis, and protected by the monsters who are much more scared of her than a child might imagine.

The ride will take over the former home of Superstar Limo. Even Mickey lays an egg every once in a while; this dark ride through Tinseltown in a top-down purple limousine was not much of a California adventure and was shut down after a very short, unimpressive run.

WELCOME TO DISNEY'S CALIFORNIA ADVENTURE

The park is made up of an entrance plaza and four major lands:
- Golden State (including Condor Flats, the Bay Area, Grizzly Peak Recreation Area, Golden Vine Winery, and Pacific Wharf)
- Paradise Pier
- The Hollywood Pictures Backlot
- A Bug's Land, including Flik's Fun Fair

Most visitors will enter from the main gate from the entry plaza that stands between Disneyland and Disney's California Adventure. From there, Hollywood Pictures Backlot is to the left, A Bug's Land straight ahead, Golden State off to the right, and Paradise Pier deep into the park and to the right.

Guests at Disney's Grand Californian Hotel and Disney's Paradise Pier Hotel have their own entrances into the Paradise Pier section of the park.

Power Trip: Do Drop In

The top draw at Disney's California Adventure is the Twilight Zone Tower of Terror. If you're up for an out-of-control elevator ride, head to the left side of the park immediately and get on board—or grab a Fastpass for a scheduled appointment.

The other big lures at Disney's California Adventure are the three major thrill rides deep in the park at Paradise Pier: California Screamin', Maliboomer, and Sun Wheel. Also at the top of the list for most excitement-seeking visitors: the oh-so-real simulated thrills of Soarin' Over California.

If you've got the need for speed or the want to go get high (in a Disneyfied family-friendly kind of way), arrive early with your track shoes on.

Pass through the Golden Gateway and bear to the right of Sunshine Plaza, between the sun icon and Grizzly Peak. Make a quick detour to pick up a Fastpass at the entrance to Soarin' Over California. Then return to the middle of the park and head for the lagoon (Paradise Bay), cross the bridge to Avalon Cove, and continue walking to the boardwalk.

Head directly for California Screamin'. Then move on to the Sun Wheel for a spin, and if the line is reasonable, shoot for the sky on Maliboomer. After you've done your time in Paradise Pier, head for Condor Flats and ride Soarin' Over California.

If you're a guest at Disney's Grand Californian Hotel, you can move a few steps ahead of other visitors by using the entrance from that hotel to the park; you'll set foot in the west side of the park near Grizzly River Run, about five minutes closer to Paradise Pier than the main entrance.

GOLDEN GATEWAY

The main entrance to Disney's California Adventure, across the esplanade from Disneyland, is a giant picture postcard of California landmarks. You'll walk into the park through 11-foot-high letters spelling out CALIFORNIA. Overhead, the monorail passes across the Golden Gate Bridge. The gateway is framed by dramatic tile murals. Southern California icons are to the left as you enter, Northern California landmarks on the right.

Just past the bridge is Sunshine Plaza, dominated by a 50-foot "sun" made of gold-hued titanium inlaid with tiny glass particles; the sun seems to ride the crest of a wave in the fountain below. The huge solar icon speaks of sunny California; the face you see as you enter, though, is oriented to the north. That was no major problem for Disney Imagineers: They installed a set of six computer-controlled heliostats with large mirrors. The devices track the

DISNEY'S CALIFORNIA ADVENTURE

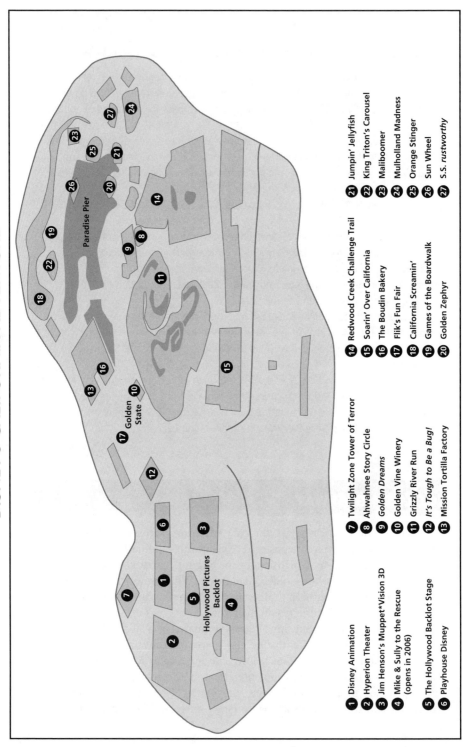

Paradise Pier

Golden State

Hollywood Pictures Backlot

1. Disney Animation
2. Hyperion Theater
3. Jim Henson's Muppet*Vision 3D
4. Mike & Sully to the Rescue (opens in 2006)
5. The Hollywood Backlot Stage
6. Playhouse Disney
7. Twilight Zone Tower of Terror
8. Ahwahnee Story Circle
9. *Golden Dreams*
10. Golden Vine Winery
11. Grizzly River Run
12. *It's Tough to Be a Bug!*
13. Mission Tortilla Factory
14. Redwood Creek Challenge Trail
15. Soarin' Over California
16. The Boudin Bakery
17. Flik's Fun Fair
18. California Screamin'
19. Games of the Boardwalk
20. Golden Zephyr
21. Jumpin' Jellyfish
22. King Triton's Carousel
23. Maliboomer
24. Mulholland Madness
25. Orange Stinger
26. Sun Wheel
27. S.S. *rustworthy*

movement of the California sun across the southern exposure and shine a golden glow on the icon from dawn to sunset. By night, the sun is handsomely lighted by high-intensity orange, red, and yellow lamps.

The plaza is one of the prime viewing points for the daily parades of the park. To the right as you enter is a full-scale replica of a streamlined California Zephyr, a railroad train with Vista-Dome cars that brought millions of travelers to the state after World War II. Today it holds shops and restaurants. Disney Imagineers found the nose of a Zephyr in a Moline, Illinois, railroad yard. The cars were built as replicas.

Paradise Pier dominates the back of the park, just past the newest mountain in the Disney Range, Grizzly Peak. Looking to the left from the entrance you'll catch a glimpse of the decrepit Twilight Zone Tower of Terror, which stands 183 feet tall, just high enough to allow its elevators to fall thirteen stories.

GOLDEN STATE

This land salutes the adventurous heritage of California and the immigrants who came looking for the golden dream. You can soar over California in the Condor Flats district, rush down a raging flume in the Grizzly Peak Recreation Area, learn about the rich tapestry of heritages and ethnicities that built the state in the Bay Area, and sample foods and wine from north, south, west, and east at Pacific Wharf.

■ CONDOR FLATS

The setting is a test pilot landing field in the high desert; all around are weathered hangars left over from man's first attempts to break the sound barrier. The streets of the district are striped with airport runway markings.

MUST-SEE Soarin' Over California ≡FAST

You've got to ride this to believe it: your own hang glider for a virtual flight down the length of the Golden State. The amazing mechanism, a Disney first, lifts three rows of seats 40 feet into an 80-foot-high dome-shaped movie screen. With your legs dangling beneath you, you move up and into the picture, banking with the hang glider as it soars from the Golden Gate Bridge in San Francisco to Mission Bay in San Diego and on to a special visit to a California icon that all started with a mouse.

The film swoops down so close to the ground and water you expect your feet to touch them and then soars up into the clouds. Your field of vision is nearly completely surrounded; Disney even adds a whiff of orange blossoms and pine trees in the farms and forests.

There is no narration to the film, and none is needed. The scenes of the film, from start to finish, include:

■ banking through clouds and then down over the Golden Gate Bridge and out to sea

■ winging down over rafters and fishermen in Redwood Creek

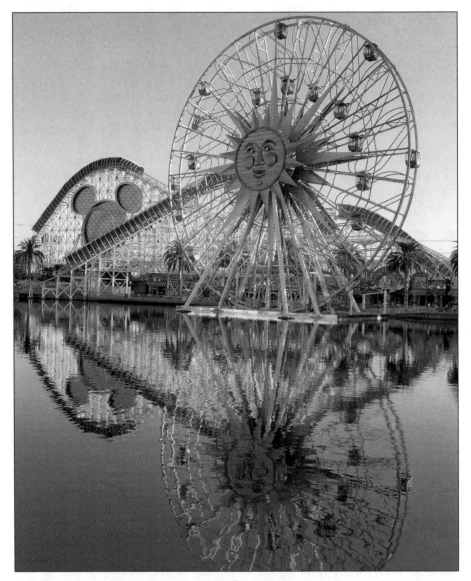

A California Screamin' train races toward the Sun Wheel. *Photo by Corey Sandler. Used by permission from Disney Enterprises, Inc.*

- flying over farmhands tending grapes in Napa Valley vineyards
- sailing out over the rugged coastline at Point Loma with fishing boats bobbing on the surf below
- swooping up the slopes of the mountains near Lake Tahoe, past oncoming skiers, and then skimming low over a tree-topped crest for a view of the lake
- banking a turn through Yosemite Valley past the falls and up toward Half Dome

- passing through fragrant orange groves near Camarillo
- flying into the rugged landscape of Anza Borrego State Park, California's largest but relatively unknown park
- encountering six jets from the Air Force Thunderbirds
- passing closely across the aircraft carrier USS *Stennis* at San Diego and following close behind a navy helicopter
- surfing along the foaming crest of ocean waves at Malibu
- cruising up the Harbor Freeway in rush-hour traffic and into downtown Los Angeles at nighttime
- visiting a party at Southern California's most famous theme park

This attraction is one of the major draws at the park and includes a large outdoor waiting area as well as a hidden maze inside the building; if you see a crowd waiting outside, consider grabbing a Fastpass ticket and coming back later.

If you do end up spending time in the waiting queue within the building, you'll have the chance to learn about some of the famous and obscure heroes of aviation in California. A photo tells the story of John J. Montgomery, who in 1883, twenty years before the Wright Brothers, took a glider flight near San Diego. There's a display about Amelia Earhart, who made many of her pioneering flights to or from California, including her success as the first person to fly from Hawaii to the mainland in 1936. Other honorees include aviation industry figures Donald Wills Douglas, Allan Lockheed, and Howard Hughes.

When you make your way to the front, the line splits to fill two identical theaters. Each holds three banks of gliders, marked A, B, and C, with three rows in each. If you have the chance, choose the center glider (B) and take a seat in the front row, marked as Row 1. You'll be rewarded with a spectacular view of nothing but the screen.

By the way, the funny safety briefing before you enter the theater stars Patrick Warburton, Elaine's annoying sometime-boyfriend "Puddy" from *Seinfeld*. He plays "Patrick," the chief flight attendant.

You can shave quite a bit off your wait by entering the "singles" line, taking any available space on the hang glider. Disney's California Adventure often opens a half hour earlier than the official starting time, and guests can shop and eat and ride Soarin' before the rest of the park is available.

The Technology Behind the Ride

To achieve the greatest clarity for Soarin' Over California, Imagineers used a 70-mm IMAX camera with a superwide-angle lens and shot at forty-eight frames per second, double the standard rate; all the scenes were shot from a helicopter.

The film is projected from above onto an upside-down IMAX screen. The seats are mounted on a simulator base with its movements linked to the scenes in the movie.

Disneyland's Star Tours, an older attraction, creates a similar illusion using larger seat movements. Through trial and error Disney engineers discovered that much smaller movements, coupled with visual screen cues, could create the same illusion. Where Star Tours seats move as much as 12 feet and pitch forty-five degrees, Soarin' Over California's seats move a scant 3 feet, with a six-degree pitch.

A critical design problem for the high-tech Soarin' Over California ride was solved with the aid of an old Erector set. The challenge was this: how to quickly load an audience of eighty-seven people into seats that would lift up and into a huge domed movie screen. Ride engineers originally intended to construct three loading ramps, with each group entering at a different level, a slow process.

Imagineers Mark Sumner and Coulter Winn had worked on creating the purposefully malfunctioning elevators for the Twilight Zone Tower of Terror at Disney–MGM Studios at Walt Disney World in Florida, and came up with a solution. To test his plan, Sumner went to the attic of his garage and brought down his thirty-five-year-old Erector set and put together a model with the toy-size girders, nuts, and bolts, and added cardboard seats. He brought the whole assemblage to work in a grocery bag.

The design allows all passengers to load on the ground floor, and then the three benches are raised into place to different levels, like a string puppet pulled into a standing position. The next challenge was to design a building to hold two of the ride systems. Winn put two theaters back-to-back and sunk the rooms 15 feet below grade so the building would not overwhelm other nearby structures in the park.

At a press event during the park's opening ceremonies, vice chairman Marty Sklar, head of Imagineering for Disney, said that all the other Disney theme parks were lobbying for the technology behind Soarin' Over California to create their own attractions. The same ride and film debuted at Epcot in Walt Disney World in Orlando in 2005.

The ride was dedicated by Dick Rutan and Jeana Yeager, who piloted *Voyager* on a nonstop trip around the world in 1986. The flight, completed in nine days, three minutes, and forty-four seconds, departed from Edwards Air Force Base in California.

■ THE BAY AREA

The small park here includes a 45-foot-high replica of the rotunda of San Francisco's Palace of Fine Arts. The real structure was built for the 1915 Panama–Pacific International Exposition and designed to look like a classical Roman ruin. A mural on the colonnade introduces the themes, characters, and stories that are told in *Golden Dreams* nearby.

MUST-SEE *Golden Dreams*

This marvelous film tells the California story through the eyes of her immigrants, including natives, Spanish explorers, a "picture bride" from Japan, a European-born moviemaker, and a dust-bowl farmer from Oklahoma. Disney considers the twenty-three-minute film the emotional heart of the park, bringing the history and heritage of California to life with drama and a bit of humor.

The narrator is Queen Califia, the namesake of the state. Spanish explorers, including Juan Rodriguez Cabrillo, among the first Europeans to see California in the sixteenth century, gave California its name based on a popular novel published in 1510 by Spanish author Garcia Ordóñez de Montalvo.

(Montalvo's book, *Las Seregas de Esplandian,* told of an island paradise called California near the Indies where beautiful Queen Califia ruled over a country of beautiful Amazon women possessed of great wealth in pearls and gold. Men were allowed to visit the island only one day a year, and only for the purposes of perpetuating the race. Explorer Hernando Cortez's men thought they had found the island in 1535 when they found pearls near today's Mexico–California border.)

In the film, Califia is portrayed by actress and comedienne Whoopi Goldberg. Appearing first when a statue alongside the stage morphs into her image, Califia/Goldberg appears Zelig-like throughout the history of California, popping in and out of scenes to help out like a fairy godmother, dressed in the costume of the period.

The film is underlaid with historical accuracy. Disney brought together a group of California historians, sociologists, and culturalists as advisors. The panel included cultures from Native Americans to the variety of ethnic peoples who have immigrated to California.

Among the dramatic moments re-created in the film is a scene among the native Chumash, who settled in California over thirteen thousand years ago. The scene was filmed at Montaña de Oro State Park near Morro Bay.

The arrival of the Spanish in 1769 brings a legacy of language, architecture, and rich colorful traditions. Califia meets Father Crespi and his band of Spanish missionaries just after an earthquake threatens their settlement.

You'll see a scene from the California Gold Rush of the mid-1800s that brought people from every corner of the globe to California.

Another scene shows William Mulholland opening the California aqueduct high in the mountains above Azusa to bring water from the mountains to Los Angeles. Because it had to look brand new, Disney had to build its own section of aqueduct for the shooting.

Another scene takes you to the immigration of the Chinese, who built the first railroads that linked California to the rest of America. One of the most emotional scenes is the arrival of a Japanese "picture bride," who has come to meet her husband-to-be in 1913. Restrictions blocked new immigration except for immediate family, so marriages were arranged through the exchange of photos. In the scene, a shy girl and her unexpectedly older fiancé are pelted with tomatoes by protestors. The scene was shot in Vallejo; an old steamboat blocks the view of the modern Mare Island shipyards.

We see scenes from the creation of Yosemite as a national park at the turn of the twentieth century and the 1936 mass immigration of thousands of farm workers when they left the dust bowl of the Midwest in search of a better life.

You'll see some history of the movie industry, with a scene from the making of *The Wizard of Oz.* We meet Eastern European immigrant Louis B. Mayer, who arrived in California a poor man and went on to create MGM, one of Hollywood's most successful studios.

Another scene takes place during World War II, when thousands of manual labor jobs were opened to women in the many aircraft factories and other military suppliers that flourished across the state.

In the 1950s and 1960s, you'll mingle with the beatniks and the hippies.

Union organizer Cesar Chavez is seen speaking with Mexican farm workers who have come to el Norte to work in the orange groves. From there it's on to the rise of the computer generation, including the introduction of Apple Computer by Californians Steve Jobs and Steven Wozniak, leading to the state's new gold strikes in Silicon Valley.

The film closes with the song, "Just One Dream," underscoring a montage of images representing the diversity of California's landscape. Included are characters from the film as well as famous modern-day figures from today's California. Among the faces that spin by quickly are those of Walt Disney, Ansel Adams, Gene Autry, Joan Baez, the Beach Boys, Sonny Bono, Johnny Carson, Cesar Chavez, Miles Davis, James Dean, Dianne Feinstein, Jodie Foster, Jerry Garcia, Danny Glover, Bob Hope, the Jackson 5, Billie Jean King, Sandy Koufax, Michelle Kwan, Bruce Lee, Richard Nixon, Carlos Santana, Charles Schultz, Tiger Woods, and Chuck Yeager.

Golden Dreams, shot in 70-mm, was directed by Polish filmmaker Agnieszka Holland, who directed such acclaimed films as *Europa, Europa* and *The Secret Garden.* The film used a cast of thousands over the course of sixteen days of dawn to dusk shooting at sixteen locations around the state.

■ GRIZZLY PEAK RECREATION AREA

The newest mountain in the Disney Range is a granite peak shaped by nature (and the Imagineers) to resemble the head of a growling grizzly bear. Grizzly Peak towers 150 feet over a High Sierra landscape of pine- and snow-covered slopes.

Disney Imagineers carefully created the mountain to resemble a natural rock configuration that just happens to look like a bear. The mountain began as a series of intricately sculpted models. Computer technology and a laser scanner then measured the models; the computer was later used to actually shape the underlying metal rebar to replicate the rock formations. The metal frame was then overlaid with wire mesh, which was then sprayed with plaster. The final plaster was hand-sculpted by artists, many of whom worked on the Tree of Life at Walt Disney World's Animal Kingdom.

On a real granite boulder on the side of the mountain you can learn a Native American legend about the peak. It seems that Ah-há-le, the coyote, called on the bear, Oo-so-ó-ma-te, to watch over and protect the land. The bear at first stood strong against those who threatened the animal realm. But when it seemed he could no longer resist, the coyote turned the grizzly to stone so that he could never be moved.

The legend of the mountain: "To this day people claim they can hear the great bear's spirit in the wind that roars through the caverns and trees of Grizzly Peak."

⋮MUST-SEE⋮ Grizzly River Run ≡*FAST*

From the base of the mountain, a 300-foot-long gold-mining conveyor lifts eight-passenger rafts to what Disney claims is the world's highest, longest, spinningest, and fastest river rafting ride. More than 130,000 gallons of water roar down the flume each minute, spinning the rafts through swirling rapids 45 feet above the valley and sending them into waterslides, caverns, and mine shafts, ending up in a wet plunge into a geyser field.

The six-minute ride marks the first time drops have been incorporated into a river rafting ride; the biggest plunge is 45 feet. In all, Grizzly River Run boasts two over-the-falls descents, one of which propels spinning rafts, one after another, over the rapids in a steep 22-foot fall. You will get slightly to very wet, depending on the wind, the weight and distribution of the passengers in the spinnable raft, and the luck of the splash.

The story behind the ride is this: The Eureka Gold and Timber Company mined and logged the mountain of all of its resources from the 1800s through the 1930s and then abandoned the area. Over time, the mountain reclaimed itself; trees grew back and the water rushed through once

Wet guests on Grizzly River Run head toward a geyser in front of Disney's Grand Californian Hotel. *Photo by Corey Sandler. Used by permission from Disney Enterprises, Inc.*

more. Now a group of young people have transformed it into a contemporary river rafting company that takes guests on the Grizzly River Run expedition.

Around the raft load areas are rusting ore crushers and donkey engines abandoned by prospectors and recovered from Sierra Nevada gold country.

Redwood Creek Challenge Trail

Three fire ranger towers loom over vantage points at a child-size recreation and workout area with smoke-jumper cable slides, net climbing, and swaying bridges.

Check out the map posted at the entry so you're sure not to miss any of the highlights, including the Tunnel Tree Crawl Thru, the Hoot-n-Holler Logs, Pine Peril Bridge, Cliff Hanger, Hibernation Hollow, and the Sequoia Smokejumpers Training Tower.

Overlooking the campground are three ranger stations: Mount Lassen Lookout, Mount Shasta Lookout, and Mount Whitney Lookout, where Disney park rangers in wide-brimmed hats, hiking boots, and hunter green uniforms tend watch.

At the Sequoia Smokejumpers Training Tower, kids can grab a pulley system to zoom down an overhead cable. The Hoot-n-Holler Logs send guests sliding from an upper level of the recreation area to the wilderness floor, while the Cliff Hanger rock climb dares adventurers to traverse its rocky surface and make it back to the safety of the campground.

Down below in the redwoods, storytellers spin tales of nature and the forest on a stage within a downed redwood tree at the Ahwahnee Story Circle.

There's a small stand of real redwood trees nearby, a young forest with hundreds of years of life ahead; the varieties (aptos blues and soquil browns) look like their Northern California cousins but are better adapted to the warmer climate of Anaheim.

■ GOLDEN VINE WINERY

Robert Mondavi brings a bit of the wine country to Anaheim with a small vineyard of about 350 grapevines and hands-on demonstrations of the winemaking process. Out on the plaza is a wine-sampling bar and a high-end delicatessen; above is a gourmet restaurant serving Mediterranean fare . . . and wine.

A small screening room presents *Seasons of the Vine,* a short film about winemaking. How's this for civility: Adults are invited to bring a glass of wine to their seats.

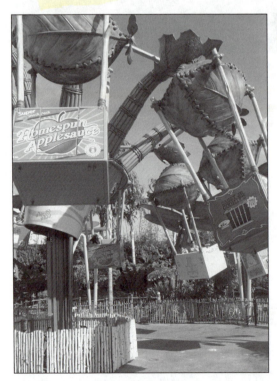

Flik's Flyers in A Bug's Land. *Photo by Corey Sandler. Used by permission from Disney Enterprises, Inc.*

A BUG'S LAND

Disney has installed a trap that draws ants, caterpillars, grasshoppers, ladybugs, pill bugs . . . and thousands of kids. The lively area, loosely based on the hit animated film *A Bug's Life*, includes the Flik's Fun Fair, *It's Tough to Be a Bug!* attraction, and Bountiful Valley Farm.

MUST-SEE FLIK'S FUN FAIR

Flik's Fun Fair is a lively children's playland within A Bug's Land, inspired by characters and settings from the Disney-Pixar animated film *A Bug's Life*. The five new attractions give visitors a look at the world from a bug's point of view, with the creatures and vegetation built on a scale that stretches one inch into two feet.

- **Flik's Flyers.** A simulated bug-size hot-air balloon ride, starring Flik the hero ant.
- **Tuck and Roll's Drive 'Em Buggies.** A drive-it-yourself pill bug car ride inside P. T. Flea's circus tent.
- **Heimlich's Chew Chew Train.** A miniature railroad ride that salutes the voracious Bavarian caterpillar.
- **Francis's Ladybug Boogie.** Spin-'em-yourself ladybugs.
- **Princess Dot Puddle Park.** A playground that surrounds a giant lawn sprinkler.

▓ MUST-SEE ▓ *IT'S TOUGH TO BE A BUG!* ≡*FAST*

In an underground theater, an imaginative 3-D film shows us humans who's really in charge. According to some scientist who has made a count, there are 10,000,000,000,000,000,000 (ten quintillion) bugs in the world. A handful of the most talented star in Disney's 3-D film, *It's Tough to Be a Bug!*

If you're lucky, you'll be personally greeted by Flik, who works the entrance to the show. Flik usually hangs around near a huge coral tree imported to the site; it will bloom in season.

You'll enter the "anty"-room of the 425-seat theater to pick up bug-eyed glasses. When the doors open, pick out a place to sit on a log and admire the tangled-root and vine architecture all around. The orchestra of creatures tunes up below while a buzzing can be heard from the wasp nest projection booth.

The show is ready to begin. The announcer has a request: Please refrain from buzzing, chirping, stinging, . . . or pollinating.

With your 3-D "bug glasses" in place, you're right in the midst of things. Flik, the ant master of ceremonies, welcomes visitors as honorary bugs and introduces us to some of the cast of millions.

"Take it from an ant. It's tough to be a bug," says Flik. "That's why we've developed some amazing survival techniques."

Assisted by a pair of acorn weevils equipped with a sling shot, Chile the Chilean Tarantula demonstrates his ability to throw poison quills. Yes, they're zooming out toward the audience.

Next, a belligerent, acid-spraying soldier termite, "the Termite-ator," defends his mound by spraying intruders—that's us—in the seats below. The stinkbug soloist, Claire DeRoom, fills the room with her haunting yet malodorous performance.

But the big artillery arrives with a villainous grasshopper, a bug on a mission to wipe out the audience of intruders. "You guys only see us as monsters!" he says. "Maybe it's time you honorary bugs got a taste of your own medicine!" Suddenly we're under assault by a giant flyswatter, then a blinding fog of "Bug Doom" spray, and finally, a nasty hornet squadron.

I won't spoil the ending, but it does have a certain biting edge. When the butterfly curtain closes, the audience is reminded to remain seated while all the lice, bedbugs, maggots, and cockroaches exit first.

The film is loosely based on *A Bug's Life,* the animated feature from Disney and Pixar. The movie featured the voices of actors Dave Foley as Flik, Cheech Marin as Chile, and Jason Alexander as Acorn Weevil.

Try to sit in the middle of the theater—midway in from both sides and halfway back from the screen—for the best 3-D effects.

■ BOUNTIFUL VALLEY FARM

In some ways all of California is a farm; the state is the nation's number-one producer of at least 350 different varieties of farm products including citrus, dates, nuts, olives, artichokes, cotton, and grapes. Here at Disney's two-and-a-half-acre showplace you'll find displays of many of the products at the Farmers' Market, a tractor yard, and a water play Irrigation Station.

■ PACIFIC WHARF

In a setting reminiscent of Monterey's Cannery Row you'll find a trio of food factories that are themselves part of the story of California.

At **San Francisco's Boudin Bakery** on Fisherman's Wharf, you can learn about, watch the making of, and then enjoy the company's legendary sourdough bread.

Inside the bakery, comic and former talk-show host Rosie O'Donnell and Colin Mochrie, the rubber-faced comedian from the show *Whose Line Is It Anyway?* star in a video that explains the unusual process of making sourdough bread. Among the details: Boudin (pronounced *BO-deen*) has used the same batch of starter yeast, called *lactobacillus San Francisco,* for nearly a century.

At **Mission Tortillas,** corn or wheat meal is made into fresh wrappers. The machine is a small version of a factory production machine, producing twenty-five tortillas per minute; the real thing at the Mission Foods plant in Rancho Cucamonga can crank out two thousand per minute. After you've watched the process you can go next door to **Cucina Cucamonga Mexican Grill** and enjoy tortillas with a variety of fillings.

PARADISE PIER

The glory days of California's beachfront amusement piers—long before the dawning of the day of Disney—are recalled at Paradise Pier.

Dominating the skyline in this land is a mile-long roller coaster with a grand loop-de-loop through the ears of Mickey Mouse, a huge Ferris wheel with golden sun spokes, and a giant catapult that sends riders to the top of a Disneyfied version of a carnival strongman game. This section of the park is especially dramatic by night with the lights of the rides reflected in the lagoon at the base of the "pier."

At the north end of the lagoon, the **Boardwalk** recalls the classic roadside stands of Route 66: giant hamburgers, hot dogs, dinosaurs, and oranges. There's a real wooden boardwalk; Disney Imagineers worked to get exactly the right type of boards that would hold up to millions of visitors each year and still yield the distinctive echo of lumber. One of the patterns for the boardwalk was Santa Rosa's amusement pier, among the last remaining original woodies.

Lumber for Paradise Pier's boardwalk was crafted from a hearty hardwood from Paraguay and designed with authentic Coney Island boardwalk screw patterns. Landscaping includes tropical palms, sea grapes, and succulents.

▦ MUST-SEE ▦ CALIFORNIA SCREAMIN' ≣*FAST*

In true Disney style, the ultimate wooden roller coaster of Paradise Pier looks like an antique classic but is actually constructed with an ultramodern steel superstructure.

Twenty-four-passenger cars scream from a standstill to fifty-five miles per hour in just under five seconds using high-tech linear motors in the track; there's no clickety-clack chain here.

Waves from the Paradise Pier lagoon crash against the jetty along the launch area at takeoff time; the waves are generated by a high-tech wave machine positioned in the lagoon. Cars zoom out over the water at the edge of Paradise Bay and then climb by momentum 120 feet to begin a run of 6,072 feet.

The four-minute ride is the world's longest steel looping roller coaster. The maximum drop, 108 feet at an impressive fifty degrees, comes midway through the ride, not at first.

The steel design delivers an unusually smooth ride. And then there is the tight loop that passes through Mickey's ears; at night, the ears light up each time the train passes. At peak times, cars pass through every thirty-six seconds.

The cars have an on-board sound system. I have to admit I didn't hear the music the first time I rode; I was concentrating on the laws of physics as they applied to my particular fast-moving seat.

California Screamin' can be seen from almost every vantage point in the park. "We knew we wanted a big backdrop to the park," said Imagineer and Paradise Pier designer Tim Delaney. "And the coaster was perfect. It's about a thousand feet across as your eye scans it from a distance."

The coaster was designed to mirror the wooden look of coasters of yesteryear but with twenty-first-century technology.

"Scream tunnels" at several locations along the track provide a bit of extra excitement and help muffle the shrieks of riders climbing up, dropping down, and speeding across the steel-reinforced track.

The induction motor system that powers California Screamin' is hidden beneath the ground in a concrete, earthquake-proof, climate-controlled bunker.

By the Clock

Here's the official measurement of ride times for attractions at Disney's California Adventure. The clock starts running when the wheels start turning; sometimes the shortest ride times end up with the longest waiting lines.

▶ California Screamin': 3.2 minutes

▶ *Golden Dreams:* 20 minutes

▶ Golden Zephyr: 4.1 minutes

▶ Grizzly River Run: 6 minutes

▶ Jim Henson's Muppet* Vision 3D: 15 minutes

▶ Jumpin' Jellyfish: 2.4 minutes

▶ King Triton's Carousel: 5.5 minutes

▶ Mulholland Madness: 2.2 minutes

▶ Orange Stinger: 4.2 minutes

▶ Soarin' Over California: 7.4 minutes

▶ Sun Wheel: 9 minutes

▶ Twilight Zone Tower of Terror: 2 minutes

Five-thousand-amp motors create traveling magnetic waves that thrust the vehicles forward as they glide along magnetic fields. As each car passes key points on the track, sensors gauge its speed and adjust the electromagnetic force to either speed it up or slow it down.

MUST-SEE SUN WHEEL

Golden beams radiate from a grinning sun-god face at the hub of the massive Ferris wheel. Eight red, six-seat gondolas ascend to the top of the 168-foot-high structure; sixteen others—purple and orange—are attached to ellipsoid tracks within the wheel and they slide forward and backward as it rotates. There are only two other wheels like this in the world: the venerable Wonder Wheel at Coney Island in New York, and another in Japan.

The cars seem to descend below the water of the lagoon; the loading platforms are hidden in a well. Three cars load at once on the first slow rotation and then the wheel makes one more complete circuit before unloading begins.

The 5.8-million-pound Sun Wheel takes two minutes to make a complete revolution; a two-rotation ride including loading takes about nine minutes.

From the top of the wheel you can see most of Disney's California Adventure. To the east you can see some of the landmarks of Disneyland, including Space Mountain and the Matterhorn. To the west, on a clear day, is the coast and Catalina Island. By night, the Paradise Pier glows with neon and strobes.

A disappointment for some is the screen mesh that covers the windows of the cars; taking photographs from the Sun Wheel is a difficult challenge.

The Sun Wheel is a major draw at the park, but not part of the Fastpass system. The line for the red, nonsliding cars will usually be much shorter than the queue for the ones on the moving track.

MUST-SEE MALIBOOMER

Here's your chance to ride a carnival strongman sledgehammer in a rocket to the bell at the top.

Three steel girder towers hold carriages that catapult riders an impressive 180 feet straight up in just two seconds and then let them fall and rise again like a bungee jump. Disney has put its own colors on a pretty common amusement park ride here; a similar tower exists at nearby Knott's Berry Farm.

One newer Disney "feature": a clear plastic shield sits in front of the faces of the riders. Protection for the riders? For those walking below? Sound barriers for the neighbors? I'd guess all of the above. The ride begins with several spine-tingling false starts before the real blastoff.

The best views of Disneyland can be seen from the top of tower 3; tower 1 faces toward Anaheim. Me, I was looking at my feet.

■ MULHOLLAND MADNESS =FAST

An amusement park wild-mouse ride sends "woody-wagon" vehicles careening across a map of the Hollywood Hills and Santa Monica Mountains. The top of the ride is only 30 feet above ground and water, and the drops are small . . . but the turns are very tight and fast.

The Maliboomer in midflight. *Photo by Corey Sandler. Used by permission from Disney Enterprises, Inc.*

S.S. *RUSTWORTHY*

A waterside playground on a wreck of a fireboat (the "T" of *Trustworthy* has rusted away) with all sorts of bells, whistles, and leaking water pipes. There are buttons to press, ropes to yank, water cannons to shoot, and other entertainments for kids and those lucky enough to come with them.

GOLDEN ZEPHYR

Looking like something out of a 1930s Buck Rogers science fiction adventure, zeppelin-shaped stainless steel spaceships are suspended by cable from a rotating 85-foot-high tower. Six vehicles each hold twelve passengers.

ORANGE STINGER

A giant California orange is peeled back to reveal another carnival favorite, a swing ride with just a bit of sting. Within the huge fruit are forty-eight single-seat "bees" suspended from a central tower that rises and falls and tilts as it spins.

Riders are accompanied by the sounds of bumblebees and a whiff of oranges in the air. The ride is wilder than it may appear; if you want to reduce the thrill a bit, choose a chair on the inner circle.

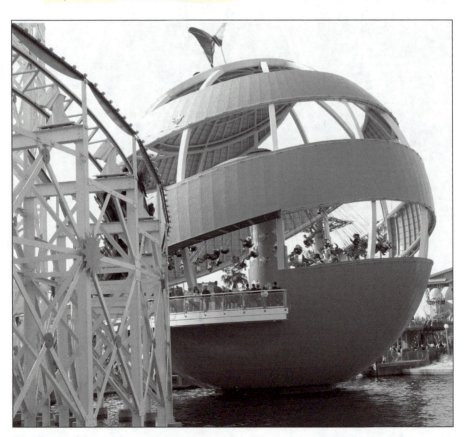

The Orange Stinger. *Photo by Corey Sandler. Used by permission from Disney Enterprises, Inc.*

KING TRITON'S CAROUSEL

This is no ordinary merry-go-round. "Aquestrians" whirl around the Little Mermaid's undersea world; fifty-six creatures including hand-carved dolphins, sea lions, flying fish, sea horses, and otters circle to the sounds of surfer and beach songs pumped out on a classic band organ.

Selections include "Catch a Wave," "Surfin' Safari," "Sea Cruise," "The Tide Is High," "I Get Around," and "Sea of Love."

JUMPIN' JELLYFISH

Young folk have their own scaled-down, gentler version of Maliboomer. Jellyfish-like capsules lurch up a 50-foot tower and then bounce down and back up again below a parachute. There are six two-passenger fish on each of the two towers.

GAMES OF THE BOARDWALK (THE MIDWAY)

On the walkway that stands between California Screamin' and the Maliboomer is the Midway—a corndog, T-shirt, ice cream, pizza kind of place with a surfin' beat. Here you can try your hand at carnival games. Most cost a dollar or two per try; with luck you may win a stuffed animal worth about half what you paid.

- **Boardwalk Bowl.** A Disney version of Skeeball.
- **Shore Shot.** Think you can sink a basketball field goal? Maybe, but those hoops look a bit smaller than regulation size.
- **San Joaquin Volley.** Softballs bounce into—and usually out of—the fruit basket targets.
- **New Haul Fishery.** Dangle a magnetic lure into the moving river in search of a prize.
- **Angels in the Outfield.** Knock down a doll with a hardball and walk home with a gift.
- **Dolphin Derby.** As many as ten players compete to land a ball in a target and push their dolphin racers across the finish line.
- **Cowhuenga Pass.** Land a ball in a milk can to make the cow moo.

HOLLYWOOD PICTURES BACKLOT

To much of the world, California is Hollywood, celebrated here with some of the icons of classic and modern-day television and movies.

The Grand Entrance to the backlot is through studio archways flanked by giant golden statues of elephants. The inspiration for the gateway dates back to 1917 when D. W. Griffith built a colossal set for *Intolerance* right in the middle of Hollywood Boulevard. The Babylonian palace courtyard set covered several blocks along the busy boulevard for many years.

Hollywood Boulevard re-creates the feeling of great backlots constructed for major motion pictures. Klieg lights and cameras stand on scaffolding in front of Art Deco and Spanish landmarks of the real Hollywood Boulevard, including the Pantages Theater and the former Bullock's-Wilshire department store.

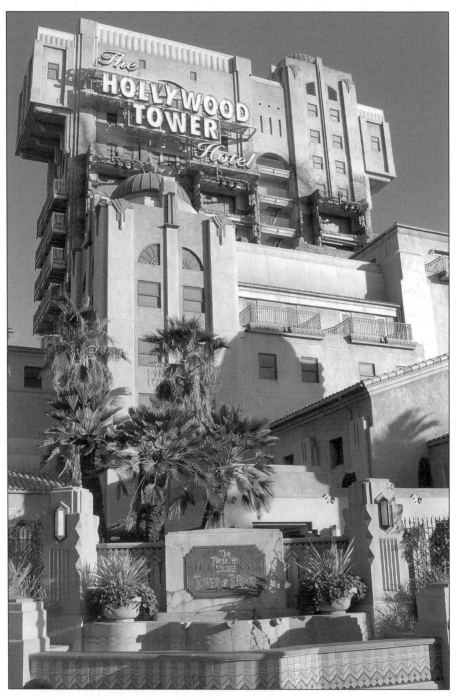

Twilight Zone Tower of Terror, open for business. *Photo by Corey Sandler. Used by permission from Disney Enterprises, Inc.*

Behind the sets are shops, outdoor performance areas, soundstages, and studios for attractions.

┊MUST-SEE┊ TWILIGHT ZONE TOWER OF TERROR

Behold the mysterious Hollywood Tower Hotel, a relic of Tinseltown's golden age gone full circle from California to Florida and back to Anaheim. It's an unusual place to visit, complete with a set of high-speed elevators guaranteed to fail on a regular basis.

The attraction at Disney's California Adventure is based on the original at Disney–MGM Studios at Walt Disney World in Florida, in turn based upon Rod Serling's classic television series, *The Twilight Zone.*

Even before you enter the lobby of the abandoned hotel, there are signs of danger high up on the side of the tall building—sparking electrical wires in a sign hanging above a gaping hole in the tower walls.

Legend says a full guest wing was once attached to that damaged wall. What happened to the wing? And more important, what happened to the people who were in the tower when it disappeared?

Once inside, the introduction begins in the darkened hotel library as a flash of lightning energizes a television in the corner. Our host, Rod Serling (long dead, but that doesn't matter in *The Twilight Zone*), tells the story of the dark and stormy night—Halloween 1939, to be exact—when the guests disappeared from their elevator and stepped into a nightmare. "This elevator travels directly to . . . The Twilight Zone."

The Twilight Zone series never included a story about a haunted elevator at the Hollywood Hotel, but that didn't stop Disney Imagineers. Rod Serling's introduction to the ride was patched together from various unrelated segments of the show and augmented by a Serling imitator.

We learn that when the lightning bolt struck, all the main elevators of the building were lost; only the creaky old service elevators still function.

And then the library doors open to reveal the entrance to the hotel's basement, a creepy world of boilers, generators, and electrical boxes. It even smells like a basement.

Finally, you are in the vertical elevator shaft in the most severely damaged part of the hotel; your cab rises higher and higher. At the very top, you reach the damaged elevator motors; they are sparking and flashing ominously.

The doors open for a view of the park; guests watching from outside should be able to catch a glimpse of the elevator cab hanging in space for a few seconds.

Inside the cab there's a brief moment of panic when the elevator cables seem to snap in a shower of electrical sparks. The cab plunges downward, falling faster than the force of gravity. Then it lurches back upward, only to fall again and again.

The elevator cab is actually driven downward by high-power motors so that it travels faster than it would in free fall. The rest of the way down, the cab travels in what the engineers call "controlled deceleration." That means putting on the brakes.

The new attraction in Anaheim is the same as the original in Orlando, only different: The elevator cabs still plunge thirteen stories, although the hotel building stands only 183 feet tall in California, about 16 feet shorter than the Florida structure. At Disney's California Adventure, though, the elevator shafts sink 20 feet below ground. And there are six cabs that share three shafts; in Florida, the very popular attraction has four cabs that alternate in two shafts.

Here, the Hollywood Tower Hotel stays a bit closer to a local architectural style, called Pueblo Deco. A number of buildings in Southern California used this sort of ornamentation in the late 1920s, including the Los Angeles City Hall and Union Station.

The sign out front reads THE HOLLYWOOD TOWER HOTEL; watch it for a few moments as it changes to THE TWILIGHT ZONE TOWER OF TERROR.

The same introductory video produced for Florida and starring the electronically reconstructed Rod Serling, is shown in Anaheim; the only changes are a few shots of the exterior of the California hotel.

If you get the chance, linger a bit in the hotel lobby to soak up the amazing details that Disney Imagineers have placed there. There are old suitcases, umbrellas (because it is raining in the preshow video), and newspapers. The *Los Angeles Examiner* on the desk is dated October 31, 1939—the night of the incident in the tower. The headline reads, "Ruth Judd Gives Self Up After Six Days, Returning to Asylum." Winnie Ruth Judd was the "Trunk Murderess," accused of shooting two of her young roommates to death in 1931 in Phoenix, cutting them up and stashing the pieces in a steamer trunk that was discovered at Union Station in Los Angeles. Sentenced to hang, she was instead held in prison for thirty years; she escaped six times but was recaptured each time.

You'll be invited into one of two libraries to view a preshow video. Before you enter the library, take a glance to the left and right. Those huge formal paintings are for real: To the right is Napoleon III, and to the left is his wife the Empress Eugenia; the portraits were produced by a court painter to Queen Victoria and picked up by Disney Imagineers who may have known more about their value than the seller.

The two libraries are slightly different. The exit from the right library leads directly into the basement; the exit from the left library goes to a set of stairs that lead to an upper level in the two-story boiler room.

Again, try to use some of your time there to look for delicious details, including more than a few wink-and-a-nod references to episodes from *The Twilight Zone* series. Here are a few:

■ A thimble in the display case at the right side of the room, as in "The After Hours." In that 1960 episode, actress Ann Francis goes shopping in a department store that seems to have a floor just for her, selling only the exact thimble she seeks.

■ A tiny spaceman, a nod to "The Invaders." This 1961 show starred Agnes Moorhead who faces an assault by itsy-bitsy aliens.

■ A trumpet, as seen in "A Passage for Trumpet." In that 1961 episode, Jack Klugman receives lessons on life and music in a visit to limbo.

■ A pair of eyeglasses, from the poignant "Time Enough at Last." This 1959 classic starred Burgess Meredith as a myopic bank clerk who hides in a vault to catch up on his reading, emerging to find that a nuclear bomb has destroyed the city around him. At last he can read all he wants. Now where are those glasses . . .

When you exit the library, details include some of the employee areas of the hotel. Look for the time clock and bulletin board for notices. Many of the names written on the wall and on the board are drawn from *Twilight Zone* episodes.

And now you're in the creepy two-story basement of the hotel. The two-level boiler room allows two cabs to share a single elevator shaft; one cab is loading while the other is rising and falling.

Many of the pieces of equipment were salvaged from old buildings; some of the gauges came from a disused power plant in Redondo Beach. Some of the items have been modified by Disney Imagineers to add speakers that produce appropriately creepy clicking and pinging noises.

The elevator cabs seat twenty-one guests, hooked into place with seat belts. Before you enter the cab, a ghostly bellhop will organize visitors into six rows that correspond to particular seats. Rows one and six fill the front of the cab, closest to the outside world; rows two and five fill the middle row of the cab, which offers the best view of the special effects in the shaft.

Once all guests have been seated and buckled into place, the elevator door closes and the cab moves backward into the shaft.

The new California ride is missing the "starfield" introduction that is part of the Florida version, a section of the attraction where the cabs move laterally into the shaft. The Anaheim version presents all of the show scenes within the shaft itself, and one new scene is a stop in the hotel vestibule. Guests see themselves reflected in an old mirror; a lightning bolt flashes, and the bodies are transformed to ghosts.

At the top of the shaft, the doors open for a view of the outside world; if your eyes are open you'll catch a glimpse of the Hyperion Theater in Disney's California Adventure and in the distance, the Matterhorn in Disneyland.

There is, of course, a gift shop. And a hidden camera will snap a picture of guests in the elevator cab; you can purchase a copy of the photo at "Picture, If You Will," a shop whose title is a puckish nod to one of Rod Serling's favorite phrases.

The attraction was specifically designed so that the movement of the elevator cabs in the shafts can be varied; in Orlando, Disney has made many changes in the action of the ride over the years. In California, the sequence of the show scenes in the shaft can also be varied.

Imagineers estimate that the California attraction can handle about 1,700 guests per hour. The ride was designed specifically for Disney's Fastpass system, with direct entry through the front gates for ticket holders. Standby guests enter a queue to the left.

▓MUST-SEE▓ JIM HENSON'S MUPPET✳VISION 3D ☰FAST

Don't pass by this extraordinary multimedia show. If you don't have a kid with you, you can pretend you're with the ones in front of you in line.

The film, a masterpiece of corn and puns, was imported lock, stock, and whoopee cushion from the original show at Walt Disney World's Disney–MGM Studios. (The 3-D effects of the 1991 film are good but nowhere near as impressive as those seen in the more current film, *It's Tough to Be a Bug!*)

Nevertheless, the film—and especially the preshow—is among the funniest presentations in the park. As you stand waiting to enter the theater, don't miss the overhead message board that alternately demands that you read various silly orders and then asks you to look away.

Spend the time to read the posters and signs around you within the Muppet 3-D FX Labs. Among my favorites: The 2-D department is a flat painting on the walls. Check out the supply of gags, including tongue inflators, volcanic ashtrays, and anvil repair kits. After a promised visit from Disney's corporate mouse, Rizzo the Rat appears with fake ears: "They're tourists. What do they know?"

We meet Sam Eagle who forthrightly explains the upcoming film as "a salute to all nations, but mostly America."

But the real fun is within the attractive 575-seat theater, which is decidedly more opulent than your neighborhood quintupleplex, although someone really should do something about those cracks in the plaster and the leak in the roof.

There's a robotic all-penguin orchestra in the pit (they took the job just for the halibut) and a private box at the front for Waldorf and Statler. The film includes some marvelous 3-D special effects, as well as flashing lights, a bubble-maker, smell-o-vision, and a surprise from the skies.

▓ PLAYHOUSE DISNEY–LIVE ON STAGE!

Kids have a rollicking show of their own at Disney's California Adventure at Playhouse Disney—Live On Stage!

The show, presented several times daily, features live performers, puppetry, and stories of friendship from popular Disney Channel Playhouse Disney programs, including:

▪ *Rolie Polie Olie.* This Emmy Award–winning series chronicles the touching and sometimes hilarious world of Olie, a six-year-old robot boy who lives with his family in a magical, all-robot world.

▪ *Stanley.* Stanley takes guests into the life of a very curious little boy with a passion for facts, who searches the animal world for clues about how things work.

▪ Jim Henson's *Bear in the Big Blue House.* Bear, the seven-foot-tall, warm, friendly, and understanding host, invites the audience into his Big Blue House every day to play, learn, sing, and dance with his friends in this Emmy- and Parents Choice Award–winning television series.

The twenty-minute stage show opens with a visit from Bear and his animal friends. Bear, who does a mean cha-cha, wants to dance with all his friends.

Jamie, the show's host, reads from a giant storybook, with chapters featuring characters from the Playhouse Disney shows, each teaching the importance of friendship.

The attraction replaced the quirky *ABC Soap Opera Bistro* in mid-2003. The bistro had featured "sets" from daytime dramas and a cast of waiters and waitresses who stayed within the sob stories of the shows.

⬛ *MUST-SEE* WHO WANTS TO BE A MILLIONAIRE—PLAY IT! ≡FAST

Together for the first time, two of Disney's biggest stars: Mickey . . . and Regis Philbin.

Philbin handed the "keys to the hot seat" to a crew of theme park hosts charged with re-creating the drama delivered in the game show, *Who Wants to Be a Millionaire?*

Guests experience *Millionaire* in exacting detail, in a 600-seat replica of the high-tech set, complete with the dramatically lit hot seat. The one difference: Guests play for points, not dollars, winning unique prizes along the way.

Like the television show, the fastest finger determines the first contestant to sit in the coveted hot seat. All audience members play along, using individual keypads as their scores are tallied throughout the session. They also get involved when players use the "ask the audience" lifeline. Other guests can be called upon for help with the "phone a complete stranger" lifeline. The "phone a stranger" phones are spread around the theme park.

Note: At press time, this attraction was operating seasonally. Please call Customer Relations for information.

⬛ *MUST-SEE* HYPERION THEATER: DISNEY'S ALADDIN ≡FAST

The handsome Hyperion Theater, a thoroughly modern 2,000-seat facility inspired by the great movie palaces of the past at the end of Hollywood Boulevard, became home to a rollicking live musical in 2003, offered several times daily to park visitors. The façade and marquee recall the old Los Angeles Theater. The theater is a false front outside of a cement box. Within, though, you'll find one of the great surprises of the park: as handsome a theater as you'll find anywhere, with near-Broadway-quality lighting and stage equipment.

Disney's Aladdin is a forty-minute, single-act musical based on the animated film *Aladdin.* The show tells the story of Aladdin, Jasmine, the evil Jafar, and the hysterical wish-granting Genie with stunning designs, high-tech stagecraft, and music, including "To Be Free," a new song from acclaimed composer Alan Menken, who was responsible for the film.

Among the highlights of the show: a flying carpet ride across the top of the orchestra and a parade of phantasmagorical elephants and other creatures that move out into the audience. The show includes eighteen scene changes and 250 costume changes. At the opening the show employed two alternating casts of twenty-eight as well as another backup cast and two stage crews.

The show is kept topical with some hilarious ad-libs and asides, mostly by the

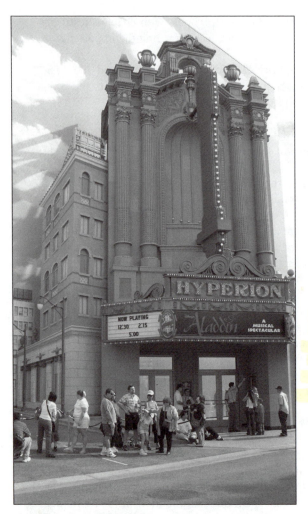

The classic design of the Hyperion Theater hides a thoroughly modern auditorium and stage within. *Photo by Corey Sandler. Used by permission from Disney Enterprises, Inc.*

Genie. "I've been 10,000 years in the lamp," he told us. "I missed every episode of *The Sopranos*. Did you tape them?" We also heard references to Britney Spears, Enron, Pete Rose, and *Survivor*.

Fastpass tickets for the show are available when the park opens, although a large number of seats are kept available for guests willing to wait in line for one of the scheduled shows.

As you walk up the road toward the entrance, stop for a moment to admire the amazing forced-perspective painting out front that expands the street scene up a skyscraper and into an astonishingly blue California sky.

The largest and tallest structure at the park, the theater includes orchestra seats and first- and second-balcony seating in a semi-circle. The balconies are close to the stage, but very high above it. The ultra-modern stage is 60 feet wide with spacious wings—larger than the one at the New York State Theater at Lincoln Center—and a 90-foot fly space above for sets.

You'll choose your seating level before you enter the building; the outdoor waiting line branches into three separate queues. The balconies are well set back from the stage. All rows are steeply raked, with good sight lines. If the line for the orchestra is not too long, I'd suggest you go there. Almost every seat down low is better than one in the stratosphere.

The theater's name is a tribute to Walt Disney's first studio on Hyperion Avenue in Los Angeles, where Mickey Mouse was born in 1928.

The Genie amazes Aladdin with a surprise dish in a scene from *Disney's Aladdin* in the Hyperion Theater. *Photo by Corey Sandler. Used by permission from Disney Enterprises, Inc.*

■ DISNEY ANIMATION

The Disney Animation pavilion is Hollywood Boulevard's most architecturally unique structure, designed in classic Art Deco style. The façade of the 30-foot-tall purple marquee atop the building is made of blue glass panels featuring a collage of classic animated characters.

Glass murals at the entrance evoke Hollywood landmarks, including the famed Pantages Theater, Max Factor Makeup Studios, and the Chapman Market.

Within the doors is the **Courtyard Gallery,** the most spectacular indoor space in the park, a total immersion into the world of animation with sixteen large-scale screens of moving and still images from classic films. The selections repeat every twenty-two minutes. Branching off from the center Courtyard Lobby are the four animation attractions featured in the pavilion.

Parents: All of the attractions in the building exit back into the central court-yard, allowing kids to be set free to explore.

Within the pavilion is the **Sorceror's Workshop,** where visitors can lay their hands on some of the tools of the animator. The Magic Mirror Realm contains early animation devices including zoetropes, whirling drums, and turning cubes. At a workbench you can draw your own simple animation series and put it into

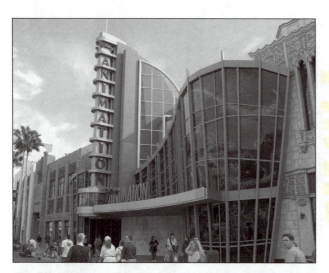

The Disney Animation building at the Hollywood Pictures Backlot. *Photo by Corey Sandler. Used by permission from Disney Enterprises, Inc.*

one of the devices to bring it to life.

At **Enchanted Books** you can enter into the Beast's Library where you can take a computerized personality test hosted by Lumiere and Cogsworth from *Beauty and the Beast.* The test determines which animated hero or villain you resemble the most.

Spend a few moments here to appreciate some of the tricks of the Imagineers. The room itself comes to life about every four minutes; special effects change the environment of the room from the dark and somber mood of the library under the curse of the Beast to the bright and happy place it becomes when the curse is broken. Video flames flicker in a fireplace and projected petals fall from a rose under glass.

In **Ursula's Grotto,** you can play some Disney karaoke: Choose a character from *The Little Mermaid* or another Disney classic and sing or speak the lines from a scene. When you're finished with your audition, sit back and listen to your effort as it is replayed.

At **Drawn to Animation,** an actor interacts with videos and the audience to portray the process or character development of an animated feature from concept through finished personality. Mushu, the reluctant dragon of *Mulan* (voiced by Eddie Murphy), disputes the artist's version of the story of his birth.

The set is an animator's work area, complete with crumpled balls of waste paper that missed the basketball hoop over the trash can. Among the things we learn is that Mushu's face was modeled on a camel, something that Mushu makes clear is not something he wants to know.

Outside of Drawn to Animation, the **Art of Animation Gallery** displays animation art from classic Disney films; the pieces are changed several times a year.

Animator's Screening Room presentations include *One Man's Dream,* a marvelous biopic about Walt Disney. The film is introduced by Disney chairman Michael Eisner, decked out in his best Mickey Mouse tie. Some of the oldest images show Walt in a Red Cross ambulance unit in France during World War I. When he was hired as an artist in Kansas City, some of his first cartoons were based on drawings he made while in France. Included in the film is a glimpse of his first successful character, Oswald the Lucky Rabbit; Disney lost control of the rights in a contract dispute.

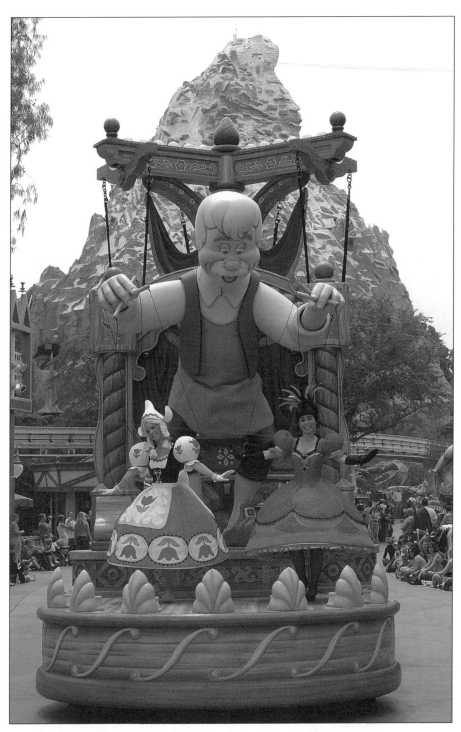

Pinocchio on parade. *Photo by Corey Sandler. Used by permission from Disney Enterprises, Inc.*

Disney Imagineers decided that no one could tell Disney's story better than Walt Disney himself. Many of the sound recordings were of poor quality, recorded in Disney's backyard by his daughter for a series of magazine articles she was writing; engineers had to work around chirping birds, the squeaky noises of the hammock Walt was sitting in, and passing airplanes and cars. Twenty hours of recordings were distilled to about ten minutes of audio for the film. Imagineers also digitized and edited films and photos of Walt, some almost one hundred years old.

We see early incarnations of Mickey Mouse, and see Disney's important transition to the Silly Symphonies cartoons, a series of musicals without a central character. We learn how Disney put up the family fortune in 1935 to finance *Snow White*. With the profits of that film he built the studio that made the company a global success. In short order came classics *Pinocchio, Bambi,* and *Fantasia*.

Some of the images in the film show Disney's formative years on the farm in Marceline, Missouri; pictures on display at the exhibit include old images of Marceline that show how it influenced the design of Main Street, U.S.A. at Disneyland and the Magic Kingdom.

PARADES AT DISNEY'S CALIFORNIA ADVENTURE

Everything old is new again; in this case the new park became home to **Disney's Electrical Parade,** a slightly updated edition of the famed Main Street Electrical Parade that was a longtime fixture at Disneyland and later traveled to other company theme parks. The parade brings many classic Disney animated features to life through three-dimensional floats covered with thousands of colorful lights. Among the most impressive scenes are the 23-foot-tall clock tower over Cinderella's Ball, complete with light-covered ballroom dancers, and the smoke-breathing, tail-wagging Elliott the dragon from *Pete's Dragon*. The parade is presented on Friday, Saturday, and Sunday nights, and on special holiday evenings.

Other entertainment includes "Goofy's Beach Party Bash," a wacky seaside spoof on the Hollywood Backlot Stage; a cast of friendly Disney characters who entertain throughout the park; and Road Trip, a talented rock band that cruises as it plays.

At its opening, Disney's California Adventure debuted **Eureka! A California Parade,** celebrating many of the Golden State's cultures and lifestyles.

EATING AND SHOPPING YOUR WAY THROUGH DISNEY'S CALIFORNIA ADVENTURE

Everyone has to eat, but the overpriced junk at some theme parks is sometimes enough to put anyone on a diet. At Disney's California Adventure, the food offerings are a notch or two above ordinary. And you can also check out of the park to Downtown Disney for even finer fare.

■ THE GOLDEN GATEWAY

Just inside the entrance is **Greetings from California,** the signature store at the park. The store is ready to meet your pressing souvenir needs as you arrive or as you drag yourself out the gate at the end of the day. **Engine-Ears Toys** offers playthings with a California and Mickey Mouse connection.

Nearby you'll find **Bakers Field Bakery & Coffee Roaster** and the **Bu-r-r Bank Ice Cream Shop.** The interiors of both stands were inspired by Los Angeles's Union Station; the tower outside is similar to one at the Santa Fe Depot in San Diego. While you're indulging your sweet tooth, check out some of the old photos of trains inside the bakery.

■ GOLDEN STATE

In Condor Flats, the **Taste Pilots Grill** is housed in a Quonset hut–like hangar at the high-desert airfield. Food like that served to airplane mechanics and pilots just returned from a grueling test flight—or a few hours in a theme park—is cooked on a rocket engine grill. A replica of an X-1 jet, the first aircraft to break the speed of sound, pokes its nose through the sidewall. Open seasonally.

Also in the area is **Fly 'n' Buy,** with Condor Flats souvenirs, including jackets, caps, logos, and pins for the pilots and wannabes.

At the Grizzly Peak Recreation Area, **Rushin' River Outfitters** sells wilderness wear and sports gear; you can also purchase rain gear to take on the river raft ride.

Bountiful Valley Farm, a celebration of the agricultural abundance of the state, includes the Bountiful Valley Farmers' Market, where you can choose from fresh California fruits and vegetables as well as hot baked potatoes and turkey legs. Also in the area is **Sam Andreas Shakes** (get it?), featuring date, citrus, and milk shakes; it is open seasonally. **Santa Rosa Seed & Supply** sells gardening supplies, flowers, and plants.

At Pacific Wharf, San Francisco's famed Boudin Bakery operates the **Pacific Wharf Cafe,** which features sandwiches on sourdough bread, seafood, and soup. You can combine all three with an order of clam chowder in an edible sourdough bowl.

Also along the wharf is the **Cucina Cucamonga Mexican Grill,** featuring meat dishes wrapped in corn or flour tortillas from the tortilla factory alongside. Less traditional offerings include tortillas wrapped around hot dogs or filled with peanut butter and jelly.

The **Lucky Fortune Cookery,** which serves Korean rice dishes, Chinese dim sum, and other Asian specialties, is available only seasonally.

Rita's Baja Blenders serves margaritas with a selection of tropic flavors. Golden Vine Winery offers a gourmet restaurant, **The Vineyard Room.** The eighty-seat mission-style eatery has hand-troweled plaster walls, terra-cotta risers, a wood beam ceiling, and *plein air*–style mural. Outside on **Golden Vine Terrace** is a patio for wine tasting and al fresco dining.

Sample dishes at the Vineyard Room include seared ahi tuna with warm potato salad, bresaola with olive oil and lemon, artichoke caponata, and gorgonzola dolcelatte with roasted pears. Pasta dishes included butternut squash ravioli,

Ariel's Grotto overlooks Paradise Bay. *Photo by Corey Sandler. Used by permission from Disney Enterprises, Inc.*

saffron tagliatelle, and pappardelle with braised duck. And for a main course, offerings included gnocchi with Maine lobster, fennel-cured roasted pork loin, and braised beef short ribs with cippolini onions. A prix-fixe four-course dinner with wine costs about $42 for lunch or $50 for dinner; without wine, the bill came to about $28 for lunch or $36 for dinner.

A wine bar on the plaza offers samples of various Mondavi brands and varieties priced from about $5.00 to $8.00 per glass. You can also purchase whole bottles; they'll be waiting at the gate for your departure.

■ PARADISE PIER

The "Under the Sea" world of **Ariel's Grotto** restaurant provides a picturesque setting for family dining that features spectacular views of Paradise Pier, appearances by the Disney characters, and a selection of specialty entrees for lunch and dinner.

The restaurant's architecture was inspired by the famous Avalon Casino on Catalina Island. A pair of conical towers is rimmed with hundreds of lights; inside, the decor features shells, dolphins, and lobsters.

The table-service restaurant is a favorite beachfront stop for Disney characters including Ariel, Minnie Mouse, Goofy, Pluto, and Chip 'n' Dale. The menu features three-course meals of family-friendly comfort foods, with inspiration drawn from foods traditionally served along the American beachfront boardwalk. Entrees include home-style meat loaf, crispy battered halibut, chicken potpie, and four-layer vegetable lasagna, as well as an assortment of soups, entree salads, sandwiches, and desserts.

The children's menu features the "Octadog," a hot dog sliced to resemble an eight-armed octopus guarding his bed of shell-shaped macaroni and cheese. Other dishes, including chicken nuggets, fish sticks, and mini corn dogs, are served in souvenir sand pails with the condiments placed in a souvenir sand shovel.

Guests are encouraged to become part of the show. Sand pails full of musical seashells and sand dollars are at each table, allowing everyone to shake, rattle, or jingle along with the music. During the signature song, "Under the Sea," everyone is invited to join the Disney characters and Avalon Cove Cast Members in a high-energy, follow-the-leader-style version of the song.

The restaurant originally opened as a gourmet eatery under the direction of famed California chef Wolfgang Puck; it was apparently too *haute* for the amusement pier theme.

Along the boardwalk are a series of amusement park food shacks. The dogs are out front at **Corn Dog Castle.** Malibu and Mexican burritos come together at **Malibu-Ritos.** The ultimate surfer beach shack is **Pizza Oom Mow Mow.** Chicken and sauces are on the menu at **Strips, Dips 'n' Chips.**

Burger Invasion recalls the California Crazy architecture of Route 66 roadside stands of the 1930s. Beneath the high Big Mac is a fanciful outpost of the McDonald's burger empire. Nearby is **Catch a Flave,** serving soft ice cream with fruit flavors swirled through.

As you would expect in a seaside amusement park (and a Disney theme park) there are many places to buy those essential T-shirts and Goofy hats. Shops along the boardwalk include **Dinosaur Jack's Sunglass Shack,** another architectural joke, topped with a giant reptile.

Award Wieners serves hip hot dogs and gourmet sausages in the Hollywood Pictures Backlot. *Photo by Corey Sandler. Used by permission from Disney Enterprises, Inc.*

Avalon Cove by night. *Photo © Disney Enterprises, Inc.*

Treasures in Paradise is designed like a 1920s beachfront pavilion, a warehouse with an Art Deco spire. **Souvenir 66** would have been at home on Route 66. At **Point Mugu Tattoo,** you can purchase a temporary emblem.

■ HOLLYWOOD PICTURES BACKLOT

Near the Muppets show is **Hollywood and Dine,** a fast-food counter restaurant that salutes several once-famous Hollywood eateries including Dan the Beachcomber, Wiltshire Bowl Grill, and Villa Capri. **Award Wieners,** a modern-style diner, serves up *haute* dogs and french fries.

CHAPTER SIX

DOWNTOWN DISNEY AND DISNEY HOTELS

THE NEW GATEWAY TO DISNEYLAND and Disney's California Adventure is a twenty-acre sprawl of shops, restaurants, and entertainment clubs in four districts.

Disney says the area is a California-modern phenomenon inspired by famous European shopping and theater districts and old-town walking streets such as Copenhagen's Strøget and Tivoli Gardens.

It's also worth crediting Universal Studios Hollywood with introducing CityWalk to Southern California. Disney later created its own city in Florida at Walt Disney World's Disney West Side and Downtown Disney.

DOWNTOWN DISNEY

Starting at the central esplanade between Disneyland park and Disney's California Adventure park, the East Garden area takes its visual cues from the new Disney's Grand Californian Hotel with its early-twentieth-century Craftsmen architecture. Some of the eateries are open for breakfast (B), lunch (L), dinner (D), or parts of the day; it is relatively easy to duck out of one of the parks to eat in downtown.

The **La Brea Bakery Café** (BLD), an outpost of an old artisan baker in Los Angeles, offers cafe dining and grab-and-go bakery treats, coffee, and espresso. Specialties include a coffee and espresso bar, breads, pastries, sandwiches, soups and salads, a food preparation station with items such as freshly grilled panini sandwiches and a crostini bar that serves open-faced, appetizer-size sandwiches using fresh grilled breads. A wine bar serves by the glass and offers microbrewery beers as well.

Naples Ristorante e Pizzeria (LD) offers casual southern Italian cuisine in a Mediterranean setting; the attractive eatery is the second restaurant at Downtown Disney operated by chef Joachim Splichal. The 350-seat restaurant features a handcrafted wood-burning oven, an open kitchen, and trellises covered with bougainvillea.

Diners can watch skillful *pizzaiole* (pizza chefs) work at marble slabs, hand-patting the balls of dough and adding the fresh toppings such as imported vine-ripened plum tomatoes and *fior di latte* mozzarella. A conveyer system moves pizza pies between the kitchen and the two-story, wood-burning oven.

Naples also offers a selection of *piccoli piatti*. These small salads, similar to tapas, are offered on individual plates and include meats, seafood, and vegetables. Also on the menu are hearty pastas and other dishes prepared in the traditional Neapolitan cucina marinara style, including *pagnottelle*, which is a twice-baked sandwich made from pizza dough. For reservations, call (714) 781–3463.

An island in the center of the Wine District includes a vine-covered wine and tapas bar. The **Catal Restaurant & Uva Bar** (LD), developed by chef Splichal, combines Art Deco and Westwood Village architectural styles in a two-story, 525-seat restaurant filled with the rich colors and streamlined aesthetics of the Jazz Age. The wine and tapas bar is located under a shaded champagne-flute trellis; as many as forty different wines will be sold by the glass. Uva is the Spanish word for grapes.

The menu features Mediterranean grilled seafood, poultry and vegetables, salads, and flavorful pastas. Dishes are infused with the fragrant herbs and olive oil that characterize the cuisine of the Mediterranean rim, including southern France, Greece, Italy, and Spain. For reservations, call (714) 774–4442.

Joachim and Christine Splichal also own Pinot Bistro in Studio City, Pinot Hollywood in the heart of Hollywood's studio district, Café Pinot in downtown Los Angeles, Pinot Restaurant and Martini Bar in Pasadena, Pinot Blanc in Saint Helena, Pinot Provence in Costa Mesa, and Pinot Brasserie within the Venetian Resort in Las Vegas.

The **Center Plaza,** the heart of the district, is surrounded by an unusual mix of major restaurants and showplaces.

Tortilla Jo's (LD) features handmade tamales and tortillas, tableside preparation of guacamole, and a rotisserie oven. The main dining room seats 150, and a second floor seats 70 inside and 90 on an outdoor patio. There's an over-the-counter *taqueria* stand for those who want to grab and go. By night, there's lively entertainment. Tortilla Jo's, another operation of Splichal's Patina Group, replaced Y Arriba. For information and reservations, call (714) 535–5000.

Jamba Juice (BLD) offers blended-to-order smoothies, snacks, and soups. Concoctions include freshly squeezed juices, fruit, vegetables, nonfat frozen yogurt, dairy-free sorbet and ice, and Juice Boosts, nutritional supplements designed to provide a variety of benefits. Established in 1990, Jamba Juice has more than 350 company and franchised or licensed stores in twenty-four states nationwide.

Ralph Brennan's Jazz Kitchen (LD) brings a bit of New Orleans' Bourbon Street to Anaheim, featuring spicy Cajun cuisine and Dixieland music. The exterior of the 400-seat restaurant is straight out of the French Quarter with wrought iron balconies and gas lights.

A member of the Brennan family of Commander's Palace fame, Ralph Brennan's company includes Red Fish Grill, BACCO, Mr. B's Bistro, and the Storyville District, all New Orleans' French Quarter restaurants. For information, consult www.rbjazzkitchen.com. For reservations, call (714) 781–3463.

The **House of Blues** (LD) is styled as a Carolina plantation estate house and seats as many as 500 for Delta-inspired cuisine. Live performances of blues, rock, rhythm-and-blues, and Latin music are planned.

The House of Blues restaurant features an open-air kitchen serving fresh rotisserie items and Delta-inspired cuisine. Menu items include Memphis-style ribs, cedar plank–smoked salmon with watercress and jicama salad, and Voodoo shrimp with rosemary cornbread. A specialty is the Sunday gospel brunch, with a southern-style buffet which features performances by local and touring gospel groups. For information, consult www.hob.com. For reservations, call (714) 781–3463.

Near the Disneyland Hotel at the West Side Garden, design themes return to Art Deco and celebrate the golden age of glittering Hollywood movie palaces in restaurants, theaters, and the Downtown Disney monorail station.

The **Downtown Disney Monorail Station** connects directly to Tomorrowland within the Disneyland park. As part of the development of Downtown Disney, the monorail station was moved across the street from the Disneyland Hotel. There is no station within Disney's California Adventure.

The **Rainforest Cafe** (BLD) uses touches of Inca palace architecture merged with a concrete block house, "La Minatura," built in California in the 1920s by Frank Lloyd Wright. The central atrium is filled with hundreds of live jungle plants. Other Rainforest Cafes are located at Walt Disney World and Disneyland Paris. For information, consult www.rainforestcafe.com. For reservations, call (714) 772–0413.

ESPN Zone (LD, B on weekends) is a sports entertainment bar and restaurant featuring satellite transmitters and receivers and more than 165 video monitors. The Studio Grill is inspired by sets from *ESPN SportsCenter* and other ESPN broadcast shows. The Screening Room is a theater to watch broadcast sports and live interviews of sports figures. The Sports Arena features interactive and competitive games, including the 30-foot Xtreme Glacier rock wall. ESPN is part of ABC, which in turn is owned by the Disney Company. For information, call (714) 300–3776.

ENTERTAINMENT AT DOWNTOWN DISNEY

If the Disneyland park or Disney's California Adventure is not quite enough excitement for you, or if you're looking for nighttime entertainment aimed at adults, Downtown Disney offers jazz, blues, salsa, rock and roll, sports talk, and twelve screens of movies.

AMC Theatres. Twelve auditoriums with a total of 3,000 seats with modern amenities, including stadium seating and high-tech sound systems. For show times and ticket reservations, call (714) 769–4262 or consult www.movietickets .com.

ESPN Zone. Guests can watch broadcasts and taping of ESPN radio and television talk shows as well as broadcasts of major professional and college sports. For schedules, call (714) 300–3776 or consult http://espn.go.com/espninc/zone/ espnzoneanaheim.html.

House of Blues. Live musical performances several nights per week, plus the Sunday Gospel Brunch. For information and tickets, call (714) 778–2583 or consult www.hob.com.

Ralph Brennan's Jazz Kitchen. A house band and special guests perform. For information, call (714) 776–5200 or consult www.rbjazzkitchen.com.

■ SHOPPING AT DOWNTOWN DISNEY

And, of course, you can shop at Downtown Disney.

The flagship store here is the **World of Disney,** a full acre of Disney merchandise set amid giant video screens and themed areas saluting classic films. More than 15,000 plush characters of various sizes and shapes fill one floor-to-ceiling display.

This is the second-largest Disney shopping experience on Earth, just behind the monstrous store at Walt Disney World in Orlando.

It's all about retail, of course: The shop sells all manner of Disney character merchandise including backpacks, books, boxers, children's apparel, clocks, collectibles, costumes, dolls, figurines, gifts, hats, jewelry, luggage, photo albums, plush toys, sleepwear, slippers, socks, souvenirs, stationery, sunglasses, sweatshirts, T-shirts, ties, videos, watches, and more.

Other shops include **Compass Books and Cafe,** the West's oldest independent bookstore. For information, consult www.booksinc.net.

The French cosmetics and fragrances retailer **Sephora** has a store in the district; for information, consult www.sephora.com.

The **Lego Imagination Center** stocks more than 400 Lego toy products. For information, consult www.lego.com.

A new magnet for little princesses is the **Club Libby Lu** store, which—in case you're not an insider—is described as a special secret club where superfabulous girls can get makeovers, have parties, play games, get advice, and find really cool princess paraphernalia. The store includes Libby's Laboratory, where girls can mix their own concoctions of bath and shower gels, cologne, and fairy dust. At Libby's Bedroom and Libby's Closet, girls can shop for stuff to decorate their room or their closet. For information, call (714) 772–3793 or consult www .clublibbylu.com.

Mainspring sells clocks and watches of all types.

Starabilias offers antique souvenirs and reproductions of Hollywood memorabilia. For information, consult www.starabilias.com.

Hoypoloi sells unusual glass and metal art pieces and lighting; the company's moniker plays off the name of its founder, artist Ron Hoy. For information, consult www.hoypoloi.com.

Department 56 sells its collectibles, Snowbabies, and home and holiday decorative products. For information, consult www.department56.com.

Illuminations is a national retailer of handmade candles and home-decor items. For information, consult www.illuminations.com.

At the **Build-a-Bear Workshop,** you can (in their words) make your beary own best friend at the Pawsitively Fun Family Experience.

Parking for Downtown Disney guests is located off Disneyland Drive in areas just to the north of the Disneyland Hotel and just south of Disney's Paradise Pier Hotel. Parking is by the hour; the first three hours are free, with the movie theater and some restaurants offering two more hours to customers. Additional hours cost $6.00 per hour.

HOTELS AT THE DISNEYLAND RESORT

There are three Disney-owned hotels on the grounds of the Disneyland Resort, with accommodations for about 2,300. Disney also has marketing arrangements with more than forty "Good Neighbor Hotels" nearby to the park. Many of these independent hotels offer shuttle bus service to the park and may offer discounted multiday tickets or other special features.

■ DISNEY'S GRAND CALIFORNIAN HOTEL

This handsome hotel captures the spirit of the Golden State's coastal woodlands in a deluxe six-story, 751-room resort hotel.

It is the first hotel with a direct entrance into any Disney park; a gate allows guests to come and go into Disney's California Adventure. It is also the first time the residential architecture of the Arts and Crafts movement has been applied to a structure as large as a major hotel. Reminiscent of old-style lodges such as the Ahwahnee Hotel at Yosemite or the Old Faithful Lodge at Yellowstone, the posh hotel is in many ways a West Coast version of the popular Grand Floridian Hotel at Walt Disney World in Orlando.

Planners chose the Arts and Crafts architecture that was popular for wealthy family homes in the California foothills. The style began in England in the late nineteenth century as a revolt against Victorian gingerbread and machine-made decor, and was embraced by noted architects such as Frank Lloyd Wright, Bernard Maybeck, and others. Designs strive to be in harmony with the surrounding area. Each piece of wood was carefully chosen, each rock selected to complement nature, and each piece of furniture was handcrafted by the artist. The best-known example of Arts and Crafts style in California is a Pasadena "bungalow" completed in 1908 by Charles and Henry Greene for Charles and Mary Gamble, of Procter and Gamble wealth.

Disney's implementation was designed by architect Peter Dominick, also responsible for Disney's Wilderness Lodge and Disney's Animal Kingdom Lodge at Walt Disney World in Florida.

A bungalow-style porte cochere greets guests arriving at the front entrance off Disneyland Drive. Large metal gates with a blue moon in the center guard the entrance to the hotel from Downtown Disney. Just inside the front entrance are large wooden trusses and stained glass light fixtures, recalling some of the elements of Northern California's first Craftsmen structure, the Swedenborgian church.

The star of the hotel is the impressive atrium lobby, 753 feet high with open timber trusses in the ceiling. Below are large stone porches. The floor is decorated with fabric and stone in a floral pattern inspired by the work of British designer William Morris, one of the early leaders of the Arts and Crafts movement.

To complete the building Disney searched for artists and artisans to build elements. Spend the time to find:

- A quarter-sawed oak grandfather clock with a hammered-copper face and cable-weight clockworks in the lobby
- Large ceramic vases shaped like birds with human caricatures so unique they are called "grotesqueries"
- A manhole cover with the face of the "north wind" in the pavement of the Court of Winds

Each room has its own balcony, with most of the rooms looking directly onto Disney's California Adventure park or the Downtown Disney district. Surrounding the hotel is an evergreen forest and rock-post fences. (One somewhat incongruous element: the monorail breezing by overhead in the interior Courtyard of Winds, nipping through a corner of the building.)

The Grand Californian offers a supervised activity center, **Pinocchio's Workshop,** for younger children. Guests can leave their youngsters at the center while they go to dinner or explore the parks.

Within the hotel, the **Napa Rose Restaurant** celebrates the bounties of California from seacoast to farmlands, with a special emphasis on the vineyards. The 200 seats surround an open exhibition kitchen and a large wine cellar including some of the state's premium and boutique wines.

The wine list has more than 600 California wines and sixty French champagnes. The menu places an emphasis on California produce and features foods that are in their prime season; for example, white asparagus in the spring, wild mushrooms in the fall, and fresh raspberries in the summer.

Large picture windows offer views of the park; other walls are decorated with stained glass grills and inlaid wood. Guests can watch twenty chefs and helpers at work in the kitchen; when meals are ready, a "runner" moves the dishes quickly to the table.

Storytellers Cafe is an informal setting for breakfast buffet and casual dining throughout the day. The restaurant's eight murals, done in the 1930s style of famed children's book illustrator N. C. Wyeth, celebrate the joys of reading. Disney characters including Chip 'n' Dale make regular appearances here.

Just off the lobby is the **Hearthstone Lodge,** serving gourmet coffee and baked goods in the morning and drinks and wine throughout the rest of the day. A stone fireplace is surrounded by handmade tile with century-old designs; a hand-carved redwood mural depicts an artist at work. What look like Mickey Mouse ears on some of the lamps are said to be reproductions of actual Arts and Crafts designs; we consider them hidden Mickeys, nevertheless.

The entrance to Disney's California Adventure is primarily for hotel guests, but can also be used by park guests after they have entered the main gates.

Rates for standard rooms range from about $235 to $330 per night; packages with admission tickets and meals are also offered. For reservations and information call (714) 956–6425 or consult www.disneyland.com.

■ DISNEYLAND HOTEL

The hotel across Disneyland Drive (formerly West Street) opened in 1955 and has grown over the years to become a small theme park of its own.

As part of the development of Downtown Disney and Disney's California Adventure, the hotel has been reborn. The resort spreads across sixty acres of lush, tropical gardens and offers 990 guest rooms and sixty-two suites in three towers.

The centerpiece of the **Never Land** water play area, inspired by scenes from Peter Pan, is a large swimming pool with a winding "shoreline" that depicts the lagoon from the film, accented by the Hangman's Tree and a backdrop of the Misty Mountains. Rising from the pool is a sculpture of Tick Tock, the hungry crocodile always on the lookout for Captain Hook. Nearby is a spa themed after the Mermaid Lagoon, including a figure of a mermaid atop a fountain.

Guests can follow a trail that winds its way up the slopes of the **Misty Mountain,** across a wood-and-rope suspension bridge and to the 16-foot-high "headwaters" of the pool. The way down is a 110-foot-long water slide that rushes through the mountain range and plunges into the lagoon.

The Disneyland Monorail station is across the road at the entrance to Downtown Disney, allowing easy access to Disneyland as well as a quick way out of the park for breaks at the pool or one of the restaurants. Day visitors to the Disneyland Resort can also use the restaurants at the hotel. The monorail does not stop within Disney's California Adventure; a tram links the main gate of the park to the hotel. Guests at the hotel can receive early admission to Disneyland on days when it is available.

Granville's Steak House offers steak, prime rib, lobster, and poultry specialties for dinner in a dark-wood American Southwest setting. After the lobster, steak, or seafood, see if you can polish off a chocolate fantasy cake.

Hook's Pointe & Wine Cellar is a slightly upscale nautical theme restaurant offering mesquite-grilled specialties for breakfast, lunch, and dinner; dishes are prepared in a display kitchen. The below-deck wine cellar features more than two dozen California wines by the bottle or glass.

For a somewhat less sophisticated experience, **Goofy's Kitchen** features Disney character meals including an all-you-can-eat buffet as well as lunch and dinner from a menu prepared by Chef Goofy, Pluto, and other friends.

Rates for the hotel range from about $190 to $265 per night. Package plans with airfare and tickets are also available. There is no charge for children younger than eighteen sharing a room with parents.

The Disneyland Hotel is located at 1150 Magic Way in Anaheim. For reservations call (714) 956–6425 or consult www.disneyland.com.

■ DISNEY'S PARADISE PIER HOTEL

Location, location, location: Disney's Paradise Pier Hotel is in one of the best spots in Anaheim. The fifteen-story high-rise—formerly the Disneyland Pacific Hotel—is a short walk from the Disneyland Hotel in one direction and the Anaheim Convention Center in the other.

But the clincher is the view from the upper floors of the east side of the hotel: Below you is the Paradise Pier section of Disney's California Adventure, and beyond it is Disneyland. (Disney's Grand Californian is closer to the action, but only four stories tall.)

The 502-room hotel was purchased by Disney a few years ago and has undergone a complete renovation. It includes a swimming pool and spa, two restaurants, and access to the facilities of the Disneyland Hotel.

The building's towers are festively painted and decorated to reflect the California theme. With the purchase of park admission, hotel guests can enter Disney's California Adventure through a private gate leading directly into Paradise Pier; guests can save fifteen minutes or more over walking through Downtown Disney to the main entrance of the park and can easily return to the hotel for a break from the park.

The **Pacific Coast Highway** restaurant is among the better Disney restaurants, offering specialty pizzas made in a wood-fired oven, unusual seafood such as sea bass marinated in sake, and a range of Pacific Rim entrees such as hoisin-grilled baby back ribs. In the morning the younger crowd takes over for breakfast with Minnie and friends.

Disney's PCH Grill also hosts twice-monthly wine dinners, featuring California wines that are paired with specially prepared five-course dinners. Winemakers from the featured winery are present to meet guests and answer questions.

Yamabuki, located next to the hotel's lobby, is Disneyland's only Japanese restaurant. Items include fresh sushi, tempura, sashimi, and teriyaki. A tatami room with both Japanese- and Western-style seating is available for special occasions and small groups.

Rates for the hotel range from about $160 to $235 per night. Package plans with airfare and tickets are also available. There is no charge for children younger than eighteen sharing a room with parents. For reservations, call (714) 956–6425 or consult www.disneyland.com.

PART III

UNIVERSAL STUDIOS HOLLYWOOD

CHAPTER SEVEN

UNIVERSAL STUDIOS HOLLYWOOD

UNIVERSAL STUDIOS IS A PLACE of great history in the relatively short life of the motion picture industry. Its films and television shows have gone back in time to *Jurassic Park* and Bedrock, home of the Flintstones; to ancient Rome and Greece for *Spartacus* and Mel Brooks in a toga; to the classic antiwar theme of *All Quiet on the Western Front* and the slapstick *McHale's Navy;* to the chilling horror of *Psycho* and the technological terror of *Backdraft;* way into the future and then back again in *Back to the Future.* Each of these films and many more are celebrated at Universal Studios Hollywood with exhibits, rides, stage shows, and guided tours.

In 2004, The Mummy moved into a charming little place of his own, with a high-tech, high-adrenaline themed roller coaster, **Revenge of the Mummy.** If that's not scary enough, nearby you'll find worms, scorpions, bungees, and humans tied up in *Fear Factor Live,* a live audience-participation show based on the successful television show.

If you're not scared of shopping, Universal has opened a new shop that sells some of the clothing worn by actors and actresses in some of the daytime dramas, soap operas, and movies filmed at the studios. Each piece of apparel comes at a discount and is accompanied by a certificate of authenticity that traces its moment of stardom.

There are four main areas at Universal Studios Hollywood; plan on a full day to see them all. The entrance to the park evokes the great movie palaces and themes of the past and leads into the upper-level Entertainment Center, which is home to the stage shows—including *Waterworld*—and most of the park's eateries, as well as the astounding **Back to the Future . . . The Ride.**

Off to the right and down a long escalator is the loading area for the Backlot Tram Tour. At the back left corner is the first of a series of four long escalators

MUST-SEES

Revenge of the Mummy
(he's got you coming and going)

Terminator 2 3-D
(he's back . . .)

Jurassic Park—The Ride
(take a shower with the dinos)

Earthquake
(Backlot Tram Tour)

King Kong
(Backlot Tram Tour)

Jaws
(Backlot Tram Tour)

Back to the Future . . . The Ride

Waterworld—A Live Sea War Spectacular

The Wild Wild Wild West Stunt Show

Fear Factor Live

Backdraft

Special Effects Stages

Animal Planet Live!

Shrek 4-D

that take you down to the Studio Center for more rides, including the spectacular **Jurassic Park—The Ride.**

Finally there is the **Universal CityWalk,** a collection of unusual shops, clubs, and restaurants well worth a visit for lunch, dinner, or late-night entertainment. You don't even need an admission ticket to visit there, but if you're at the park it's a great place to duck out for lunch or dinner.

Universal Studios is about forty-five minutes by car from Anaheim, or fifteen minutes from downtown Los Angeles; driving times can more than double during the extended rush hours.

You can ride the Red Line of the Metro subway to a station at the base of the Universal City hill; Universal Studios Hollywood offers a free shuttle bus from the train to the park.

A UNIVERSAL HISTORY

Universal Studios was established in 1912 with the founding of the Universal Film Manufacturing Company, started at the time of the nickelodeon in a cluster of tiny offices in New York City. Under the leadership of Carl Laemmle the company became a major force in the industry.

When Laemmle decided to consolidate production facilities from both coasts to one site, he purchased a 130-acre chicken ranch in North Hollywood, and construction of what was to become Universal City began in 1914.

Because the property in Cahuenga Pass was far removed from what passed for the modern conveniences of Los Angeles at the time, the company installed its own power, water, and other facilities.

At the grand opening in 1915, Thomas Edison was on hand to officially start the studio's electrical equipment, and showman Buffalo Bill Cody was a special guest. Ten thousand sightseers were also there to view the dawn of the motion picture industry on the West Coast.

Almost immediately, Universal was the world's busiest motion picture studio; early filmmakers included the legendary John Ford, Eric von Stroheim, and Irving Thalberg.

UNIVERSAL STUDIOS HOLLYWOOD

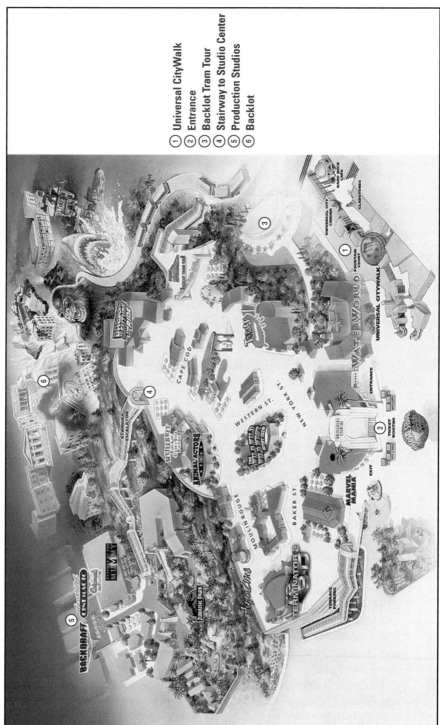

1. Universal CityWalk
2. Entrance
3. Backlot Tram Tour
4. Stairway to Studio Center
5. Production Studios
6. Backlot

Power Trip: The Jurassic Dash and the Terminator Trot

You'll be damned if you do . . . and disappointed if you don't, so thrill seekers should head first for **Revenge of the Mummy**, which is sure to be one of the top draws, along with *Fear Factor Live*. (At some times of the year, the lower Studio Center opens later than the upper part of the park; call ahead and plan accordingly.)

The other big draws at the park are **Terminator 2 3-D**, and—especially on hot days—the splashdown at **Jurassic Park**. Dry yourself off and then visit Backdraft and the **Special Effects Stages**.

By now most of the other visitors will have taken the tram tour and will be heading your way. Grab an early lunch to avoid hungry crowds later, and then go against the flow, back up the escalator to the Entertainment Center. If the waiting line at **Back to the Future** is reasonable (half an hour or less), go on in; if not, go down the other side of the hill to the Backlot Tram Tour and return to **Back to the Future** later.

In early afternoon visit the shows, including *Animal Planet Live!, Shrek 4-D,* and *The Wild Wild Wild West Stunt Show.*

A burst of growth took place during World War II; government regulations prohibited excess profits during wartime, so the company poured cash into new soundstages and other construction.

In 1946 Universal expanded in a merger with International Pictures. In following years, the studio lured director Alfred Hitchcock and later Steven Spielberg and George Lucas. The Music Corporation of America (MCA) purchased the Universal studio facilities and land in 1959 and Universal Pictures itself in 1962. During the next two decades, MCA opened the Universal Studios Hollywood theme park, fourteen modern soundstages, the Universal Amphitheatre, and many other facilities including office buildings, hotels, shops, and restaurants.

In 2004, the French company Vivendi Universal and General Electric Co. completed a merger of Universal's Hollywood studio, its theme park empire, and other U.S. entertainment assets with GE's television network NBC and cable television holdings, which include CNBC, MSNBC, Telemundo, the USA Network, and the Sci-Fi Channel.

The deal created a new company called NBC Universal, which will compete with entertainment giants Walt Disney, Viacom, and News Corp, owner of Fox and DirecTV. NBC Universal is 80 percent owned by GE; Vivendi was granted the option to sell its 20 percent stake at market prices beginning in 2006.

Universal is the country's third-largest motion picture studio, behind Sony and Disney's Buena Vista. Some analysts say the new company may sell off its theme park operations to concentrate on television and film holdings.

UNIVERSAL STUDIOS HOLLYWOOD, TODAY

Since public tours were established at Universal Studios Hollywood in 1964, more than 100 million people have visited the former chicken farm as paying guests. Today, more than five million come to Universal Studios Hollywood each year.

Universal Studios Hollywood is located in Universal City between Hollywood and the San Fernando Valley, off the Hollywood Freeway (U.S. Highway 101), at either the Universal Center Drive or Lankershim Boulevard exits.

The park is open daily except for Thanksgiving and Christmas. Operating hours in the summer are generally 8:00 A.M. to 10:00 P.M. and for the rest of the year from 9:00 A.M. to 7:00 P.M.

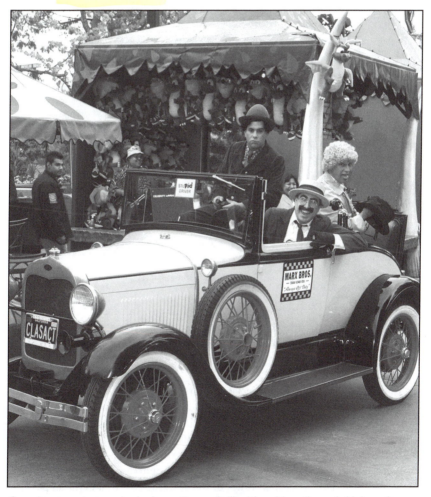

Groucho, or an actor who looks pretty much like him, drives through Universal Studios Hollywood with Chico and Harpo look-alikes. *Photo by Corey Sandler*

Universal Studios Hollywood Tickets

Prices were in effect in 2005 and are subject to change; prices do not include a 2 percent Los Angeles County tax. For information, call (818) 622–3801 or consult www.universalstudioshollywood.com. Discounts for multiday and other tickets are sometimes offered online. Annual passes are available for not much more than the cost of a one-day ticket; call for details.

ONE-DAY PASS	ADULT	CHILD (3 to 7 or under 48")
	$53.00	$43.00

Parking: $8
Preferred Parking: $13

FRONT-OF-THE-LINE PASS	$89.75	$89.75

Priority entry privileges for an entire day on all attractions, limited to two times per attraction. Reserved seating at shows including *Animal Planet Live!* and *Waterworld—A Live Sea War Spectacular.*

VIP EXPERIENCE	$139.00	$139.00

Includes private trolley for a tour of front lot production facilities, including soundstages, sound mixing rooms, and the property warehouse, subject to production restrictions. The trolley then visits the backlot. Guests also receive front-of-the-line privileges at attractions.

HOLLYWOOD CITYPASS	$72.00	$49.00

Valid for one admission to seven Hollywood attractions over a thirty-day period. Participating attractions are Universal Studios Hollywood, Museum of Western Heritage, Kodak Theatre Guided Tour, Hollywood Entertainment Museum, and Starline Tours of Hollywood.

SOUTHERN CALIFORNIA VALUE PASS	$94.00	$76.00

Unlimited admission to Universal Studios Hollywood and SeaWorld San Diego for fourteen consecutive days.

You can see all of the park in one very full day. In recent years Universal Studios has regularly offered **second-day free promotions** during low-season; these allow you to come back to the park within seven days. A two-day visit is a good way to combine the park with the dining and entertainment venues at Universal CityWalk.

You may want to purchase special combination tickets, such as the **Southern California Value Pass,** which offers unlimited admission to Universal Studios and SeaWorld San Diego over a fourteen-day period, or the **Hollywood CityPass** with admission to Universal Studios plus seven museums and attractions in the area.

And if you plan to visit Universal Studios for more than one day of your trip or make two or more visits within a year, you should also consider purchasing an annual pass. During certain times of the year, the cost of an annual pass can be as little as the price of a one-day ticket; in recent years the price has been no more than the cost of two tickets.

By the way, a quick and easy way to save some money is to eat breakfast before you arrive or pack a meal to eat outside the gates. That is, unless you prefer paying $3.29 for a sticky bun and $2.50 for a tiny carton of orange juice. There are lockers near the exits of the parking garages at Universal CityWalk.

ENTERTAINMENT CENTER

MUST-SEE *TERMINATOR 2 3-D*

He's back . . . and with a vengeance. This Universal attraction is a tour de force of film and computer special effects that puts the audience in the middle of an epic battle between and among the fearsome "cinebotic" robots, live actors, and reunited stars of *Terminator 2*: Arnold Schwarzenegger, Linda Hamilton, Robert Patrick, and Edward Furlong, along with director James Cameron and special effects wizards from the movie series.

In this Terminator adventure—which begins in the present day and jumps to the Los Angeles of 2029 as depicted in the film—Cyberdyne Systems, the dreaded creators of Skynet and its fearsome Terminator cyborgs, has moved its corporate headquarters to Universal Studios Hollywood in the back corner of the Upper Lot, to the left of the entrance. And the sinister company is determined to showcase its advanced technologies to the world.

Guests twist and turn in their seats as menacing Cyberdyne Systems "T-70" cinebotic warriors train their sights on random targets, firing across the theater. The audience leaps back in three-dimensional shock when the T-1000 Terminator "cop" from *Terminator 2* morphs to life before their very eyes, then cheers with relief as Schwarzenegger's T-800 cyborg literally charges off the screen to save the day astride a 1,500-pound Harley Davidson "hog," which lands on the stage and then dives back into the screen and into the scene.

And I don't want to spoil the fun, but you'll want to hold on to your seats for the jaw-dropping finale. You'll understand what I mean when your feet are back on solid ground.

The show begins with a "super" entertaining preshow sales pitch by Kimberly Duncan, Cyberdyne's director of community relations and media control. "Imagine a world where butterflies run on batteries," Cyberdyne suggests, expecting you to do so with happy anticipation, "where human error is a thing of the past. Our goal is complete control of global communication."

It's all really "super." Really.

The associate unveils Skynet, a computer-controlled defense system, and then suddenly something goes wrong with the promotional video: It seems that hackers have broken into the system to warn us against Cyberdyne.

Terminator creator James Cameron, who directed this third installment of the saga as well as the blockbuster *Titanic,* regards *Terminator 2 3-D* as a true sequel to the earlier Terminator films. "It's definitely the next film," he says. "The only difference is this film is only twelve minutes long and you can't see it in just any theater."

Because the audience is in the present day, the film script uses T-70 cinebots, a design of robots not seen in the movies, which take place several decades in the

Lockup

A room full of lockers to store stuff you don't want to drag through the park can be found just inside the entrance gates on the right side; boxes rent for several dollars a day.

future. The six T-70s each stand 8 feet tall; they rise from hiding places along the walls of the theater with the aid of a sophisticated hydraulic system.

This film marks the first time interlocking 3-D images have been projected onto multiple screens, surrounding guests in 180 degrees of action. For the climactic third act, the film opens up from one center screen to simultaneous projection on three screens, arranged at sixty-degree angles from each other.

According to Universal Studios, the twelve-minute-long film is, frame for frame, the most expensive motion picture ever produced.

Live-action scenes for the film took place at Kaiser Eagle Mountain, an abandoned steel foundry in Desert Center, California; the area was rebuilt in spectacular fashion to resemble Los Angeles in the aftermath of a nuclear war. More than a hundred cars, trucks, and buses were hauled in from wrecking yards and strewn about the one-million-square-foot location set.

The background consisted not of mockups but of actual buildings that were blown up during two weeks of filming, lending a scale of authenticity that surpasses many big-budget Hollywood action flicks.

Additional scenes were shot on a Los Angeles soundstage, where an elaborate 24-foot "miniature" of Skynet, the pyramid-shaped headquarters of Cyberdyne Systems, was constructed. Through the magic of cinema trickery it appears to be 800 feet tall on screen.

The best seats for the 3-D effects are from the middle to the back of the theater; the best seats to see the live action, including the arrival of the Harley on stage and the finale, are in the third or fourth row, center.

The Terminator show is nearly identical to one at Universal Studios Florida.

MUST-SEE BACK TO THE FUTURE . . . THE RIDE

Dive into the world of the record-breaking movie trilogy *Back to the Future* in Universal's incredible simulator adventure. It's a roller coaster of an attraction that never moves more than a few feet in any direction.

Coming Attraction

If you have really sharp eyes and a good sense of balance, keep an eye out during your wild Back to the Future ride for the movie poster on the wall in Hill Valley; it advertises *Jaws 19.*

It seems that weird Doc Brown is back home conducting new time-travel experiments. He has created his newest vehicle—an eight-passenger time vehicle that is faster and more energy-efficient than anything before . . . or since. That's the good news. The bad news is that Biff Tannen has broken into the Institute of Future Technology and threatens to end the universe as we know it! It's up to you to jump into your own DeLorean and chase down Biff.

Surrounded by images and sound and buffeted by the realistic motion of your flight simulator, you soar into Hill Valley in the year 2015, blast back to the Ice Age for a chilling high-speed encounter with canyons

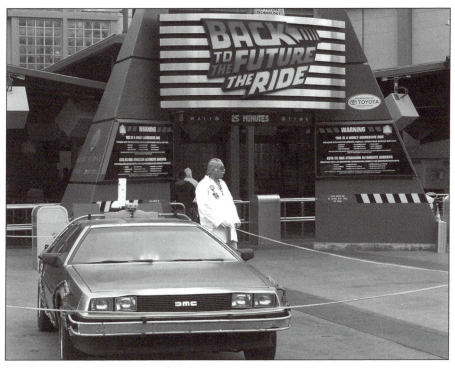

Doc Brown waits for volunteers at Back to the Future . . . the Ride. *Photo by Corey Sandler*

of sheer ice, explode into the Volcanic Era for a once-in-a-lifetime encounter with a Tyrannosaurus rex, and then go through a volcano and over the edge of a molten lava fall.

This is a state-of-the-art attraction that combines a spectacular 70-mm Omnimax film with simulator ride vehicles. The 80-foot-diameter domelike screens of the Omnimax theater occupy all of the viewer's peripheral vision, making the screen seem to vanish by taking the viewer into the scene.

There are three levels of twelve eight-seater DeLorean cars in the theater dome. Universal insiders say the very best experience can be had by sitting in the front row of the center car on the second tier. This particular vehicle is in the absolute center of the movie dome, and you cannot easily see any surrounding cars that might distract from the illusion. If you are concerned about motion sickness, you may want to try to get a seat on the lower level of the ride. (I prefer a Dramamine in the morning and the middle car.)

The Institute of Future Technology in the waiting

Don't Say You Weren't Warned

Back to the Future is described as a "dynamically aggressive ride." Visitors suffering from maladies including dizziness, seizures, back or neck problems, claustrophobia, motion sickness, and heart disorders, or pregnant women, are advised to sit this one out. The ride also won't work for persons of a certain size or shape who cannot fit into the seats and safety harness.

The Working Studio

Just inside gates on the right side is the Daily Shooting Schedule, which reports on movie and television projects under way in the studios and backlots. It's a matter of pure luck whether you'll see a show being filmed or run into a celebrity while on the backlot tram tour.

Keep your eyes peeled as you are taken past the studios—watch for dressing room trailers and equipment trucks. From time to time, one or another star makes a point of waving to a passing tram, or more. According to studio lore, one day a crazed man dressed in a granny dress and waving an ax ran screaming out of the Bates Motel from *Psycho* in the backlot; it turned out to be Jim Carrey, taking a break from the filming of *The Grinch* to play with visitors.

area features actual props from the *Back to the Future* movie series including hoverboards (specially adapted skateboards without wheels) and the all-important flux capacitors for time travel.

Check out the bulletin board in the waiting area, where you see the names of some of the visiting scientists who have offices in the building. They include Thomas Edison, Albert Einstein, and Francis Bacon.

Some of Doc Brown's inventions are found in the waiting area outside the simulators. Check out the Time Man personal time travel suit prototype. There are lots of clocks on the walls including ones for Greenwich, Moscow, Tokyo, Sydney, Hollywood, Hill Valley, Mexico City, and Orlando. Hill Valley is set about five minutes ahead of Hollywood.

When you enter the holding room for the simulator, try to maneuver next to the door to get a seat in the front of the car. (Some visitors find the small waiting room a bit confining; you can ask the attendant to leave the door open if you feel it necessary. Trust us: A much more intense experience is coming.)

As you wait to board, pay attention to the short movie about the essentials of time-travel safety; we enjoyed watching crash dummies Fender and Bender at work. When you feel a rumble beneath your feet, you'll know your car has arrived.

The preshow film and the movie shown in the ride itself were made specially for the simulator. Doc Brown (Christopher Lloyd) and Biff Tannen (Thomas Wilson) make special appearances, but Marty McFly (Michael J. Fox) has missed his date with destiny.

The director of the film used in the Back to the Future ride is renowned movie special effects designer Douglas Trumbull, who created special effects for hits including *2001: A Space Odyssey* and *Close Encounters of the Third Kind.* The four-minute, 70-mm movie portion of the ride took two years to make and cost as much as a feature film. Elaborate hand-painted miniatures were created for the filming.

The glass case in the preflight waiting rooms includes some juicy details for fans of the film. The cabinets include communication devices such as telepathic projectors, a multilingual translator, and a telekinetic projector; there are also emergency supplies, including first aid, travel rations, and dog biscuits. You'll also find hoverboards being energized in case they are needed.

The DeLoreans themselves rise about 8 feet out of their garages at the start of the movie. When in the air, four actuators—three for vertical movement and one for fore-and-aft movement—drive the car. Although it may feel as if your car is soaring and dropping hundreds of feet, the entire range of movement for the vehicle is about 2 feet.

To give the feeling of traveling through space, the cars are surrounded by a fog made from liquid nitrogen.

▓MUST-SEE▓ *WATERWORLD—A LIVE SEA WAR SPECTACULAR*

A seaplane crashes through a wall of jagged steel, exploding straight at terrified onlookers. Underwater warriors rise from the sea to battle invaders on jet skis. A fiery figure falls 50 feet, turning a lagoon into a blazing inferno.

And it's all presented live at Universal's *Waterworld* stunt show, based on the spectacular but flawed movie of the same name. We don't have to worry about the movie, though: We can enjoy the spectacular live stunt show they've made here, with some sixty stunts and special effects and water vehicles including jet skis, motorboats, and airboats. Don't pay much attention to the corny script; it only gets in the way of the stunts and pyrotechnics.

Visitors pass through a collection of some of the movie props into another century after the polar cap has melted and turned planet Earth into Waterworld. They'll find themselves seated with a view of the atoll, a floating island of boats, barges, driftwood, and debris; it's a dangerous day to pay a visit. Roving pirates of the future are swarming on the atoll, led by the Hellfire Gunboat.

Alarms sound. Nets drop. Flares explode in the sky. And high-pressure water cannons aimed at slaloming hovercraft and jet skis blast past the audience. A dive-bomber makes a low-level run, tearing off a chunk of the wall and showering the visitors with salt spray. Avoid the green-painted "wet seats" unless you are looking for a free shower with your clothes on. Special effects in the show include a submerged catapult that slingshots a jet skier from beneath the water and onto the watery stage.

Above it all, the Legendary Mariner and Deacon—the leader of the cutthroat pirates—struggle for the fate of the future in hand-to-hand combat that climaxes in a death-defying plunge and an explosive firestorm that destroys the set . . . at least until the next performance.

The 2,800-seat stadium eats up lines pretty quickly, and at busy times of the year there are as many as eight performances a day. Lines are at their maximum by midday; head for the show early or late to avoid the crowds. And be aware that the complex special effects and outside forces such as high winds can sometimes cause cancellation of some of the stunts; on one of our visits, the spectacular seaplane never got off the ground.

▓MUST-SEE▓ *THE WILD WILD WILD WEST STUNT SHOW*

Yee-ha! This is a very silly, very entertaining live show with some spectacular stunts, bad jokes, and enough gunfire and explosions to rattle *Fear Factor* next door. The storyline goes something like this: The professional stunt coordinator rides onto the set aboard his trusty steed to introduce a demonstration of western skills only to find that his cast of cowboys has been kidnapped by Ma

Hopper and her mean and ugly sons. The Hopper family proceeds to wreak havoc with guns, dynamite, and gross and dumb jokes, culminating in a shoot-out that literally brings down the house.

The twenty-minute show is well worth a visit. Parents be warned: The explosions and gunfire may upset young visitors.

FEAR FACTOR LIVE

Are you ready to pay $50 for the privilege of eating worms, sticking your head in a tub of scorpions, or diving off a helicopter into a 3-foot-wide tub of grape Jell-O? Me neither.

Volunteers at the new *Fear Factor Live* show at Universal Studios will be spared from *some* of the most frightening or disgusting stunts from the successful television reality show, but there should be more than enough ee-yoos and aahs to satisfy the viewers in the audience. The show, which replaces the *Spider-Man Rocks!* show, is the first major crossover resulting from the purchase of Universal Studios by GE, which also owns NBC, where the television show is a major factor.

In each show park guests will compete against each other in a progression of extreme stunts. The stunts were developed with help from *Fear Factor*'s creators and are designed to test the physical and emotional limits of each contestant. Members of the audience can pitch in by blasting contestants with water and air and controlling obstacles on stage. In addition, audience members can spin the "Wheel of Fear" and confront their own phobias.

Participants will take part in a series of progressively extreme stunts, guided by a host who will reinforce the complexity and risks associated with the stunts performed in the attraction. Just like the television show, the host will begin the show with a disclaimer: "The stunts you are about to see were designed and supervised by trained professionals. They are extremely dangerous and should never be attempted by anyone, anywhere, anytime." Except right here in a Universal Studios theme park, I guess.

Outside of the theater will be a casting call booth where guests will be invited to audition to take part in the show. Each selected contestant will be videotaped to later air during their performance.

Employing the same technology utilized in "live" television broadcasts, the videotaped highlights will be transmitted electronically to an elaborate *Fear Factor Live* editing booth located within the attraction. The footage will be edited and readied for close-circuit broadcast during each contestant's performance.

Each performance will involve as many as eighteen volunteers, and each show will be different because of the varying mix of participants. The heart of the show involves three extreme stunts; at the completion of each, two participants will exit via the "walk of shame" until one winner remains.

Among the stunts planned for the show:

■ **The Endurance Hang.** Six contestants stand, harnessed atop horizontal trusses 30 feet in the air. A small platform protrudes at their feet and a thin trapeze-like bar suspended by two cables hangs before them. At the proper moment, the platform falls from beneath them and the six contestants attempt to hang on as long as possible. (Just to make it interesting, while they are hanging there, two children from the audience will have the chance to try to distract the contestants by blasting them with "air cannons" that send out pulses of offensive odors.)

■ **The Eel Tank Relay.** Hanging from an overhead bolt, four contestants dangle in shackles inches above the ground. In this multitask stunt, the contestants must free themselves from the shackles and sprint across a giant spinning turntable until they reach the tank of slithering eels. A collection of signature yellow *Fear Factor* flags lie beneath the eels. The first two contestants to successfully plunge into the tank of eels, grab and secure the flags to a designated pole suspended above the rotating turntable, and ingest an unusual mixture of blended ingredients—a secret *Fear Factor Live* smoothie—move to the final challenge.

■ **Shock 'n' Awe.** In a setting reminiscent of Frankenstein's laboratory, the two final contestants are lowered onto tables and outfitted with electrical wire contraptions. With their arms extended in front of them, the contestants are directed to rotate spinning wheels located on either side of the tables. The faster the wheels spin the more electricity they generate; the first contestant to release the spinning wheel is eliminated; the loser is launched backward via an elaborate reverse bungee pull which ignites a pyrotechnical explosion. Huge electrical sparks splash across the stage . . . and into the audience.

Just to keep things moving, while the contestants on stage are preparing for their big stunts, members of the audience (mostly kids) will get to take part in smaller excitements. Some may include:

■ **You Are What You Eat!** Entomophagy (the art of eating insects) is practiced worldwide, delivering a delicious high-protein dinner. All of the delicacies served in *Fear Factor Live* are FDA approved. Two opposing teams of young volunteers will compete for the honor of devouring the most chocolate-covered insects.

■ **The Desert Hat Challenge.** The lucky volunteer sits on stage with a large Plexiglas box carefully placed on his or her head. The goal: Keep inside the box after it is filled with a load of emperor scorpions. (The emperor scorpion is the largest of all known scorpions with some giants reaching up to 8 inches in length and weighing over two ounces. Emperor scorpions are not deadly, though their sting could be painful.)

Fear Factor Live will be produced similar to a live broadcast, with eight fixed cameras strategically positioned throughout the attraction and accompanied by several roving cameras. Technicians will capture action as it occurs and feed it back to an elaborate editing suite, where the footage will be cut and broadcast onto a pair of ten-foot-tall screens.

Each thirty-minute show will accommodate as many as 1,500 guests. A similar show was opened at Universal Studios Florida, replacing the *Wild Wild Wild West Show.*

■ FIEVEL'S PLAYLAND

It's a small outdoor playground where the kids can burn off a bit of energy on some interesting props and slides related to the cartoon feature *An American Tail.*

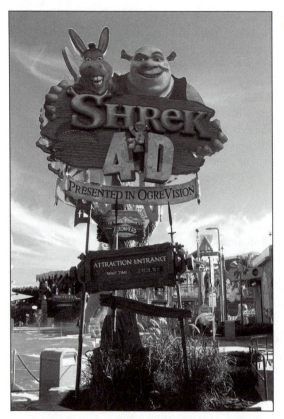

Shrek 4-D . . . in OgreVision. *Photo by Corey Sandler*

MUST-SEE *SHREK 4-D*

A 4-D presentation . . . in OgreVision, no less, that continues the fractured fable of Shrek.

Shrek 4-D marks the first time an Oscar-winning animated film has been developed as a film-based theme park attraction. The film also debuted at Universal Studios Orlando.

The show is presented in dual-chambered theatrical settings designed to introduce OgreVision sensory immersion, including images, sound, a bit of touch, a smidgen of smell, and a few well-timed splashes.

The fifteen-minute animated film includes a spectacular swamp-dwelling, 700-pound ogre with poor hygiene, picking up the tale where the Academy Award–winning Best Animated Feature *Shrek* left off. The experience reveals the tale of Shrek's honeymoon with the beautiful Princess Fiona and their persistent companion, Donkey.

Shrek 4-D bridges the story between Shrek and the recently released DreamWorks Pictures sequel, *Shrek II*.

Guests are ushered into a forbidding preshow chamber based on the dark and dank recesses of Lord Farquaad's dreaded dungeons. Via multiple screens, they are greeted by the vertically challenged Farquaad himself, who, in his first posthumous appearance, informs guests of his ghostly scheme to haunt Shrek, Fiona, and their donkey companion.

Once settled in specially designed seats in the main auditorium, guests don OgreVision glasses to be transported to the fairy-tale realm of Duloc, as the screen and the theater itself come alive with the tale of the Shrek–Fiona honeymoon adventure. Surprising sensory elements help propel the narrative experience through seats equipped with tactile transducers, pneumatic air propulsion, and water spray nodules capable of both vertical and horizontal motion.

You've got to listen carefully to catch all of the puns and wickedly bad jokes. Duloc is described as "the happiest totalitarian dictatorship on Earth. Well, the second-happiest," with a nod toward the house of the Mouse.

The opening greeting from the face in the mirror announces, "Welcome to Lord Farquaad's castle. Run for your lives!" And before you are ushered into the theater for the movie, you'll hear a recap of the original story: "Shrek saved the princess . . . and his ass."

Shrek 4-D marks the first animation to be created for a theme park attraction by PDI/DreamWorks, whose invention of the Fluid Animation System was recognized with a technical achievement Oscar by the Academy of Motion Picture Arts and Sciences. The addition of three-dimensional depth to the animation by PDI/DreamWorks and the creation of in-theater effects by attraction designers at Universal Creative resulted in the introduction of the OgreVision multisensory experience.

In both Hollywood and Orlando, the Shrek film is housed in its own castle-like building with an hourly capacity of as many as 2,400 guests.

The original film was based on the children's book by William Steig. In the film, an ornery ogre named Shrek (voiced by Mike Myers) finds his solitude shattered by an invasion of annoying fairy-tale characters. Suddenly there are blind mice in his food; a big, bad wolf in his bed; and three little homeless pigs in his personal space. All of them have been banished from their kingdom by the evil Lord Farquaad (John Lithgow).

Shrek strikes a deal with Farquaad to rescue the beautiful princess Fiona (Cameron Diaz) to be Farquaad's bride and get the unexpected visitors out of his hair. He sets off with the Donkey (Eddie Murphy) on a great expedition that reveals a deep, dark, and twisted secret.

NICKELODEON BLAST ZONE

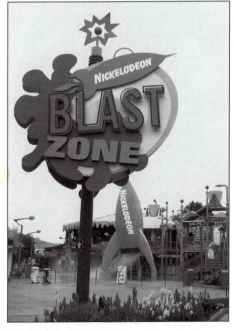

Children have a place of their own in the Nickelodeon Blast Zone, an adventure zone that includes an elaborate water play area based on programs such as *SpongeBob SquarePants;* "Wild Thornberry's Adventure Temple," a ball play area with more than twenty-five thousand molten lava–colored foam balls; "Nick Jr.'s Backyard" for children under the age of six to slide, crawl, and climb through; *Blue's Clues; Little Bear;* and *Dora the Explorer.*

Also in the zone is *Animal Planet Live!*

The Nickelodeon Blast Zone. *Photo by Corey Sandler*

╪MUST-SEE╪ *ANIMAL PLANET LIVE!*

Animal stars, including more than a few rescued from animal shelters, take center stage at *Animal Planet Live!* The show brings Animal Planet television network's favorite shows together with behind-the-scenes movie magic.

Animal Planet Live! features special video clips from such popular Animal Planet television shows as *Emergency Vets, The Planet's Funniest Animals, The Jeff Corwin Experience, Wild on the Set,* and the network's lively animal sports programs.

Many of the animal stars featured in *Animal Planet Live!* have credits in film and television production. Almost all of the dogs and cats were rescued from shelters and pounds.

BACKLOT TRAM TOUR

Sit down and relax for a guided motorized tour through a large part of the famed backlot of Universal Studios, a place where many of the most celebrated movies and television shows of all time have been made.

Universal Studios Hollywood is unusual among theme parks in that the audience is delivered by chauffeured tram to the attractions for about half of its exhibits. There's just a single line to wait in; after you are loaded onto the large tram you'll be driven to and through sets and props for movies and TV shows, including *Back to the Future; Murder, She Wrote; Psycho; Jurassic Park;* and much more. And you'll go right into exciting re-creations of thrillers, such as *Earthquake* and *Jaws.*

The tram vehicles include LCD screens that display scenes from movies and television shows along with the occasional outtake. Tour guides, many of whom are wannabe actors, get to mug for a camera that displays their faces through the cars, too. The guides get to select from a library of more than a hundred video clips to match their patter and deal with any detours along the way.

The latest wrinkle allows guides to punch up pictures of passengers way back in the bus getting splashed, flamed, and frightened; if you don't recognize the guests, remember that you are in a movie studio: The scenes were filmed for your entertainment.

On a recent visit, as the tram crossed Court House Square, the LCDs showed the set as it was used in the *Back to the Future* series. At Spartacus Square the screens showed scenes from the movie *Spartacus.*

The loading queue for the tram is located down the hill at the back of the main Entertainment Center level of the park. Lines are shortest when the park first opens, and usually again in early afternoon; the last tram departs about two hours before the park closes. The length of each tour can vary depending on how busy the park is and shooting schedules that may affect parts of the backlot, but each tour generally lasts about sixty to ninety minutes.

When you load onto the tram, try to avoid sitting just behind the motor or you will end up breathing a fair amount of diesel fumes on your journey. Despite

A set from the film *War of the Worlds* along the tram route. *Photo by Corey Sandler*

what the guide might say, don't worry about a "wet" or "dry" side of the tram; not much water makes its way into the tram on the tour. For the record, the right side (facing forward) of the tram is closest to the cascading waters in the *Earthquake* set, and the left side is nearest the flash flood in the backlot.

Cameras are welcome throughout the tour; there are no restroom stops, and there is no way to get off the tram short of an emergency.

The introduction to the tour is from director and actor Ron Howard. As you descend from the loading area to the soundstages below, the tram passes a time-line of some of the 8,000 movies made on the Universal lot.

The order of the tour as presented here may be different when you visit the park because of television or movie production schedules; sometimes entire sections have to be skipped because the cameras are rolling on the lot.

Front Lot Soundstages

Depending on shooting schedules and the time of year the backlot tour may give you a brief glimpse of part of the front lot—the soundstages. If you're lucky you may see a television or movie star strolling by, or perhaps grab a quick glimpse inside the open door of one of the large soundstages there; otherwise, you're going to see a lot of blank walls.

Universal's facilities are in almost continuous use for productions of television series and movies. Stage 27 housed Houston Mission Control for *Apollo 13*. Stage 28 holds the historic Paris Opera House set used in the classic *Phantom of the Opera* and many other films since. The Sultan of Strangeness Michael Jackson (and sister Janet Jackson) installed a flying saucer in Stage 24 for the "Scream" music video.

A small-scale model used in the film *U-571* floats on a backlot pond. *Photo by Corey Sandler*

Colonial Street

Where else but in Hollywood could you expect to find a neighborhood that includes the homes of Beaver Cleaver, Herman Munster, Jessica Fletcher, the Hardy Boys, Elvis Presley, Casper, Ronald Reagan in *Bedtime for Bonzo,* Buffy in *Buffy the Vampire Slayer,* and many more? And where else would you find *The Best Little Whorehouse in Texas* at the end of the street? (The whorehouse was created within Stage 12, and the movie was filmed there; the set was later moved to its outdoor location.)

The official address is Colonial Street, and your tour guide will point out such sites as Frank and Joe Hardy's house from the *Hardy Boys* TV mysteries of the 1970s. Next-door to the Hardys is the home occupied by James Garner and Doris Day in *The Thrill of It All.* Just a bit farther down the road is an old Colonial mansion that, among other roles, served as the sanitarium in James Stewart's beloved film *Harvey.*

At 1313 Mockingbird Lane is the home of the Munsters, nearby to one of Faber College's sorority houses from *Animal House.*

Then we're on to a portion of the town of Cabot Cove, made famous in the *Murder, She Wrote* series, one of Universal's most successful television projects.

> ## AAA S.O.S.
>
> Card-carrying members of AAA can receive a 10 percent discount at most shops within Universal Studios.

The brick building on the street has served as both the Cabot Cove Savings Bank and the Cabot Cove Town Hall; back in the '60s it was where the Beaver went to school in *Leave It to Beaver.*

Many of the homes on Colonial Street were used in the film *The Burbs* starring Tom Hanks and Carrie Fisher. And then the same street became Memphis, Tennessee, for an episode of *Quantum Leap* in which Sam leaps into the body of the King himself, Elvis Presley. Yet another remake made it one of the homes of Casper the Friendly Ghost.

Industrial Street

Many of the homes in this area are actual residences that were purchased for as little as $1.00 each and moved to the backlot to be used in the classic film *To Kill a Mockingbird,* starring Gregory Peck and a then-unknown actor named Robert Duvall.

Old Mexico

In addition to standing in for some scenes in *Murder, She Wrote,* this area has been used for many old films and contemporary television shows. It was home of many scenes in the comedy *Three Amigos* with Steve Martin, Martin Short, and Chevy Chase.

Old West

Across the border from Mexico is the oldest section of the Universal Studios backlot, a filmmaker's re-creation of the Old West also known as Six Points, Texas. Many of the buildings, which appear to be made of brick or stone, are actually constructed of wood, chicken wire, and modern products such as foam rubber or fiberglass.

Note that some of the doors seem out of scale. Small doors were used to make small actors appear bigger and more threatening than they really were; oversize doors shrank tall cowboys and cowgirls down to size for the camera.

Old West was the home of stars including John Wayne, Tom Mix, Hoot Gibson, Audie Murphy, Ken Maynard, and others. Among the television series made there was *Wagon Train.* In more recent times, it was used in the United Artists' film *Wild Bill.*

At its height, there could be six films under way on the six streets at the same time; since the movies were silent, all the directors had to worry about was the possibility of an actor making a wrong turn from one film to another.

Old West's basic setup includes a hotel, bar, bank, and sheriff's office. A bad guy could stroll into town, get a drink, spend the night, rob the bank, and end up in jail.

When It Rains . . .

. . . you will get wet. Most of Universal Studios Hollywood is outdoors. The Backlot Tram is exposed to the elements, and most of the shows are uncovered.

Flimsy plastic rain jackets appear magically at shops, priced at about $6.95; umbrellas are priced about $16.95. If the skies are at all threatening, I'd suggest you make a stop at a discount store outside the park and pick up ponchos or umbrellas to bring with you. Some of the shows may be canceled because of rain.

If the skies really open—something that doesn't happen that often in Southern California—the park may issue guests a "rain check" that allows them to return for free on another day.

Prop Storage

A prop on a movie set is just about anything that isn't nailed down. Some are small and some are huge; some are ordinary and some are one of a kind. More than a million of the studio's props are kept in the property warehouse at the back corner of the backlot, but many of the larger pieces are scattered outdoors. The tram tour does not enter the prop building; guests on the more expensive VIP Tour, though, are allowed an inside peek.

Along the course of the tram tour you'll pass by bits and pieces of the past and future from *Back to the Future,* fossils and props from *Jurassic Park,* and various vehicles from dozens of familiar movies.

In the middle of the props area is a tiny lake—more of a pond, really. This body of water served as the entire Pacific Ocean every week in the popular TV series *McHale's Navy.* The pond was also used for some of the shooting in the 1977 film *Midway.* Scale models of battleships and cruisers made war on the pond; some of the vessels were painted in Allied colors on one side and Japanese colors on the other so that they could serve double duty in the war.

After you exit Sound Stage 50 you'll have another view of the pond. It was also used as the home of *The Creature from the Black Lagoon* in 1954.

You will see a large metal tank that has been used in many underwater scenes including the original *Jaws.* The actors and props are placed within the tank while cameras and crew are outside, looking in through windows.

You may see some of the old wagons used in *Wagon Train* and *The Virginian.* Nearby on one of my trips was a gigantic football helmet and a huge shopping cart, both from the film *The Incredible Shrinking Woman* with Lily Tomlin. Another time the tram caught a glimpse of a chariot from *The Ten Commandments.*

Psycho House

Is there any house more famous than Mrs. Bates's pleasant Victorian up on the hill over the Bates Motel?

You'll approach the house alongside the small swamp used by Norman Bates (Anthony Perkins) to bury the car of Marion Crane (Janet Leigh) in the 1960 Alfred Hitchcock classic, *Psycho.* Later on in the tour you'll approach Psycho House a bit closer.

The house was built to three-quarter scale, which helped make Anthony Perkins look taller and more menacing as he posed in the foreground. When the house itself was pictured, it was always shot from below to look larger.

The house is a shell with a complete outside but nothing within except for the beams that help keep it standing; well, okay, some wag did stick a dummy that looks like Norman's mom in the second floor window. It is a dummy, right? Indoor scenes were all shot on a soundstage.

Nearby is the Bates Motel, more or less as it was created for the original film. The archway entrance in front did not appear in any of the *Psycho* films but was added in 1986 for a television movie of the week called *Bates Motel.*

Spartacus Square

Parts of the classic film *Spartacus* were filmed in the section that is named in its honor; the same section was again used as ancient Rome in the great Mel Brooks spoof, *History of the World, Part I.*

Little Europe

This section of old buildings stood in for Greece in Brooks' *History of the World.* More recently it was Pamplona, Spain, for the opening sequence of *City Slickers.* Way back when, Little Europe was home of the classic antiwar film, *All Quiet on the Western Front.*

When Brenda and Donna left *Beverly Hills 90210* to go to France, they actually went just across town to Little Europe. Other television shows that have used this area include *Sea Quest DSV* and, of course, the ubiquitous *Murder, She Wrote.* The quirky television series *Moonlighting* filmed its takeoff of *The Taming of the Shrew* here.

Real film history can be glimpsed in the Court of Miracles, built in 1919 for the film *The Miracle Man* starring Lon Chaney. But it is most famous for the monster movie classics that followed, including Chaney in 1923's *The Hunchback of Notre Dame* and again in 1925's *The Phantom of the Opera.* In 1930, Bela Lugosi was *Dracula* here; later classics included *Frankenstein, The Bride of Frankenstein, The Son of Frankenstein, Abbott and Costello Meet Frankenstein, The Wolf Man, The Mummy,* and *The Invisible Man.*

The same area was used more recently for some of the scenes in Touchstone's *Pirates of the Caribbean.* On a visit in 2004, filming was under way in the European streets, re-created as the capital city of Genovia for *Princess Diaries 2.*

▓▓▓▓▓ *MUST-SEE* ▓▓▓▓▓ Earthquake

Quiet, now: You've got a green light to drive right into Stage 50, a real working soundstage. Well, it's sort of a real stage (and still in occasional use for special projects), but it's mostly given over to a spectacular re-creation of a scene from the 1974 disaster epic, *Earthquake.*

Bigger . . . (and certainly better) than the real thing, Universal's Earthquake unleashes a tremendous temblor beneath your feet.

The earth falls out from under tramloads of visitors, trapping them in an underground subway station with sparking wires, out-of-control trains, and even a fuel truck that crashes through the ceiling and onto the tracks. Just to cap it all, water pipes let loose and trigger a 15-foot-tall wall of water in a 60,000-gallon flood.

Every detail of the simulation was based on the re-creation of real earthquakes. The soundstage was built with concrete pilings sunk 25 feet into the ground below the tram to withstand 600,000 pounds of force more than 200 times a day. The ceiling slab that falls into the subway station weighs 11,000 pounds.

The simulated earthquake is the equivalent of an 8.3 event on the Richter scale, which is the same level as the huge temblor that destroyed San Francisco in 1906. By comparison, the 1971 Sylmar quake measured 6.6, and the 1985 Mexico City disaster was an 8.1 event.

The simulation lasts about two-and-a-half minutes. After your tram exits the soundstage, the entire set resets in fifteen seconds.

If it makes you feel better, engineers say the soundstage is built to withstand a genuine 8.3 quake, making it one of the safest places in the world to be during a real earthquake.

The *Earthquake* set was used for a scene in *Beverly Hills Cop 3,* which took place in a fictional amusement park. Just outside the *Earthquake* set is Stage 747, which includes full-size mock-ups of airplane interiors used regularly as sets in films and television shows.

Courthouse Square

The year is 1955. The date is November 5. And the time is 10:03 P.M. Down this road—with the aid of a great deal of movie magic—Marty McFly drove Doc Brown's time-traveling DeLorean at precisely eighty-eight miles per hour hoping to catch the lightning bolt just in time to get back to 1985.

You'll see the Hill Valley courthouse more or less as it appeared in the film *Back to the Future* and its sequel, *Back to the Future 2.* It has also been used in many other films during the years.

MUST-SEE King Kong

One of the most realistic sets at Universal Studios Hollywood can be found within a soundstage just past the Courthouse Square. It's a re-creation of lower Manhattan . . . and it smells suspiciously like bananas.

Your tram driver will take you and other passengers directly into an attraction that celebrates the spectacular 1976 version of the classic film, *King Kong.* The remake starred Jeff Bridges, Charles Grodin, and an unknown actress by the name of Jessica Lange, who went on to be an Academy Award winner.

King Kong rises out of the East River, towers over the Brooklyn Bridge, rips down power lines, attacks a hovering news helicopter, and then even tries to throw Universal's trams into the river as they move across the bridge. Kong comes within a few feet of the tram—so close you can smell the bananas on his breath.

Computers control twenty-nine facial movements from nodding his head to curling his lip to showing his vicious teeth. (Movements are controlled mostly by pneumatic air pipes.)

The $6.5 million leading man really throws his weight around. He's seven tons of fur, steel, and computers, and stands 30 feet high.

New York Street

Welcome to an all-purpose downtown home of scenes from *Columbo, McCloud, McMillan and Wife, Kojak, Ironside, The Rockford Files, The Streets of San Francisco, The Mod Squad, Baretta, The Night Stalker,* and many more.

In 1969 these streets were walked by Elvis himself for his final film role in *A Change of Habit,* also starring Mary Tyler Moore. Four years later New York

Street became Chicago in the Academy Award–winning film *The Sting* starring Robert Redford and Paul Newman.

In 1977 New York Street was used to film scenes from the Warner Bros. classic movie *Dirty Harry* starring Clint Eastwood. A few years later it was turned into modern-day Chicago for *The Blues Brothers,* which starred John Belushi and Dan Aykroyd. It became London for *Wayne's World 2* and then transformed back to 1930s New York in many scenes from *The Shadow* starring Alec Baldwin.

Nearly all of New York Street was destroyed in a fire in 1991, but the street in the Big Apple was re-created.

On one of my visits a few years back many of the buildings were draped with fake icicles for a scene depicting the aftermath of a visit by Mr. Freeze in the movie *Batman & Robin.* Some of the brownstones appeared in *Bruce Almighty,* and the streets stood in for Boston for some scenes in the TV series *Ally McBeal.*

Collapsing Bridge

A bridge somewhat like this one at Universal was built in 1915 for a silent film. More recently it was used in television shows, including *The Six Million Dollar Man* and *Quantum Leap.*

In the *Bionic Woman* series star Lindsay Wagner was shown jumping up from the water to the bridge. Actually a stuntwoman jumped backward from the bridge to the water and the film was reversed. If you ever see the scene, note the TV director's goof: Her hair was not tied down and defies the law of gravity as she seems to fly upward.

These days the bridge has been fixed up so that it falls down . . . as the tram passes over the top. Don't worry, though: Most passengers survive to make it to the souvenir shops.

Vehicles

The "boneyard" of the backlot includes dozens of vehicles from movies and television shows. You may spot one of several red Ferraris used in the television series *Magnum P.I.* starring Tom Selleck. Nearby on a recent visit was the much less impressive Mousemobile driven by John Candy as Uncle Buck in the film of the same name.

You may also see some small vehicles from *The Little Rascals,* DeLoreans used in *Back to the Future,* and some retro-military gear from *Waterworld.*

Bedrock and Jurassic Park

Still standing on both sides of the road is a piece of Bedrock, as it was constructed for *The Flintstones.* You'll see Barney and Betty Rubble's house and their car. Check out the welcoming sign with the town's claim to fame: BEDROCK: FIRST WITH FIRE.

Parked alongside the road just past Bedrock is the jeep that was nearly torn to pieces by a T. rex in *Jurassic Park.* Most of that film was filmed inside soundstages at Universal Studios Hollywood with just a small amount of exterior footage taken in Hawaii.

Flash Flood

The road that leads down toward Old Mexico was covered with dirt to become the Appian Way for *Spartacus* in 1960; hundreds of Roman soldiers marched right into ancient Rome.

Today's tour-goers, though, are given a watery treat as movie special effects are used to simulate a raging flash flood that roars down the hill on the left side of the tram. Some 10,000 gallons of water drop down from the top of the hill; it's all pumped back up for the next visitors. The flash flood scene was used in the film *Fletch Lives* in 1989.

MUST-SEE Jaws

Welcome to Amity Island, the reconstructed scene of some of the action from the classic 1975 fish-food movie, *Jaws*. Jaws Lake not only serves as the backdrop for the shark, but also stood in for Cabot Cove, Maine, in exterior scenes from (yes, again) *Murder, She Wrote.* The hairpin turn that leads past the lake is where Jessica Fletcher rode her bicycle every week at the beginning of the show. The pond setting was first built for use in *The Great Race,* starring Jack Lemmon, Tony Curtis, and Natalie Wood.

Past the lake you come to the small home where Lansbury/Fletcher did her gardening. The same house has also been used in other productions including *Quantum Leap* and the mostly forgotten film *Shout* starring John Travolta.

Nearby is a light-colored house with green trim that was the home of Ben Matlock from the *Matlock* TV series. Next to Matlock's house is the home used in the classic Vincent Price horror film, *The House of the Seven Gables.*

Some of the scenes from the *Casper* movie were also shot near the lake.

Jaws emerges from the lake to menace guests on a backlot tram. *Photo by Corey Sandler*

Wilderness

As your tram begins to approach the wilderness area, you will come to a large log cabin that was used in *The Great Outdoors* and then later as an important element of the Paramount comedy *Naked Gun 33⅓*.

The wilderness, covered with fake snow, became the Antarctic for the remake of *The Thing*. A large painted backdrop behind a small lake was used for the splashdown scene for 1995's *Apollo 13*. It was also used as the blue wall that marked the boundary of Jim Carrey's world in *The Truman Show*.

Just past the lake, your tram enters a tunnel . . . and into Gomorrah, a dizzying salute to the film *Scorpion King*. Over the years the same tunnel stood in for the Tomb of Imhotep from *The Mummy,* before then as a fiery hell for *Dante's Peak,* and before then as an icy avalanche zone. Whatever, if you're prone to dizziness, take the opportunity to close your eyes and take a short nap.

The tunnel was used in a scene from *The Six Million Dollar Man,* and according to studio legend, star Lee Majors became so dizzy he had a major problem staying upright long enough to get through his part.

STUDIO CENTER

The Studio Center is located down the hill from the Entertainment Center at the bottom of a series of three long escalators, a 200-foot drop down a 1,200-foot-long cascade of moving stairs.

The long trek down to the center is a good reason why you'll want to plan your day at Universal. It is not a minor thing to go from one area to another at the park. (There is, by the way, alternate shuttle transportation between the upper and lower parts of Universal Studios for disabled guests.)

MUST-SEE REVENGE OF THE MUMMY

If an encounter with the Mummy is not scary enough for you, how about meeting up with the creepy guy while zooming forward and backward and on your side . . . in near-total darkness. There's a bit of weightlessness, some 3.5 gs. Oh yes, there's also a flaming ceiling.

You'll enter the Museum of Antiquities, which is actually the set of yet another Mummy movie. Strolling among the cameras, klieg lights, and costumes you'll see some snippets of a behind-the-scenes documentary being made about the new movie. Wonder of wonders: It seems that strange things have been happening on the set. Some members of the crew think the place may even be . . . cursed. It seems possible that this movie set may actually be a real archaeological dig, and that perhaps there's been a bit of extracurricular grave robbing.

Be that as it may, we're all given the extraordinary opportunity to take a little train ride into the Mummy's catacombs. The vehicles are industrial carts used by the archaeologists to bring supplies into the dig, and take discoveries out. The train starts out slowly, like a dark ride.

It won't take much of a ride before you realize that things really are a bit askew: Parked off to the side is another train, this one filled with tourists just like you, wearing theme park T-shirts, holding cameras . . . and quite mummified. This is not a good thing.

One of the mummies manages to croak out a warning, but then the chief mummy appears with the ultimate threat: He'll be happy to take our souls. The train moves on to a dark room and suddenly animatronic warriors burst out of the walls toward the train. Huge flames erupt from an altar, and the ceiling is filled with fire. As the train rolls forward toward a descending stone door, it suddenly drops below.

That may sound like a successful escape, but actually the train has now arrived at what is obviously a dead end. After that sinks in for a moment, the train suddenly is launched backward and uphill into a roller coaster ride through the interior of the tomb. The track never goes completely upside down, but there are turns banked as much as eighty degrees and a few very sharp drops in total darkness.

Along the way, we'll see computer-generated special effects and creatures projected onto fog and mist and hear a sound track intense enough to wake the dead.

The Mummy is a very successful merger of a scary dark ride, cinematic special effects, and a state-of-the-art roller coaster using linear induction motors, which allow smooth and rapid launches of the trains in either direction and varying speeds. The ride builds and improves on other fabulous rides like Indiana Jones at Disneyland and its cousin Dinosaur at Disney's Animal Kingdom, Journey to Atlantis at SeaWorld Orlando, and one of the archetypes for indoor thrill rides, Space Mountain at Disneyland and Walt Disney World.

The ride, ten years in research and development, debuted simultaneously at both Universal Studios Hollywood and Universal Orlando.

"This is in many ways the next sequel of *The Mummy*," said director Stephen Sommers, who consulted with Universal on the ride.

The ride launch system uses the same technology employed in futuristic magnetic levitation trains, thrusting riders forward, backward, and forward again. Utilizing engineering techniques gleaned from the Mars robotic range vehicle, the attraction includes a skeleton warrior who literally leaps into the passenger vehicle to defend his netherworld tomb.

Universal's ride producers traveled to Egypt and the British Museum in London to make the ride's shadowy interior environment more realistic. Details range from glistening golden amulets to dusty canopic jars containing the grisly remains of the haunted, long-deceased royalty portrayed in the ride.

The ride replaced the "superannuated" E.T. Adventure in Hollywood.

⌗⌗⌗⌗ MUST-SEE ⌗⌗⌗⌗ JURASSIC PARK—THE RIDE

A spectacular ride millions of years (and $100 million) in the making: Jurassic Park—The Ride is the big splash of the lower level of the park.

The attraction, one of the most expensive and technologically advanced theme park adventures ever created, fulfills Universal Studio's promise to allow visitors to "ride the movies," in this case Steven Spielberg's version of Michael Crichton's bestselling novel and one of the most popular motion pictures of all time, ancient and modern.

You'll enter through the 35-foot-tall wooden gates of Jurassic Park. As you wait your turn to board your exploration raft, you'll see a multimedia preshow presented on massive video walls. The film features John Hammond, founder and owner of Jurassic Park; as in the movie, Hammond is played by distinguished actor Sir Richard Attenborough.

The journey begins as a gentle exploration of Jurassic Park's dinosaur habitat. The rafts explore the misty fog banks, brilliantly colored foliage, and exotic vegetation of "herbivore country," home of the vegetarians of the dinosaur world. Not to worry, though: The swift velociraptors and the ferocious Tyrannosaurus rex are securely contained nearby in Carnivore Canyon behind a sparking 10,000-volt electrified fence.

The boats gently cruise through radiant Ultrasaur Lagoon with gentle waterfalls and clear tide pools. Just a finger away sits a gigantic 50-foot ultrasaurus cooling off at the water's edge. The boat is nudged by what seems to be a rock below the surface, but it turns out to be a surprised baby ultrasaurus, who eyes the riders curiously.

As the rafts glide out of the river two rambunctious psittacosauruses frolic nearby, splashing water across the boat's bow. Erupting geysers spew billows of white steam as the boat arrives at Stegosaur Pond, where mother and baby stegosauruses seem happy to have company. Small dinosaurs known as "compys" shriek their greetings.

Riding an increasingly swift current, the boat moves into Hadrosaur Cove. Suddenly the waters begin racing and the raft is driven dangerously off-course into Carnivore Canyon, very close to the velociraptor pen. And bad news: There's a jagged, gaping hole in the electrified fence. The vicious velociraptors are nowhere to be seen, and signs of danger surround guests on the raft as it continues to veer out of control and deeper into unknown territory. A wrecked land cruiser dangles perilously from a nearby guardrail.

An empty abandoned raft drifts by; suddenly a "spitter" rears his multicolored crown and bares his teeth in a sinister smile.

Jurassic Park's water pumping station is bedlam. Alarms blare as catwalks collapse and some of the station's pipes give way, spraying scalding water in the path of the raft. A pack of voracious raptors spring forward and begin to pursue the runaway raft.

And then . . . well, we're not going to spoil all of the scary fun except to say that sooner or later the rafts plunge into an 84-foot drop in total darkness,

The Park at Jurassic Park

The re-created world of Jurassic Park includes some spectacular greenery. There are some 353 palm trees of 11 species, including Sago, King, Queen, Kentia, and Canary Island Date. Gardeners put in 926 additional trees of 33 species, including Flame, Golden Rain, Orchid, Australian Tree Fern, Giant Bird of Paradise, and Dragon. Finally, there are 7,441 shrubs, plants, and 76 species of flowers, including star jasmine, breath of heaven, rattlesnake grass, tasmanian tree fern, shell ginger, mystery gardenia, sugar bush, bougainvillea, and giant burmese honeysuckle. Scattered about are 300 bamboo plants of 6 varieties.

A splash landing at Jurassic Park. *Photo by Corey Sandler*

splashing into the lagoon at speeds of nearly fifty miles per hour. (It's claimed to be the longest, fastest water plunge at any theme park.) To make things even more interesting, the drop includes a "vertical curve" (you might call it a bump) that makes riders feel that their boat is being lifted straight up before it nearly tips over and smashes to the lagoon below.

The ride technology includes some of the most advanced animatronic dinosaurs anywhere, using a new technique dubbed "compliant reactivity" to model the interaction of different parts of a body as it moves. Many of the dinosaurs are programmed to react to the presence of visitors, some attacking at speeds of up to 25 feet per second with the quickness of a striking rattlesnake.

Stars of the park include ultrasaurus, tall as a five-story building; the armor-plated 18-foot-tall stegosaurus, 40 feet long from nose to tail; and the relentlessly pursuing Tyrannosaurus rex.

The twenty-five-passenger boats are the largest amusement ride watercraft ever built; they are free-flowing, not on tracks. The boats are paced by computer to travel at least thirty seconds behind the boat ahead, propelled along by 1.4 million gallons of rushing water.

The sixteen boats can move about 3,000 visitors per hour through the park for the ride, which lasts about five-and-a-half minutes. That still won't be enough to eliminate long lines from midmorning through dinner; arrive early or late.

The minimum height to ride is 42 inches.

A restaurant, **Jurassic Cove Cafe,** and a retail shop, Jurassic Outfitters, are included in the compound. Look in the cement outside the restaurant for director Steven Spielberg's autograph and a special message to riders.

And I hope you've read down this far before riding: You can purchase inexpensive ponchos just outside the entrance to the ride. The front seats of the boats are usually the wettest.

The Starway escalators descend to the lower lot. *Photo by Corey Sandler*

⋮⋮⋮⋮ ᴹᵁˢᵀ⁻ˢᴱᴱ **BACKDRAFT**

A backdraft is a fire that has consumed all the oxygen in a room, leaving only superheated gas waiting for a fresh breath of air. *Backdraft* is also the name of a successful thriller by director Ron Howard, celebrated here in a spectacular demonstration.

You'll learn how the film included real blazes set in old warehouses in Chicago. Actor Scott Glenn tells about how flame-retardant underwear he wore in one important scene worked not quite long enough for comfort; he also exposes some of the secrets of the Ashmatic, a machine created for the movie that shot burning ash over the cast.

Backdraft includes a spectacular re-creation of some of the wildest scenes from the movie; in fact, the effects in this show are a lot more real than some of the movie magic seen in the film. As many as 200 times a day the Backdraft soundstage becomes a fiery furnace with ruptured fuel lines, superheated air, and scalding heat.

When you first enter the soundstage you'll watch a backdraft flame spinning wildly around the fictitious Nikolas Randall and Company chemical building. That is, of course, merely the overture: Suddenly there's a massive explosion of fuel drums, which in turn causes overhead pipes to burst and spew their flammable contents toward the audience. The flames become a firestorm, reaching more than 2,000° F. The soundstage was built as a completely fireproof building; a special invisible "air curtain" protects visitors from the flames that march toward them.

There's a control room behind a glass window at the back of the Backdraft room where a technician supervises the show for safety purposes. Abundant fire extinguishers and other safety equipment are also in the room. Construction of the building required special dispensation from the Hollywood Fire Department.

Lucy, I'm home!

The original "Lucy" show was unusual in that the creators worked with three or four permanent sets that stood side-by-side in the studio, avoiding the flimsy-looking sets typical of television shows at the time. The permanent setting also allowed for more advanced lighting, permitting cameras to move quickly from one area to another. All of the sets were painted in carefully chosen shades of gray to control the contrast of the finished black-and-white film.

■ LUCY: A TRIBUTE

If you are a fan of Lucille Ball and everyone around her, you'll be enthralled at this collection of photos, scripts, memorabilia, and a continuous showing of episodes from her television show. Among my personal favorites is Lucy as part of a barbershop quartet.

There is a diorama showing how the original television show was filmed in front of a live audience. The show was shot on 35-mm black-and-white film on one large set; episodes were edited and combined for the final show.

You'll see part of the script from *Mame*, which in 1974 marked Lucy's final return to the big screen, and a display of her five Emmy awards. There's also a Lucy trivia quiz including questions like, "What was the biggest laugh in Lucy history?"

Here's a hint: The answer involves Lucy, Ricky, a bunch of raw eggs, and a wild and romantic dance. You figure it out.

On display are photos of Lucille Ball's home on Roxbury Drive in Beverly Hills where she lived for thirty-five years. Next-door neighbors were the Jack Benny family, and the Jimmy Stewart family lived across the street. There's also a selection of home movies narrated by Luci Arnaz and a collection of stereoscopic slides of Lucy's family taken in the 1950s.

Desi Arnaz was born Desiderio Alberto Arnaz y de Acha III in Santiago, Cuba, in 1917. The son of a Cuban senator, he lived in great luxury until the Cuban revolution of 1933 when the family left the country. Arnaz worked at various jobs, including cleaning birdcages for 25 cents.

Eventually he got a job in a band and soon became one of the top band leaders in New York City. Signed to the lead in the New York City musical *Too Many Girls,* he played a Latin football player. When he went to Hollywood to play his role in the movie version of the musical, he met the studio ingenue Lucille Ball, and in late 1940 they began a bicoastal marriage.

After World War II, looking for a way to work together in Los Angeles, Lucy and Desi hired the writers of Lucy's radio show "My Favorite Husband" and produced a pilot for *I Love Lucy.* Their company, Desilu Productions, became the largest television and film production company in Hollywood. Arnaz died in 1986. Lucy passed on in 1989.

■ SPECIAL EFFECTS STAGES

At Stage One, visitors are introduced to a "virtual studio" showcasing green-screen compositing techniques and computer-generated imagery (CGI) such as was used to bring the *Jurassic Park* dinosaurs back from extinction and to animate *The Mummy.* Two adult volunteers step into the movies, playing with a gigantic pussycat projected through a window, and sitting down to dinner with *The Nutty Professor.*

Stage Two showcases Universal's historical "creature factory." Guests see some rare, behind-the-scenes footage of special effects pioneered by makeup artist Jack Pierce for *Frankenstein, Dracula,* and the original *Mummy*. There's also an introduction to the elaborate makeup techniques used to transform Jim Carrey into the Grinch, a process that took as many as four hours per day.

You'll learn some of the insider secrets of "stage blood." In black-and-white movies, like *Psycho,* Janet Leigh bled Hershey's chocolate syrup. For color films, technicians worked with colored corn syrup; some modern special effects departments use colored dish detergent, which has the added advantage of being easy to clean up.

Visitors also meet Fluffy, a "robotic" creature controlled by an audience volunteer—or so it seems. The attraction concludes at Stage Three, which features the art of Foley sound effects production, a technique pioneered by Universal's legendary sound man, Jack Donovan Foley, in the 1920s. Guests participate in re-creating sound effects such as those used in *U-571, Shrek,* and *The Scorpion King.*

EATING YOUR WAY THROUGH UNIVERSAL STUDIOS HOLLYWOOD

Soft drinks at Universal Studios are pricey at about $2.50 for a regular-size cup and nearly $4.00 for a large drink. One "deal" offers a souvenir cup of soda for $7.99, with unlimited 99 cent refills. You'll also find beer wagons at several locations.

The **Saddle Ranch Chop House,** an Urban Cowboy–like eatery modeled after the original on Sunset Boulevard, opened in late 2003 just outside the gates of the park.

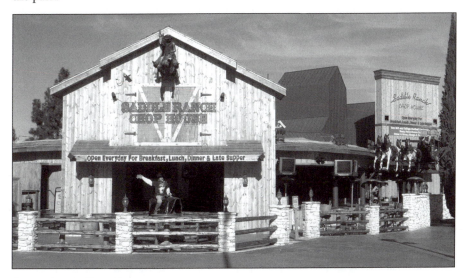

Saddle Ranch Chop House. *Photo by Corey Sandler*

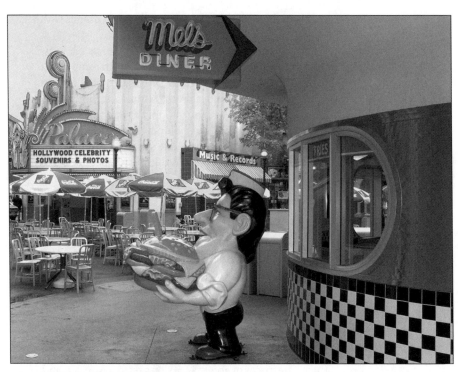

Mel's Diner on the upper lot. *Photo by Corey Sandler*

■ ENTERTAINMENT CENTER

Doc Brown's Fancy Fried Chicken. Chicken dinners, biscuits, and corn on the cob. A three-piece basket of fried chicken is priced at about $6.00; a full dinner with potatoes and gravy is priced about a dollar higher. (Open in season only.)

Hollywood Cantina. Fajitas, tacos, burritos, nachos, enchiladas, and other Mexican favorites, priced from about $4.00 for soft tacos to $6.00 for fajitas. Platters, including rice and beans, sell for about a dollar more.

Louie's Pizza & Pasta. Pizza, hot dogs, ice cream, pies and pastries, salads, sandwiches, and espresso and cappuccino, with entrees priced from about $4.00 to $8.00.

Mel's Diner. A remake of a 1950s diner reminiscent of the eatery in *American Graffiti.* Load up on burgers, fried chicken, hot dogs, and other fine fare, priced from about $3.00 to $6.00.

Roman Noodle #1. A Tuscan-style Italian cafeteria serving pizza, lasagna, fresh pasta, and garlic sticks. Entrees range from about $5.50 to $7.00. Open seasonally.

■ STUDIO CENTER

Jurassic Cove Cafe. Bronto burgers, ribs, and salads . . . much fresher than the Jurassic period.

Margarita Bar. Margaritas, beer, and lemonade. Open seasonally.

Studio Commissary. Philly steak sandwiches, tostada salads, and pizzas. Open seasonally.

UNIVERSAL CITYWALK

In typical Hollywood fashion, Universal Studios saw a place where there should be a city—a clean, safe, and fun city—and so that is what was built. The concept for the development was for a street that was not an imitation of any particular place or time period, but instead a sort of architectural collage of the images and traits of Los Angeles without duplicating any buildings.

Universal CityWalk is an easy five- to ten-minute walk from the Entertainment Center of Universal Studios, making it an attractive alternative to the fast food of the theme park for lunch or dinner. See if you can convince the kids to save some of their souvenir money for the neat shops here.

Stores are open seven days a week from 11:00 A.M. to 11:00 P.M. with longer hours at peak times. By night Universal CityWalk comes alive with fabulous lighting that includes crackle-tube neon, cove and accent lighting, towers with theatrical lighting, and light-reflecting panels that splash color throughout the plazas. The Museum of Neon Art displays vintage neon signs along the street.

CityWalk has been a big success, and was nearly doubled in size in 2000 with new shops and restaurants and a multimedia sound and light system. CityWalk connects to the 6,200-seat Universal Amphitheatre, the eighteen-screen Universal City Cinemas, and the Universal Studios theme park.

You'll have to pay to park your car at Universal Studios; some of the clubs and theaters offer reimbursement or special deals for car owners.

Universal CityWalk regularly offers a special deal that includes parking, a first-run movie, and dinner at any of six restaurants (Cafe Tu Tu Tango, Daily Grill, Gladstone's, Hard Rock Cafe, Shanghai & Mein, or Wasabi at CityWalk). The deal, available daily after 4:00 P.M., cost $19.95 per person in 2005, with a minimum of two people in the party; it can be purchased at Universal City Cinemas.

■ ENTERTAINMENT AT CITYWALK

B. B. King's Blues Club and Memphis Restaurant. Authentic southern cuisine and live blues music seven nights a week at the Los Angeles version of the original club on Beale Street in Memphis. (818) 622–5464.

Hard Rock Cafe Hollywood. Down-home American food seasoned with a bit of rock 'n' roll; includes occasional live performances. There is, of course, a gift shop. (818) 622–7625. www.hardrock.com.

Howl at the Moon. Dueling pianos.

Imax 3D Theater. Six-story-high screen featuring high-tech projectors and Sonics Proportional Point Source loudspeaker system.

Jillian's Hi Life Lanes. Multilevel rock 'n' roll bowling alley and interactive game room.

NASCAR Silicon Motor Speedway. A virtual racing experience.

Rumba Room. A multilevel Latin dance club featuring live salsa, Latin jazz, merengue, and rock Español, accompanied by tapas and drinks.

Universal Amphitheatre. One of the hottest live performance venues anywhere with no curfew, no sound restrictions, and no seat more than 150 feet from the stage. (213) 252–9497. www.uniconcerts.com/uniamp.

Universal City Cinemas. Eighteen screens and more than 6,000 seats with the latest technology, including DTS digital, THX, and Dolby sound systems. Highly popular among residents of the San Fernando Valley, it is one of the nation's busiest theater complexes. (818) 508–0711. www.loewscineplex.com/locations/ca/index.html.

■ RESTAURANTS AT CITYWALK

Buca di Beppo Restaurant. A quirky family-style southern Italian eatery with an inside joke of a name: Buca means basement, and Beppo is southern Italian slang for Giuseppe, or Joe. So the name translates to "Joe's Basement," a nod to the location of the first restaurant in this chain. You can dine in mock-splendor at the pope's table or at a kitchen table. (818) 509–9463. www.bucadibeppo.com.

Cafe Tu Tu Tango. An eclectic menu of appetizer-size tapas dishes to be shared around the table. Designed like an artist's loft in Barcelona with brushes on the table and spontaneous performances by musicians and dancers. (818) 769–2222. www.cafetututango.com.

Camacho's Cantina. Andy Camacho, owner of the popular El Paseo Inn on Olvera Street in Los Angeles, brings authentic Mexican cuisine including many unusual dishes and a mariachi band. (818) 622–3333.

Daily Grill Short Order. High-tone short-order cooking favorites like potpie, meat loaf, and Cobb salad. (818) 760–4448. www.dailygrill.com.

Gladstone's Universal. A popular California seafood restaurant featuring live Maine lobsters as well as local fare. Fish doesn't get much fresher than this. The restaurant includes several huge saltwater tanks, an oyster tank, and sawdust on the floor. Out front is the San Pedro light buoy, which marked channels in and out of San Pedro Harbor from 1942 until its decommissioning in 1971. (818) 622–3474. www.gladstones.com.

Karl Strauss Brewery Garden. An onsite brewery serving handcrafted beers and American cuisine. (818) 753–2739. www.karlstrauss.com.

Shanghai & Mein. Casual Chinese food, featuring dim sum and noodles.

Tony Roma's. An open kitchen with a view of the ribs on the grill. (818) 763–7662. www.tonyromas.com.

Upstart Crow Cafe. A simple cafe alongside a friendly bookstore with sections for adults and children. The name of the place comes from a critical comment on the writing and acting abilities of William Shakespeare by a rival, one Robert Greene. (818) 763–1811. www.upstartcrowtrading.com.

Wasabi at CityWalk. Fresh sushi by day and disco by night. (818) 622–7224.

Wolfgang Puck Cafe. The celebrated chef brings his famous pizza as well as rotisserie fare to an outdoor cafe. (818) 985–9653. www.wolfgangpuck.com.

■ FAST FOOD AT CITYWALK

Cafe Puccino. An attractive European-style bakery and cappuccino cafe, plus an Italian deli serving gourmet pizza, salads, and sandwiches. (818) 622–2233. www.cafepuccino.com.

Hollywood FreeZway. Pay no mind to the '57 Chevy bursting through the Hollywood FreeZway sign; the ice cream parlor features Häagen-Dazs and is just begging you to cruise on in. (818) 622–2653.

Jamba Juice. Healthful fruit juices and shakes. (818) 761–9816.

Jerry's Famous Deli. From matzo ball soup to pastrami on rye.

Jody Maroni's Sausage Kingdom. The king of the *haute* dog, a California favorite on Venice Beach and at Dodger Stadium. Specialties include hot and sweet Italian, Portuguese fig and pinenut, Bombay curried lamb, and chicken and duck with shallots and tarragon. (818) 622–5639. www.maroni.com.

Panda Express. Quick Chinese food.

Pit Fire Pizza Co. Wood fire–grilled pizzas.

Rubio's Baja Grill. Quick Mexican cuisine.

Smoothie King. Creamy fruit smoothies.

Tommy's Original World Famous Hamburgers. A venerated burger joint, specializing in chili-dripping burgers and fries.

Tropic Nut Company. Warm roasted nuts, trail mixes, and honey served in a rustic Caribbean-style shack. (818) 622–6889.

Versailles Restaurant. Authentic Cuban food including garlic-drenched chicken and fried plantains.

Wetzel's Pretzels. Fresh-baked, hand-rolled in at least ten flavors.

■ FASHION AT CITYWALK

Atomic Garage. Snowboard, skateboard, fashion apparel, and accessories.

Hollywood Harley Davidson. Motorcycle-theme apparel, merchandise, and collectibles.

Quiksilver Boardrider's Club. Men's and women's surfwear.

Skechers USA. Lifestyle footwear (some call them sneakers) and casual shoes.

UCLA Spirit. Books, clothing, and other samples of the college's Westwood campus. (818) 754–6719.

Universal Studio Store. Fashion, accessories, and character merchandise. (818) 622–8000.

Vans. Shoes from toddler to adult, as well as a full line of skateboarding equipment; there's a half-pipe skateboarding ramp inside the store.

■ GIFTS AT CITYWALK

Abercrombie & Fitch. Preppy clothing with an edge, in a large store at the core of CityWalk. (818) 752–7530.

Adobe Road. Native American jewelry, belts, skins, shirts, musical instruments, and wall hangings. (818) 622–3623.

All Star Collectibles. Autographed and authenticated sports memorabilia. (818) 622–2222.

Awesome Atom's. Scientific games and educational toys.

Cirque De Bijoux. Designer costume and body jewelry.

Dapy. Originating in Paris, offering a collection of unusual toys and gifts. Dapy is part of Spencer Gifts, which is in turn owned by Universal Studios. (818) 622–3279. www.spencergifts.com.

Fossil. Fashion watches. (818) 985–8209.

Glow. Glow-in-the-dark clothing, stationery, art, jewelry, paint, toys, and gifts. (818) 761–3270.

Hot Topic. Apparel, accessories, gifts, and music for teenagers.

Martin Lawrence Gallery. Arts and crafts. (818) 508–7867.

The Nature Company. An indoor rain forest at the entrance, and gifts, garden accessories, and educational playthings within. (818) 508–7867.

Out Takes. Computer-generated composite photography placing visitors into famous movie or television scenes. (818) 752–1262.

Retro Rad. Vintage and nostalgic clothing and accessories.

Sam Goody Superstore. A large collection of CDs, tapes, and videos, and a piano-shaped coffee cafe. (818) 763–4301.

Sparky's. Vintage and reproduction toys. (818) 622–2925.

Sunglass Hut. (818) 505–8446.

THEM! Science-fiction movie memorabilia.

Things From Another World. From Dark Horse Comics, all manner of games, aliens, creatures, and videos. (818) 622–8464.

The Wound & Wound Toy Co. Thousands of wind-up toys.

CHAPTER EIGHT

KNOTT'S BERRY FARM

IT ALL BEGAN WITH A BISCUIT AND JAM, thirty years before Walt Disney arrived in Anaheim. Today Knott's Berry Farm has more than 165 attractions, rides, live shows, restaurants, and shops spread across 150 acres—about the combined size of Disneyland and Disney's California Adventure and about fifteen minutes away.

Now part of the Cedar Fair family, the park has seen a steady stream of investment in thrill rides, including the astounding **Silver Bullet** suspended coaster, which opened at the end of 2004. At the same time the park remains committed to family entertainment and kiddie rides.

In 2003 the park added the amazing **Xcelerator** coaster, which rides up the side of a near-vertical hill before plunging straight down the other side. In recent years the bodacious **Perilous Plunge** water ride made a big splash at the back of the park, while the front was transformed with the addition of **GhostRider,** a gigantic old-style wooden roller coaster. In the middle of the park came a spectacular space shot known as **Supreme Scream.** A completely new second gate, **Soak City U.S.A.,** opened across the road.

Kiddies will find an amphitheater for Snoopy and Peanuts shows in Camp Snoopy.

THE STORY OF KNOTT'S BERRY FARM

Knott's Berry Farm traces its history to 1920 when Walter and Cordelia Knott began farming twenty acres of leased land in Buena Park. They had spent the three years before unsuccessfully trying to homestead in the Mojave Desert.

Most of the family's savings went to purchase equipment and berry plants, and the business nearly died in the first year when a series of unusually heavy frosts nearly wiped them out. In the second year berry prices plummeted.

What saved the business was Walter Knott's decision to market his produce by himself. He built a roadside stand to sell his berries to summer vacationers

MUST-SEES

Silver Bullet

Xcelerator

GhostRider

Supreme Scream

Perilous Plunge

Timber Mountain Log Ride

Jaguar!

Montezooma's Revenge

Boomerang

Bigfoot Rapids

Mystery Lodge

Camp Snoopy
(unaccompanied adults excused)

Soak City U.S.A.
(second-gate water park)

who drove past the farm on Grand Avenue, now known as Beach Boulevard or Highway 39.

There was competition, though, from other berry stands, so Knott combined his marketing skills with some agricultural engineering. In 1922 he read a newspaper article about an unusual berry that was larger than other berries; it was a cross between a dewberry and a loganberry, and named youngberry. Knott tracked down the source to a farm in Alabama and imported them to Southern California for the first time, developing a business selling the berries to visitors and the plants to other area farmers.

By 1927 business was successful enough to allow Knott to purchase land to build a home and a larger berry stand on the property. To make ends meet on their farm, Cordelia Knott began serving hot biscuits and homemade preserves to customers of the road-side berry stand.

The original berry farm stand was located at La Palma Avenue at Beach Boulevard, which today is in the first corner of the park as you come in; the stand has been replaced by a statue of westward pioneers that's visible from the road.

About the same time Knott's growing fame as a berry farmer brought him in contact with Rudolph Boysen of Orange County, the city parks superintendent and an amateur botanist who had conducted experiments with a cross between a blackberry, a raspberry, and a loganberry. Boysen had abandoned his experiment, and it took some searching to find the last six surviving vines; they were brought back to life and eventually transplanted at Knott's farm.

They were named boysenberries and were an immediate success at the Knott's Berry Farm roadside stand. In June 1934 the momentous day came when Mrs. Knott decided to expand her menu to include fried chicken at 65 cents per full meal; the first day she served just eight meals on her own wedding china. By 1940 visitors were standing in line for hours to enjoy plates of Walter's boysenberries and Cordelia's chicken. Today the restaurant serves more than one and a half million meals per year.

As long as all those people were standing in line, why not find something else for them to spend their money on? In 1940 Knott built Old West Ghost Town next door. The family started with an artistic cyclorama known as the Covered Wagon Show, a detailed mural enhanced with real objects in the foreground; it depicted the journey of the Knotts to California. Knott found the Old Trails Hotel in Prescott, Arizona, and moved the 1848 structure to the farm to hold the

KNOTT'S BERRY FARM

Courtesy Knott's Berry Farm

Power Trips

FOR ADULTS AND OLDER CHILDREN

The latest and wildest is **Silver Bullet,** and if you're determined to take a hit, head there first or last. The good news is that Silver Bullet will likely reduce some of the lines at those other amazing thrill rides, **Xcelerator, Supreme Scream,** and **Ghost Rider.** If you'd rather ride one of them, head there first.

Move on to **Boomerang, Montezooma's Revenge,** and **Mystery Lodge.** As it starts to get warm, take a ride on **Perilous Plunge** and then **Bigfoot Rapids.** You can dry off just a bit at the **Log Ride.** Use the afternoon to see some of the shows, including the **Stunt Show.**

The lines at Silver Bullet and Xcelerator will build through the day; come back at dinnertime or near the end of the day when the crowds will be else-where.

If you are going to stay until evening, think about ducking out for an early dinner (chicken, anyone?) and return to the park when others are heading for the feed lot.

FOR CHILDREN

The big draws for kids are in Camp Snoopy, which will become crowded by midmorning. Arrive there early if you can.

Working counterclockwise from Camp Snoopy, visit whichever of the rides in Fiesta Village your youngsters can handle. These might include **Gran Slammer, Tumbler,** and **WaveSwinger.** The **Carousel** is in Fiesta Village, too.

Amusement park rides that may appeal to some kids include **Wilderness Scrambler,** all but guaranteed to make adults dizzy. Most kids enjoy the **Bumper Cars** near the Charles M. Schulz Theatre. Adventuresome kids will love **Perilous Plunge;** bring a change of clothes or a rain jacket on a cool day.

Children are sure to enjoy **Lucy's Tugboat.**

Ghost Town will appeal to children of all ages. Youngsters will particularly enjoy **Big Foot Rapids** on a warm afternoon. So, too, a ride on the **Ghost Town & Calico Railroad** and the **Butterfield Stage.**

Very young children will probably not enjoy **Mystery Lodge;** save it for school-aged visitors.

cyclorama. He added a saloon (without alcohol) and soon expanded with other buildings, including a Kansas schoolhouse, a blacksmith's shop, and shacks from mining territories.

In 1952 Walter Knott purchased one of America's last operating narrow-gauge railroads, the Denver and Rio Grande, moving its rolling stock in its entirety to the farm. It originally traveled a 76-mile route from Denver to Colorado Springs. Installed at the park, the steam-powered train was renamed the Ghost Town & Calico Railroad.

most massive wooden roller coaster in Southern California. Then there is the terrifying Silver Bullet.

■ HOURS OF OPERATION

Summer hours: Open every day from 9:00 A.M. to midnight. (The summer season runs from about June 16 to September 3.)

Winter hours: Open 10:00 A.M. to 6:00 P.M. during the week, 10:00 A.M. to 10:00 P.M. Saturday, and 10:00 A.M. to 7:00 P.M. Sunday. Closed on Christmas. Extended hours during seasonal periods.

DRIVING INSTRUCTIONS TO KNOTT'S BERRY FARM

From West Los Angeles: Santa Monica Freeway (Interstate 10) East to Santa Ana Freeway (Interstate 5) south. Stay on Santa Ana Freeway south to the Artesia Boulevard/Knott Avenue exit. Stay in one of the two right-hand lanes of the off-ramp. Go straight, making no turns. You will be on Knott Avenue, which leads directly to the park.

From Orange County and Disneyland Area: Santa Ana Freeway (I–5) north to Highway 91 west to the Beach Boulevard exit, which leads into Knott's Berry Farm.

Here's an alternate route from Disneyland: Santa Ana Freeway (I–5) north to the Beach Boulevard exit. Bear right off the exit, and turn right (south) onto Beach Boulevard, which leads to the entrance to the park.

From Hollywood/San Fernando Valley: Hollywood Freeway (U.S. Highway 101) south to Santa Ana Freeway (I–5) south. Stay on Santa Ana Freeway south to the Artesia Boulevard/Knott Avenue exit. Stay in one of the two right-hand lanes of the off-ramp. Go straight, making no turns. You will be on Knott Avenue, which leads to the park.

GHOST TOWN

A rough-and-ready 1880s Old West boomtown of cowboys, cancan dancers, stunt fights, stagecoaches, a steam train, a log ride, old-time melodramas, and panning for real gold. Ghost Town is a fun place to walk about and explore.

Knott bought the California ghost town of Calico before he developed his own amusement park; the unofficial name for the ghost town is Calico because of that original purchase.

▓ MUST-SEE ▓ SILVER BULLET

The **Silver Bullet** threads its way through the front of Knott's Berry Farm, a magical solution for whatever ails you . . . unless you have an unreasonable fear of overbanked curves, cobra rolls, and corkscrews.

The newest thrill ride at the park transforms the look of the place once again, placing a chrome-plated state-of-the-art steel coaster right across the entrance plaza with various elements touching many of the other parts of the park, including Reflections Lake, Ghost Town, Fiesta Village, and Indian Trails. The $16 million Swiss-designed ride stretches over 3,125 feet of track; the cars are lifted to 146 feet above the ground with an initial drop of 109 feet.

Riders are suspended from an overhead track in a floorless train. The ride is similar in design to Batman at Six Flags Magic Mountain. The designer, Bolliger & Mabillard, is also responsible for the twin-track Dueling Dragons at Universal Studios Islands of Adventure in Orlando.

That's just the beginning: There's a vertical loop of 105 feet in diameter and six inversions along the course of the two-and-a-half-minute-long excursion. Elements of the ride include an outside loop, an overbanked curve, a cobra roll, zero-gravity roll, an elevated spiral, corkscrew, and a double spiral. Top speed is about fifty-five miles per hour, and each of the two trains can carry thirty-two passengers at a time.

Guests must be 54 inches or taller to ride.

MUST-SEE ▪ GHOSTRIDER

The longest, tallest, most massive wooden roller coaster in Southern California, GhostRider sprawls over 4,530 feet of track, with a spectacular 108-foot drop. The modern woodie delivers a remarkably smooth ride, too.

Three trains of twenty-eight seats transport about 1,600 guests each hour. Towering 118 feet at its highest point, the coaster delivers a maximum g-force of 3.14.

GhostRider's L-shaped track begins near the **Gold Mine,** soaring high above Grand Avenue to a former parking lot, making four high-speed passes over the road.

Built of yellow pine, the weathered look of the coaster blends nicely with Knott's Berry Farm's celebrated Old West atmosphere. GhostRider dominates the front of the park, its huge framework easily visible from busy Beach Boulevard.

According to insiders, designers at Knott's Berry Farm set out to create a wooden coaster that was longer and higher than the venerable Colossus at Six Flags Magic Mountain. Colossus's tower reaches to 115 feet, 3 feet shorter than GhostRider's peak.

Many roller-coaster fans believe that wooden coasters are preferable to modern steel designs because the former have more give. According to the designer of GhostRider, the structural flexibility of the classic wooden coaster intensifies the passengers' sensation of weightlessness. "GhostRiders feel as if they are moving, shifting, and swaying with the structure."

MUST-SEE ▪ TIMBER MOUNTAIN LOG RIDE

A Knott's Berry Farm classic, it was originally named the Calico Logging Company. When it opened in 1968 it was the first log flume theme ride in the country; today, it is still considered one of the best. Traveling in hollowed logs, guests float through animated scenes of the inner workings of an old-time sawmill.

There is a false drop in the dark, and then you are in a wilderness scene with wildlife; the room smells like a pine forest. The log moves out onto a track with a view of the outside world, very near to the tracks of **Jaguar!**

Eventually the logs reach the end of their tour within Timber Mountain and plunge down a 50-foot waterfall. Riders receive only a tiny splash; the ride was developed when most visitors came to the park to go to a chicken dinner and didn't want to get wet.

■ GHOST TOWN & CALICO RAILROAD

Think the New York City subways are unsafe? The Knott's Berry Farm train line is held up by bandits more than 10,000 times a year. The train circles the park on a ½-mile tour that takes fifteen minutes (including a scheduled robbery).

The GT&C operates two locomotives: #41, *Red Cliff,* from the Rio Grande South-

A Timber Mountain Log Ride boat heads for a splash-down. *Photo by Corey Sandler*

ern, and #40, *Green River,* from the Denver & Rio Grande and the Denver & Rio Grande Western. Both were built by the Baldwin Locomotive Works in 1881, two of only twelve C-19 narrow-gauge freight engines built by Baldwin. Together, the engine and loaded tender weigh about 127,260 pounds. The engine's wheel configuration is 2-8-0.

The stable of coaches for the GT&C includes:

■ **Combine #351.** Built in 1880, and rebuilt in 1937 as a parlor-buffet car for service on the San Juan Express.

■ **Closed Vestibule Coaches #310, #325, and #326.** Built by Pullman in 1887.

■ **Parlor Car #105,** *Durango.* Built in 1880; one of only three narrow-gauge parlor cars still in operation.

■ **Special Car B-20,** *Edna.* Used as a private business car for Otto Mears, president of the Rio Grande Southern. Originally lit by oil lamps, at one time it included mahogany-wood finish and crimson plush upholstery. Inside was sleeping space for six with a private bedroom with bathroom, kitchen, and dining room.

The Calico Railroad just minutes from a scheduled robbery. *Photo by Corey Sandler*

In January and February the two steam engines are regularly given time off, and service on the GT&C is provided by the *Galloping Goose,* a gasoline-fueled railway car built in 1931 for the Rio Grande Southern. Originally powered by a Pierce-Arrow engine, it now uses a GMC truck engine.

Engineers conduct guided tours of the park's roundhouse; you can purchase tickets at the Train Junction shop in Ghost Town.

■ SCREAMIN' SWING

For just a few dollars more, you can be launched from the earth 70 feet in the air with a blast of compressed air on Screamin' Swing, the first ride of its kind. The swing reaches a top speed of about sixty miles per hour.

The ride is located near the Calico Mine Ride and the former location of the Haunted Shack. Guests are charged an additional $5.00 for the privilege.

■ *SIEGE OF FORT KNOTT STUNT EXTRAVAGANZA*

Join the audience to cheer on the ever-resourceful U.S. agent Jebadiah Casy as he attempts to hold down the legendary Fort Knott from the gold-hungry likes of Welby Weed and his evil cohort, Frank Fargo.

Note that some of the seats are out in the sun; if you want to be sure of shade, arrive early and choose one of the covered stagecoaches that ring the top of the small amphitheater. There also are two stagecoaches and some seats on the stage itself; they are up close to some of the action but don't offer the best view for events going on at the other end of the stage.

The Old Trails Hotel

The first building erected in Ghost Town, the hotel was built in 1868 in Prescott, Arizona, and moved to the farm in 1940 to house the Covered Wagon Show, Knott's first attraction. The show is a cyclorama, a combination of costumed figures and artifacts with a painted backdrop; the exhibit is still in place and is open to the public for a few hours each day. Inside the hotel is a mirror backed with diamond dust and a key rack missing a hook for unlucky Room 13.

The Bottle House

All 3,082 empty wine and whiskey bottles that form the walls of the Bottle House face inward; if they didn't, they'd whistle in the wind. Built at Knott's Berry Farm in 1946, the Bottle House was inspired by similar structures in turn-of-the-twentieth-century mining towns throughout the West. While wood was scarce because it was needed in the mines, empty liquor bottles were plentiful.

Old School House

Everything in this old building—books, desks, chalkboard, and potbelly stove—is authentic and dates from about 1875.

Thomas A. Edison Inventors' Workshop

Children of all ages can take time out to learn at the Thomas A. Edison Inventors' Workshop, which moved into the former Bonnet Shop in 2004. California's only collection of Edison artifacts and memorabilia, it includes early experimental light-bulbs and hand-written notes by Edison. There are hands-on exhibits demonstrating the invisible forces of electricity and magnetism.

Gold Mine

Take a pan to the sluice in Ghost Town and sift out a few grains of gold. Each year, guests take home more than $70,000 in real gold dust from Knott's Gold Mine in Ghost Town; more than $3 million has been taken from the stream since the park opened. The sluice is stocked with gold flakes each morning to increase your chances. In 2005 the fee was $5.00.

Western Trails Museum

A most eclectic collection of things more-or-less Western. Some of the materials began from Walter Knott's own gatherings, but during the years many of the items in the Western Trails Museum were donated by guests.

You'll see old china from the early mining ghost towns of Colorado and California, period photos of Bat Masterson and Annie Oakley, and many guns and knives. On the back wall, look for an unusual picture of the Rock Island Line train system; based on an original black-and-white photo from 1900, it was hand-colored on mother-of-pearl. The work was created in 1916 for E. J. Goreman, president of the railroad, for his office. Set near Colorado Springs, Pikes Peak is the snow-covered point at the right side of the range.

Another interesting exhibit is a display of cigarette-box cards that offer a glimpse

The Gold Mine is one of the oldest attractions at Knott's Berry Farm. *Photo by Corey Sandler*

at what were considered naughty pictures at the turn of the century; there's nothing there to shock a modern-day visitor.

Butterfield Stagecoach
The last regularly scheduled stagecoach line in America circles a portion of Ghost Town. Five of Knott's six stagecoaches are authentic and more than one hundred years old; many were used on the Oregon Trail in the 1880s and 1890s. The one replica, the Knott's coach, was built on the Farm in 1956. Knott's maintains a stable of more than fifty horses to pull the coaches around the park.

Medicine Show
Be on the lookout for Dr. I. Will Skinnem and his old-time medicine show; the fast-talking pitchman has a cure for whatever ails you.

Bird Cage Theatre
A meticulous replica of the Bird Cage Theatre in Kingston, Arizona, near Tombstone, it was claimed by Knott's as the oldest continually operated melodrama theater in the United States. The theater is open for special events only; check with the park for schedules.

Main Street Windmill
A century-old import from England, the windmill was originally intended by Walter Knott to serve as the boundary for the park. Today it stands in roughly the middle of Knott's Berry Farm. The mill was brought to California in the 1860s by an English syndicate that first laid out and subdivided Riverside.

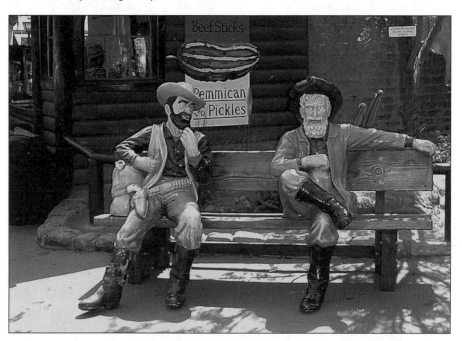

Handsome Brady and Whiskey Jim in Ghost Town. *Photo by Corey Sandler*

Seated Statues

Knott's four sets of seated character statues—Handsome Brady and Whiskey Jim, the cancan girls in Ghost Town, the Mexican ladies in Fiesta Village, and the flapper girls in the Boardwalk—are favorite stops for visitors to the park. A fifth pair, Cecilia and Marilyn, sit in front of the Calico Saloon and are modeled after actual saloon performers of the 1850s. They have a recorded patter that is remarkably suited to the actions of some of the females and most of the males who sit down beside them.

At one time nearly all Kodak film was processed in one plant in Rochester, New York, and Knott's received phone calls from Kodak wanting to know who these people were and why they kept turning up in thousands of photographs.

Old Betsey

Parked near the windmill, *Old Betsey* is a wood-burning engine that had been used in the early days of borax mining on the desert in Death Valley. The locomotive was a distinct improvement over the twenty-mule team that used to haul borax from the mines. The mineral borax has a number of industrial uses as a water softener and as part of the foundry process. The engine was retired to the park in 1941.

Berry Stand

In a nod to local history, the original stand that launched the Knott's Berry Farm empire is preserved as a refreshment counter.

Attached to the side of the stand are some old photos. Alongside is a Ford Model A, the vehicle driven by Walter and Cordelia Knott when they came to California. Out back is a small patch of boysenberry plants, the only berries still grown within the park.

Boot Hill

Most of the grave markers in this boneyard across the way from the Western Trails Museum are authentic relics of the Old West; the graves themselves were left behind. The painted backdrop to Boot Hill is the backside of the Good Time Theatre.

Check out the grave of Hyram McTavish. Legend has it the heart will beat again after one hundred years—any visitor who places his or her foot on the grave will feel . . . something. Our favorite epitaphs? "Butch Youngman 1857. Here lies Butch, we planted him raw. He was quick on the trigger, but slow on the draw." And, "Here lies Lester Moore. 4 slugs shot from a 44. No less and no more."

Alas, in 2001 the **Haunted Shack** faded away. The quirky, crooked residence of Shifty Sam and Slanty Sadie, a place where water ran uphill and the worst (or best) puns in the park took flight, was closed.

CAMP SNOOPY

The official home of the Peanuts gang, Camp Snoopy is a six-acre kids' paradise themed like a section of California's High Sierra. Camp Snoopy features thirty attractions for the youngest visitors.

Woodstock's Airmail is a smaller, gentler version of Supreme Scream, but I imagine it looks big enough to little eyes. Nearby is **Charlie Brown's Speedway,** a mini NASCAR track.

Camp Snoopy's Bear-y Tales Playhouse is a just-for-kids world that includes winding corridors and all sorts of unusual surprises.

Other rides include the **Red Baron** planes, the **Twister** mini coaster, the **Rocky Road** cars, and a kid-size Ferris wheel.

Among recent additions to the area:

■ **Joe Cool's GR8 SK8,** an eight-person lift-and-slide ride like a giant skateboard.

■ **Camp Snoopy Theatre,** home to a live show that changes annually.

■ **Lucy's Tugboat,** where visitors can set sail in a rocking and rolling sea voyage—just thrilling enough for kiddies—departing directly behind the refurbished Peanuts' Playhouse. The boat rises to a height of 21 feet and rolls and spins; but fear not: Captain Lucy Van Pelt is at the helm and eventually all will return safely to port.

FIESTA VILLAGE

A salute to California's Spanish legacy, Fiesta Village is also the prowling ground for Knott's Jaguar! adventure.

MUST-SEE JAGUAR!

Knott's unusual roller coaster prowls through a large portion of the village like a cat stalking its prey, speeding up and slowing down as it threads the needle through thrill rides and circles the lake.

Passengers board the coaster at the Temple of the Jaguar, a five-story Mayan pyramid in Fiesta Village. The temple was inspired by the architectural style of the famed Tikal pyramid, which featured a decorative crown cap depicting a supernatural figure holding a jaguar mask.

According to Mayan and Aztec legend, there exists in this temple a deity who could transform himself into a mighty fire-breathing cat. As you make your way through the queuing area inside the Temple of the Jaguar, you will hear and see evidence of the cat and feel his presence.

The waiting line passes through detailed corridors and chambers as it moves its way toward the columned Hall of Egress. Still within the temple, passengers board sleek twenty-four-seat trains. As you board your train, it becomes apparent that you have become the cat.

Immediately after departure riders climb 60 feet into the air and then dive back through the temple's crown tower to begin a twisting, spiraling expedition above Knott's Berry Farm. Jaguar! is a very quiet ride and actually travels low to the ground in most places.

Halfway through your journey, the trains return to the temple tower through fog, fire effects, strobe lights, and sound.

Along the way, Jaguar! passes right through the middle of the loop of another Knott's Berry Farm coaster, Montezooma's Revenge, and then careens within inches of the Timber Mountain Log Ride.

Before it is done, Jaguar! winds its way through all of Fiesta Village and parts of Camp Snoopy. The track crosses the path of the park-circling Grand Sierra Scenic Railroad in eight places.

The steel structure runs about 2,700 feet with a pair of 60-foot drops. There are no guardrails to block the view from the cars, which travel just fast enough to give a thrill in places; the cars do not turn upside down.

For much of its run, Jaguar! is more like an aerial tour of the park. The trip, about two-and-a-half minutes, is a ride that most everyone in the family will enjoy.

Three twenty-four-passenger trains can carry a total of 1,500 guests per hour. The wait for the ride can build to as much as an hour during the summer and on holidays; come early or off-season to avoid the crowds.

⬛ MUST-SEE ⬛ MONTEZOOMA'S REVENGE

From zero to fifty-five miles per hour in just over three seconds, heading for two circles within a vertical loop, Montezooma's Revenge zooms riders through a 76-foot-high, 360-degree loop to the apex of a 148-foot tower; the train pauses at the top and then races backward through the loop and up a 112-foot tower at the opposite end of the track.

La Revolucion

A giant eggbeater, with seats. Not for the faint-of-stomach.

Calico Mine Train

Built in 1966, it was the first ride on Knott's Berry Farm and one of the first dark rides at any park. The walkway to the loading platform is decorated with old mining equipment. The scene is reminiscent of Disneyland's Thunder Mountain Railroad, but trust us: This is not a thrill ride.

The train chugs its way into the Calico Mine. Among the first sights is an old mine elevator like the ones used in the diggings of the West.

La Revolucion in mid-spin. *Photo by Corey Sandler*

You'll visit some interesting animated dioramas of miners at work and then arrive at the highlight of the trip: an otherworldly cavern of stalactites and stalagmites with a simulated organ providing musical accompaniment.

The mine train cars seat about ten persons with five cars per train; traffic is pretty constant on a busy day.

Dentzel Carousel

The oldest working carousel at any amusement park in the country, it was one of the first two-level carousels built. It was created by Gustav A. Dentzel in 1902 at G. A. Dentzel Steam and Horsepower Carousel Builder in Germantown, Pennsylvania. Before coming to Knott's in 1955, it entertained guests at Hershey Park in Hershey, Pennsylvania, and before then at Brady Park in Canton, Ohio.

Of the fifty-four animals on the ride, forty-eight are original, hand-carved works of art. Collectors have paid as much as $100,000 for original, hand-carved Dentzels. The animal menagerie includes lions, tigers, ostriches, camels, zebras, giraffes, pigs, cats, and horses that have real horsetail hair.

Music is provided by a pair of turn-of-the-twentieth-century organs, a Wurlitzer and a Gavioli band organ, which is capable of producing the sound of twenty-two instruments.

Church of the Reflections

Originally the First Baptist Church of Downey, California, the building was moved to Knott's in 1955 to provide a nondenominational respite for farm employees and visitors. More than one hundred weddings are performed in the small church each year. Bride and groom sometimes ride off in a stagecoach; Snoopy is available as the best man.

The church was moved in 2004 to make way for the Silver Bullet roller coaster that will travel over the lake; it's still in the area, but not quite with a waterfront address. Nearby is a place of discomfort. Doctor Walker's dentist office was hauled in from the Ozarks in 1953. Dating back to the nineteenth century, the walls of the office include some frightening tools.

THE BOARDWALK

Hear ye, hear ye: The Supreme Scream is in session. While you're in the neighborhood, you can also plunge over a watery cliff at Perilous Plunge and enjoy the looping action of Boomerang. Alas, the hopelessly quaint Kingdom of the Dinosaurs receded into ancient history and was closed in 2005.

▓ MUST-SEE ▓ XCELERATOR

Grab your leather jacket and cool shades; the wind will slick back your hair on Xcelerator, the '50s-themed roller coaster that arrived at Knotts in mid-2002. The high-octane coaster fires up its engines on the Boardwalk, dispatching a fleet

Xcelerator goes over the top at Knott's. *Photo by Corey Sandler*

of chrome-plated, flip-top, flame-decorated '57 Chevy cars across 2,202 feet of cool coral track.

Xcelerator trains are hydraulically launched to eighty-two miles per hour in just over two seconds, and up through a 205-foot ascent and immediate descent at a ninety-degree angle. That's right: straight down. The two trains have a capacity of twenty people each, carrying as many as 1,330 guests per hour.

The coaster occupies the former home of Windjammer.

⋮MUST-SEE⋮ PERILOUS PLUNGE

The name pretty much sums it up: You'll ride a boat up, up, up . . . and then over a cliff and into the water below.

The ride, which opened in 2000, is claimed as the highest, steepest, fastest, and wettest waterfall plunge in the world. The ride, unfortunately, lived up to its name in 2001 with a fatal accident; it was closed for nearly a year while safety issues regarding the safety harnesses were addressed.

Boats plunge down a record 115-foot drop at a seventy-five-degree angle, hitting a speed of fifty miles per hour and generating an amazing 45-foot, 180-degree splash.

The boats load in a sunny California setting of palm trees, beach, and oil derricks. The ride is open year-round; designers built in a system that allows operators to slow down the boats and reduce the splash on cold days.

Three twenty-four-passenger boats travel a ninety-second track, accommodating 1,900 riders an hour. State-of-the-art water pumping technology pumps 40,000 gallons of water up the 121-foot lift per minute.

Universal Studios' Jurassic Park attractions in California and Florida drop guests 84 and 85 feet, respectively.

⋮MUST-SEE⋮ BOOMERANG

A high-speed, high-energy, European-designed thriller, Boomerang turns riders upside down six times—three times forward and three times backward—in less than a minute.

The blue tracks of Boomerang take off from a loading station next to the Sky Jump. Riders sit two abreast, held in place by overhead restraints.

The train is pulled backward up a hill; at the top, the cars are suddenly released. The train races down the hill, back through the loading station and into a twisting turn one way and then the other, into a 360-degree double loop, and up another hill.

When you reach the top, you drop back through the same course, this time backward.

Boomerang's tracks are very close to the walkways of the park in the Boardwalk; passersby can get right up close to wonder why people would pay good money to subject themselves to such an experience.

Boomerang replaced Corkscrew, the first inverted 360-degree looping coaster in the country; Corkscrew was moved to a park in Coeur d'Alene, Idaho.

⋮MUST-SEE⋮ SUPREME SCREAM

Supreme Scream is a "vertically descending thrill adventure"; what that means is that riders fall from a great height. The ride boasts a towering, 325-foot triangular steel structure, making it taller than any skyscraper in Orange County and 75 feet taller than Knott's landmark Sky Tower.

How does it feel? Think of jumping off the roof of a thirty-story building.

Each of the three towers accommodates twelve riders who are harnessed in outward-facing seats with their legs dangling freely. They are sent soaring by a blast of compressed air; after a brief pause at the top, Supreme Scream plunges them straight down. But wait: Another heart-pounding wallop is ahead with an abrupt bounce halfway back up the tower before a final touchdown to the launch pad.

The ride has a capacity of about 1,300 riders per hour. It replaced the anemic XK-1 ride.

The ride is a near-twin to the Power Tower, which opened in 1998 at the Cedar Point amusement park in Sandusky, Ohio. It is also similar to the Maliboomer at Disney's California Adventure.

The Supreme Scream takes off. Unlike a similar ride at Disney's California Adventure, seats are open to the rush of wind. *Photo by Corey Sandler*

RipTide

Like a giant threshing machine gone wild, RipTide delivers "720 degrees of attitude" to thirty-eight passengers. Stadium-like rows of seats go up and over in tight circles, eventually soaring to 59 feet in the air before descending perilously close to jets of water coming up from the base. The ride, called TopSpin by its manufacturer, replaced the Hammerhead ride at Knott's.

Wave Swinger

An old amusement park ride—formerly called Slingshot—that still thrills; visitors sit in a swing suspended by chains from an overhead canopy. The whole apparatus spins, rises, and then tilts. Riders must weigh less than 230 pounds.

Sky Cabin

Knott's landmark Parachute Sky Jump, inspired by the classic Coney Island landmark, was closed at the end of 1999, the victim of old age. The ride lifted riders 235 feet into the air and then dropped to earth beneath a billowing parachute canopy. The Sky Cabin, a slowly revolving enclosed cabin, still climbs the tower.

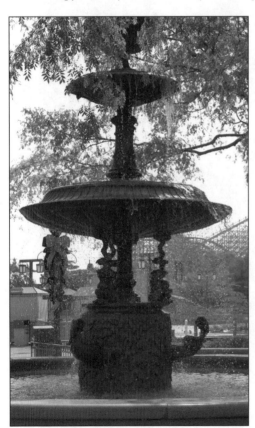

The Charleston Circle Fountain played a role in *Hello, Dolly! Photo by Corey Sandler*

Buffalo Nickel Arcade

This video arcade is neither in Buffalo nor involves nickels (Buffalo design or otherwise) or pennies. You'll need lots of quarters to get through the modern electronic games and old-time skeeball alleys.

Charleston Circle Fountain

The unusual waterworks located in the circular plaza that opens to Ghost Town, the Charleston Circle Fountain was originally part of the set for the 20th Century Fox movie *Hello, Dolly!,* starring Barbra Streisand.

Charles M. Schulz Theatre

In the summer and at Christmastime, the stage (formerly known as the Good Time Theatre) features a live Broadway-style musical extravaganza with dazzling lights, spangled costumes, and special effects. Admission to shows is usually free and part of the general ticket for the park.

The Christmas entertainment usually features a Snoopy ice show. Summer performances have included an Elvis review and other rock performances. In 2005 the summer feature was "Snoopy's Summer Vacation."

Wilderness Scrambler
A spinning carnival ride; in late 1999 it was moved from within its dark building to an outdoor setting. The ride was originally called HeadSpin.

Wheeler Dealer Bumper Cars
A classic favorite, this ride is near the Charles M. Schulz Theatre.

INDIAN TRAILS

Here is a celebration of the lore, legends, crafts, music, and dance of Native American tribes. The 27-foot Knott's Totem Pole at the entrance to Indian Trails is said to be the largest totem ever carved from incense cedar. The pole's figures include a Native American with child, buffalo, burro, turtle, owl, Knott's pioneer with covered wagon, grizzly bear, and eagle.

At Knott's Indian Trails, Native Americans produce intricate arts and crafts. The architectural styles include an authentic Big House and tepees of the Blackfoot, Nez Percé, Cheyenne, Crow, and Kiowa tribes.

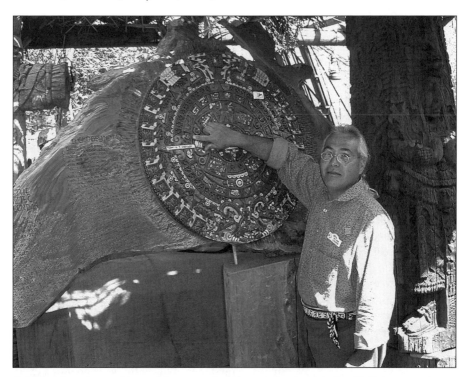

A Native American guide explains an ancient Aztec calendar at Indian Trails. *Photo by Corey Sandler*

The Big House is in the style of the Kwak'wala-speaking people. The building's façade and the hand-carved house posts near its entrance were created by Richard Hunt, a Kwak'wala artist from British Columbia.

Children's Camp at Indian Trails

Young visitors can create traditional honor bonnets as well as learn beadworking and sand painting. Native American storytellers recount living history, and kids can have their faces painted in authentic tribal fashion.

WILD WATER WILDERNESS

The Wild Water Wilderness recaptures the beauty of a California river wilderness park of the early 1800s. The trees, all indigenous to the Far West, include California black oak, coast redwood, and Torrey pines. Colorful wildflowers blossom throughout the wilderness, including poppies, bluebells, daffodils, larkspurs, and lilies.

MUST-SEE BIGFOOT RAPIDS

The whitewater river raft ride is a lot of fun if you don't mind getting a bit wet; depending on your luck, you may even get soaked. There: You have been warned. Now go and have fun.

(By the way, a sign at the Rapids tells visitors that garbage-bag rain gear is not allowed. It seems that everyone wants to be a fashion critic.)

MUST-SEE MYSTERY LODGE

Legends tell of a magical place known as **Thunder Falls** that's located deep within the luxuriant green forests of the Northwest Coast. It's a place of miracles, where grand waterfalls crash into a running river with such force that the canyon reverberates with the sound of thunder. Some say that the roar of the thunder brings forth mystic images of the distant past.

Visitors enter Thunder Falls through an ornate wooden archway, continuing across a re-creation of a traditional boardwalk like the ones that connect Northwest Coast tribal houses to the ocean.

The lights dim, and the sounds of a multimedia preshow set the scene. Suddenly lightning fills the sky, and guests are invited into the lodge to take refuge from the approaching storm.

Deep within the lodge a mystical old storyteller begins to spin his tale. It's a story of life, of birth and love and marriage and children and old age and the approach of eternal rest . . . and it presents a mystical calm to all who hear it. The message is that if we can share the mysteries of life with the wonder of a child, life will always be full of magic.

Master dancer Bill Cranmer, a hereditary chief of

Special Ks

Knott's Berry Farm's equivalent of Disney's "Hidden Mickeys" are the park's several dozen "Hidden Ks" that are woven into structures and decorations in the park. For example, look for the designs made out of twigs in the windows of the Art Gallery across from the Bottle House.

A Bigfoot Rapids raft spins through whitewater. *Photo by Corey Sandler*

the 'Namgis people and chairman of the U'mista Cultural Society, choreographed the traditional dance movements in the show, and he serves as the voice of the presentation. Kwak'wala musicians, including drummers and singers, perform the show's musical score.

I'm not about to destroy the illusions of the Mystery Lodge with an explanation of the magic, but I will tell you this much: The show combines a real actor on stage with spectacular lighting and special effects. The preshow and main lodge presentations total twenty-six minutes; the hourly capacity is 1,440 visitors.

The façade of Mystery Lodge, designed by Native American artists, includes images from the lore and legends of the Northwest tribes. The stonework includes four towering waterfalls dropping into Thunder Lake. At night bursts of fire, fog, and strange images issue forth from the building.

Aspects of the Mystery Lodge are based on traditions of the 'Namgis people of Alert Bay, Cormorant Island, British Columbia, Canada. The 'Namgis are one band of the Kwak'wala-speaking people, the native North American group who live on the northeastern coast of Vancouver Island, the central coast of mainland British Columbia, and the small islands in between.

Before contact with European settlers, the Kwak'wala-speaking people numbered about 7,000 persons. With the introduction of European diseases in the nineteenth century, the population was reduced to fewer than 2,000 by 1929. Today, the population is about 5,000 people.

Because of the groundbreaking work of the German-American anthropologist Franz Boas in the late 1800s, the Kwak'wala traditions are among the most fully documented of all North American Indian traditions.

Today the descendants of Boas's guide George Hunt are among the cultural leaders of their people, and the Hunt family of carvers produced some of the elements of Knott's Indian Trails area.

Skilled canoeists, fishers, and sea hunters, the Kwak'wala also excelled as carvers of totem poles, masks, and other ritual objects. They originated some of the most spectacular rituals of the Northwest Coast culture, including the potlatch ceremony.

Potlatch means "to give" and is a ceremony common to all tribes in the area. Occasions for holding a potlatch include marriages, naming children, mourning the dead, and transferring rights and privileges from a retiring chief to his successors. Dancers dressed in dramatic masks and robes invoke theatrical magic to act out the legends and stories of their people in dances that are traditional to a particular family. The host distributes gifts as payment to his guests for witnessing the ceremony. By accepting the gifts, guests validate the host's claims to the dances.

Mystery Lodge Store and Museum
At the exit to the Mystery Lodge is an attractive shop offering a variety of handmade native crafts to view and purchase. A hand-carved Coast Salish canoe depicting a killer whale design hangs from the ceiling beams. The canoe was carved at Knott's Berry Farm during a canoe-making demonstration begun in 1992 to commemorate the opening of the Indian Trails area. Also on display are intricately carved house posts and other craft work.

Items for sale include bentwood boxes made from a single piece of cedar and used to store blankets and prized family possessions; carvings in argillite, a slatelike stone; handwoven baskets; and a selection of native silver jewelry.

Nature Center at Wild Water Wilderness
After your ride on Bigfoot Rapids, stop to ask park rangers about Sasquatch, the elusive creature known to some of his friends as Bigfoot. You'll see some photos and footprints that suggest that the huge beast really does exist. Rangers will also show displays of insects, tarantulas, scorpions, and native plants, plus a glassed-in apiary that puts you about as close as you ever may want to get to a buzzing beehive.

The ranger station is located in the old Maizeland School, the first school in the Rivera District, constructed in 1868.

The Wilderness Dance Hall in Wild Water Wilderness once stood on the Burbank farm of Jim Jeffries, one-time American heavyweight boxing champion. Jeffries used the barn to train promising young fighters. Today the barn is home to an antic assortment of entertainers, from bluegrass pickers to Smoky Mountain cloggers.

EATING YOUR WAY THROUGH KNOTT'S BERRY FARM

Mrs. Knott's Chicken Dinner Restaurant. The winner and still local champion is this sprawling eatery, which regulars and employees call the CDR. Mrs. Knott's Chicken Dinner Restaurant seats more than 1,000 people in eight sep-

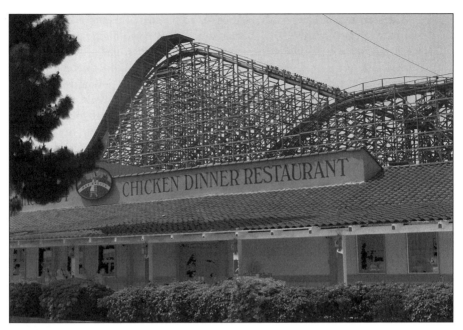

GhostRider rises over the old Chicken Dinner Restaurant. *Photo by Corey Sandler*

arate dining rooms and employs as many as 375 people during the summer.

The classic dinner, served from 11:00 A.M. until closing, is priced about $12 and includes four pieces of fried chicken, cherry rhubarb, mashed potatoes and gravy, vegetable, soup or salad, as many buttermilk biscuits as you can eat, beverage, and boysenberry pie. You can also order broiled chicken breast, chicken and dumplings, chicken potpie, barbecued beef ribs and chicken, or chicken-fried steak for the same price.

Today, the CDR is the largest single-location chicken restaurant in the country and the single-largest user of chickens in California. The part of the restaurant that faces Grand Avenue is the original restaurant that was built in and around the Knotts' home. You can ask to sit in one of the straight-back wooden chairs under the paddle fans in the original dining room.

Check out the guest register on the wall in the waiting area. Among notable diners in early years were Eddie Fisher, Elizabeth Taylor, and Jane Russell.

The biggest days of the year are typically Mother's Day, Easter, and Thanksgiving. (The restaurant is closed on Christmas Day.) The biggest day on record at the restaurant was Mother's Day 1982, when 8,400 meals were served. Over the course of a year, the restaurant seats 1.5 million visitors.

Auntie Pasta's Pizza Palace. Located in the California Marketplace, this restaurant features Italian fare including an all-you-can-eat special for $7.95 for adults and $5.95 for children.

Chicken to Go/Deli. You can buy a chicken and a boysenberry pie to go or pack up a picnic basket of fried chicken, sandwiches, or salads to take into the park. Located in the California Marketplace.

Coasters Diner. The Boardwalk area took a big step backward a few years ago with the opening of this 1950s-themed diner. Coasters combines neon, stainless steel, and glass block with cheeseburgers, french fries, and extra-thick milk shakes. Several restored vintage or re-created cars and a 22-foot neon tower lure park guests to the restaurant's location at the back of Knott's Boardwalk area.

Fireman's Brigade Barbecue. Chicken, ribs, corn on the cob, and more, in Ghost Town. A stand offers huge dill pickles to properly top off your meal.

Hollywood Hits. Your basic burger, hot dog, and pizza joint, in the back corner of the park near the Wheeler Dealer Bumper Cars. It was formerly known as the Hollywood Wok, and before that the Hollywood Beanery.

La Cocinita and Herdez Cantina. Mexican specialties in Fiesta Village.

SPECIAL EVENTS AND PRESENTATIONS

Independence Hall. A free exhibit outside the gates of Knott's Berry Farm. Within the reproduction is a replica of the Declaration-signing chamber; you'll see live performances by actors portraying Ben Franklin, Thomas Jefferson, Patrick Henry, and others.

There is an exact replica of the Liberty Bell, down to its crack. The only real difference lies upstairs where there is a large auditorium that is used for guest orientations, private parties, and special events.

Easter EggMazeMent. A hands-on family event with elaborate walk-through adventure mazes. Held each year for a two-week period on either side of Easter Sunday.

Independence Day. Annual fireworks show and special events.

Knott's Scary Farm. The park offers elaborate walk-through mazes that have ghastly storylines, live performances, and awesome special effects. Several rides are re-themed with disorienting special effects, music, and many monsters. Among the special live shows are *The Hanging,* an annual satirical send-up in Calico Square. More than 1,000 costumed and made-up performers haunt the park, mazes, and rides.

The Scary Farm is a special-ticket event not covered by general admission, and tickets sell out in advance each year. Tickets go on sale in August at Knott's, and at Ticketmaster outlets throughout the West. Not recommended for young children. Held weekends in October and Halloween night.

Knott's Scary Farm Halloween Haunt, first begun in 1972, is considered both the world's largest annual Halloween party and the largest annual event in the amusement park industry.

On the last two weekends of October, look for **Camp Spooky,** a daytime nonscarified Halloween celebration for kids eleven and younger that includes trick-or-treating, costume contests, and other activities.

Knott's Merry Farm. The park is transformed into an 1880s Victorian Christmas shopping and entertainment village, complete with lavish decorations, dozens of artisans, special holiday foods, continuous Christmas shows,

Santa's workshop, strolling carolers, choirs, and more. Held from about Thanksgiving to Christmas Eve. (The park is closed on Christmas Day.)

Classic Christmas Celebration. The annual party includes a holiday ice show and other festivities.

SOAK CITY U.S.A.

Ocean waves now lap at the shores of Knott's Berry Farm at Soak City U.S.A., a thirteen-acre water park, opened in a former parking lot adjacent to Independence Hall, across Beach Boulevard from Knott's Berry Farm.

The park includes twenty-one water rides and attractions catering primarily to families and preteens, drawing on legendary south California beach towns such as Huntington, Newport, and Malibu for its decoration and theming.

Among attractions are sixteen high-speed tube and body slides, the **Tidal Wave Bay** wave pool, the **Sunset River,** the **Zuma Express** family tube ride, and **Gremmie Lagoon,** a children's activity pool.

San Onofre Falls features three high-speed slides: **Blackball, Point Break,** and **Riptide; Malibu Run,** including four tube and two body slides named **Wipeout, Dropoff, Over the Falls,** and **Goofyfoot; Laguna Storm Watch Tower,** with three tube slides dubbed **Typhoon, Tornado,** and **Cyclone. Kowabunga Falls** offers a six-lane speed slide.

Soak City U.S.A. operates from May to September. Tickets are available for the water park, in combination with Knott's Berry Farm, and in packages including hotel accommodations.

PART V

SIX FLAGS CALIFORNIA

CHAPTER NINE

SIX FLAGS
MAGIC MOUNTAIN

SIX FLAGS MAGIC MOUNTAIN is a thriller of a theme park, with roller coasters at every turn, and turns on every coaster like you'll not see anywhere else. Things change, but with sixteen roller coasters and nearly 10 miles of track, Magic Mountain may well hold the record for the most such rides in a single theme park.

The park—about 34 miles north of Los Angeles or 62 miles from Disneyland—lays claim to the title of the world's "Xtreme Park." But not everything is all adrenaline: It is also the home of Tweety Bird and Bugs Bunny.

Over the last five years, the largest capital investment in the park's history brought forth the amazing **Déjà Vu,** the astounding **X,** and for the pint-size crowd, the amusing kiddie coaster **Goliath Jr.**

The latest almost indescribably astonishing ride is **Scream!,** a topless, floorless, and all-but-bottomless coaster.

It's a place where the vital statistics for rides include their "g" rating, something that visitors will share in common with jet fighter pilots and astronauts. One g is a measure of ordinary earth gravity; 3 gs, for example, means that the forces pulling on a rider are three times normal. You may also experience zero gs, or near to it, in drops.

Among Six Flags' zoomers is the world's tallest and fastest roller coaster (**Superman: The Escape,** 415 feet and one hundred miles per hour, which blasts off from the Fortress of Solitude at the top of the mountain); the world's tallest and fastest super boomerang (Déjà Vu, 196 feet and sixty-five miles per hour); the world's tallest and fastest stand-up roller coaster (**The Riddler's Revenge,** 156 feet and sixty-five miles per hour); and the world's tallest looping coaster (**Viper,** 140 feet).

Goliath, a massive steel coaster, comes face-to-face with the park's classic wooden coaster, **Colossus.**

These are just the latest additions to the park's world-class collection of roller coasters. Earlier members of the local flying Hall of Fame include the aforementioned Viper, the largest looping roller coaster in the world; **Flashback,** the world's only hairpin-drop roller coaster; **Psyclone,** a traditional boardwalk woodie; **Ninja,** a suspended roller coaster; **Gold Rusher,** the original thriller at the park; **Revolution,** a 360-degree looper; and the spectacular **Batman The Ride,** which almost defies description.

There's even the **Wile E. Coyote Coaster,** a mini ride for the up-and-coming thrill-seeker.

For younger visitors, **Bugs Bunny World** features sixteen rides and attractions with an interesting twist: Kids and parents can ride together.

The *Looney Tunes Nites Parade* takes place on selected nights from late May through late September. Grab a spot to watch some forty cartoon superstars, including Granny and Tweety . . . with Sylvester not far behind, Wile E. Coyote, Foghorn Leghorn, the Tazmanian Devil, Yosemite Sam, Pepé Le Pew, and Daffy Duck. And there's also Superman and the Justice League of America and Batman.

THE STORY OF SIX FLAGS

Land baron Henry Mayor Newhall bought the Spanish land grant known as the Rancho San Francisco in the mid-1800s. The Santa Clarita Valley was the site of California's first gold discovery in 1842 and of the state's first commercial oil well in 1875.

The amusement park opened its gates on May 29, 1971, a joint venture of subsidiaries of SeaWorld and the Newhall Land and Farming Company. Intended as a draw for the housing developments in the area, Magic Mountain originally featured thirty-three rides, attractions, and shows, as well as a local landmark, the 384-foot-tall Sky Tower. America's Bicentennial celebration in 1976 was the occasion for the introduction of the Great American Revolution—the world's first 360-degree looping roller coaster (now known as the Revolution).

In 1979 the park was purchased by the Six Flags Corporation of Arlington, Texas. Under the new management, Roaring Rapids was added in 1981—the

MUST-SEES

X
(the spot to be)

Déjà Vu
(you haven't been here before)

Goliath

The Riddler's Revenge
(a stand-up challenge)

Superman: The Escape

Flashback

Log Jammer

Colossus

Batman The Ride

Freefall

Scream!

Psyclone

Ninja

Revolution

Roaring Rapids

Viper

Bugs Bunny World
(for kids and the adults with them)

Power Trip: The Big Coasters for Breakfast

True thrill-seekers are going to make a beeline for the new Déjà Vu or X coasters, which may relieve some of the lines at the still-fabulous Goliath and The Riddler's Revenge stand-up coaster, and from there on to Superman: The Escape and the venerable Batman The Ride.

Arrive at the park early, at least half an hour before the gates officially open.

PLAN A
Head directly for Déjà Vu at the back of the park in Cyclone Bay. When you wobble off, take advantage of the fact that all the other coaster fanatics are heading your way. Here's your chance to jump on the older rides. Later in the day, the lines at X should be more manageable, and you can also ride Déjà Vu all over again. Catch lunch early or late and complete your tour of the park.

PLAN B
Head for the older coasters first and enjoy the shorter lines on The Riddler's Revenge, Superman: The Escape, and the others. By lunchtime and early afternoon, the lines at Déjà Vu and X will be a bit shorter. Catch lunch early or late and complete your tour of the park.

West's first white-water rafting ride on a 2½-mile-long, man-made river.

Six Flags was the dream of a Texas oil man who came back from a trip to Disneyland in its early days, determined to create a mega-amusement park of his own. Angus Wynne Jr., together with Hollywood director Randall Duell, created the first park in 1961: Six Flags Over Texas.

That first park, located between Dallas and Fort Worth, was divided into six "lands," which had the themes of the six national flags that had flown over Texas in its history.

Six Flags was subsequently purchased by Time Warner, whose properties included Warner Bros. Motion Pictures and Television (home of *Batman*), HBO, and *Time, People,* and *Sports Illustrated* magazines. This brought "cwazy wabbit" Bugs Bunny and his Looney Tunes cartoon compatriots to the park as mascots. The toon people stuck around after Time Warner sold off its division in 1998.

In 2005 Six Flags owned and operated thirty parks in North America. In the spring of 2005, the company opened a new water park, Six Flags Hurricane Harbor near Chicago, part of the Six Flags Great America theme park.

If you watched any television at all in 2005, it would have been all but impossible to miss being introduced to the company's corporate symbol, the dancing fool Mr. Six. The spry, bald man travels around the country in a retro bus, inviting children and their adults to climb on board and travel to the nearest Six Flags park; the music, by the way, is a snippet of "We Like to Party" by the

Six Flags Magic Mountain Ticket Prices

Rates were in effect in mid-2005 and are subject to change. Note that general admission tickets apply to all visitors more than 48 inches tall. Check for online specials at www .sixflags.com.

GENERAL ADMISSION	$47.99
Children (under 48 inches)	$29.99
Seniors (55+)	$29.99
Children (2 and younger)	Free
Fast Lane Boarding Pass (4 one-time passes)	$17 additional
Two-park combo ticket with Hurricane Harbor	$57.99

Parking: $9

Vengaboys. Mr. Six has appeared on talk shows, has his own blog, and (of course) you can buy merchandise with his face. His identity, though, has remained a closely held secret.

Among Six Flags properties are Six Flags Magic Mountain (Six Flags Magic Mountain and Six Flags Hurricane Harbor); Six Flags Over Texas and Six Flags Hurricane Harbor in Arlington, Texas; Six Flags Over Georgia in Atlanta; Six Flags St. Louis; Six Flags Astro-World and Six Flags WaterWorld in Houston; Six Flags Great Adventure and Six Flags Wild Animal Safari Park in Jackson, New Jersey; Six Flags Fiesta Texas in San Antonio; Six Flags Great America between Chicago and Milwaukee; Six Flags Worlds of Adventure in Cleveland; and Six Flags New England in Agawam, Massachusetts.

International properties include La Ronde in Montreal; Walibi Aquitaine in Roquefort, France; Warner Bros. Movie World in Bottrop, Germany; Warner Bros. Movie World in Madrid; and Six Flags parks in Mexico City, Mexico; Biddinghuizen in The Netherlands; and Wavre, Belgium.

VITAL INFORMATION

The park is set in the Santa Clarita Valley, about thirty minutes north of downtown Los Angeles, at the Magic Mountain Parkway exit off Interstate 5 in Valencia.

Six Flags Magic Mountain operates daily from late March through early October. For the remainder of the year, the park is open on weekends and during school holidays, including Christmas school vacation through New Year's Day, with the exception of Christmas Day itself. Check for special offers at the park and at nearby merchants for deals.

Consult the section on Six Flags Hurricane Harbor for spring and summer operating hours for that park. Ordinary hours run from 10:00 A.M. to 6:00 P.M.; in the heart of summer and on holidays the park stays open to 10:00 P.M. or even midnight. Call (661) 367–5965 to confirm hours or consult www.sixflags.com/magicmountain.

Special events include a Kids Fest in June with events for the smallest visitors of the park. There's also a major Fourth of July celebration.

On three weekends in October, Six Flags is transformed into a ghost town for Fright Fest, which features strolling skeletons, ghouls, and goblins, as well as creepy graveyards, mazes, and live entertainment.

In the busy summertime, the largest crowds are usually found from Wednesday through Saturday. Sunday is the least-busy weekend day, and Monday and Tuesday are usually the quietest weekdays.

Fast Lane Boarding Pass. Time is money, even at a theme park; at Six Flags, visitors can purchase a pass that allows them to move to the front of the line at major thrill rides including X, Revolution, Arrowhead Splashdown, Colossus, The Riddler's Revenge, Roaring Rapids, Viper, and Goliath.

Here's the way it works: Each pass costs $15, and allows four detours around waiting lines. The pass can be used at four different rides, or for four people at one ride, or other combinations. The park sells only a limited number of the passes each day.

SIX FLAGS PLAZA

Just past the entrance to Six Flags Magic Mountain is a mini history of amusement parks in this century. To your left is a classic eighty-three-year-old merry-go-round; to the right is a modern, stomach-dropping stacked roller coaster. It's like that throughout much of the park, with old and new, machine and nature side by side.

▐MUST-SEE▌ FLASHBACK

This is the world's only hairpin-drop roller coaster, with six head-over-heels dives and a 540-degree upward spiral. It's all packed into a relatively small area with 1,900 feet of track stacked above each other. The drops are severe, producing a free-fall experience on the plunges; fast steel switchbacks connect the turns just before trains fly into the gravity-defying upward spiral.

Trains reach a maximum of thirty-five miles per hour, with a 3-g force on the one-and-a-half-minute ride. Flashback debuted in 1992.

▐MUST-SEE▌ LOG JAMMER

A log-ride classic dating from the early days of the park and featuring a pair of straight-down drops.

▮ GRAND CAROUSEL

A lovingly restored and maintained 1912 merry-go-round with moving wooden horses. Built by the Philadelphia Toboggan Company, it was operated at the Savin Rock Amusement Park in West Haven, Connecticut, for fifty years before it was brought to California. The carousel has sixty-six seats, including sixty-four horses and two carriages; rides last three minutes.

ORIENT EXPRESS
At the back left corner of the plaza is an inclined railway up the mountain to the rides and observation tower on Samurai Summit. The people-mover is a much easier route up the hill than the stairs and ramps that lead from the back of the park.

PALACE GAMES
A Skeeball and arcade center. Nearby is the Palace Hoop Shoot, a basketball carnival stand.

HIGH SIERRA TERRITORY

One of the prettiest spots in a pretty park, the High Sierra Territory is beautifully landscaped with trees and plants of the mountains. All that said, the entrance to the area is through the General Sam Tree, a 140-foot-tall artificial sequoia tree—a world-record holder for such replicated greenery, according to the park.

SIERRA TWIST
A fast-spinning sled ride on an inclined platter.

YOSEMITE SAM SIERRA FALLS
Splash down 760 feet of twisting, turning water slides aboard two-person rafts. Warning: You will get wet or even soaked. The heavier the riders, the more the water will fly.

GRANNY GRAN PRIX
A mini-car ride for minis and an adult, if they want.

BUGS BUNNY WORLD

The corner of the park devoted to the youngest thrill-seekers has been completely revamped with more than a dozen rides and attractions. And, for more fun, parents can join their youngsters on the rides.

Goliath Jr.
Kiddies too small to ride Goliath, one of the park's signature rides, have their own downsized version here. The little coaster has a lift of 20 feet, reaching a top speed of ten miles per hour over a 350-foot-long track; that will still seem pretty awesome to young kids trying out their first thrill ride. Children under 48 inches must be accompanied by an adult.

Watch Your Back

Six Flags Magic Mountain is a thriller of an amusement park, and many of the rides carry with them important safety and health restrictions. Pregnant women and anyone with back, heart, or other health problems are advised against taking a trip on some of the wilder roller coasters and other rides. Some rides have height restrictions; these are intended to make sure passengers are safely held in place by safety bars, belts, or other restraining devices.

▶ **Must be at least 54 inches to ride:**

Batman The Ride	Viper
Goliath	Scream!
Superman: The Escape	The Riddler's Revenge

▶ **Must be at least 48 inches to ride:**

Colossus	Psyclone
Déjà Vu	Revolution
Flashback	X
Gold Rusher	

▶ **Must be at least 42 inches to ride:**

Atom Smasher	Sandblasters
Freefall	Sierra Twist
Grinder Gearworks	Skycoaster
Ninja	Swashbuckler
Roaring Rapids	Tidal Wave

▶ **Under 48 inches must be accompanied by adult; children not permitted to sit on adult's lap:**

Goliath Jr.

▶ **Under 42 inches must be accompanied by adult; children not permitted to sit on adult's lap:**

Buccaneer	Arrowhead Splashdown
Circus Wheel	Jolly Roger
Grand Carousel	Log Jammer
Granny Gran Prix (must be over 48 inches to drive)	Yosemite Sam Sierra Falls

▶ **Must be at least 36 inches tall:**

Scrambler

Looney Tunes Lodge

An interactive fun zone filled with thousands of foam balls for throwing, catapulting, and blasting, plus slides and much more.

The Canyon Blaster

A roller coaster that offers pint-size thrills for the kids (and their parents).

Daffy's Adventure Tours

A wild ride on an out-of-control bus, with Daffy Duck behind the wheel.

Elmer's Weather Balloons

Check the weather from these high-flying balloons with Mr. Fudd in charge.

Foghorn Leghorn's Barnyard Railway

A ride into Foghorn's barn on a real coal-burning choo-choo.

Merrie Melodies Carousel

Pick your favorite steed.

Sylvester's Pounce and Bounce is a kiddie-size version of Freefall. *Photo by Corey Sandler*

Pepé le Pew's Tea Party

Go for a ride as Pepé chases the love of his life in a whirling teacup ride.

Sylvester's Pounce and Bounce

Kids and their parents shoot to the sky and then bounce down to a smooth landing on this scaled-down version of the park's Freefall ride.

Tweety's Escape

Jump in a Tweety cage and watch out for Sylvester in this classic ride.

Taz's Trucking Company

The best little Bigfoot trucks in the west.

Yosemite Sam's Flight School

Take a lesson in high flying from the master of the air, Yosemite Sam.

Wile E. Coyote Critter Canyon

Here's your chance to take part in the time-honored pursuit of tame sheep, goats, ducks, and other critters you can pet. Display areas feature more than fifty species of rare and exotic animals.

Animal Action Show

Animals from exotic to household friends perform in a stage show presented in the Carrot Club Theater.

COLOSSUS COUNTY FAIR

MUST-SEE SCREAM!

The name for the sixteenth major coaster at Six Flags Magic Mountain gets right to the point: This is a breathtaking ride that features a unique floorless train that sends guests through a series of seven up-and-over, 360-degree inversions across 4,000 feet of track.

Riders are strapped into trains with thirty-two "flying chairs" with their feet dangling in the air, no track above their head, and no coach around their seats. They begin their trip with a 150-foot drop at sixty-five miles per hour into a huge 128-foot vertical loop. Next is a plunge into a gut-wrenching 96-foot dive loop followed by a dramatic heartline camelback designed to enhance the feeling of flying.

(Let me define that "dive loop" for you: The train climbs the loop on the outside, then rolls underneath the track across the top of the loop before diving down on the inside of the loop. You can scream now.)

Next up is a cobra roll at 78 feet above the ground before a straight plunge down into a high-speed sharp turn and then into a nearly ninety-degree high-speed helix. Finishing out the flight, riders scream over a banked turn, into a speed hill, and end up with two interlocking corkscrews and one more hill.

The ride, designed by coaster experts Bolliger & Mabillard of Switzerland, is the only ride of its kind in Southern California. The capacity is about 1,600 riders per hour; guests must be at least 54 inches tall to ride.

MUST-SEE COLOSSUS

The county fair serves as the backdrop for the colossal Colossus coaster, one of the largest dual-track wooden roller coasters in the world with nearly a mile of track times two courses.

An old-style speed demon, the Colossus features cars that reach speeds of up to sixty-two miles per hour and experience g forces of up to 3.23 on the three-and-a-half-minute ride. (That's a long ride in roller-coaster terms.)

Colossus covers ten acres of land, climbing to 115 feet above the ground at its highest point. There are fourteen hills in all with two drops of more than 100 feet each (a world record at the time of its construction in 1978) and a climactic triple jump near the end.

There are two six-car trains on each of the two tracks; each car seats four riders. The maximum capacity of the ride is about 2,600 guests per hour. That's among the largest capacities of any thrill ride in the world. Colossus is a good place to head when lines are long elsewhere.

After dark, Colossus becomes a multicolored light show. A computer-controlled lighting system bathes the entire ride in color; as many as 128 different color combinations can be created.

▓ MUST-SEE ▓ GOLIATH

Towering 255 feet above the earth, the massive steel superstructure has one of the world's tallest drops, and at eighty-five miles per hour it is one of the fastest roller coasters anywhere.

Combining traditional coaster thrills with a few new twists, the three-minute ride travels over 4,500 feet of track that includes sharp plunges, sweeping spirals, zero-gravity drops, and a 120-foot-long tunnel in total darkness.

The modern steel coaster Goliath plunges alongside the classic woodie Colossus. *Photo by Corey Sandler*

Seated two-abreast in fireorange trains, the cars climb high above the Colossus coaster and near the peak of Superman: The Escape. The sixty-one-degree first drop plunges 255 feet to the ground . . . and beyond into darkness of the black hole. Emerging from the tunnel, the trains race up into a giant sweeping turn where steel coaster technology meets a traditional woodie as the track soars 100 feet up and over the Colossus. From there it is into camelback hills and a high-speed spiraling curve, followed by a carousel dive outside the station.

Buccaneer

A rocking pirate ship swings back and forth, gathering momentum until it finally turns upside down.

Circus Wheel

Round and round you'll go; only the operator knows where you'll stop.

Swashbuckler

A spinning swing set.

Center Ring Games

Video machines, carnival games, and your chance to cut your own audio- or videotape singing with a professional backup group.

GOTHAM CITY BACKLOT

The dark world of the Caped Crusader is re-created in Gotham City Backlot, the newest of Six Flags Magic Mountain's theme areas. You'll know you're in town when you hear the rumble of the awesome Batman ride and the screams of the visitors who paid good money to climb on board.

You'll enter through the portals of the city and into Bruce Wayne's beautifully landscaped Gotham City Park. As you move a bit farther into the park, though, you begin to hear some strange sounds and see some unsettling sights, including a crashed police car, a broken fire hydrant, and other indicators that all is not well with Gotham City. And then you are into the somewhat menacing tunnels beneath Gotham City, tunnels that lead up to Batman's newest crime-fighting device, The Ride.

⁝ *MUST-SEE* ⁝ BATMAN THE RIDE

You'll clamber aboard one of two sleek, black, ski-lift-style trains, each carrying thirty-two passengers sitting four across. Unlike standard roller coasters, though, the trains are missing something: the floor! You'll be locked into place with padded over-the-shoulder and belt-locking harnesses.

Traditional roller-coaster trains travel atop a track and inside of loops; Batman The Ride sends you soaring 360 degrees around the outside of a loop, a very different sensation. Passengers experience a maximum of 4 gs on the 2,700-foot track. Reaching speeds of up to fifty miles per hour, the trains enter into two vertical loops (77 feet and 68 feet tall), two single corkscrews (each 40 feet long), and a one-of-a-kind, 224-foot "heartline" spin that delivers a zero-g weightless force with nothing but air below your feet.

The heartline spin comes after the first loop when riders go through a twisting spin centered around the middle of your body. It's a quick trip from a 4-g loop into a zero-gravity roll, which is something you don't do every day unless you are a professional coaster rider.

Is Batman the ultimate in roller coasters? Well, the experts point out that there are faster, higher, and wilder coasters—including the Viper at Six Flags Magic Mountain—but Batman is unusual because the lower bodies of the riders are hanging free. Think of it as a ski lift gone crazy and you get the idea. Hardcore roller-coaster fans rank Batman The Ride among the most bodacious in America. I know it is on my personal list of terrors.

Six Flags also deserves credit for the good job of applying the ride's theme in the waiting areas. You'll walk through a crumbling neighborhood, past the steaming wreck of a police car, and into the decrepit innards of a factory on the way to your appointment with the ride.

(In the world of amusement park technology, the Batman ride is called an inverted coaster, whereas the Ninja is known as a suspended coaster because it has enclosed train cars hanging from an overhead track.)

The capacity of the Swiss-made ride is about 1,400 passengers per hour.

■ ATOM SMASHER

A whirling, wobbly turntable ride set within the industrial walls of the ACME factory.

■ GRINDER GEARWORKS

Let centrifugal force plaster you to the wall as the platform spins at a forty-five-degree angle. Riders stand up in a whirling cage that goes round and round and then turns on its side with prisoners, er, passengers stuck to the exterior by centrifugal force.

THE MOVIE DISTRICT

The Riddler is the star of the "ultimate backlot experience," the former Monterey Landing area of Six Flags Magic Mountain.

▦ MUST-SEE THE RIDDLER'S REVENGE

Turn on the superlative machine: Among the latest and greatest at Six Flags is The Riddler's Revenge, the world's tallest and fastest stand-up roller coaster.

Looming 156 feet tall and reaching a top speed of sixty-five miles per hour and maximum g-force of 4.2, the coaster sends riders looping head-over-heels six times during nearly a mile of twisting, looping, and spiraling green steel track. Did we mention that riders stand up through the entire three-minute ride?

The ride's theme is based on the character Edward Nygma—the Riddler—from the Batman series. Guests are drawn through a glaring green neon question mark entrance into Riddler's laboratory.

Standing four abreast and strapped in sleek green bullet-nosed trains, riders climb sixteen stories before plummeting almost straight down the first 146-foot drop. There are six inversions: a 360-degree vertical loop at a height of 124 feet, a 360-degree oblique loop, two over-the-top diving loops, and a pair of 150-foot-long barrel rolls. There's also a 250-foot-long, high-speed spiral.

The ride, designed by a Swiss company, has a capacity of 1,800 riders per hour. Guests must be at least 54 inches tall to ride.

▦ MUST-SEE FREEFALL

Here's an elevator ride you won't soon forget. Your car will rise to the top of a 98-foot tower, move out onto a platform . . . and then drop straight down. You'll reach fifty-five miles per hour in about two seconds and then zoom out on a curved rail at the bottom.

Each of the eight cars carries four passengers per trip; one car drops every twelve seconds. A state-of-the-art system applies brake pressure according to the weight of each car plus its passengers at forty different sensor locations along the slow-down pathway.

By the way, professional and amateur theme park enthusiasts consider this ride to be a roller coaster, albeit in a class of its own.

GOLD RUSHER

The first roller coaster at Six Flags, this runaway mine train was built in 1971. By comparison to the big coasters, it's rather tame with a top speed of thirty-five miles per hour, but it still has its thrills. The ½-mile track is built into the hillside with its track very close to the ground; this is an excellent beginner coaster ride that lasts about two-and-a-half minutes.

SANDBLASTERS

Every amusement park worth its name has a bumper car ride; if that's what you're looking for, here's a fine example.

TIDAL WAVE

The wettest water flume that features twenty-passenger boats plunging over a 50-foot waterfall.

BATMAN & ROBIN LIVE ACTION SHOW

Based on the film *Batman & Robin,* the *Batman & Robin Live Action Show* brings the hit movie to life with a behind-the-scenes look at big Hollywood stunts. The show is presented from about Memorial Day until Halloween.

The explosive stage production features elaborate set designs, incredible stunts and special effects, plus athletic hijinks, such as in-line skating performed by Mr. Freeze's Icemen, and an assortment of unusual high-tech Batgadgets, including a souped-up Batmobile.

The action begins as the diabolical Mr. Freeze teams up with the lovely but deadly Poison Ivy to seize and freeze Gotham City. Poison Ivy, the result of a laboratory mishap, releases Mr. Freeze from the Arkham Asylum where he has been imprisoned; he promptly unleashes a new kind of frozen terror. However, Batman and Robin, along with superhero Batgirl, turn on the heat to melt Mr. Freeze's icy grip on the good citizens of Gotham.

Scrambler

This human eggbeater spins and rocks a two-seater car on an uneven platform.

Spin Out

As the cage spins faster and faster, the floor drops out below you.

CYCLONE BAY

A Southern California equivalent of a beachfront boardwalk and much more attractive than Coney Island in New York, this bay runs alongside the Psyclone wooden coaster.

[MUST-SEE] DÉJÀ VU

Wanna see the world's tallest and fastest suspended roller coaster with a super boomerang loop? Wanna see it again?

Strapped in ski-lift-style chairs suspended from the track above, riders plummet 196 feet and fly at sixty-five miles per hour over the outside of a vertical loop and into a 110-foot-tall boomerang turn with nothing but the sky above their feet. The first drop could not be any steeper: a ninety-degree free fall. The 1,203-foot-long track includes one vertical loop 102 feet in the air and a boomerang turn 110 feet up. Maximum gravitational forces reach a significant 4.5 g. The cars go through the track one time forward and one time backward: Déjà Vu all over again.

Each train carries twenty-four passengers, seated four abreast in a sleek V-shape design. The ride has a capacity of 1,100 riders per hour; expect long lines at midday. Guests must be at least 48 inches tall to ride.

[MUST-SEE] PSYCLONE

A traditional wooden coaster opened in 1991, Psyclone is a replica of the legendary 1927 Cyclone in Coney Island, New York. How realistic? Well, in addition to the feel of the steep drops and high-banked twists and turns, you'll also hear the somewhat unnerving sounds of creaking wood and screaming steel wheels.

There is more than ½ mile of steel track, eleven hills, and five high-speed banked turns; the track also drops into a 183-foot-long, pitch-black tunnel. Riders are treated to a maximum g force of 3.

Built in 1991 the ride required 450,000 board-feet of treated southern pine, unpainted to emphasize the ride's natural beauty. It's held together with 16,000 pounds of nails and 125,000 pounds of bolts. One more useless but interesting factoid: The ride required something like 40,000 man-hours to build; if one carpenter had done the job by himself, it would have taken him twenty years to finish the job.

Psyclone features a 95-foot first drop angled at fifty-three degrees, ten additional steep hills, and average speeds of up to fifty miles per hour.

■ DIVE DEVIL

A strange cross between a giant backyard swing, bungee jumping, hang-gliding, and skydiving, and you get to pay for the privilege!

The ride apparatus consists of a soaring 173-foot-tall steel arch with four suspended steel cables; alongside is a pair of launch towers. At the end of each pair of cables is an attachment for up to three flight suits.

The riders are placed in the suits and stretched out parallel to the ground, and then pulled backward by cable behind the arch to the top of the launch towers, about 152 feet off the ground. When a rider pulls a ripcord, they all swoop down headfirst in free fall about 50 feet before they zoom past their starting point. When they reach the bottom of the fall, they are about 6 feet off the ground and moving about sixty miles per hour.

The forward motion of the fliers carries them about 90 to 100 feet up in the air in front of the arch, reaching a weightless free-fall stall in midair before they swing back in the other direction. The fliers swing back and forth about a dozen times before they come to a stop at the bottom.

To ride Dive Devil, you'll have to fork over an additional fee. For flights with three fliers in the harness, admission will be about $16 per flier; for two-person flights, the charge will be about $22; and for solo flights the fare will be about $28. Riders must be at least 42 inches tall.

■ ARROWHEAD SPLASHDOWN

A pleasant tour aboard a jet boat with a splashy 57-foot-plunge finale. Arrowhead Splashdown is less likely to soak riders than the Log Jam ride, but don't discount the possibility of the occasional damp touchdown. The loading platform for the ride is a circular turntable that is synchronized to the speed of the moving boats. Arrowhead Splashdown was previously known as Jet Stream.

Entertainment at Cyclone Bay includes Sharkey's Shooting Gallery and the Boardwalk Bandstand. Check the daily schedule for performances.

Muscle Beach Arcade

A video-game parlor.

SAMURAI SUMMIT

MUST-SEE SUPERMAN: THE ESCAPE

Look, up in the sky: That roller coaster is accelerating from zero to one hundred miles per hour in just seven seconds and delivering six-and-a-half seconds of weightlessness. Only Superman: The Escape could perform such feats. In fact, Six Flags claims its unusual ride was the first to reach one hundred miles per hour.

We're not going to quibble over a few miles per hour or notches on the g-force belt; we do know that this ride is super-awesome.

The L-shape dual-track ride travels more than 900 feet (three football fields) from its launch pad on Samurai Summit on a track that suddenly curves into a climb straight up a 415-foot-tall tower.

The Superman adventure begins in the Fortress of Solitude, a crystalline ice cavern high atop the mountain ridge at Six Flags. Confronted by enemy forces inside the Fortress, the only escape for guests is to board fifteen-passenger aerodynamically designed vehicles. Electromagnetic motors blast the six-ton vehicles out of the Fortress through a special effects tunnel; the cars accelerate to one hundred miles per hour and 4.5 gs and then climb the forty-one-story tower, reaching near-total weightlessness when they reach the top and free-fall straight down the skyscraper.

The linear synchronous motors apply acceleration that has been compared with an F-18 jet fighter rocketing off an aircraft carrier.

The construction of the Swiss-designed ride—at a cost of roughly $10 million—changed the look of the park. Other alterations to the scene include a bridge over the lift for the venerable Gold Rusher coaster, which circles all around the loading station for the Superman ride.

⬛ MUST-SEE NINJA

The Black Belt of coasters, this is the West Coast's fastest suspended roller coaster. Trains swing 180 degrees side to side while hanging from an overhead track and traveling at speeds of up to fifty-five miles per hour. Riders are treated to nearly 4 gs in the second spiral.

Completed in 1988, the ride takes about two minutes to travel 2,700 feet of track. Each of three trains carries a total of twenty-eight riders sitting two abreast. The maximum capacity of the ride is about 1,600 riders per hour.

Orient Express
The people-mover down the mountain to Six Flags Plaza.

Sky Tower
The thirty-eight-story landmark offers a spectacular view of the entire park and much of the Santa Clarita Valley. The elevator ride to the top is part of the thrill.

RAPIDS CAMP CROSSING

Entertainment at Rapids Camp Crossing includes the Mining Town Arcade and Mining Town Games.

⬛ MUST-SEE ROARING RAPIDS
America's first man-made, white-water river. Twelve-passenger boats splash through waves, crosscurrents, and rapids.

BAJA RIDGE

MUST-SEE X

Welcome to the fourth dimension of roller-coaster technology, a trip where riders for the first time will travel in vehicles that can independently spin 360 degrees forward or backward as they move down the track. On X, once the train leaves the station, there is no up, down, left, or right.

The huge 20-foot-wide, wing-shaped vehicles each carry twenty-eight passengers seated four-abreast; the cars each weigh 10,000 pounds. Riders plummet 200 feet to the ground, headfirst and facedown; then they race at seventy-six miles per hour, spinning through acrobatic head-over-heels loops along the course of the 3,600-foot twisting steel maze.

Stop for a minute and consider that first statistic: The trains are 20 feet wide. Riders sit two abreast on each side of a large central control mechanism that rotates their seats. There are four rails beneath the huge trains; two hold the trains and the other two rotate the seats.

The first drop—the one that plummets 200 feet—produces a maximum 4 gs. The track includes a twisting front flip, two back flips, and a pair of raven turns.

The ride has a capacity of 1,600 riders an hour; passengers must be at least 48 inches tall to ride.

MUST-SEE REVOLUTION

You say you want a revolution? This giant looping steel roller coaster was the first of its kind when it was built in 1976. It included the world's first 360-degree vertical loop, 90 feet above the Grand Carousel.

The white steel track is built into the lush hillsides and features a fast-and-furious series of steep dips and serious dives inspired by old-fashioned wooden roller coasters.

The two-and-a-half minute ride travels over 3,457 feet of track; each train carries twenty riders in five cars sitting two abreast. The maximum capacity is about 2,000 riders per hour.

Riders experience a maximum positive g force of 4.94 entering the vertical loop, which soars 90 feet high in a 45-foot-diameter loop. The difference between the rider's lowest point at Valencia Falls and the highest point at the top of the lift is 113 feet.

MUST-SEE VIPER

The largest looping roller coaster in the world, with a top speed of seventy miles per hour, three vertical loops, a double-barrel boomerang, and a classic corkscrew. Some roller enthusiasts consider the Viper among the most frightening rides on the planet.

Riders are turned upside down seven times, and there are sixteen changes in elevation; the first drop is a gargantuan 188 feet, seven stories higher than the colossal Colossus.

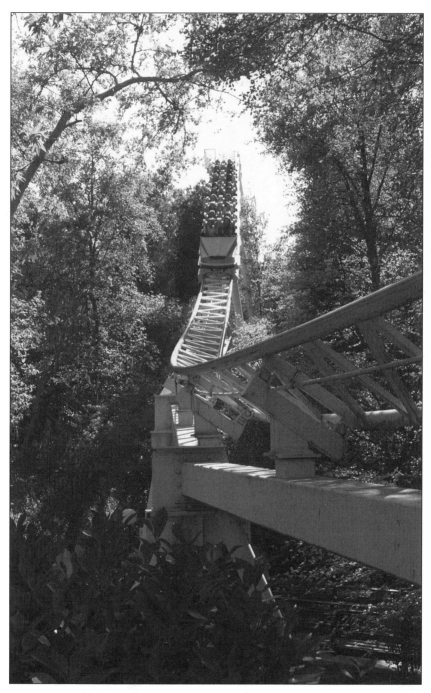

Revolution hugs the hillside. *Photo by Corey Sandler*

The Viper in Baja Ridge. *Photo by Corey Sandler*

The two-and-a-half-minute ride travels a 3,830-foot track; each of the three trains carries twenty-eight riders in seven cars, seated two across. The maximum capacity of the ride is about 1,700 riders per hour.

About those vertical loops: The first one rises and falls 114 feet, making it among the world's tallest; the second is a mere 90 feet in height, and the last 62 feet tall. The boomerang rotates riders upside down twice; it rises 60 feet from the lowest to highest point. The corkscrew is 40 feet high and 200 feet long.

If you need a bit of reassurance before you strap yourself into the over-the-shoulder locking harness for the ride, consider that the construction of the Viper in 1990 required one million pounds of steel and 600,000 tons of concrete.

EATING YOUR WAY THROUGH SIX FLAGS MAGIC MOUNTAIN

Eateries at Six Flags run from the most basic of fast food—burgers and dogs—to a talking moose head to a sit-down family restaurant with a spectacular mountaintop view.

◼ SIX FLAGS PLAZA

Chicken Plantation. Crispy fried chicken with all the fixings. Open in high-season.

Plaza Café. Sandwiches, salads, and desserts set beside Valencia Falls.

Suzette's Bakery. Essentials like funnel cakes and other sweets.

◼ HIGH SIERRA TERRITORY AND BUGS BUNNY WORLD

Mooseburger Lodge. The mooseburgers aren't really made out of moose, and the restaurant isn't really a hunting lodge in the High Sierras, but you could be fooled by both. This is an attractive, fun, family restaurant that features a trio of robotic moose heads who are aided and abetted by singing waiters and waitresses who will be glad to perform the Moose Muffle Shuffle just for you. In addition to the big burgers, you'll also find ribs, a buffet, and special desserts including (of course) chocolate mousse. Entrees range from about $7.00 to $10.00.

Wascal's. A kiddie-oriented burger and fries stand.

■ THE MOVIE DISTRICT
Eduardo's Grill. Mexican specialties.

Waterfront Commissary. A burger and fries, and chicken strips eatery. Prices range from about $5.00 to $7.00, including a drink.

■ RAPIDS CAMP CROSSING
Katy's Kettle. Hamburgers, turkey burgers, and fries.

■ CYCLONE BAY AND SAMURAI SUMMIT
Los Cuates Mexican Grill. A palsy joint for tacos, burritos, and more.

Surfside Grill. What would you expect from a restaurant under a jumbo hot dog? Frankfurters, chili dogs, icees, and more.

■ COLOSSUS COUNTY FAIR AND PIRATES COVE
Carousel Grill. Philly cheesesteaks, chicken clubs, and other specialties.

Food Etc. An indoor food court offering a wide range of delectables, including Mexican food, pasta, pizza, and more.

■ GOTHAM CITY BACKLOT
The Pizza Vector. Like the sign says.

SIX FLAGS HURRICANE HARBOR

Whoosh! Hurricane Harbor sits alongside Six Flags Magic Mountain offering a cooling antidote to the sometimes hot park; its cool waters, though, are not without some extreme thrills of their own.

The twenty-two-acre park, in the shadow of Colossus and Flashback at Magic Mountain, tells the watery story of a lost lagoon in a forgotten world. Set amid the fringes of a tropical jungle, you'll find the remains of a disappeared civilization, hidden pirate treasures, playful sea creatures, ancient ruins, shipwrecks, girls in bikinis, guys in muscle shirts, kids in wave pools, suntan lotion, hot dogs, ice cream . . . you get the idea.

Daring visitors are willingly sucked into **Tornado,** an extreme tubing ride. The thrills begin 75 feet in the air with a plunge down a 132-foot-long tunnel that leads to a huge open-ended funnel. The ride's specially designed four-person cloverleaf-shaped tubes hug the inside of the funnel, splashing back and forth in 5,000 gallons of swirling water. When gravity finally takes hold, the tubes

Hurricane Harbor Ticket Prices

Rates were in effect in 2005 at Six Flags Hurricane Harbor and are subject to change. Check for online specials, including deep discounts for spring and fall seasons, at www .sixflags.com.

GENERAL ADMISSION	$23.99
Hurricane Harbor/Magic Mountain combo ticket	$57.99
Children under 48 inches	$16.99
Children (2 and younger)	Free
Seniors (55+)	$16.99

Parking: $9

exit through the mouth of the funnel into a catch pool below.

A viewing platform lets riders and guests watch the action. Tornado is located next to the Forgotten Sea wave pool. Riders must be 48 inches or taller.

Six Flags expects that most visitors will spend a day at either Magic Mountain or Hurricane Harbor. Combination tickets for separate days are available. Some visitors, though, might choose to visit the water park in the day and cross through to the theme park at night. The parks share the same parking lot.

The operating schedule for Hurricane Harbor is dependent upon the weather, but plans call for it to be open on weekends only from early May and then daily from Memorial Day through Labor Day from 10:00 A.M. to 6:00 P.M.; the park will stay open until 8:00 P.M. on summer weekends. After Labor Day, Hurricane Harbor will remain open on weekends only through the end of September.

Be sure to confirm the schedule; call (661) 367–5965.

Rafts are required at Lightning Falls, Tiki Falls, Lost Temple Rapids, and the River Cruise. All visitors can use free tubes provided by the park; on busy days it may make sense to rent a personal tube for an additional charge.

▉MUST-SEE▉ BLACK SNAKE SUMMIT

The hot news at this cool park, the area features five speed slides, including the tallest enclosed speed slides in Southern California—two totally enclosed twisting slides, one almost vertical plunge, and two totally enclosed twisting tube slides.

The twin queens of this hill are Twisted Fang and Coiled Cobra, enclosed body slides each 500 feet long and dropping from the 75-foot level. Nearby is Venom Drop, an open slide that extends only 300 feet.

Sidewinder and Boa Constrictor are 59-foot-tall enclosed tube slides that extend 650 feet.

▉MUST-SEE▉ LIZARD LAGOON

This just-over-three-acre activity area includes a 3½-foot-deep pool that has basketball hoops, beach volleyball courts, a lizard slide, and the Reptile Ridge tower with five body slides.

■ REPTILE RIDGE

Five gentle body slides descend from the 35-foot-tall summit. There are two 130-foot-long enclosed twisting slides, Gecko Gully East and West, and Gator Gorge, a 70-foot-long enclosed straight drop. A pair of open flume body slides are the 230-foot-long twisting slide Iguana Ravine and the gentle Croc Creek, 255 feet long.

▦ MUST-SEE ▦ BAMBOO RACER

A six-lane racing slide from a 45-foot tower. Entrants plunge headfirst, side by side on water toboggans down 625-foot-long lanes.

■ CASTAWAY COVE

Designed exclusively for the littlest swashbucklers (less than 54 inches tall), Castaway Cove is one of the largest children's water play areas in California. Adventures include a variety of pint-size water slides, including a pair of cannon slides. Little visitors will also find waterfalls; a bamboo rain tree; friendly sea creatures; an organ that squirts water as guests play the keys; hidden pirate treasures; and a kiddie fortress loaded with waterfalls, gadgets, swings, slides, and more. Youngsters can also splash in the secluded tide pools of Octopus Island, where a giant eight-legged creature stands guard.

■ SHIPWRECK SHORES

The place where Red Eye the Pirate first dropped anchor is now a splashy lagoon that offers more than thirty-two family activities, including a huge skull that dumps thousands of gallons of water onto intruders every few minutes and weeping sails that shed continuous streams. Visitors enter through the rickety remains of Red Eye's ship, mysterious ancient ruins from a lost civilization. Around the shoreline are eight 11-foot-tall water-spraying statues and the old temple entrance to the volcano.

■ GEYSER PEAK

Towering 45 feet above the harbor between Castaway Cove and Shipwreck Shores is the volcano where Red Eye the Pirate once hid his plunder.

■ THE RIVER CRUISE

Guests board rafts that circumnavigate Castaway Cove and Shipwreck Shores on a 1,300-foot-long lazy river at the center of the park. The 3-foot-deep river moves at about two miles per hour, and a complete circuit takes about eight minutes. Along the river banks are nine 15-foot-tall tikis, replicas of the famous statues of Easter Island, as well as the Rainbow Reef, an overgrown tropical rain forest.

▦ MUST-SEE ▦ FORGOTTEN SEA WAVE POOL

Hurricane Harbor's tide pool with a constant tide of 2-foot waves. The 480,000-gallon pool slopes to a depth of 6 feet.

⠿ MUST-SEE ⠿ TABOO TOWER

The park's showcase attraction—visible from I–5—is the crumbled remains of an ancient temple; three speed slides, including a completely dark tube, are built into the 65-foot-tall ruins. They include the 300-foot-long Daredevil Plunge, with a forty-five-degree straight drop; the bumpy, 260-foot-long Escape Chute; and the Secret Passage, an enclosed 325-foot spiraling slide.

◼ LIGHTNING FALLS

Three twisting, turning, 400-foot-long open tube slides named after island storms drop about 42 feet; look for Typhoon Tube, Tornado Twist, and Thunder Trough.

◼ TIKI FALLS

Visitors splash through the mouths of Hurricane Harbor's three most famous tikis: Old Shut Eye, a 395-foot enclosed slide; Stone Face, a 385-foot enclosed tube; and Bright Eyes, a semienclosed 400-foot tube.

◼ LOST TEMPLE RAPIDS

A 560-foot-long, six-person family rafting adventure down the island's ancient aqueduct.

PART VI

SLEEPING AND EATING FOR LESS

CHAPTER TEN

NEGOTIATING FOR A ROOM

DON'T BUY A ROOM. Negotiate a room. Hotel rooms, like almost everything else, are subject to negotiation and change.

Here is how to pay the highest possible price for a hotel room: Walk up to the front desk without a reservation and say, "I'd like a room." Unless the NO VACANCY sign is lit, you're going to pay the "rack rate," which is the published maximum nightly charge.

Here are a few ways to pay the lowest possible price:

1. Join associations and clubs that offer discounts to their members, such as AAA or AARP. And don't overlook direct offers from hotels and chains published in newspapers and magazines.

2. Get on the Internet and check out the Web sites for major chains and independent hotels. Be on the lookout for Internet specials that may be less than the price you will be quoted on the phone.

You can also make an Internet visit to travel portals—hotel booking and travel agency Web sites—that offer searches by location. Travel portals are usually more convenient, but in my experience, best prices are usually found by going directly to the hotel Web sites.

3. If you want to try to get an even better deal, pick up your telephone and call your best candidates directly. (Don't call the central booking number for hotel chains; they rarely have the best deals.)

Start by asking for the room rate. Then ask them for their best rate. Does that sound like an unnecessary second request? Trust us, it's not: We can't begin to count the number of times the rates have dropped substantially when we ask again.

Here's a true story: I once called the reservation desk of a major hotel chain and asked for the rates for a night at a Chicago location. "That will be $149 per night," I was told. "Ouch," I said. "Oh, would you like to spend less?" the reservationist asked. I admitted that I would, and she punched a few keys on her key-

Here's My Card

Membership in AAA brings some important benefits for the traveler, although you may not be able to apply the club's usual 10 percent discount on top of whatever hotel rate you negotiate. (It doesn't hurt to ask, though.) Be sure to request a Tour Book and a California map from AAA, even if you plan to fly to California; they are much better than the maps given by car rental agencies.

AARP members also receive a discount. Most hotels also offer senior discounts, accepting your driver's license or your gray hair as proof of age.

Weekly, Not Weakly

Are you planning to stay for a full week? Ask for the weekly rate. If the room clerk says there is no such rate, ask to speak to the manager. He or she may be willing to shave a few dollars per day off the rate for a long-term stay.

board: "They have a special promotion going on. How about $109 per night?"

Not bad for a city hotel, I reasoned, but still I hadn't asked the big question: "What is your best rate?" "Oh, our best rate? That would be $79," said the agent.

But, wait: "OK, that's good. I'm an AAA member, by the way." Another pause, and then the reservation agent said, "That's fine, Mr. Sandler. The nightly room rate will be $71.10. Have a nice day."

When you feel you've negotiated the best deal you can obtain over the phone, make a reservation at the hotel of your choice. Be sure to go over the dates and prices one more time, and obtain the name of the person you spoke with and a confirmation number if available.

4. But wait: When you show up at your hotel on the first night, take a look at the marquee to see if the hotel is advertising a discount rate. Use your cell phone to make a few phone calls to neighboring hotels to check their rates. Many of the hotels in the Disneyland area adjust their prices based on attendance levels at the park. It is not uncommon to see prices change by $10 or more over the course of a day.

If the hotel you chose is still offering the best rate and you're going to stay, here's where you need to be bold. Walk up to the desk as if you did not have a reservation, and ask the clerk: "What is your best room rate for tonight?" If the rate they give you as a walk-up is less than the rate of your reservation, you are now properly armed to ask for a reduction in your room rate.

Similarly, if the room rate advertised out front on the marquee drops during your stay, don't be shy about asking that your charges be reduced. Just be sure to ask for the reduction before you spend another night at the old rate, and obtain the name of the clerk who promises a change. If the hotel tries a lame excuse like "that's only for new check-ins," you can offer to check out and then check back in again—that threat usually works. And you can always check out and go to the hotel across the road that will usually match the rates of its competitor.

5. Here is the way to play lowball roulette only in the low-season: Come without a reservation and cruise one of the motel strips near Disneyland. Check the outdoor marquees for discount prices and make notes. Find a phone booth and make a few phone calls to the hotels with attractive rates. Once again, be sure to ask for the best price. The later in the day you search for a room, the more likely you are to find a hotel ready to make a deal.

Except for the busiest periods of the year—the time from Christmas through New Year's and the heart of summer among them—you're not going to have any trouble locating a place to stay near Disneyland. In fact, the biggest problem facing most visitors is choosing among the various places to stay.

The opening of Disney's California Adventure in 2001 remade the hotel market in and around the Disneyland Resort. Disney's Grand Californian Hotel is a handsome addition and is the first Disney-owned hotel with a direct entrance into a theme park.

Disney also upgraded the already-fine Disney's Paradise Pier Hotel (the former Disneyland Pacific Hotel) and the Disneyland Hotel.

With the opening of the new theme park in Anaheim, there are approximately 17,400 hotel rooms within a mile of Disneyland, an increase of 3,400 rooms from recent years. And several thousand more places to sleep are under construction or are planned to be built in the first decade of the twenty-first century.

Wrong Numbers

Be sure you understand the telephone billing policy at the motel. Some establishments allow free local calls, while others charge as much as a dollar for such calls. (We're especially unhappy with service charges for 800 numbers.) Be sure to examine your bill carefully at checkout and make sure it is correct. We strongly suggest you obtain a telephone credit card and use it when you travel; nearly all motels tack a high service charge on long-distance calls, and there is no reason to pay it.

ANAHEIM AREA

(Price ranges are approximate and subject to change and adjustments in busiest seasons; ratings are relative for the area. Rates near the park are often the lowest in the area because of the intense competition, except during the busiest times of the year when the hotels may be sold out. You may have to stay in nearby communities, including Buena Park, Costa Mesa, Huntington Beach, Newport, Orange, and Santa Ana. Each is within about fifteen minutes of Disneyland; Buena Park is home of Knott's Berry Farm.)

The hotels listed here represent the best deals and best quality in the area; not every hotel is included. Properties marked with an *Econoguide* ★ are relatively better than others in the area.

Properties marked with a ➋ icon are within five minutes of Disneyland.

Legend

$	Budget: less than $50
$$	$50–$99
$$$	$100–$149
$$$$	Luxury: $150 and more
★	*Econoguide* Bests
➋	Near Disneyland

➋ **Abby's Anaheimer Inn.** 1201 West Katella Avenue. (714) 774–0211 or (800) 933–6222. www.stayanight.com/anaheimerinn. $$

➋ **Anaheim Angel Inn.** 800 East Katella Avenue. (714) 634–9121 or (800) 358–4400. anaheimangel.tripod.com. Shuttle, pool. $–$$

★ ➋ **Anaheim Carriage Inn.** 2125 South Harbor Boulevard. (714) 740–1440 or (800) 345–2131. www.carriage-inn.com. Continental breakfast, shuttle, pool. $–$$

➋ **Anaheim Days Inn Disneyland/West.** 1030 West Ball Road. (714) 520–0101. www.daysinn.com. $$

★ ➋ **Anaheim Desert Inn and Suites.** 1600 South Harbor Boulevard. (714) 772–5050 or (800) 433–5270. www.anaheimdesertinn.com. Continental breakfast, shuttle, pool. $$

★ ➋ **Anaheim Desert Palm Inn and Suites.** 631 West Katella Avenue. (714) 535–1133 or (800) 635–5423. www.anaheimdesertpalm.com. Shuttle, pool. $$

★ ➋ **Anaheim Fairfield Inn By Marriott.** 1460 South Harbor Boulevard. (714) 772–6777 or (800) 228–2800. www.anaheimfairfieldinn.com. Shuttle, pool. $$

★ ➋ **Best Western Anaheim Inn.** 1630 South Harbor Boulevard. (714) 774–1050 or (800) 854–8175. www.stovallshotels.com. Shuttle, pool. $$

➋ **Best Western Anaheim Sportstown.** 1700 East Katella Road. (714) 634–1920 or (800) 634–1920. www.bestwestern.com. Pool. $$

➋ **Best Western Anaheim Stardust.** 1057 West Ball Road. (714) 774–7600 or (800) 222–3639. www.bestwestern.com. Shuttle, pool. $$

Best Western Courtesy Inn. 1070 West Ball Street. (714) 772–2470 or (800) 233–8062. www.bestwestern.com. Pool. $$

★ ➋ **Best Western Park Place Inn.** 1544 South Harbor Boulevard. (714) 776–4800 or (800) 854–8175. www.stovallshotels.com. Continental breakfast, pool. $$–$$$

★ ➋ **Best Western Pavilions.** 1176 West Katella Avenue. (714) 776–0140 or (800) 854–8175. www.stovallshotels.com. Shuttle, pool. $$

★ ➋ **Best Western Raffles Inn and Suites.** 2040 South Harbor Boulevard. (714) 750–6100 or (800) 654–0196. www.bestwestern.com. Shuttle, pool. $$–$$$

➋ **Best Western Stovall's Inn.** 1110 West Katella Avenue. (714) 778–1880 or (800) 854–8175. www.stovallshotels.com. Shuttle, pool. $$

★ **Candy Cane Inn.** 1747 South Harbor Boulevard. (714) 774–5284 or (800) 345–7057. www.candycaneinn.net. Shuttle, pool. $$

➋ **Carousel Inn and Suites.** 1530 South Harbor Boulevard. (714) 758–0444 or (800) 854–6767. www.carouselinnandsuites.com. Continental breakfast, pool. $$–$$$

Safety First

The small safes available in some hotels can be valuable to the traveler, but be sure to inquire whether there is a service charge for their use. We've been in hotels that apply the charge regardless of whether we used the safe or not; look over your bill at checkout time and object to any charges that are not proper. In any case, we'd suggest that objects valuable enough to lock up should probably be left home.

★ ◪ **Clarion Hotel–Maingate.** 616 Convention Way. (714) 750–3131 or (800) 228–5151. Shuttle, pool. $$–$$$

★ ◪ **Comfort Inn & Suites.** 300 East Katella Way. (714) 772–8713 or (800) 982–8239. www.comfortinns.com. Continental breakfast, shuttle, pool. $$

◪ **Comfort Inn & Suites West.** 727 South Beach Boulevard. (714) 220–0100. www.comfortinns.com. Pool. $$

◪ **Days Inn Anaheim/Disneyland/Maingate Convention Center.** 620 West Orangewood Avenue. (714) 971–9000. www.daysinn.com. Pool. $–$$

◪ **Days Inn Suites.** 1111 South Harbor Boulevard. (714) 533–8830. www.daysinn.com. Pool. $–$$

◪ **Days Inn Suites at Anaheim Resort/Convention.** 2029 South Harbor Boulevard. (714) 971–5000. www.daysinn.com. Pool. $–$$

★ ◪ **Disney's Grand Californian Hotel.** 1600 South Disneyland Drive. (714) 635–2300. www.disney.com. Pool. $$$$

★ ◪ **Disney's Paradise Pier Hotel.** 1717 Disneyland Drive. (714) 999–0990. www.disney.com. Pool. $$$–$$$$

★ ◪ **Disneyland Hotel.** 1150 West Cerritos Avenue. (714) 778–6600. www.disney.com. Monorail, pool. $$$$

★ **Embassy Suites Anaheim.** 3100 East Frontera. (714) 632–1221 or (800) 362–2779. www.embassysuites.com. Shuttle, pool. $$–$$$

★ **Embassy Suites Hotel Anaheim South.** 11767 Harbor Boulevard, Garden Grove. (714) 539–3300. www.embassysuites.com. Pool. $$–$$$

★ **Hawthorn Suites Limited Hotel.** 1752 South Clementine Street. (714) 535–7773 or (800) 992–4884. www.hawthorn.com. Shuttle, pool. $$–$$$$

★ ◪ **Hilton Anaheim.** 777 Convention Way. (714) 750–4321 or (800) 222–9923. www.hilton.com. Shuttle, pool. $$$–$$$$

★ ◪ **Holiday Inn Anaheim at the Park.** 1221 South Harbor Boulevard. (714) 758–0900 or (800) 545–7275. www.holiday-inn.com. Shuttle, pool. $$

Holiday Inn Anaheim Resort Area. 1915 South Manchester Avenue. (714) 748–7777. www.holiday-inn.com. Pool. $$

◪ **Holiday Inn Express–Anaheim Maingate.** 435 West Katella Avenue. (714) 772–7755 or (800) 833–7888. www.holiday-inn.com. Shuttle, pool. $$

Holiday Inn Hotel & Suites. 1240 South Walnut Street. (714) 535–0300. www.holiday-inn.com. Pool. $$

★ **Howard Johnson Express Inn.** 1930 East Katella Avenue, Orange. (714) 639–1121. www.hojo.com. Pool. $$

★ ◪ **Howard Johnson Hotel.** 1380 South Harbor Boulevard. (714) 776–6120 or (800) 422–4228. www.hojo.com. Shuttle, pool. $$

★ **Hyatt Regency Orange County Disneyland Park.** 11999 Harbor Boulevard. (714) 750–1234 or (800) 233–1234. www.hyatt.com. Shuttle, pool. $$–$$$$

★ ◪ **Jolly Roger Inn.** 640 West Katella Avenue. (714) 782–7500 or (800) 446–1555. Pool. $$

★ ◪ **Marriott Anaheim.** 700 West Convention Way. (714) 750–8000 or (800) 228–9290. www.marriott.com. Shuttle, pool. $$$–$$$$

★ ◪ **Park Inn Anaheim.** 1520 South Harbor Boulevard. (714) 635–7275 or (800) 828–4898. www.parkinn.com. Shuttle, pool. $$–$$$$

★ ◗ **Park Vue Inn.** 1570 South Harbor Boulevard. (714) 772–3691 or (800) 334–7021. www.parkvueinn.com. Pool. $–$$$

★ ◗ **Peacock Suites Hotel.** 1745 South Anaheim Boulevard. (714) 535–8255 or (800) 522–6401. Shuttle, pool. $$–$$$

★ ◗ **Radisson Hotel–Maingate.** 1850 South Harbor Boulevard. (714) 750–2801 or (800) 333–3333. www.radisson.com. Continental breakfast, shuttle, pool. $$

★ **Radisson Resort Knott's Berry Farm.** 7675 Crescent Avenue. (714) 995–1111 or (800) 422–4444. www.radisson.com. Shuttle, pool. $$–$$$$

◗ **Ramada Inn Near Disneyland Park.** 1331 East Katella Avenue. (714) 978–8088 or (800) 228–0586. www.ramada.com. Shuttle, pool. $$

◗ **Ramada Limited Disneyland Area.** 800 South Beach Boulevard. (714) 995–5700. www.ramada.com. Pool. $–$$

◗ **Ramada Limited Main Gate North.** 921 South Harbor Boulevard. (714) 999–0684 or (800) 235–3399. www.ramada.com. Shuttle, pool. $–$$

◗ **Ramada Limited Suites Anaheim Convention Center.** 2141 South Harbor Boulevard. (714) 971–3553. www.ramada.com. Pool. $–$$

◗ **Ramada Maingate/Saga Across from Disneyland Park.** 1650 South Harbor Boulevard. (714) 772–0440 or (800) 854–6097. www.ramada.com. Continental breakfast, shuttle, pool. $$

◗ **Ramada Plaza Anaheim Resort.** 515 West Katella Avenue. (714) 991–6868. www.ramada.com. Pool. $–$$

◗ **Red Roof Inn Anaheim Maingate.** 100 Disney Way. (714) 520–9696 or (800) 843–7663. www.redroof.com. $–$$

★ **Residence Inn Anaheim/Disneyland.** 1700 South Clementine Street. (714) 533–3555 or (800) 331–3131. www.residenceinn.com. Shuttle, pool. $$$$

★ ◗ **Sheraton Anaheim Hotel.** 900 South Disneyland Road. (714) 778–1700 or (800) 331–7251. www.sheraton.com. Shuttle, pool. $$$–$$$$

◗ **Super 8 Motel.** 415 West Katella Avenue. (714) 778–6900 or (800) 800–8000. www.super8.com. $–$$

Super 8 Motel–Buena Park. 7930 Beach Boulevard, Buena Park. (714) 994–6480 or (800) 800–8000. www.super8.com. Near Knott's Berry Farm. $

◗ **Super 8 Motor Inn.** 915 Disneyland Drive. (714) 778–0350 or (800) 248–4400. www.super8.com. Shuttle, pool. $–$$

◗ **Travelodge Anaheim at the Park.** 1166 West Katella Avenue. (714) 774–7817. www.travelodge.com. $–$$

Travelodge Anaheim/Buena Park. 705 South Beach Boulevard. (714) 761–4200. www.travelodge.com. $–$$

★ **Travelodge Buena Park.** 7039 Orangethorpe Avenue, Buena Park. (714) 521–9220 or (800) 854–8299. www.travelodge.com. $–$$

★ **Travelodge International Inn.** 2060 South Harbor Boulevard. (714) 971–9393 or (800) 251–2345. www.travelodge.com. Continental breakfast, shuttle, pool. $–$$

◗ **Tropicana Inn.** 1540 South Harbor Boulevard. (714) 635–4082 or (800) 828–4898. www.bei-hotels.com. Shuttle, pool. $$

LONG BEACH AREA

Long Beach is about thirty minutes away from Anaheim, although traffic delays can double the commute.

Best Western Golden Sails Hotel. 6285 East Pacific Coast Highway. (562) 596–1631 or (800) 762–5333. www.bestwestern.com. **$$–$$$**

Best Western of Long Beach. 1725 Long Beach Boulevard. (562) 599–5555. www.bestwestern.com. **$$–$$$**

Courtyard Long Beach Downtown. 500 East First Street. (562) 435–8511 or (800) 321–2211. www.courtyard.com. Pool. **$$$**

★ **Hilton Long Beach.** 701 West Ocean Boulevard, at World Trade Center. (562) 983–3400 or (800) 445–8667. www.hilton.com. Pool. **$$$**

Holiday Inn Long Beach. 2640 Lakewood Boulevard. (562) 597–4401 or (800) 465–4329. www.holiday-inn.com. Pool. **$$–$$$**

★ **Hotel Queen Mary.** 1126 Queens Highway. (562) 435–3511 or (800) 437–2934. www.queenmary.com. Staterooms on the *Queen Mary.* **$$$**

★ **Hyatt Regency Long Beach.** 200 South Pine Avenue. (562) 491–1234 or (800) 233–1234. www.hyatt.com. Pool. **$$$–$$$$**

★ **Renaissance Long Beach Hotel.** 111 East Ocean Boulevard. (562) 437–5900 or (800) 228–2800. www.renaissancehotels.com. Pool. **$$–$$$$**

★ **The Westin Long Beach.** 333 East Ocean Boulevard. (562) 436–3000 or (800) 937–8461. www.westin.com. Pool. **$$$–$$$$.**

LOS ANGELES DOWNTOWN

Best Western Dragon Gate Inn. 818 North Hill Street. (213) 617–3077. www.dragongateinn.com. **$$**

Best Western Mayfair Hotel. 1256 West Seventh Street. (213) 483–1313 or (800) 821–8682. www.bestwestern.com. **$$–$$$**

Best Western Westwood Pacific Hotel. 11250 Santa Monica Boulevard. (310) 478–1400. www.bestwestern.com. **$$–$$$**

★ **Days Inn Downtown.** 711 North Main Street. (213) 680–0200 or (800) 223–2223. www.daysinn. com. Free parking. **$$**

Days Inn Hotel. 457 South Mariposa Avenue. (213) 380–6910. www.daysinn.com. **$$**

Figueroa Hotel–Convention Center. 939 South Figueroa Street. (213) 627–8971 or (800) 421–9092. www.figueroahotel.com. Across from Staples Center. Outdoor pool. **$$$**

★ **Hilton Checkers Hotel.** 535 South Grand Avenue. (213) 624–0000 or (800) 996–3426. www.hilton.com. Outdoor pool. **$$$$**

★ **Holiday Inn City Center.** 1020 South Figueroa Street. (213) 748–1291 or (800) 465–4329. Outdoor pool. **$$$**

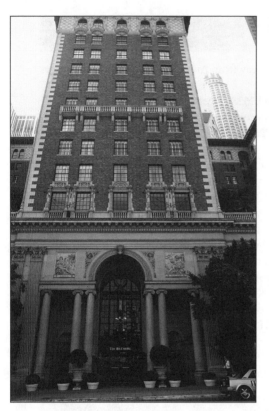

The Millennium Biltmore in Los Angeles. *Photo by Jeff Hyman, © Corel Corporation*

Holiday Inn Los Angeles Downtown. 750 South Garland Avenue. (213) 628–9900 or (800) 628–5240. www.sixcontinentshotels.com. Outdoor pool, free parking. $$

★ **Hyatt Regency Los Angeles.** 711 South Hope Street. (213) 683–1234 or (800) 233–1234. www.hyatt.com. Outdoor spa. $$$–$$$$

InnTowne Hotel Los Angeles. 913 South Figueroa Street. (213) 628–2222. Outdoor pool. $$

Kawada Hotel. 200 South Hill Street. (800) 752–9232, ext. 608. www.kawadahotel.com. $$$

★ **Los Angeles Athletic Club.** 431 South Seventh Street. (213) 630–5264 or (800) 421–8777. www.laac.com. Continental breakfast, indoor pool. $$$

★ **Los Angeles Marriott Downtown.** 333 South Figueroa Street. (213) 617–6027 or (800) 325–3535. www.marriott.com. Outdoor pool. $$$$

Miyako Inn & Spa. 328 East First Street. (213) 617–2000 or (800) 228–6596. www.miyakoinn.com. Health spa. $$$

★ **Millennium Biltmore Hotel.** 506 South Grand Avenue. (213) 624–1011 or (800) 245–8673. www.regalbiltmore.com. $$$$

★ **The New Otani Hotel.** 120 South Los Angeles Street. (213) 629–1200 or (800) 421–8795. www.newotani.com. Japanese garden. $$$$

Quality Inn & Suites Downtown. 1901 West Olympic Boulevard. (213) 385–7141 or (888) 385–9889. www.qualityinns.com. Indoor pool, free parking. $$

Radisson Hotel Midtown. 3540 South Figueroa Street. (213) 748–4141 or (800) 333–3333. www.radisson.com. Outdoor pool. $$–$$$

Radisson Wilshire Plaza. 3515 Wilshire Boulevard. (213) 381–7411 or (800) 333–3333. www.radisson.com. Outdoor pool. $$$–$$$$

Ramada Inn Commerce. 7272 Gage Avenue, Commerce. (562) 806–4777 or (800) 547–4777. www.ramada.com. Outdoor pool, free parking. $$

Ramada Inn–Los Angeles Downtown. 611 South Westlake Avenue. (213) 483–6363 or (800) 688–8389. www.ramada.com. Free parking. $$

Stillwell Hotel. 838 South Grand Avenue. (213) 627–1151 or (800) 553–4774. $–$$

★ **The Westin Bonaventure Hotel and Suites.** 404 South Figueroa Street. (213) 624–1000 or (888) 625–5144. www.starwood.com/westin. Outdoor pool. $$–$$$

★ **Wilshire Grand Hotel & Centre.** 930 Wilshire Boulevard. (213) 688–7777 or (888) 773–2888. www.wilshiregrand.com. $$$–$$$$

LOS ANGELES WEST SIDE AND BEVERLY HILLS

The Argyle Hotel. 8358 Sunset Boulevard, West Hollywood. (323) 848–6620 or (800) 225–2637. www.argylehotel.com. $$$–$$$$

★ **Avalon Hotel.** 9400 West Olympic Boulevard, Beverly Hills. (310) 277–5221. www.avalon-hotel.com. $$$–$$$$

Best Western Royal Palace. 2528 South Sepulveda Boulevard, Los Angeles. (310) 477–9066. www.bestwestern.com. $$

★ **Beverly Hills Hotel.** 9641 Sunset Boulevard, Beverly Hills. (310) 276–2251 or (800) 283–8885. www.beverlyhillshotel.com. $$$–$$$$

Beverly Hills Inn. 125 South Spalding Drive, Beverly Hills. (210) 278–0303 or (800) 463–4466. $$–$$$

Beverly Hilton. 9876 Wilshire Boulevard, Beverly Hills. (310) 285–1299 or (800) 445–8667. www.hilton.com. $$$–$$$$

The Beverly Plaza. 8384 West Third Street, Los Angeles. (323) 658–6600 or (800) 624–6835. www.beverlyplazahotel.com. $$–$$$

Bevonshire Lodge Motel. 7575 Beverly Boulevard, Los Angeles. (213) 936–6154. $–$$

Courtyard Los Angeles Century City/Beverly Hills. 10320 West Olympic Boulevard, Los Angeles. (310) 556–3593 or (800) 321–2211. www.courtyard.com. $$$

Crescent Hotel Beverly Hills. 403 North Crescent Drive, Beverly Hills. (310) 247–0505. www.crescentbh.com. $$–$$$

DoubleTree Hotel, Los Angeles–Westwood. 10740 Wilshire Boulevard, Los Angeles. (310) 475–8711 or (800) 472–8556. www.doubletree.com. $$$

★ **Four Seasons Hotel at Beverly Hills.** 300 South Doheny Drive, Los Angeles. (310) 273–2222. www.fourseasons.com/losangeles. $$$$

★ **Mondrian Hotel.** 8440 Sunset Boulevard, West Hollywood. (323) 650–8999 or (800) 525–8029. www.mondrianhotel.com. Outdoor heated pool. $$$$

Park Hyatt Los Angeles at Century City. 2151 Avenue of the Stars, Los Angeles. (310) 277–1234 or (800) 233–1234. www.hyatt.com. $$$$

Radisson Los Angeles Westside. 6161 Centinela Avenue, Culver City. (310) 348–4517. www.radisson.com. $$$–$$$$

Ramada Plaza Hotel and Suites West Hollywood–Beverly Hills. 8585 Santa Monica Boulevard, West Hollywood. (310) 652–6400 or (800) 272–6232. $$$

★ **The Regent Beverly Wilshire.** 9500 Wilshire Boulevard, Beverly Hills. (310) 275–5200 or (800) 427–4353. www.regenthotels.com. $$$$

★ **Sofitel Los Angeles.** 8555 Beverly Boulevard, Los Angeles. (310) 278–5444 or (800) 763–4835. www.sofitel.com. $$$$

Sunset Marquis Hotel & Villas. 1200 North Alta Loma Road, West Hollywood. (310) 657–1333. www.sunsetmarquishotel.com. $$$$

Westin Century Plaza Hotel. 2025 Avenue of the Stars, Los Angeles. (310) 277–2000 or (800) 937–8467. www.centuryplazala.com. $$$$

HOLLYWOOD AREA

(Price ranges are approximate and subject to change and adjustment during the busiest seasons; ratings are relative for the area.)

Banana Bungalow Hollywood @ The Gershwin West. 5533 Hollywood Boulevard. (323) 464–1131 or (800) 446–7835. www.bananabungalow.com. Budget hostel with dorms and private rooms. Free airport, bus, or train pickup. Beach and Disneyland shuttle available. $–$$

Best Western Hollywood Hills. 6141 Franklin Avenue. (323) 464–5181 or (800) 528–1234. www.bestwestern.com. Outdoor pool. $$

★ **Best Western Hollywood Plaza.** 2011 North Highland Avenue. (323) 851–1800 or (800) 232–4353. www.bestwestern.com. Outdoor pool. $$

★ **Beverly Garland's Holiday Inn at Universal Studios Hollywood.** 4222 North Vineland Avenue, North Hollywood. (818) 980–8000 or (800) 238–3759. www.beverlygarland.com. Outdoor pool, lighted tennis courts. $$$

Days Inn. 5410 Hollywood Boulevard, Central Hollywood. (323) 463–7171. www.daysinn.com. $$

Days Inn. 7023 Sunset Boulevard. (323) 464–8344 or (800) 329–7466. www.daysinn.com. Heated pool. $$

Econo Lodge Hollywood. 777 North Vine Street. (323) 463–5671 or (800) 446–3916. www.econolodge.com. $$

Econo Lodge Wilshire. 3400 West Third Street. (213) 385–0061 or (800) 266–0061. www.econolodge.com. $$

Hilton Universal City and Towers. 555 Universal Terrace Parkway, Universal City. (818) 506–2500 or (800) 445–8667. www.hilton.com. $$$–$$$$

★ **Holiday Inn–Hollywood.** 2005 North Highland Avenue. (323) 850–5811 or (800) 465–4329. www.holiday-inn.com. Heated pool. $$–$$$

Hollywood Hotel & Conference Center. 1160 North Vermont Avenue. (323) 660–1788 or (800) 272–6232. www.ramadahollywood.com. Pool. $

Hollywood Orchid Suites. 1753 North Orchid Avenue. (323) 850–7465 or (800) 537–3052. www.orchidsuites.com. $$–$$$

★ **Hollywood Roosevelt Hotel.** 7000 Hollywood Boulevard. (323) 466–7000 or (800) 950–7667. www.hollywoodroosevelt.com. Historic hotel, site of the first Academy Awards, restored in 2002. $$$–$$$$

Magic Castle Hotel. 7025 Franklin Avenue. (323) 850–7465 or (800) 741–4915. www.magiccastlehotel.com. Part of the famed magician's clubhouse. $$–$$$

★ **Sheraton Universal.** 333 Universal Terrace Parkway. (818) 980–1212 or (800) 325–3535. www.starwood.com/sheraton. $$$–$$$$

Super 8 Motel–Hollywood. 1536 North Western Avenue. (323) 467–3131 or (888) 534–2293. www.stayanight.com/super8hlywd. $$

★ **Valadon Hotel.** 8822 Cynthia Street, West Hollywood. (310) 854–1114 or (800) 835–7997. www.valadonhotel.com. Formerly Le Rêve Hotel. Rooftop heated pool. $$$–$$$$

LAX AIRPORT AREA

Best Western Airpark. 640 West Manchester Boulevard, Inglewood. (310) 677–7378 or (800) 233–8060. www.bestwestern.com. $$

Best Western Airport Plaza Inn. 1730 Centinela Avenue, Inglewood. (310) 568–0071 or (800) 528–1234. www.bestwestern.com. $$

Best Western Suites Hotel. 5005 West Century Boulevard, Los Angeles. (310) 677–7733 or (800) 424–5005. www.bestwestern.com. $$–$$$

Crowne Plaza Los Angeles Airport. 5985 West Century Boulevard, Los Angeles. (310) 642–7500 or (888) 315–3700. www.crowneplaza.com. $$$–$$$$

Days Inn Airport Center. 901 West Manchester Boulevard, Inglewood. (310) 649–0800 or (800) 231–2508. www.daysinn.com. $$

Days Inn Airport South. 15636 Hawthorne Boulevard, Lawndale. (310) 676–7378 or (800) 231–2508. www.daysinn.com. $$

Embassy Suites Los Angeles International Airport North. 9801 Airport Boulevard, Los Angeles. (310) 215–1000 or (800) 362–2779. www.embassy suites.com. $$$

Four Points Hotel Los Angeles International Airport. 9750 Airport Boulevard, Los Angeles. (310) 648–7007 or (800) 529–4683. www.fourpointslax.com. $$$

Hampton Inn. 10300 La Cienega Boulevard, Los Angeles. (310) 337–1000 or (800) 426–7866. www.hamptoninn.com. $$

Hilton Los Angeles Airport. 5711 West Century Boulevard, Los Angeles. (310) 410–4000 or (800) 445–8667. www.hilton.com. $$$–$$$$

Holiday Inn Los Angeles International Airport. 9901 La Cienega Boulevard, Los Angeles. (310) 649–5151 or (800) 624–0025. www.ichotelsgroup.com. $$–$$$

Howard Johnson Hotel International LAX. 8620 Airport Boulevard, Los Angeles. (310) 645–7700. www.hojo.com. $$–$$$

Marriott Los Angeles Airport. 5855 West Century Boulevard, Los Angeles. (310) 641–5700 or (800) 228–9290. www.marriott.com. $$$–$$$$

Quality Hotel LAX. 5249 West Century Boulevard, Los Angeles. (310) 645–2200 or (800) 266–2200. www.qualityinn.com. $$–$$$

Ramada Plaza Hotel LA Airport North. 6333 Bristol Parkway, Culver City. (310) 484–7014 or (800) 321–5575. www.ramada.com. $$

Renaissance Los Angeles Hotel Airport. 9620 Airport Boulevard, Los Angeles. (310) 337–2800 or (800) 568–3571. www.renaissancehotels.com. $$$–$$$$

Sheraton Gateway Hotel Los Angeles Airport. 6101 West Century Boulevard, Los Angeles. (310) 642–4885 or (800) 325–3535. www.sheraton.com. **$$$–$$$$**

Travelodge Hotel at LAX Airport. 5547 West Century Boulevard, Los Angeles. (310) 649–4000 or (800) 421–3939. www.travelodge.com. **$$**

Westin Los Angeles Airport. 5400 West Century Boulevard, Los Angeles. (310) 216–5858 or (800) 228–3000. www.starwood.com/westin. **$$$–$$$$**

CHAPTER ELEVEN

An Eclectic Selection of Restaurants in Anaheim and Los Angeles

THE SPRAWLING COUNTY of Los Angeles and the outlying areas of Orange County include a wide variety of gustatory options from funky California cuisine to fancy French food, from Pacific Rim to old Italy, and from down-home barbecue to the unusual zests of Vietnam, Thailand, and India.

In this chapter you'll find an eclectic selection of some of the best restaurants, selected for value and quality. Price ranges listed are estimates based on dinner entrees; lunch entrees are usually lower.

You'll also find listings of restaurants at Downtown Disney and Universal CityWalk.

Be sure to call to check on hours and to make a reservation, if needed, before heading out to any of the restaurants listed.

RESTAURANTS AT DOWNTOWN DISNEY

(For details, see Chapter 6)

Catal Restaurant & Uva Bar. (714) 774–4442. www.patinagroup.com/catal.htm.

ESPN Zone. (714) 300–3776. espn.go.com/espninc/zone/espnzoneanaheim.html.

House of Blues. (714) 778–2583. www.hob.com/venues/clubvenues/anaheim.

La Brea Bakery. (714) 490–0233

Naples Ristorante e Pizzeria. (714) 776–6200

Rainforest Cafe. (714) 772–0413. www.rainforestcafe.com.

Ralph Brennan's Jazz Kitchen. (714) 776–5200. www.rbjazzkitchen.com.

Tortilla Jo's. (714) 535–5000. www.patinagroup.com.

RESTAURANTS NEAR DISNEYLAND AND ANAHEIM

Following is an eclectic selection of the best or more interesting restaurants and the best deals in and around Disneyland and Anaheim. I've left out all the McDonald's, Denny's, Taco Bells, Red Lobsters, and other franchises you could ever want (or not); you'll find at least one of each within a mile or so of the park. See also the listings for restaurants at Downtown Disney and the three Disneyland resort hotels in Chapter 6.

Acapulco Restaurant. 1410 South Harbor Boulevard, Anaheim. (714) 956–7380. Family-style Mexican fare. **$–$$**

Anaheim White House. 877 South Anaheim Boulevard, Anaheim. (714) 772–1381. www.anaheimwhitehouse.com. Northern Italian specialties in a landmark 1909 home. **$$**

Azteca Mexican Restaurant and Crooner's Lounge. 12911 Main Street, Garden Grove. (714) 638–3790. www.elvislounge.com/arhistory.html. Mexican specialties, with an Elvis collection. **$–$$**

Benihana. 2100 East Ball Road, Anaheim. (714) 774–4940. www.benihana.com. Japanese steakhouse and teppanyaki dishes. **$$–$$$**

The Catch Seafood and Steakhouse. 1929 South State College Boulevard, Anaheim. (714) 634–1829. Local seafood favorite. **$$**

Cattleman's Wharf. 1160 West Ball Road, Anaheim. (714) 535–1622. Steak and fresh seafood. **$$–$$$**

Charley Brown's. 1751 South State College Boulevard, Anaheim. (714) 634–2211. Slow-roasted prime rib, steaks, chicken, and seafood, and pasta dishes. **$$**

Citrus City Grille. 122 North Glassell Street, Orange. (714) 639–9600. www.citruscitygrille.com. California cuisine in the heart of Old Town Orange. **$$**

Crazy Horse Steakhouse & Saloon. 11580 Brookhollow Drive, Santa Ana. (714) 549–1512. Corn-fed steaks, roasted prime rib, and fresh fish. **$$–$$$**

Fresca's Mexican Grill. 2085 East Katella Avenue, Anaheim. (714) 935–0666. Indoor and outdoor seating. **$–$$**

Gulliver's. 18482 MacArthur Boulevard, Irvine. (714) 833–8411. www.gulliversrestaurant.com. Prime rib, Yorkshire pudding, creamed corn, and English trifle, as well as seafood specialties served in an Old English atmosphere. **$$$**

Legend

Prices are for typical dinner entrees.

$	Entrees under $15
$$	Entrees $15 to $30
$$$	Entrees above $30

Hard Rock Cafe Newport Beach. 451 Newport Center Drive, Newport Beach. (714) 640–8844. www.hardrock.com. An outpost of the rock 'n' roll eatery. **$$**

The Hobbit. 2932 East Chapman Avenue, Orange. (714) 997–1972. High-tone contemporary/continental cuisine with a world-class wine cellar. Six-course prix-fixe dinner. **$$$**

King's Fish House. 1521 West Katella Avenue, Orange. (714) 771–6655. www.kingsfishhouse.com/loc.html. Local seafood favorite. **$$**

Koisan Japanese Cuisine. 1132 East Katella Avenue, Orange. (714) 639–2330. Traditional Japanese cuisine. $$

Market Broiler Restaurant. 20 City Boulevard, Orange. (714) 769–3474. www.marketbroiler.com. Casual seafood eatery. $$

Mr. Stox. 1105 East Katella Avenue, Anaheim. (714) 634–3994. www .mrstox.com. Continental fare, with a renowned wine cellar. $$–$$$

Mrs. Knott's Chicken Dinner Restaurant. Knott's Berry Farm, 8039 Beach Boulevard, Buena Park. (714) 220–5067. www.knotts.com/camplace/dine_ restaurant.shtml. World famous fried chicken. $$

P.J.'s Abbey. 182 South Orange Street, Orange. (714) 771–8556. www.pjs abbey.com. A renovated church, complete with stained glass windows. $$

Spaghetti Station Restaurant & Old West Museum. 999 West Ball Road, Anaheim. (714) 956–3250. www.spaghetti-station.com. Spaghetti, ribs, chicken, pizza, and more set among western arts and artifacts. $$

Thai and Thai Restaurant. 150 Katella Avenue, Anaheim. (714) 635–3060. Family-style authentic Thai cuisine. $–$$

Yamabuki. Disney's Paradise Pier Hotel, 1717 South West Street, Anaheim. (714) 956–6755. Fine Japanese dining. $$–$$$

Zorba's. 195 West Harbor Place, Anaheim. (714) 999–5075. Lively food and entertainment. $$

RESTAURANTS AT UNIVERSAL CITYWALK

(For details, see Chapter 7) See www.citywalkhollywood.com/dining_restaurants.html for details on many restaurants at CityWalk.

B. B. King's Blues Club and Memphis Restaurant. (818) 622–5464. www .bbkingbluesclub.com/Los_Angeles.php.

Buca di Beppo Restaurant. (818) 509–9463. www.bucadibeppo.com.

Cafe Tu Tu Tango. (818) 769–2222. www.cafetututango.com.

Camacho's Cantina. (818) 622–3333. www.camachosinc.com/restaurants .html.

Daily Grill Short Order. (818) 760–4448. www.dailygrill.com/dgcitywalk .html.

Gladstone's Universal. (818) 622–3474.

Hard Rock Cafe Hollywood. (818) 622–7625. www.hardrock.com.

Jamba Juice. (818) 761–9816. www.jambajuice.com.

Karl Strauss Brewery Garden. (818) 753–2739. www.karlstrauss.com/ restaurants/kscw/start.html.

Tony Roma's. (818) 763–7662. www.tonyromas.com.

Upstart Crow Cafe. (818) 763–1811. www.upstartcrowtrading.com/about .cfm.

Wasabi at CityWalk. (818) 622–7224.

Wolfgang Puck Cafe. (818) 985–9653. www.wolfgangpuck.com.

LOS ANGELES DOWNTOWN

Atlas Supper Club. 3760 Wilshire Boulevard, Los Angeles. (213) 380–8400. www.atlassupperclub.com. Eclectic fare in a setting from the twenties. $$

Azalea. The New Otani Hotel & Garden. 120 South Los Angeles Street, Los Angeles. (213) 253–9235. www.newotani.com/restaurantazalea.htm. California cuisine with continental and Asian influences. $$

Back Door Pub. The Milner Hotel, 813 South Flower Street, Los Angeles. (213) 627–6981. www.milner-hotels.com/la.html. Casual Spanish-American specialties. $

Bonaventure Brewing Co. Westin Bonaventure Hotel, 404 South Figueroa Street, Suite 418A, Los Angeles. (213) 236–0802. www.bonaventurebrewingco .com. An indoor-outdoor beer garden high above the streets of downtown. $$

Cafe Pinot. 700 West Fifth Street, Los Angeles. (213) 239–6500. www.patina group.com/therestaurants_pinots_cafe.htm. Parisian bistro near the central library. $$

California Pizza Kitchen. At Wells Fargo Center. 330 South Hope Street, Los Angeles. (213) 626–2616. www.cpk.com. Unusual pies. $$

Cardini Ristorante. Wilshire Grand Hotel & Centre, 930 Wilshire Boulevard, Los Angeles. (213) 896–3822. www.wilshiregrand.com/english/restaurants/ cardini.html. Northern Italian fare in an elegant setting. $$

CBS Seafood Restaurant. 700 North Spring Street, Los Angeles. (213) 617– 2323. Cantonese specialties and dim sum. $

Ciao Trattoria. 815 West Seventh Street, Los Angeles. (213) 624–2244. www .ciaotrattoria.com. Italian in an Art Deco setting. $$

City Grill. Wilshire Grand Hotel & Centre, 930 Wilshire Boulevard, Los Angeles. (213) 627–4289. wilshiregrand.com/english/restaurants/citygrill.html. Light American fare. $

Ciudad. 445 South Figueroa Street, Suite 100, Los Angeles. (213) 486–5171. www.millikenandfeniger.com/ciudad/ciu/ciu.htm. Latin fare from Havana to Barcelona. $$

El Cholo. 1121 South Western Avenue, Los Angeles. (323) 737–7718 or (800) 789–2172. www.elcholocafe.com. Landmark Mexican restaurant, now in its ninth decade. $

El Paseo Inn. 11 East Olvera Street, Los Angeles. (213) 626–1361. Authentic Mexican food in Old Los Angeles. $

Engine Co. No. 28. 644 South Figueroa Street, Los Angeles. (213) 624–6996. www.engineco.com. Bar and grill in a century-old fire station. $$

Epicentre. Kawada Hotel, 200 South Hill Street, Los Angeles. (213) 621–4455 or (800) 752–9232. www.kawadahotel.com/restaurants.htm. Contemporary cuisine with an earthquake motif. $$

Fox Sports Sky Box. 1111 South Figueroa at Staples Center, Los Angeles. (213) 742–7345. www.staplescenter.com. Sports bar. $

Frying Fish. 120 Japanese Village Plaza Mall, 350 East First Street, Los Angeles. (213) 680–0567. Contemporary Japanese and sushi. $–$$

Garden Grill. The New Otani Hotel & Garden, 120 South Los Angeles Street, Los Angeles. (213) 253–9263. www.newotani.com/restaurantgardengrill.htm. Teppanyaki and Japanese steakhouse. $$

Gill's Cuisine of India. Stillwell Hotel, 838 South Grand Avenue, Los Angeles. (213) 623–1050 or (800) 553–4774. www.gillsindiancuisine.com. Clay oven Indian cuisine. $

Golden Dragon Restaurant. 960 North Broadway, Los Angeles. (323) 721–0774. Popular Chinese eatery. $

Grand Cafe. Omni Los Angeles Hotel at California Plaza, 251 South Olive Street, Los Angeles. (213) 617–3300. www.omnihotels.com/hotels/default.asp?h_id=61. Fine dining in theater and museum district. $$

Harry's Bar & American Grill. 2020 Avenue of the Stars, Century City. (310) 277–2333. Venetian and Florentine specialties in a room modeled after the famous original Harry's in Florence, Italy. $$

Jyokamachi Japanese Restaurant. 404 South Figueroa Street, Suite 601, Los Angeles. (213) 629–9929 or (888) 629–2977. Teppanyaki, shabu-shabu, and sushi. $$

Kyoto Japanese Cuisine. Wilshire Grand Hotel & Centre, 930 Wilshire Boulevard, Los Angeles. (213) 896–3812. www.wilshiregrand.com/english/restaurants/kyoto.html. $$–$$$

La Golondrina Cafe. W-17 Olvera Street, Los Angeles. (213) 628–4349. www.lagolondrina.com. Popular Mexican restaurant in 1850s brick building in Old Los Angeles. $$–$$$

Les Freres Taix French Restaurant. 1911 Sunset Boulevard, Los Angeles. (213) 484–1265. www.taixfrench.com. Reasonably priced French country cuisine at a Los Angeles landmark. The Taix family are the third and fourth generations of a family of sheepherders and bakers from the "hautes-alpes" in southeastern France who immigrated to Los Angeles around 1870. The original Taix restaurant opened in 1927. $$

McCormick & Schmick's. The Library Tower, 633 West Fifth Street, Los Angeles. (213) 629–1929. www.mccormickandschmicks.com. Lush seafood shrine. $$

Moody's Bar & Grille. Los Angeles Marriott Downtown, 333 South Figueroa Street, Los Angeles. (213) 617–6023. New York–style bar and grill. $$

The Orchid Gardens. Best Western the Mayfair Hotel, 1256 West Seventh Street, Los Angeles. (213) 484–9789. hometown.aol.com/mayfairla/index.html. Art Deco restaurant popular for its lunch buffet. $$

Original Pantry Cafe. 877 South Figueroa Street, Los Angeles. (213) 972–9279. Landmark casual twenty-four-hour eatery. $

Pacific Dining Car. 1310 West Sixth Street, Los Angeles. (213) 483–6000. www.pacificdiningcar.com. Classic steak and seafood. $$$

Patinette at MOCA. 250 South Grand Avenue, Los Angeles. (323) 626–1178. www.patinagroup.com/patinettecafes_patinette.htm. Light Mediterranean fare at the Museum of Contemporary Art. $$

Pavan Pacifico. Hyatt Regency Los Angeles, 711 South Hope Street, Los Angeles. (213) 683–1234. California cuisine with Asian influences. $

Philippe the Original. 1001 North Alameda Street, Los Angeles. (213) 628–3781. www.philippes.com. Simple family fare, famous for its French dip sandwich. $

Plum Tree Inn. 937 North Hill Street, Los Angeles. (213) 613–1819. Mandarin and Szechuan fare. $$

Rendezvous Court. The Biltmore Hotel, 506 South Grand Avenue, Los Angeles. (213) 624–1011. Lush setting of an indoor garden for lunch and high tea. $$

The Restaurant at the Standard. 550 South Flower Street, Los Angeles. (213) 892–8080. Eclectic fare at an agreeably bizarre hotel. $$–$$$

Saka-E. Radisson Wilshire Plaza, 3515 Wilshire Boulevard, Los Angeles. (213) 381–7411. Tempura, teppanyaki, and sushi. $$

San Antonio Winery & Restaurant. 737 Lamar Street, Los Angeles. (323) 223–1401. www.sanantoniowinery.com. Winery and historic landmark. $

Seoul Jung. Wilshire Grand Hotel & Centre, 930 Wilshire Boulevard, Los Angeles. (213) 688–7880. www.wilshiregrand.com/english/restaurants/seoul jung.html. Korean barbecue. $$

Smeraldi's Ristorante. The Biltmore Hotel, 506 South Grand Avenue, Los Angeles. (213) 612–1562. Pasta and California specialties. $

The Sonora Cafe. 180 South La Brea Avenue, Los Angeles. (323) 857–1800. Mexican and southwestern specialties. $$$

Tesoro Trattoria. 300 South Grand Avenue, Los Angeles. (213) 680–0000. Tuscan specialties. $$

Three Thirty Three. Los Angeles Marriott Downtown, 333 South Figueroa Street, Los Angeles. (213) 621–1513. Casual California cafe. $–$$

Water Grill. 544 South Grand Avenue, Los Angeles. (213) 891–0900. www.watergrill.com. Northwest seafood specialties. $$

Windows Steaks & Martinis. 1150 South Olive Street, Los Angeles. (213) 746–1554. Retro-1960s steakhouse high over downtown. Weekdays for lunch and dinner; Saturday lunch only. $$$

HOLLYWOOD

Bob's Big Boy. 4211 West Riverside Drive, Burbank. (818) 843–9334. A state burger-landmark restored to its 1949 heyday, complete with carhops. The eatery has appeared in several movies, including *Heat*. $

Cafe Sierra. Universal City Hilton and Towers, 555 Universal Terrace Parkway, Universal City. (818) 509–2030. Favored for its lunch buffets, Friday seafood buffet, and Sunday brunch. $$

Hard Rock Cafe Hollywood. 1000 Universal Center Drive, Suite 99, Universal City. (818) 622–7625. www.hardrock.com. Another gift shop with a menu. $$

Patina. 5955 Melrose Avenue, Los Angeles. (323) 960–1760 ext. 22. www.patinagroup.com/therestaurants_patina.htm. Flagship of Joachim Splichal's empire, serving regional specialties. $$$

Pink's Famous Chili Dogs. 709 North La Brea Avenue, Los Angeles. (323) 931–4223. www.pinkshollywood.com. Just like the sign says. $

Pinot Hollywood. 1448 North Gower Street, Los Angeles. (323) 461–8800. www.patinagroup.com/therestaurants_pinots_hollywood.htm. Bistro dining. $$

Theodore's. Hollywood Roosevelt Hotel, 7000 Hollywood Boulevard, Hollywood. (323) 466–7000 or (800) 950–7667. www.hollywoodroosevelt.com/food_&_fun.htm. California fare for power lunchers and dinner dealers. $$

Yamashiro. 1999 North Sycamore Avenue, Hollywood. (323) 466–5125. www.yamashirorestaurant.com. Seafood, sushi, sashimi, and tempura with a panoramic setting. $$$

LOS ANGELES WEST SIDE

Cafe Le Parc. 733 North West Knoll Drive, West Hollywood. (310) 855–8888. www.leparcsuites.com/cafe.html. Mediterranean cafe. $$$

Cava Restaurant & Tapas Bar. Beverly Plaza Hotel, 8384 West Third Street, Los Angeles. (323) 658–8898. Spanish specialties including tapas. $$

Celestino an Italian Steakhouse. 8908 Beverly Boulevard, West Hollywood. (310) 858–5777. www.celestinodrago.com. High-tone Italian. $$$

Chaya Brasserie Restaurant. 8741 Alden Drive, Los Angeles. (310) 859–8833. www.thechaya.com. French, Japanese, and Italian cuisine. $$

The Dining Room. The Regent Beverly Wilshire, 9500 Wilshire Boulevard, Beverly Hills. (310) 275–5200 ext. 5103. www.regenthotels. com. California specialties in a tony setting. $$$

Ed Debevic's. 134 North La Cienega Boulevard, Beverly Hills. (310) 659–1952. www.eddebevics.com. Classic short-order diner from the fifties. $

Griff's. The Beverly Hilton, 9876 Wilshire Boulevard, Beverly Hills. (323) 274–7777. American and continental. $$

Hard Rock Cafe. 8600 Beverly Boulevard, Los Angeles. (310) 276–7605. www.hardrock.com. A gift shop with a menu. $$

House of Blues. 8430 Sunset Boulevard, West Hollywood. (323) 848–5100 or (800) 848–5194. www.hob.com/venues/clubvenues/sunsetstrip. American regional fare with a bluesy setting. $$

Il Pastaio. 400 North Canon Drive, Beverly Hills. (310) 205–5444. www.celestinodrago.com/ilpastaio.htm. A favorite neighborhood trattoria. $$

Jaan. Raffles L'Ermitage Hotel. 9291 Burton Way, Beverly Hills. (310) 278–3344 or (800) 323–7500. www.lermitagehotel.com. Modern French, with a touch of Asia. $$

Junior's Restaurant, Delicatessen & Bakery. 2379 Westwood Boulevard, Los Angeles. (310) 475–5771 or (800) 475–3354. www.jrsdeli.com. Classic Jewish deli. $

Lawry's the Prime Rib. 100 North La Cienega Boulevard, Beverly Hills. (310) 652–2827. www.lawrysonline.com/primerib/f_bhills.html. Seafood, steaks, and the signature prime rib, carved tableside. $$

McCormick & Schmicks–Beverly Hills. Two Rodeo Drive, Beverly Hills. (310) 859–0434. www.mccormickandschmicks.com. Seafood specialties. $$

The Palm Restaurant. 9001 Santa Monica Boulevard, Los Angeles. (310) 550–8811. www.thepalm.com/sitemain.cfm?site_id=5. Steak and seafood, in the lush style of the New York original. $$$

The Polo Lounge. The Beverly Hills Hotel, 9641 Sunset Boulevard, Beverly Hills. (310) 276–2251. www.beverlyhillshotel.com. California fare with Asian accents in a fabled setting. $$$

Ruth's Chris Steak House. 224 South Beverly Drive, Beverly Hills. (310) 859–8744. www.ruthschris.com. Outpost of a national steak and seafood empire. $$$

San Gennaro Cafe. 140 Barrington Place, Brentwood. (310) 476–9696. Neighborhood Italian trattoria. $$

Spago Beverly Hills. 176 North Canon Drive, Beverly Hills. (310) 385–0880. www.wolfgangpuck.com/myrestaurants/fine_dining/home/frame.php. A trendy "in spot" for celebrities, from Wolfgang Puck. $$$

The Stinking Rose. 55 North La Cienega, Beverly Hills. (310) 652–7673. www.thestinkingrose.com. Regional and Italian fare, featuring lots of garlic. $$$

Terrace Il Ristorante. Century Plaza Hotel & Tower, 2025 Avenue of the Stars, Los Angeles. (310) 551–3359. Fancy Mediterranean fare. $$

Trader Vic's. Merv Griffin's Beverly Hilton, 9876 Wilshire Boulevard, Beverly Hills. (310) 276–6345. www.tradervics.com. Beef, seafood, and poultry in a South Seas setting. $$

BEACH CITIES

Andiamo. Hilton Los Angeles Airport, 5711 West Century Boulevard, Los Angeles. (310) 410–4000. Elaborate menu of northern Italian specialties. $$

Andre's. 21333 Hawthorne Boulevard, Torrance. (310) 540–0500. www .hiltontorrance.com. California, Chinese, and continental specialties. $$

Benihana Japanese Steakhouse–Torrance. Village Del Amo, 21327 Hawthorne Boulevard, Torrance. (310) 316–7777. www.benihana.com. Teppanyaki and steakhouse specialties. $$

Border Grill. 1445 Fourth Street, Santa Monica. (310) 451–1655. www.milliken andfeniger.com/BG2002/BGSM/bgsm.htm. Modern, bold Mexican specialties from chefs Mary Sue Milliken and Susan Feniger. $$$

Chelsea Restaurant. Queen Mary Seaport, 1126 Queen's Highway, Long Beach. (562) 435–3511. www.queenmary.com. Seafood specialties aboard the *Queen Mary* in Long Beach harbor. $$

Drago Ristorante & Bar. 2628 Wilshire Boulevard, Santa Monica. (310) 828–1585. www.celestinodrago.com/drago.htm. Another Italian gem from chef Celestino Drago. $$$

Gladstone's 4 Fish. 17300 Pacific Coast Highway, Pacific Palisades. (310) 454–3474. www.gladstones.com. Local favorite for seafood, with an ocean view. $$

Gotham Hall. 1431 Third Street Promenade, Santa Monica. (310) 394–8865 or (800) 394–8865. www.gothamhall.com. California grill, with pool tables and a disco. **$**

Harbor House Restaurant. 4211 Admiralty Way, Marina del Rey. (310) 577–4555. www.harborhouse-mdr.com. Seafood and steaks at the marina. **$$**

Il Boccaccio. 39 Pier Avenue, Hermosa Beach. (310) 376–0211. www .ilboccaccio.com. Italian regional fare. **$$**

Landry's. Sheraton Gateway, 6101 West Century Boulevard, Los Angeles. (310) 642–1111. California cuisine. **$$**

Rix. 1413 Fifth Street, Santa Monica. (310) 656–9688. Updated supper club offerings. **$$**

Rockenwagner. 2435 Main Street, Santa Monica. (310) 399–6504. www .rockenwagner.com. Fancy California and French offerings. **$$$**

Schatzi on Main. 3110 Main Street, Santa Monica. (310) 399–4800. www .schatzi-on-main.com. California and Austrian specialties at this trendy place founded by actor and governor of California, Arnold Schwarzenegger, and his wife, newscaster Maria Shriver. **$$$**

Sir Winston's Restaurant. Queen Mary Seaport, 1126 Queen's Highway, Long Beach. (562) 435–3511. www.queenmary.com. California and continental menu onboard the *Queen Mary* in Long Beach harbor. **$$$**

Waterfront Bar and Grille. Marina del Rey Hotel, 13534 Bali Way, Marina del Rey. (310) 301–1000 or (800) 442–8000. www.marinadelreyhotel.com. California and continental specialties at the marina. **$**

PART VII

BEYOND THE THEME PARKS

CHAPTER TWELVE

FESTIVALS

TOURNAMENT OF ROSES PARADE

The Tournament of Roses Parade is a New Year's Day tradition. It dates all the way back to 1890 and then, like now, was meant as a proclamation to the world about Southern California's temperate climate. Today the parade through the streets of Pasadena is broadcast around the world, and don't you think that makes the Chamber of Commerce happy?

Although a handful of the elaborate floats are still built by volunteers from community organizations, most are put together by professional parade construction companies (there's a unique job description, don't you think?). Some floats take nearly a year to build, at a cost of hundreds of thousands of dollars. Tournament rules say the displays must be completely covered with flowers, greenery, or some other organic material, with an average float requiring up to 100,000 blossoms.

The whole shebang is accompanied by the traditional trappings of modern parades: marching bands, horses, television cameras, second-tier celebrities, and corporate logos.

The parade starts pretty early in the day, and many spectators spend the night or arrive at the crack of dawn to grab the best curbside viewing places. Officially, the city of Pasadena allows occupancy of curbside space along the route beginning at noon on December 31. For more information about the rules for walk-up viewing and overnight parking on some Pasadena city streets near the route, call the Pasadena Police Department at (626) 744–4598.

A limited number of grandstand seats are available for sale; they're usually spoken for well before the parade begins.

For information, contact the Tournament of Roses Association at (626) 449–4100 or (626) 449–7673, or write to the association at 391 South Orange Grove Boulevard, Pasadena, CA 91184. You also can consult www.tournament ofroses.com. Further information is available from the Pasadena Convention & Visitors Bureau, at (800) 307–7977 or www.pasadenacal.com.

The official marketers of grandstand seating for the Rose Parade include:

Sharp Seating Company. (626) 795–4171. www.sharpseating.com. More than 70,000 tickets are available from February 1 through December 31, and range in price from $40 to $85.

LRB Entertainment. (626) 440–9731. www.lrbentertainment.com. Tickets for the 2005 parade were priced from $65 to $67.

Marsden Brothers. (310) 454–3511.

Tickets for the parade and for some overnight parking spaces may be purchased—at a hefty premium—from ticket brokerages including:

A-1 Tickets, Inc. (800) 938–9929. www.aonetickets.com.

Al Brooks Rose Bowl Tours. (213) 626–5863. www.albrooks.com.

Southern California Ticket Service. (800) 888–7287. www.socaltix.com.

JANUARY

Annual New Year's Day Swim. San Pedro. The Cabrillo Beach Polar Bears go for a dip at noon, a tradition that dates back to 1936. (310) 833–1377. New Year's Day.

Chinese New Year. Celebrate the Lunar New Year with firecrackers, dragons, and a colorful parade in Chinatown. Contact the Chinese Chamber of Commerce. (213) 617–0396. www.lachinesechamber.org. Late January or early February.

Golden Globe Awards. Beverly Hills. The Hollywood Foreign Press awards for achievement in the television and motion picture industry. Spectators can watch on the sidelines or purchase bleacher seats. (310) 274–7777. www.the goldenglobes.com.

Greater Los Angeles Auto Show. Los Angeles. (310) 444–1850. www.laauto show.com.

King Festival of the Arts. Exposition Park, Los Angeles. Arts and crafts. (213) 735–1261.

Rose Bowl Game. Pasadena. Champions of the Pac-10 and Big Ten Conference. (626) 449–4100. www.rosebowl.com. New Year's weekend.

Rose Parade Float Viewing. Paloma Street and Sierra Madre Villa Avenue, Pasadena. (626) 449–7673. January 1 and 2.

Tournament of Roses Parade. Pasadena. (626) 449–4100. www.rosebowl .com. New Year's Day.

FEBRUARY

Academy Awards. Kodak Theatre, Hollywood. Your chances of getting tickets for the ceremony itself are about as good as your chances of winning an Oscar, but there is always a lot of excitement in the streets of Hollywood. Bleachers are set up near the award site for those who want to ogle the stars as they arrive. For information, consult www.oscars.org. Late February or early March.

Feria De La Mujer. Los Angeles. Fashion show, cooking demonstrations, food booths, and other activities. (213) 468–5213. Mid-February.

Presidents' Day Lawn Party and Road. 40 Presidential Drive, Simi Valley. Presidential look alikes, storytelling, music, singing, dancing, 5-K run, and family fun run. (800) 410–8354. Mid-February.

***Queen Mary* Scottish Festival.** *Queen Mary,* Long Beach. Pipe bands, highland dancing, parades, competitions, exhibits, performances, Scottish food, and drinks. (562) 435–3511 or (562) 499–1650. www.queenmary.com. Mid-February.

Santa Monica Pier Winter Music Series. Santa Monica Pier, Santa Monica. Music and dance. (310) 458–8900. www.santamonicapier.org. February through June.

Southern California Boat Show. Los Angeles. (714) 633–1427. www.scma .com.

Whiskey Flats Days. An Old West festival in Kernville. (760) 376–2629 or (800) 350–7393. www.kernvalley.com/news/whiskey. Mid-February.

Winter Wonderland. Brand Park, Glendale. (818) 548–2000. Sledding on mountains of man-made snow. Late February.

MARCH

Catalina Island Marathon. Catalina Island. (714) 978–1528. Mid-March.

Festival of the Whales. Dana Point. The annual migration of the California gray whales is celebrated with a parade, a street fair, whale-watching cruises, exhibits, lectures, and an art show. (714) 496–1555 or (888) 440–4309. www.dp festivalofwhales.com. Early to mid-March.

Los Angeles Marathon. Los Angeles. World's fourth largest running event, passing through many of Los Angeles's neighborhoods. (310) 444–5544. www .lamarathon.com. Early March.

Los Angeles Marathon Bike Tour. 900 Exposition Boulevard, Los Angeles. Course begins and ends at Exposition Park, passing through Koreatown, Hancock Park, and Hollywood. (310) 444–5544. www.lamarathon.com. Early March.

Los Angeles Marathon Finish Line Celebration. Los Angeles. Huge block party with exhibitors of athletic gear, arts and crafts, live entertainment, and food. (310) 444–5544. www.lamarathon.com. Early March.

Return of the Swallows to Capistrano. A celebration of the miraculous return of thousands of swallows to the ruins of Mission San Juan Capistrano each March 19 (of course, some swallows also come on March 18 and March 20, but there's no party for them). (949) 234–1300, ext. 322. www.missionsjc.com.

APRIL

Earth Day Fair and Beach Clean-Up. 3720 Stephen White Drive, San Pedro. (310) 548–7562. Late April.

Easter Sunrise Service. 309 Esplanade, Redondo Beach. (310) 376–6911.

Easter Sunrise Service. Forest Lawn Memorial Park, 6300 Forest Lawn Drive, Los Angeles. (800) 204–3131. www.forestlawn.com.

Easter Sunrise Service at the Bowl. Hollywood Bowl, 2301 North Highland Avenue, Hollywood. (213) 896–1700. www.hollywoodbowl.org.

Feria de los Niños. Hollenbeck Park, Los Angeles. Hispanic folk festival for children. (213) 261–0113. Late April.

San Fernando Valley Street Fiesta. San Fernando Road and MacClay Street, San Fernando Valley. Games, carnival rides, food booths, arts and crafts, and live entertainment. (562) 495–5959. Mid-April.

Santa Anita Derby Day. 285 West Huntington Drive, Arcadia. Microbrew festival, 5-K run, fan fest, and family fun day. (626) 574–7223. www.santa anita.com. Early April.

Toyota Grand Prix of Long Beach. Indy cars race through the seaside community. (562) 436–9953. www.longbeachgp.com. Mid-April.

MAY

Carnival on the Beach. Ocean Boulevard, Long Beach. Carnival rides, food booths, arts and crafts. (562) 495–5959. Mid-May.

Cinco de Mayo at MacArthur Park. Wilshire Boulevard, Los Angeles. (562) 495–5959. May 5.

Cinco de Mayo Celebration. Dancing, singing, eating, and more in a movable Mexican feast around Los Angeles, including Olvera Street. Check newspaper coverage.

Memorial Day Parade. Canoga Park. Celebrities, floats, clowns, marching bands, antique and classic cars. (818) 884–4222.

Pasadena Cinco de Mayo Street Fest. 100 North Garfield Avenue, Pasadena. Carnival rides, food, arts and crafts, and entertainment. (562) 495–5959. May 5.

San Bernardino County Fair. Victorville. Old-style agricultural and crafts fair. (619) 245–6506. www.sbcfair.com. Mid-May.

Strawberry Festival. Village Green, Garden Grove. Strawberries, a parade, strawberries, music, strawberries, and more. Did we mention the strawberries? (714) 638–0981. www.strawberryfestival.org. Late May.

JUNE

IFP Los Angeles Film Festival. Various locations. (866) 345–6337. www.lafilmfest.com. Mid-June.

Juneteenth Festival. William Grant Still Arts Center, 2520 West View Street, Los Angeles. Live concert performances featuring blues, jazz, and gospel music commemorating the end of slavery in 1865. (323) 734–1164. Mid-June.

Juneteenth Celebration. 4700 Western Heritage Way, Los Angeles. Demonstrations, reading of the Emancipation Proclamation, music, workshops, and lectures. (323) 667–2000. Mid-June.

San Fernando Valley Fair. Hansen Dam Sports Center, Lake View Terrace. Three days of exhibits, carnival rides, entertainment, and the Los Angeles County Beauty Pageant. (818) 557–1600. www.sfvalleyfair.org. Early June.

JULY

Fireworks at Huntington Beach. Huntington Beach. (714) 374–1535. July 4.

Fourth of July at *Queen Mary*. 1126 Queen's Highway, Long Beach. Fireworks, carnival rides, games, and dancing to live bands. (562) 435–3511. www.queenmary.com.

Fourth of July at Starlight Bowl. Lockheed View Drive, Burbank. (818) 545–3721.

Fourth of July Celebration. 2200 Crenshaw Boulevard, Torrance. Fireworks, games, food, carnival, train rides, and entertainment. (310) 618–2930.

Fourth of July Dance and Barbecue Dinner. 1 Casino Way, Avalon. Barbecue buffet dinner, music of the USC Marching Band, and fireworks over Avalon Bay. (310) 510–1520. July 4.

Fourth of July Fireworks Display. Marina del Rey. The fireworks display can be viewed from Burton Chace Park, Fisherman's Village, and waterside restaurants. (310) 821–0555. July 4.

Fourth of July Fireworks Display. Sunset Boulevard and Temescal Canyon Road, Pacific Palisades. (310) 459–7963. July 4.

Fourth of July Parade. Avalon, Catalina Island. Golf-cart parade featuring the USC Marching Band. (310) 510–1520. July 4.

Independence Day Picnic and Parade. Ontario. Marching bands, floats, street fair, arts and crafts, food, classic-car display, and picnicking on the Guinness World Record's longest picnic table. (909) 395–2020. July 3 and 4.

Kaboom Celebration. McKinley Avenue, Pomona. Carnival, stage entertainment, chili cook-off, classic-car show, pony rides, games, and fireworks. (909) 623–3111. July 4.

Malibu Summer Festival and Art Show. Malibu Civic Center, Malibu. (310) 456–9025. Late July.

Old-Fashioned Family Fourth of July. Presidential Drive, Simi Valley. Carnival games, storytelling, president look-alikes, face painting, pie-eating contest, and live music. (800) 410–8354. July 4.

Orange County Fair. Orange County Fair and Exhibition Center, Costa Mesa. Rides, exhibits, and entertainment. (714) 708–3247. www.ocfair.com. Late July.

Pacific Palisades Americanism Parade. Pacific Palisades Park, Pacific Palisades. Floats, marching bands, celebrities, and politicians. (310) 459–7963. July 4.

Ramona Pageant. 27400 Ramona Bowl Road, Hemet. Asian-Pacific culture featuring entertainment, dragon boat races, flower show, art exhibits, children's activities, and ethnic food. (800) 645–4465. Mid-July.

Shakespeare Festival. Citicorp Plaza, downtown Los Angeles. (213) 481–2273. www.shakespearefestivalla.org. July and August.

Surf City Celebrates. Main Street, Huntington Beach. Marching bands, floats, and 5-K run. (714) 374–1535. July 4.

Valley of the Stars and Stripes. Northridge. Car show, carnival rides, games, live entertainment, food, skydivers, and fireworks. (818) 368–3235. July 4.

AUGUST

African Marketplace & Cultural Faire. 5001 Rodeo Road, Los Angeles. Arts, crafts, games, soccer tournament, African business expo, and entertainment. (323) 734–1164. Late August and early September.

Model Boat Regatta. Long Beach. Youths race hand-built model boats. (562) 570–1725. Late August.

Nisei Week. Little Tokyo, Los Angeles. Parade and celebration of Japanese culture in America. (213) 687–7193. www.niseiweek.org. Early August.

Old Spanish Days. Santa Barbara. Weeklong celebration of Spanish culture. (805) 962–8101. www.oldspanishdays-fiesta.org. Early August.

SEPTEMBER

Annual Flea Market. Civic Center Way, Malibu. (818) 706–0233. Late September.

Annual Route 66 Rendezvous. Between Second and Fifth Streets, Los Angeles. Vintage cars, street rods, food, carnival rides, and live entertainment. (909) 889–3980. Late September.

Danish Days. Solvang. Parade, dance, and music. (805) 688–6144 or (800) 468–6765. www.solvangusa.com. Third weekend of September.

Festival of Philippine Arts and Culture. Point Fermin, San Pedro. Dance, arts and crafts. (213) 389–3050. www.filamarts.org. Mid-September.

Grecian Festival by the Sea. Colorado Street, Long Beach. Dancing, music, food, and crafts celebrating Greek culture. (714) 220–0730. Early September.

Greek Festival. Santa Anita Racetrack, Arcadia. (626) 574–7223. Late September.

Korean Festival. Korean Community Center, Koreatown, Los Angeles. (213) 730–1495. Late September.

Los Angeles County Fair. County Fairgrounds, Pomona. The largest agricultural fair in the country, plus rides, racing, and entertainment. (909) 623–3111. www.fairplex.com. Second and third weeks of September.

Oktoberfest. Old World, Huntington Beach. Food, beer, entertainment, and beer. (714) 895–8020. Mid-September to late October.

Taste of Newport/Sandcastle Contest. Newport Beach. Food and art. (949) 729–4400. www.tasteofnewport.com. Mid-September.

OCTOBER

Autumn Sea Fair. 3720 Stephen White Drive, San Pedro. Swashbuckling pirates, dunk tanks, carnival games, sand-castle building, live bands, and food. (310) 548–7562. Late October.

Calico Days. Calico Ghost Town, Yermo. (760) 254–2122. www.calicotown.com. Early October.

Halloween Carnival at Wilson Park. 2200 Crenshaw Boulevard, Torrance. Halloween games, costume parade, and food. (310) 618–2930. October 31.

Halloween on South Lake Avenue. Between Colorado and California Boulevards, Pasadena. Wicked witch, ghostly magic show, creepy crawly critter show, pumpkin hunt, and a costume contest. (626) 792–1259. October 31.

Halloween Terror Fest. *Queen Mary,* Long Beach. The engine room of the *Queen Mary* is transformed into a maze with monsters, goblins, and gruesome creatures. (562) 435–3511. www.queenmaryshipwreck.com. Late October.

International Sail and Power Boat Show. Long Beach Convention Center, Long Beach. (714) 633–1427. www.scma.com. Mid-October.

Knott's "Scary" Farm. Knott's Berry Farm, Buena Park. A Halloween conversion of the amusement park. See chapter on Knott's Berry Farm in this book for information. (714) 220–5200. www.knotts.com.

Pier Days. Ocean Avenue and Colorado Street, Santa Monica. Antique-car show, fireworks, sailing race, fishing derby, face painting, live bands, and more. (310) 458–8900. Early October.

Redondo Lobster Festival. Harbor Drive and Beryl Street, Redondo Beach. Eating contest, exhibit, displays, demonstrations, Maine lobster meals, food tasting from area restaurants, and live entertainment. (310) 376–6911. Mid-October.

Silverado Days. William Peak Park, Buena Park. A carnival, a parade, entertainment, food, and arts and crafts. (714) 521–0261. Mid-October.

South Bay Greek Festival. Redondo Beach. Cultural booths, ethnic food, music, dance, arts, crafts, and costumes. (310) 540–2434. Early October.

West Hollywood Halloween Carnival. Between La Cienega and Doheny Streets, West Hollywood. Festival booths, live entertainment, costume contest, and parade. (323) 848–6547. October 31.

NOVEMBER

Doo Dah Parade. Holly Street, Colorado Boulevard, and Pasadena Avenue, Pasadena. A riotous spoof of the Tournament of Roses parade, featuring more than 1,200 marchers that in past years have included synchronized briefcase drill teams, marching political pundits, midget gospel singers, and dogs in drag. (626) 440–7379. www.pasadenadoodahparade.com. Third week of November.

Hollywood Christmas Parade. Sunset and Hollywood Boulevards, Hollywood. Celebrities, marching bands, and classic cars in a parade from Mann's Chinese Theatre. Grandstand seats available for a fee. (213) 469–2337. www .hollywoodspectacular.com. Sunday after Thanksgiving.

DECEMBER

Annual New Year's Eve Shipwalk Party. *Queen Mary,* Long Beach. Live music and entertainment, and fireworks. (562) 435–3511. www.queenmary.com.

First Night Fullerton. Downtown Fullerton. Music and arts. (714) 738–6575. New Year's Eve.

Hanukkah at the Skirball. 2701 North Sepulveda Boulevard, Los Angeles. Art workshops, children's sing-along, live music, candle-lighting, treasure hunt, special food, and more. (310) 440–4500. www.skirball.com. Date varies.

Holiday at South Lake Avenue. Colorado Boulevard and California Avenue, Pasadena. Santa on a red fire engine, strolling Dickens carolers, and hay rides. (626) 792–1259. Early December.

Las Posadas. El Pueblo de Los Angeles Historic Monument, downtown Los Angeles. Candlelight procession depicting the journey of Mary and Joseph to Bethlehem. (213) 628–1274. Late December.

Los Angeles County Holiday Celebration. Dorothy Chandler Pavilion. Annual free festival on Christmas Eve, in and around the Music Center. (213) 974–1343. Late December.

Newport Harbor Christmas Boat Parade. Newport Beach Harbor, Newport Beach. More than 150 decorated and illuminated kayaks, canoes, small boats, and million-dollar yachts. (714) 729–4400. www.christmasboatparade.com. Late December.

New Year's Eve at Two Harbors. Catalina Island. Dinner and party. (310) 510–2800. New Year's Eve.

New Year's Eve Bash at the Beach. 17300 Pacific Coast Highway, Malibu. Dinner, laser show, and countdown. (310) 454–3474. New Year's Eve.

New Year's Eve on Catalina Island. Catalina Island. Black-tie gala with dancing to big-band music. (310) 510–1520. New Year's Eve.

New Year's Eve on Pine Avenue. Long Beach. Music, street performers, street dancing, and confetti shower. (562) 437–7700. New Year's Eve.

Tree Lighting at *Queen Mary.* *Queen Mary,* Long Beach. Holiday sing-alongs, refreshments, and choir performances. (562) 435–3511. www.queenmary.com. Early December.

CHAPTER THIRTEEN

GRIFFITH PARK AND LOS ANGELES MUSEUMS

GRIFFITH PARK

Griffith Park, a hilly green space in the foothills of the eastern Santa Monica mountain range, is the largest municipal park and urban wilderness area in the United States. The park, with elevations ranging from 384 to 1,625 feet above sea level, encompasses more than 4,100 acres of wild sage, manzanita shrubs, and California oak trees.

The park includes several major museums and attractions including the famed Griffith Park Observatory and Planetarium (currently under reconstruction and due to reopen in 2006), the Museum of the American West, the Travel Town Transportation Museum, the Los Angeles Zoo, and recreational facilities including a merry-go-round, pony and wagon rides, several golf courses, and an amphitheater. On the slopes below the planetarium is the site—off limits to the public—of the celebrated Hollywood sign.

Over the decades Griffith Park has been the setting for dozens of Hollywood movies with its valleys and hillsides standing in for locations around the world. The lower slopes of the park were once occupied by Native American tribes. The land was originally part of Rancho Los Feliz, a Spanish land grant given to scout and explorer Corporal Jose Vicente Feliz in 1796.

Today the park bears the name of its controversial former owner, Griffith J. Griffith. Born in South Wales in Great Britain, Griffith immigrated to the United States in 1865; he made a considerable fortune speculating on gold mines in California, parlaying some of the inside information he obtained as a newspaper reporter into investments. Griffith settled in Los Angeles in 1882 and purchased what is now the parkland, a property that stretched northward from the northern boundaries of the Pueblo de Los Angeles.

Described by his contemporaries as insufferably pompous (he insisted upon being called "Colonel Griffith" although there is no record he ever held a military title higher than major of riflery practice with the California National Guard), he gave his Rancho Los Feliz estate as a grandiose Christmas gift to the people of Los Angeles in 1896.

In 1903, he was put on trial for the attempted murder of his wealthy society wife, Christina Griffith. In perhaps the first of California's continuing string of celebrity trials, Griffith was portrayed as an alcoholic with a paranoid delusion that his wife was in league with the pope to poison him, steal his money, and commit treason against the nation. He was sentenced to two years in prison; while he was locked away, the city renamed the park's mountain from Mount Griffith to Mount Hollywood, the name it bears today.

Out of prison, Griffith tried to rebuild his standing, offering $100,000 to the city to build an observatory in 1912, and another $50,000 for the construction of Greek Theatre in the park the following year. Politicians were besieged by petitions and rallies calling for them to reject the money from a morally suspect source.

It took more than twenty years—well after Griffith's death in 1919—before the city accepted the money. Greek Theatre was built in 1930, and the Griffith Observatory and Planetarium was constructed in 1935.

The City of Los Angeles Department of Recreation and Parks maintains a Web site about Griffith Park, at www.ci.la.ca.us/rap/dos/griffithPK/.

■ GRIFFITH PARK OBSERVATORY AND PLANETARIUM

One of the stars of Southern California has been dimmed for several years, but plans for the renovated **Griffith Park Observatory and Planetarium** promise a supernova at the top of Mount Hollywood when it reopens in mid-2006. During the three-year reconstruction, the entire area at the top of the mountain will be closed to the public. During the construction period, a limited number of planetarium shows are presented in a temporary theater in the northeast corner of Griffith Park near the L.A. Zoo. For information on programs, call (323) 664–1181.

If the observatory at the top of the south slope of Mount Hollywood in Griffith Park looks vaguely familiar, it may be because of its starring role in a number of motion pictures and television shows over the years. Plans call for every piece of the observatory to be restored to its original grandeur and improved. Excavations under the building and part of its front lawn will allow a doubling of the interior space without changing the classic appearance of the structure. New features will include a presentation theater, two large exhibit areas, a restaurant, and an expanded bookstore.

The **planetarium,** which museum officials acknowledge was world famous for having the most uncomfortable seats in the entire Milky Way Galaxy, will be completely renewed and feature a new all-dome laser projection system, as well as a new Zeiss Mark IX sky projector . . . and better seats.

GRIFFITH PARK

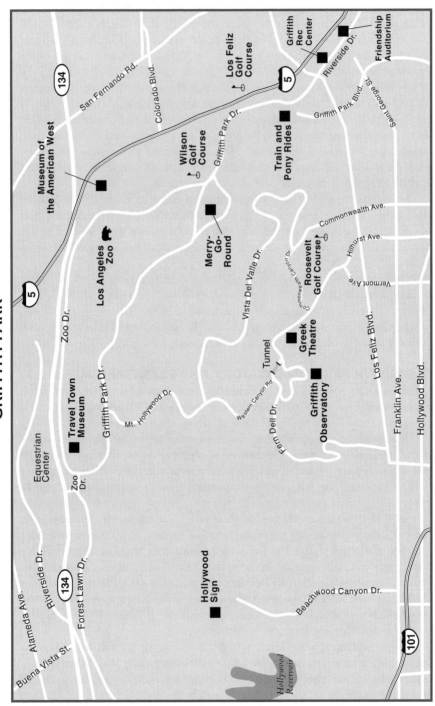

The main rotunda, noted for its massive **Foucault Pendulum,** custom marble, travertine, and mosaic work will be restored to its original architectural grandeur of the 1930s. The Hugo Ballin murals covering the ceiling of the main rotunda were damaged in an earthquake in 1994 and will be restored. The panels depict the scientific achievements of a variety of national groups, including the English, Italian, Chinese, Egyptian, Greek, Arab, and Mexican (Aztec) peoples.

The new 200-seat theater, the **Leonard Nimoy Event Horizon,** was partly funded by a $1 million gift by the actor and his wife.

When it returns, the observatory will again feature a rooftop observatory that has spectacular views of the city on all sides and the heavens above; that is, when the smog clears. The 12-inch Zeiss telescope is one of the largest public telescopes in the world.

The **Hall of Science** within will once again feature a collection of meteorites and geological specimens. A popular exhibit expected to return is a working World War II periscope, which was originally used on the USS *Blenny.* The six-power periscope extends 37 feet up, presenting a nearly 360-degree view from the top of the observatory.

To the right of the entrance to the observatory is a bust of James Dean, who died in 1955—the same year his most famous movie, *Rebel Without a Cause,* was filmed in and around the observatory. Over the shoulder of the bust is the famous Hollywood sign high up on the hills behind it. The observatory was also used as a setting in *Terminator* and as a backdrop for many other films from classic to forgettable.

For information about the observatory, call (323) 664–1191 or consult www
.griffithobs.org. You can also call (323) 663–8171 to hear a recorded message about astronomical events.

MUST-SEE   MUSEUM OF THE AMERICAN WEST

In a corner of Griffith Park is a magical place that celebrates the history of the West from sixteenth-century Spanish armor to the Emigrant Trail and the fabulous growth of modern-day California.

The Museum of the American West (formerly the Gene Autry Museum of Western Heritage) features a significant collection of artifacts including possessions of some of the wagon train Pioneers who settled the West and the cowboys who worked the trails. Run as a nonprofit organization established by the Autry Foundation, the museum includes seven theme galleries with a permanent hands-on gallery for children. It's a hidden piece of Disneyland, too; Disney Imagineers helped create animated displays that celebrate and explain the Old West.

The museum is now part of the Autry National Center, a consortium of two related collections: the Museum of the American West and the **Southwest Museum of the American Indian** in the Mt. Washington area of Los Angeles. The **Women of the West Museum** is part of the Museum of the American West.

Treasures include early guidebooks for westward travelers, such as a copy of the *Hastings Emigrant Guide,* which misled the Donner party to tragedy in the Sierra Mountains. You'll also find a gleaming brass Silsby Steam Pumper, purchased with community fund-raising in 1874 in Carson City. And there's a huge mahogany Edison Multiphone coin-operated phonograph from about 1915 and a "Los Angeles" bar from the turn of the twentieth century that was used in a Montana saloon for nearly a century.

There's a collection of sheriff's badges, Belle Starr's revolver, and a Holdout Arm Cheating Device from about 1905 that hid a card up the sleeve. One case also contains Annie Oakley's gold-plated pistols, presented to her by her husband Frank Butler in about 1900; in 1875, at age fifteen, she beat professional marksman Butler in a local shooting match in Ohio. In 1885 she joined Buffalo Bill's Wild West Show where she starred for seventeen years.

The fine-art collection features work by painters that include Frederic Remington and Seth Eastman. Remington's first sculpture, *Bronco Buster,* is also on display. A museum store offers jewelry, clothing, books, and posters.

Gene Autry, born in 1907 in Tioga, Texas, was a star of radio, music, Hollywood, and business. He began his radio career in 1928 as the result of a chance meeting with Will Rogers; his *Melody Ranch* show on CBS began in 1939 and ran for sixteen years. Autry appeared in ninety-five films and recorded more than 635 records, selling more than forty million copies. His most famous gold records include "Rudolph the Red-Nosed Reindeer," "Peter Cottontail," "Here Comes Santa Claus" (which he cowrote), "Tumbling Tumbleweeds," "Back in the Saddle Again" (cowriter), and "You Are My Sunshine."

Autry put some of his riches into business interests; he owned four radio stations in Los Angeles and Seattle, the California Angels baseball team, and other properties. He sold off majority ownership of the Angels to the Walt Disney Company in 1996. Autry died in 1998.

Located at 4700 Western Heritage Way in Griffith Park at the junction of the Golden State (Interstate 5) and Ventura (Highway 134) freeways, the Museum of the American West is open Tuesday to Sunday from 10:00 A.M. to 5:00 P.M. On Thursday the museum is open until 8:00 P.M. Closed Monday except for certain holidays; closed Thanksgiving and Christmas.

Admission: adults, $7.50; seniors (older than 60) and students (13–18), $5.00; and children (2–12), $3.00. Admission is free on Thursday from 4:00 until 8:00 P.M. Parking is free. For information, call (323) 667–2000 or consult www.autry-museum.org or www.museumoftheamericanwest.org/museum.

The Southwest Museum of the American Indian has extensive holdings of pre-Hispanic, Spanish colonial, Latino, and western American art and artifacts. The collection represents Native American cultures from Alaska to South America.

The Southwest Museum is located at 234 Museum Drive in Los Angeles, with its own station on the Gold Line train. Open Tuesday to Sunday from 10:00 A.M. to 5:00 P.M. Admission: adults, $7.50; seniors (older than 60) and students (13–18), $5.00; and children (2–12), $3.00. For information, call (323) 221–2164 or consult www.southwestmuseum.org.

A combination ticket for both museums is adults, $12.00; seniors and students, $8.00; and children, $5.00.

■ TRAVEL TOWN TRANSPORTATION MUSEUM

This museum is a free and almost-secret treasure guaranteed to enthrall children of most ages. Come see the large collection of steam locomotives, retired Los Angeles street trolleys, antique railway cars, boxcars, cabooses, and old wagons; visitors can climb aboard most of the equipment, including a 110-ton Union Pacific locomotive.

One of the more spectacular engines is Engine No. 26 from the Western Pacific Railroad, which stands almost 12 feet tall. A set of steps leads you to the controls. You will also find a 1911 Metropolitan Transportation Authority street-car and a 1902 Pacific Electric Electra car.

Located on Zoo Drive in Griffith Park, the museum is open weekdays from 10:00 A.M. to 4:00 P.M., and on weekends from 10:00 A.M. to 5:00 P.M. Parking and admission to the museum are free; there is a nominal fee for a train ride. For information, call (323) 662–9678 or consult www.laparks.org/grifmet/tt/index.htm.

Pony and Covered Wagon Rides

Crystal Springs Drive, near Los Feliz Boulevard in Griffith Park. (323) 664–3266 or consult www.ci.la.ca.us/rap/dos/parks/griffithpk/ponyrides.htm. Three small pony tracks can accommodate riders from one to one hundred pounds. Open Tuesday through Sunday from 10:00 A.M. to 4:00 P.M. Nominal fee.

Griffith Park Merry-Go-Round

A lovingly maintained 1926 wooden carousel located between the Los Angeles Zoo and the Los Feliz park entrance. The carousel hosts sixty-eight horses, all of them jumpers, with carved and jeweled bridles. The Stinson Military Band Organ plays more than 1,500 selections of marches and waltzes. Open from 11:00 A.M. to 5:00 P.M. weekends throughout the year and weekdays during the summer, and over Christmas and Easter vacations. Nominal fee. For information, call (323) 665–3051 or consult www.ci.la.ca.us/rap/dos/parks/griffithpk/mgr.htm.

LOS ANGELES AREA ART MUSEUMS

World-renowned collections of ancient Greek, Roman, and Asian works highlight the art museums of Los Angeles.

▐MUST-SEE▌ J. PAUL GETTY MUSEUM AT THE GETTY CENTER

The Getty collection includes Greek and Roman marble and bronze sculptures, paintings, vases, and other objects from 3000 B.C. to A.D. 300. Major works include the Cycladic harpist from about 2500 B.C. and the limestone and marble *Aphrodite* from the end of the fifth century B.C.

The collection of drawings and paintings includes Rembrandt's *An Old Man in Military Costume* and other portraits; Thomas Gainsborough's *Portrait of Anne, Countess of Chesterfield;* Paul Cézanne's *Young Italian Woman at a Table;* Titian's *Venus and Adonis;* Peter Paul Rubens's *Andromeda;* as well as works by da Vinci, Raphael, Goya, Renoir, Munch, and van Gogh.

The spectacular museum consists of a cluster of two-story pavilions bridged by walkways on both levels with indoor and outdoor galleries and gardens. Visitors are delivered from the parking area to the hilltop facility by an automated tram; the cars are like a horizontal elevator, gliding ⅛ inch above the track on a cushion of air.

The Getty Center is located at 1200 Getty Center Drive in Brentwood, near the San Diego Freeway (Interstate 405) and the Santa Monica Freeway (Interstate 10). Take the Getty Center Drive exit from 405 and follow the signs.

The museum is open Sunday and Tuesday to Thursday from 10:00 A.M. to 6:00 P.M., Friday and Saturday from 10:00 A.M. to 9:00 P.M. Closed Monday and major holidays. Admission is free. Advance reservations are recommended for special events. Parking is $7.00; advance reservations for spaces recommended. For information, call (310) 440–7300 or consult www.getty.edu/museum.

Getty Villa, Malibu

The spectacular building in a gorgeous setting with a fabulous endowment was created by oil billionaire J. Paul Getty to hold his personal collection. It was closed to the public in 1997 for renovation and is expected to reopen by the end of 2006 as a research and cultural center.

The building is set in a re-creation of a first-century Roman villa, built on a cliff overlooking the Pacific Ocean; it is surrounded by manicured gardens. The design for the building is based on the Villa dei Papiri, which stood outside the ancient city of Herculaneum, overlooking the Bay of Naples.

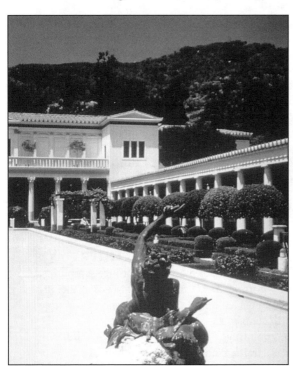

The villa's new mission includes the display of works of art from the Antiquities Collection, which now contains more than 50,000 objects. The collections will be displayed by themes such as religion and myth or on aspects of everyday life. The Villa will also have a number of galleries for temporary exhibitions of materials from other institutions and from the collections of the Getty Research Institute.

For information, call (310) 440–7300, or consult www.getty.edu/museum/villa.html.

Peristyle Garden: Getty Villa. *Photo by Alexander Vertikoff, Copyright © The J. Paul Getty Trust*

‡MUST-SEE‡ HUNTINGTON LIBRARY, ART COLLECTIONS, AND BOTANICAL GARDENS

Another art-filled monument to old money, the extensive and wide-ranging collections of railroad magnate Henry E. Huntington are housed in a group of buildings in a 200-acre botanical garden in the San Gabriel Valley. The estate was built in 1919. The library, built in 1925, contains more than half a million books and five million manuscripts, including a first folio of several of Shakespeare's plays, the Ellesmere manuscript of Geoffrey Chaucer's *The Canterbury Tales* from about 1410, and a Gutenberg Bible. The art gallery, built in 1910 as Huntington's home, showcases famous works such as Thomas Gainsborough's *Blue Boy.*

The estate's botanical gardens include a large Japanese garden with a koi fish pond; the Desert Garden is the largest such collection in the world with more than 5,000 desert plant species. Guided tours of the garden are available; call for details.

The museum is located at 1151 Oxford Road, San Marino, about 12 miles northeast of downtown Los Angeles and due east of Pasadena. Open Tuesday through Friday from noon to 4:30 P.M. and weekends from 10:30 A.M. to 4:30 P.M.; in the summer, the museum opens daily, except Monday, at 10:30 A.M.

Admission: adults, $15.00; students, $10.00; seniors, $12.00; children 5–11, $6.00; children (4 and younger) free. Admission is free to all on the first Thursday of each month.

For information, call (626) 405–2100 or consult www.huntington.org.

‡MUST-SEE‡ LOS ANGELES COUNTY MUSEUM OF ART

A sprawling collection of art from around the world including a fabulous collection of Tibetan, Indian, and Nepalese works, a gallery of Daumier prints, and a pavilion with one of the best gatherings of Japanese art outside of Asia.

The museum includes four main buildings: the Hammer Building (photography, prints, drawings, and late-nineteenth-century European art), the Bing Center, the Robert O. Anderson Building (primarily twentieth-century art), and the Ahmanson Gallery. The Ahmanson includes ancient Egyptian, Asian, Middle Eastern, pre-Columbian, and early-American art and artifacts. The Bing Theater at the Bing Center offers a family film series on Friday and Saturday evenings.

The La Brea tar pits, one of the world's most important Pleistocene-era sites, are located directly behind the museum in Hancock Park.

The museum, at 5905 Wilshire Boulevard in Los Angeles, is open Monday, Tuesday, and Thursday from noon to 8:00 P.M., Friday from noon to 9:00 P.M., Saturday and Sunday from 11:00 A.M. to 8:00 P.M. Closed Wednesday, Thanksgiving, and Christmas. Admission: adults, $9.00; students and seniors, $5.00; and children (12 and younger), free. Admission is free to all on the second Tuesday of each month. Parking is available at Wilshire Boulevard and Spaulding Avenue, and at Wilshire and Ogden Drive for $5.00, free after 7:00 P.M. For information, call (323) 857–6000 or consult www.lacma.org.

⫶ *MUST-SEE* ⫶ MUSEUM OF CONTEMPORARY ART, LOS ANGELES (MOCA)

Like many of the pieces it displays, MOCA is a bit hard to get a handle on: To begin with, this is one museum with three locations.

The main building is known as **MOCA at California Plaza,** located at 250 South Grand Avenue, Los Angeles. In the best traditions of grand museums, the building that houses the collection of modern art at MOCA is a work of art by itself; designed by Japanese architect Arata Isozaki and opened in 1986, it includes spectacular pyramidic skylights and geometric angles. For information, call (213) 621–2766 or consult www.moca-la.org.

The more mundane **MOCA at the Geffen Contemporary** in Little Tokyo, which opened while MOCA was under construction, has been kept in service as home to traveling exhibitions and some of the works from the main museum. It is housed within a converted Los Angeles Police Department garage at 152 North Central Avenue, about a mile from California Plaza. For information, call (213) 626–6222.

The most recently added piece of the pie is **MOCA at the Pacific Design Center,** at 8687 Melrose Avenue, West Hollywood. The small facility features contemporary architecture and design. For information, call (213) 621–1741.

All three of the museum buildings are closed Monday. Open Tuesday through Sunday 11:00 A.M. to 5:00 P.M. and until 8:00 P.M. on Thursday. Admission: adults, $8.00; students (12 and older) and seniors, $5.00. Free admission on Thursday from 5:00 to 8:00 P.M. One ticket is valid at California Plaza and the Geffen Contemporary on the same day, and at the Pacific Design Center within thirty days of first use. Admission to MOCA at the Pacific Design Center is only $3.00.

⫶ *MUST-SEE* ⫶ MUSEUM OF TELEVISION AND RADIO

The history of television, radio, and the Internet is collected and celebrated at the Museum of Television & Radio in Beverly Hills. The museum was founded by broadcasting pioneer William S. Paley in New York, and today maintains identical collections of programming on both coasts.

Visitors and researchers can listen to and watch more than 120,000 programs covering the history of broadcasting, including news, public affairs programs and documentaries, performing arts programs, children's programming, sports, comedy and variety shows, and commercial advertising. The collection is cataloged on computers.

Major annual screening and listening series and festivals include the William S. Paley Television Festival, Television Documentary Festival, Radio Festival, and International Children's Television Festival. Seminars feature discussions with writers, producers, directors, actors, journalists, and others involved with landmark programming. The New York and Beverly Hills museums are electronically linked to allow seminars to take place at both locations simultaneously.

Visitors can request a program from the collection and listen to or watch their selections at radio and television consoles.

The museum is located at 465 North Beverly Drive, at the intersection of North Beverly Drive and Little Santa Monica Boulevard. Open Wednesday to Sunday from noon to 5:00 P.M. Admission is free, but there is a suggested contribution of $10.00 for adults, $8.00 for students and seniors, and $5.00 for children. For information, call (310) 786–1000 or consult www.mtr.org.

🔲MUST-SEE🔲 NORTON SIMON MUSEUM OF ART

Only the best: modern nineteenth- and twentieth-century classics from Picasso, Monet, van Gogh, Renoir, Degas, Cézanne, Klee, and more, plus 2,000 years of Indian and Southeast Asian sculptures. At nearly every turn you'll see familiar works of art by famous artists.

Norton Simon, born in Portland, Oregon, in 1907, moved to Los Angeles and started a series of businesses. In 1929, at the start of the Depression, he invested $7,000 in a failing juice bottling company that became the highly successful Hunt Foods. His holdings eventually expanded to include Hunt-Wesson Foods, McCall's Publishing, Canada Dry, Max Factor, and Avis Car Rental.

Treasures include Botticelli's *Madonna and Child with Adoring Angel,* from about 1470; Peter Paul Rubens's *David Slaying Goliath;* Rembrandt's famed *Self-Portrait;* and Jean-Honoré Fragonard's *The Happy Lovers.* Modern masterpieces include Ansel Adams's famous photograph, *Moonrise, Hernandez, New Mexico;* Pablo Picasso's *The Ram's Head;* and Henri Matisse's *The Black Shawl.*

Located at 411 West Colorado Boulevard at Orange Grove Boulevard in Pasadena at the intersection of the Foothill (Interstate 210) and Ventura (Highway 134) freeways, the museum is open daily except Tuesday from noon to 6:00 P.M., and on Friday until 9:00 P.M. Admission: adults, $8.00; seniors, $4.00; children (18 and younger) and students with current ID, free. Admission is free for all on the first Friday of the month from 6:00 to 9:00 P.M.

For information, call (626) 449–6840 or consult www.nortonsimon.org.

▪ PACIFIC ASIA MUSEUM

Housed within a replica of a Chinese imperial palace is an extensive collection of Pacific Island and Asian costumes, ceramics, textiles, ornaments, and paintings. Located at 46 North Los Robles Avenue, north of Colorado Boulevard in Pasadena, the museum is open Wednesday through Sunday 10:00 A.M. to 5:00 P.M., and on Friday until 8:00 P.M. Admission: adults, $7.00; seniors and students, $5.00; children (12 and younger), free. Admission is free on the fourth Friday of the month. For information, call (626) 449–2742 or consult www.pacificasia museum.org.

▪ UCLA HAMMER MUSEUM

The twentieth-century industrialist and deal maker Armand Hammer's collection of Impressionist and Postimpressionist paintings and caricatures by Honoré Daumier highlight the exhibition. Other stars of the collection include Claude Monet, Camille Pissarro, John Singer Sargent, Mary Cassatt, and Vincent van Gogh.

Nearby on UCLA's North Campus, the Franklin D. Murphy Sculpture Garden features more than seventy sculptures by such artists as Jean Arp, Alexander Calder, Claire Falkenstein, Barbara Hepworth, Gaston Lachaise, Jacques Lipchitz, Henri Matisse, Henry Moore, Isamu Noguchi, Auguste Rodin, David Smith, and Francisco Zuñiga.

Located at 10899 Wilshire Boulevard at Westwood Boulevard in Los Angeles, the museum is open Tuesday and Wednesday 11:00 A.M. to 7:00 P.M., Thursday until 9:00 P.M., Friday and Saturday 11:00 A.M. to 7:00 P.M., and Sunday 11:00 A.M. to 5:00 P.M. Admission: adults, $4.50; students and seniors, $3.00; children (17 and younger), free. Admission is free on Thursday. For information, call (310) 443–7000 or consult http://artscenecal.com/UCLA HammerMsm.html.

■ UCLA FOWLER MUSEUM OF CULTURAL HISTORY

An eclectic collection of more than 750,000 objects representing prehistoric, historic, and contemporary cultures of Africa, Oceania, the Americas, and Asia. Admission: free. Parking $6.00. Located just west of Royce Hall on the UCLA campus, off Sunset Boulevard, the museum is open Wednesday to Sunday, noon to 5:00 P.M., and Thursday evenings until 8:00 P.M. For information, call (310) 825–4361 or consult www.fowler.ucla.edu/incEngine/.

■ BARNSDALL ART PARK

Architect Frank Lloyd Wright's first Los Angeles house was the Hollyhock House, built in 1918 for oil heiress Aline Barnsdall, who came West with hopes of developing a theater company. She donated the home and surrounding property to the city in 1927 as an arts center. The house is presently closed for rehabilitation; no opening date has been set. For information, call (323) 913–4157.

The park is located at 4800 Hollywood Boulevard, Los Feliz. One-hour walking tours are available from Wednesday to Sunday from 12:30 to 3:30 P.M. Admission: adults, $5.00, seniors $3.00. Call (323) 644–6269 for availability.

Also on the grounds is the **L.A. Municipal Art Gallery.** Admission: $5.00, $3.00 seniors. Hours are Friday, Saturday, and Sunday from noon to 5:00 P.M. On the first Friday of the month, the gallery is open from noon to 9:00 P.M. and admission is free. For information, call (323) 644–6269.

■ LONG BEACH MUSEUM OF ART

An intriguing mixture of old and new with displays of modern art, sculpture, and videos in a 1912 mansion on a bluff overlooking Long Beach Harbor and the Pacific Ocean. Admission: free. The museum, at 2300 East Ocean Boulevard in Long Beach, is open Tuesday through Sunday 11:00 A.M. to 5:00 P.M., and until 8:00 P.M. on Thursday. Admission: adults, $5.00; students and seniors, $4.00; children (12 and younger), free. Admission is free on the first Friday of each month. For information, call (562) 439–2119 or consult www.lbma.org.

■ ORANGE COUNTY MUSEUM OF ART

Twentieth-century American art with an emphasis on 200 years of California culture. The museum is located at 850 San Clemente Drive in Newport Beach, about 45 miles southeast of Los Angeles or 15 miles south of Disneyland. It is open Tuesday to Sunday 11:00 A.M. to 5:00 P.M. and Thursday until 8:00 P.M. Admission: adults, $7.00; students and seniors, $5.00; children (16 and younger), free. For information, call (949) 759–1122 or consult www.ocma.net.

MUSEUMS OF SCIENCE AND CULTURE

In southern California, sometimes it's hard to separate science and culture; they seem inextricably bound up with each other in places like the La Brea Tar Pits and the International Surfing Museum.

▓ MUST-SEE ▓ LA BREA TAR PITS/GEORGE C. PAGE MUSEUM OF THE LA BREA DISCOVERIES

The La Brea Tar Pits are one of the most unusual elements of a downtown anywhere in the world, a little bit of the Ice Age in the shadow of the skyscrapers. The museum has within it more than a million fossils of plants and animals taken from the tar pits since their discovery in 1906.

Among the skeletal remains found in the tar are saber-toothed tigers, a mammoth, and the 9,000-year-old remains of a woman. Don't promise your kids a view of dinosaurs, though: The pits are only about 40,000 years old, and the big guys had been gone tens of millions of years by then.

As you enter **Hancock Park,** home of the La Brea Tar Pits, you can smell tar and asphalt in the air. The first historic reference to the tar pools was recorded in the diary of Gaspar du Portola in 1769; the area was originally a portion of the Rancho La Brea granted by Governor Alvarado in 1840.

The lake pit along Wilshire Boulevard is a quarry where asphalt was mined in the nineteenth century; life-size fiberglass models of an imperial mammoth family stand at the east end of the lake, which is covered with an oily slick. Bubbles of methane burst through the surface of the lake regularly.

The pools of thick oil became unique death traps for countless Ice Age animals and birds, making La Brea the richest deposit of Ice Age fossils in the world. More than one hundred tons of fossil bones have been recovered.

The reconstructed Imperial Mammoth Bull alongside the lake pit is modeled after a nearly complete skeleton exhibited in the George C. Page Museum. The animal stood about 12 feet tall and weighed more than 10,000 pounds.

On a nice Sunday you will also likely find a collection of some of California's patented kooks. On one of my visits, I found a man exhibiting his pair of "psychic cats." If you held out a dollar bill, they would grab hold of it with their paws and push a lever on a cigar box to release a printed message.

The pits and museum are located at 5801 Wilshire Boulevard east of Fairfax Avenue in Los Angeles. Open weekdays from 9:30 A.M. to 5:00 P.M., weekends and holidays from 10:00 A.M.; first Tuesday of the month is free. Admission: adults, $7.00; seniors and students, $4.50; children (5–12), $2.00. Parking at the museum is $6.00 with validation.

For information, call (323) 857–6311 or consult www.tarpits.org.

▓MUST-SEE▓ LOS ANGELES COUNTY MUSEUM OF NATURAL HISTORY

A national treasure with dozens of major displays from the age of the dinosaurs to modern-day mammals and most everything in between. You'll find an insect zoo, a Hall of Birds, a sparkling collection of gems and minerals, and even a display of ancient Mayan artifacts.

Two world-famous habitat halls show African and North American mammals in their natural environments. The museum is also home to Megamouth, the world's rarest shark; the 14.5-foot-long male is one of only five of his species found since the first one was discovered in 1976. The Hall of Native American Cultures showcases more than 800 pieces from the museum's permanent collection, and the Marine Hall features intricate dioramas of sea life in California waters.

Located at 900 Exposition Boulevard in Los Angeles in Exposition Park, the museum is open daily from 9:30 A.M. to 5:00 P.M., and from 10:00 A.M. to 5:00 P.M. on weekends. Admission: adults, $9.00; students and seniors, $6.50; children (5–12), $2.00. Admission free on the first Tuesday of each month.

For information, call (213) 763–3466 or consult www.nhm.org.

Within the museum is the Discovery Center, a hands-on, interactive gallery where visitors can dig for fossils, meet live reptiles, and observe insects at their own zoo.

Next-door to the Natural History Museum is the Exposition Park Rose Garden, one of the largest displays in the country. Open daily. Admission: free.

▓ LOS ANGELES MARITIME MUSEUM

The next best thing to a life at sea: a collection of more than 600 ship models, including a cutaway model of the *Titanic,* plus all manner of maritime equipment, including diving equipment and artifacts from the old whaling and shipping days to modern times. The museum is located at Berth 84, Sixth Street and Harbor Boulevard, San Pedro, in a former ferry building with a view of the harbor. Open Tuesday to Saturday from 10:00 A.M. to 5:00 P.M., Sunday from noon to 5:00 P.M. Closed Monday. Admission: adults, $3.00; youth and seniors, $1.00. For information, call (310) 548–7618 or consult www.lamaritimemuseum.org.

Nearby at Berth 94 is the SS *Lane Victory,* a restored cargo ship built in Los Angeles in 1945. The vessel served in the latter part of World War II, Korea (at the Chosin Reservoir operation), and in Vietnam. The ship was named after Isaac Lane, who rose from slavery to become a Bishop in the Methodist Episcopal Church and founded the Lane College in Jackson, Tennessee, in 1882.

The ship has been restored to near-pristine condition, with all of its naval guns and most of its equipment in place. It is open for tours throughout the year. The vessel is regularly employed as a set for films, television shows, and commercials; call ahead to confirm hours before a visit.

Six times a year during the summer the *Lane Victory* leaves its dock to cruise to Catalina Island, as part of a re-enactment of a World War II air battle. Organizers expect a donation of at least $100 per adult for the all-day trip, including meals. Children 15 and younger, $60. For dockside visits, a donation of $3.00 per person is expected. Call (310) 519–9545 for information and schedules or consult www.lanevictory.org.

⫶MUST-SEE⫶ PETERSEN AUTOMOTIVE MUSEUM

A branch of the Natural History Museum of Los Angeles County, the permanent exhibit on the first floor traces the history of the automobile. The second floor contains five large, rotating exhibition galleries with state-of-the-art displays of race cars, classic cars, vintage motorcycles, concept cars, celebrity and movie cars, and automotive design and technology. The museum is housed in the former Ohrbach's Department Store in downtown Los Angeles and is named after benefactor Robert E. Petersen, a noted automobile enthusiast.

Located at 6060 Wilshire Boulevard, near Fairfax Avenue, the museum is open Tuesday to Sunday from 10:00 A.M. to 6:00 P.M. and is closed Monday except for holidays. Admission: adults, $10.00; seniors and students, $5.00; children (5–12), $3.00. For information, call (323) 930–2277 or consult www.petersen.org.

▪ CABRILLO MARINE AQUARIUM

Saltwater aquariums, displays of sea plants, tide pools, and mudflats located in and around a 1920s bathhouse. The museum also sponsors educational lectures, whale-watching trips, and the annual Whale Fiesta in June and Autumn Sea Fair in October.

Located at 3720 Stephen White Drive in San Pedro, the museum is open Tuesday to Friday from noon to 5:00 P.M.; weekends from 10:00 A.M. to 5:00 P.M. Admission free; suggested donation, $5.00; children, $1.00. Beach parking fee $7.00 on weekends, free on weekdays. For information, call (310) 548–7562 or consult www.cabrilloaq.org.

⫶MUST-SEE⫶ CALIFORNIA SCIENCE CENTER

A sprawling museum with hands-on explorations of science from medicine to outer space, second only in size to the Smithsonian in Washington. The two main theme areas are **World of Life** and **Creative World.** Check out the Life Tiles as you enter; art "morphs" from one image to another.

Guests who meet size and weight requirements can ride a high-wire bicycle hung 43 feet above the atrium floor of the Science Court. The bike is counterbalanced on a guy wire; you cannot fall, but you do have to overcome any fear of heights.

Suspended above the Science Court is a hyperbolic paraboloid sculpture, better known as Hypar, which is a fantastic blend of science and art made from 2,500 aluminum links. The sculpture grows from a compact cluster of 15 feet to 50 feet, maintaining its shape.

The aerospace section includes historic airplanes, spacecraft, other exhibits, and the IMAX Theater with a 70-foot-high, 90-foot-wide screen for science, nature, and travel films in 2-D and 3-D formats. Call (213) 744–7400 for IMAX schedules. Admission to IMAX films: adults, $7.50; seniors and students (13–17 and college students with ID), $5.50; children (4–12), $4.50.

The museum is located in Exposition Park at 700 State Drive, next to the Los Angeles Memorial Coliseum; the area is often used for special events. Parking is $6.00 per car, $10.00 for buses or oversize vehicles. To reach the parking structure, turn west into Exposition Park on 39th Street from Figueroa and follow the signs. The museum is open daily from 10:00 A.M. to 5:00 P.M. Admission: free to exhibits.

For information, call (323) 724–3623 or consult www.casciencectr.org.

JET PROPULSION LABORATORY

Exhibits include models of the Galileo and Cassini spacecrafts. Two-hour tours given only by reservation; currently all-day tours must be booked at least six months in advance. Children younger than ten are not permitted. The laboratory is located at 4800 Oak Grove Drive in Pasadena. Call (818) 354–9314 for information and hours. Information about the laboratory can be seen at www.jpl.nasa.gov.

HOBBY CITY DOLL AND TOY MUSEUM

More than 6,000 antique dolls and toys, with displays including a small-scale replica of the White House. Next door is **Adventure City,** an outdoor theme park for children under thirteen that includes small-scale rides, a petting zoo, and play areas.

Located at 1238 South Beach Boulevard, Anaheim. Nominal admission. For information and hours, call (714) 527–2323.

HUNTINGTON BEACH INTERNATIONAL SURFING MUSEUM

Far out, dude: a collection of wicked surfboards, including a 1930 wooden behemoth that measures more than 12 feet and weighs 135 pounds. Other exhibits include posters, artwork, surfing music, and a Hall of Fame. Free surfer music shows in the parking lot Sunday afternoons; call for schedules.

Located at 411 Olive Avenue in Huntington Beach (exit I–405 at Highway 39, Beach Boulevard), the surfing museum is open year-round, with hours changing seasonally.

For information, call (714) 960–3483 or consult www.surfingmuseum.org.

HISTORY MUSEUMS AND HISTORIC DISTRICTS

Historical museums and attractions in Southern California explore the influences of immigrants from the East, Asia, Mexico, and Central America.

AMERICAN MILITARY MUSEUM

An unusual collection of military equipment, including tanks, jeeps, and cannons. Located at 1918 North Rosemead Boulevard, El Monte, within the Whittier Narrows Recreation Area, the museum is open Friday through Sunday 10:00 A.M. to 4:30 P.M. Closed in wet weather. Admission: by donation. For information, call (626) 442–1776 or consult hometown.aol.com/tankland/museum.htm.

■ CALIFORNIA AFRO-AMERICAN MUSEUM

Art exhibitions, a library, and theater celebrating African-American culture. Located in Exposition Park at South Figueroa Street and State Drive in Los Angeles. The facility reopened in late 2005 after extensive renovations; call ahead to check on operations. Open daily except Monday, from 10:00 A.M. to 5:00 P.M. Admission: free; parking, $6.00. For information, call (213) 744–7432 or consult www.camuseum.org.

■ EL MONTE HISTORICAL MUSEUM

A small museum that celebrates El Monte's history as the end of the Santa Fe Trail, which extended some 780 miles from Independence, Missouri, to Santa Fe, New Mexico, and from there on to California. Hundreds of wagon trains made the forty- to sixty-day trip to New Mexico from about 1822 until 1880, when the Santa Fe Railroad reached the area.

The adobe-style building, a former WPA-built library, includes Victorian-era settings and a children's section with antique toys. Located at 3150 North Tyler Avenue, El Monte, the museum is open Tuesday to Friday from 10:00 A.M. to 4:00 P.M. and Sunday from 1:00 to 3:00 P.M. Donations are accepted. For information, call (626) 580–2232 or consult www.ci.el-monte.ca.us/citygov/comm_services/museum.html.

■ HERITAGE SQUARE MUSEUM

Eight Victorian-era and older buildings have been restored into a living museum with shops and displays; they are open for tours by costumed guides Saturday, Sunday, and most holidays. Buildings include the Palms Railroad Station, which has been restored and filled with railroad artifacts, plus several homes and a church from 1897. Special events include old-fashioned Fourth of July celebrations and Christmas festivals.

Located at 3800 Homer Street in Highland Park; guided tours depart frequently. The museum is open Friday, Saturday, Sunday, and most holiday Mondays. Summer hours are noon to 5:00 P.M.; winter hours are 11:30 A.M. to 4:30 P.M. Admission: adults, $10.00; seniors, $8.00; students and children (7–11), $5.00.

For information, call (626) 449–0193 or consult www.heritagesquare.org.

■ JAPANESE-AMERICAN NATIONAL MUSEUM

The story of Japanese immigrants to America told in artifacts, photos, art, and recordings.

The museum is located within the former Nishi Hongwanji Buddhist Temple, built by Japanese immigrants in 1925 as the first Buddhist place of worship in Los Angeles. The ornate structure mixes elements of a temple in Kyoto with other Japanese and Middle Eastern influences. A hub of religious and social life in thriving Little Tokyo, the structure was later used to store the belongings of Japanese Americans ordered to World War II internment camps. The temple eventually fell into serious disrepair and, in 1969, was sold to the City of Los Angeles. It was saved from demolition for use as the museum site.

Located at 369 East First Street at Central Avenue, Los Angeles, the museum is open Tuesday to Sunday 10:00 A.M. to 5:00 P.M. and until 8:00 P.M. on Thursday. Closed Monday. Admission: adults, $8.00; seniors, $5.00; students with ID and children (6–17), $4.00. Free every third Thursday and every Thursday evening from 5:00 to 8:00 P.M. For information, call (213) 625–0414 or consult www.janm.org.

KOREAN FRIENDSHIP BELL

Angel's Gate Park, San Pedro, on Gaffey Street. What is said to be the largest bell in America was a gift from the Republic of Korea to the United States for the 1976 Bicentennial celebration. The one-ton bell is rung only four times each year: July 4, August 15 (Korean Independence Day), New Year's Eve, and every September to coincide with bell ringings around the country to celebrate Constitution week. For information, consult www.sanpedrochamber.com/champint/korenbel.htm.

LUMMIS HOME

Writer and photographer Charles Lummis, who chronicled some of the early days of the Wild West, built his home—named El Alisal for a nearby stand of sycamores—between 1896 and 1910 from granite boulders, concrete, and telegraph poles from the Santa Fe Railroad. Inside are rare photos of Native Americans and other artifacts. Located at 200 East Avenue 43, Highland Park, near the Southwest Museum, the home is open Friday to Sunday from noon to 4:00 P.M. Admission: free. For information, call (323) 222–0546.

LOS ANGELES MUSEUM OF THE HOLOCAUST

A commemoration of the victims of the Holocaust, including photographs, diaries, artifacts, and oral histories. Located at 6435 Wilshire Boulevard, Los Angeles, the museum is open Monday to Thursday from 10:00 A.M. to 5:00 P.M., Friday from 10:00 A.M. to 2:00 P.M., and Sunday by appointment. Open Tuesday until 8:00 P.M. Closed Saturday. Admission: free. For information, call (323) 651–3704 or consult www.lamuseumoftheholocaust.org.

MUSEUM OF TOLERANCE, SIMON WIESENTHAL CENTER

Never again: exhibits on twentieth-century genocide, war, and oppression, from the Holocaust to the fighting in Rwanda and the Neo-Nazi movement. Some of the exhibits can be rather intense, including the Whisper Gallery where visitors walk through an audio gauntlet of racial and ethnic slurs, and the Hall of Testimony, where you will hear stories of survival and sacrifice from the Holocaust in Europe.

Simon Wiesenthal, trained as an architect, survived the Nazi death camps of World War II. After the war he became a hunter of former Nazis. The Simon Wiesenthal Center was founded in 1977.

Located at 9786 West Pico Boulevard at Roxbury Drive, Century City, the museum is open Monday through Thursday from 11:30 A.M. to 6:30 P.M., Friday from 11:30 A.M. until 3:00 P.M. in the winter and until 5:00 P.M. in the summer, and Sunday from 11:00 A.M. to 7:30 P.M. The museum is closed Saturday and

Jewish holidays. The last admission each day is two hours before closing time. Admission: adults, $10.00; seniors, $8.00; students and children (3–10), $7.00. For information, call (310) 553–8403 or consult www.museumoftolerance.com.

■ SKIRBALL CULTURAL CENTER

Jewish history and art from around the world and across time, with a performing arts center. Located at 2701 North Sepulveda Boulevard, Los Angeles, the center is open Tuesday through Saturday from noon to 5:00 P.M., Thursday until 9:00 P.M., Sunday from 11:00 A.M. to 5:00 P.M. Closed Monday. Admission to the core exhibit *Visions and Values:* general, $8.00; seniors and students, $6.00. Admission to *Einstein* (includes admission to all other exhibits): general, $12.00; seniors and students, $8.00. Free on Thursday. For information, call (310) 440–4600 or consult www.skirball.org.

■ SOUTHWEST MUSEUM OF THE AMERICAN INDIAN

An impressive collection of artifacts and crafts of Native Americans of the West, as well as elements of the Spanish colonization of California. Located at 234 Museum Drive, near Highland Park in Los Angeles, the museum is open Tuesday to Sunday from 10:00 A.M. to 5:00 P.M. Closed Monday. Admission: adults, $7.50; seniors and students, $5.00; children (7–17), $3.00. For information, call (323) 221–2164 or consult www.southwestmuseum.org.

■ WELLS FARGO HISTORY MUSEUM

A history of the rough side of development of the West including stagecoaches, the Pony Express, mining equipment, gold nuggets, and a replica of a nineteenth-century Wells Fargo office. Visitors can try their hands at a telegraph key and examine early photos and documents that trace the history of Wells Fargo Bank from its founding in 1852 into the electronic age. Located at 333 South Grand Avenue at Third Street in the Wells Fargo Bank Center, Los Angeles, the museum is open weekdays from 9:00 A.M. to 5:00 P.M. Admission: free. For information, call (213) 253–7166 or consult www.wellsfargo.com/about/museum_info.jhtml.

■ WILLIAM O. DOUGLAS OUTDOOR CLASSROOM

Nature center, family and children's hiking trails, and special educational and ecological programs. Located at Franklin Canyon Ranch, north of Beverly Hills. Admission: free. For information, call (310) 858–3834.

CHILDREN'S MUSEUMS

■ CHILDREN'S MUSEUM OF LOS ANGELES

The mother of all children's museums in Los Angeles will reopen in two new facilities by 2007. The first new facility, the **North Valley Campus,** is on an acre of land in the Hansen Dam Recreational Area located in the northeast San Fernando Valley. The museum structure will include activities for children to learn, explore, and discover all sorts of neat stuff.

The second half of the museum will be within the **Art Park,** located adjacent to the Geffen Contemporary Museum of Art and next to the Japanese-American National Museum and the Union Art center. The Art Park will include a 100,000-square-foot building celebrating the urban environment and the performing and visual arts. For information, call (213) 687–8800 or consult www .childrensmuseumla.org.

■ KIDSPACE

Children try on some of the roles of adulthood in this innovative museum that insists that visitors touch the exhibits. Children can visit a television weather set, climb on a fire truck, and much more. Children must be accompanied by an adult, and the other way around. The museum reopened in 2004 at a new location, 480 North Arroyo Boulevard, Pasadena, at the site of the former Fannie Morrison Horticultural Center in Pasadena's Brookside Park. Admission: adults and children older than 1 year, $8.00. For information, call (626) 449–9144 or consult www.kidspacemuseum.org.

■ LA HABRA CHILDREN'S MUSEUM

A converted train depot with hands-on exhibits including a real city bus, a mini market with a cash register and scales, a dino dig, and a model train village. Check out the dino topiaries at the entrance. Located at 301 South Euclid Street, La Habra, the museum is open daily from 10:00 A.M. to 5:00 P.M. and Sunday from 1:00 to 5:00 P.M. On Monday the museum closes at 1:00 P.M. Admission: $5.00. For information, call (562) 905–9793 or consult www.lhcm.org.

TRANSPORTATION MUSEUMS

■ LOMITA RAILROAD MUSEUM

Step back to the turn of the century and explore a 1921 Southern Pacific locomotive, an old train station, an antique caboose, and other railroad equipment. Located at 2137 250th Street, at Woodward Avenue, Lomita, the museum is open Wednesday to Sunday from 10:00 A.M. to 5:00 P.M. Admission: adults, $4.00; children (12 and younger), $2.00. For information, call (310) 326–6255 or consult www.lomita-rr.org.

■ THE AIR MUSEUM–PLANES OF FAME

Rare aircraft from World War I to the space age. The collection includes more than a hundred aircraft and displays spanning the history of manned flight; there are more than forty historic "war birds" in airworthy condition. Flying events the first Saturday of every month. Located at Chino Airport, 7000 Merrill Avenue, the museum is open daily from 9:00 A.M. to 5:00 P.M. Admission: adults, $8.95; children (11 and younger), $1.95. For information, call (909) 597–3722 or consult www.planesoffame.org.

ENTERTAINMENT INDUSTRY MUSEUMS

■ HOLLYWOOD BOWL MUSEUM

The history of the Hollywood Bowl in a small but rich museum. Located at 2301 North Highland Avenue, Hollywood. Admission: free. For information and hours, which vary by season, call (323) 850–2058 or consult www.hollywood bowl.org/event/museum.cfm.

■ HOLLYWOOD HERITAGE MUSEUM (THE DEMILLE BARN)

Memorabilia, costumes, and equipment from the early days of moviemaking. The museum is located in the barn where Lasky's Feature Play Company, with Cecil B. DeMille as director, produced *The Squaw Man,* the first feature-length film made in Hollywood. Objects on display include the chariot from *Ben Hur.* Reopened in 1998 after damage from a fire, the museum is located at 2100 North Highland Avenue, Los Angeles, near Hollywood Bowl. Open weekends from 11:00 A.M. to 4:00 P.M. Admission: adults, $6.00; seniors and students, $3.00; children (3–12), $1.00. For information, call (323) 874–2276 or consult www.holly woodheritage.org/museum/museum.html.

■ HOLLYWOOD WAX MUSEUM

Get up close and personal with more than 200 of Hollywood's greatest stars; just don't expect them to give you an autograph. The museum also features a Chamber of Horrors with residents including Frankenstein's monster, Dracula, Wolfman, Pinhead, Elvira, and the Phantom of the Opera, and a movie theater that shows films celebrating the old hometown. Located at 6767 Hollywood Boulevard, Hollywood, the museum is open daily from 10:00 A.M. to midnight. On Friday it stays open until 1:00 A.M. Admission: adults, $10.95; seniors, $8.50; children (6–12), $6.95.

Combo tickets may be purchased for the Wax Museum and the Guinness Book of World Records Museum across the street. Admission: adults, $15.95; seniors, $13.95; children (6–12), $8.95.

For information on the Hollywood Wax Museum, call (323) 462–8860 or (323) 462–5991 or consult www.hollywoodwax.com.

SPECIAL TOURS

■ *LOS ANGELES TIMES*

Located at First and Spring Streets, Los Angeles. The newspaper offers tours of the newsrooms and printing plant. Children ten and older only. Reservations required weeks in advance. Admission: free. For information, call (213) 237–5000.

CHAPTER FOURTEEN

HOLLYWOOD MOVIE AND TELEVISION STUDIOS

ON ANY GIVEN DAY IN LOS ANGELES, a film or television crew is shooting scenes on the streets or within a public building. They're not difficult to spot: A film crew usually travels with a phalanx of several dozen trucks with equipment, mobile dressing rooms, caterers, and carloads of technicians, production assistants, and more. They are also often accompanied by police cars.

On one of my trips, there were no fewer than two movies being filmed in and around my hotel, the Westin Bonaventure Hotel in downtown Los Angeles. In the lobby, a crew worked on *Nick of Time,* a political kidnapping story. Outside my window, Al Pacino and Robert DeNiro ran up and down the street with machine guns as a huge crew shot action scenes for *Heat.*

It used to be possible to obtain a copy of the "shoot sheets" from the **Los Angeles Film and Video Office,** with details of current permits issued for filming in the city. Alas, the practice came to an end with the security concerns that followed September 11, 2001.

You may, though, be able to find location shootings by keeping a watchful eye for the fleets of trucks and vans required by movie companies. You may also spot small cryptic signs on posts around the city, marked with directional arrows, intended to help a crew find a location.

Other than the occasional location shooting, moviemaking takes place mostly behind closed doors or on remote sets. But several major studios offer tours from simple peeks behind the curtains to elaborate theme-park-like attractions such as Universal Studios. Fans of television, from game shows to sitcoms to talk shows, may have good luck in obtaining tickets to television studios.

▓ MUST-SEE ▓ SONY PICTURES STUDIOS

The Sony Pictures Studio offers a small tour with a great deal of history on the former MGM lot in Culver City. Two-hour walking tours include glimpses of the sound stage where the yellow brick road once wound through Munchkinland in *The Wizard of Oz,* the stage where agents from *Men in Black* battled aliens, and the *Jeopardy* game show set. The studios are in heavy demand for film and television production.

The tour concentrates on Columbia and Sony projects, although the studios themselves are redolent with MGM history. There are very few remaining large outdoor sets.

The studios are located at 10202 West Washington Boulevard in Culver City. Tours begin at Sony Pictures plaza on weekdays from 9:30 A.M. to 2:30 P.M. Admission is $24; visitors must be twelve or older. For information, call (323) 520–8687 or consult www.sonypicturesstudios.com/tours.

▓ MUST-SEE ▓ UNIVERSAL STUDIOS

From the very start of the studio in 1915, when filmmaker Carl Laemmle charged 25 cents to watch movies being made, Universal has welcomed visitors.

Of course, in true Hollywood style, things have gotten a whole lot flashier and more grandiose over the years. Universal Studios Hollywood is now a major theme park, mixing glimpses of working elements of the studios with re-creations of some of filmdom's greatest hits, including *King Kong, Back to the Future,* and *Backdraft.* See Chapter 6 on Universal Studios Hollywood for more information.

Universal Studios is located in Universal City, off the Hollywood Freeway (U.S. Highway 101) at Lankershim Boulevard. For information, call (818) 508–9600 or consult www.universalstudios.com.

▓ MUST-SEE ▓ WARNER BROS. STUDIOS VIP TOUR

Follow in the footsteps of Humphrey Bogart, Bette Davis, and James Cagney; walk down the same dirt road trod by Gary Cooper and James Garner as Maverick; and step into the soundstage that once housed *The Old Man and the Sea, My Fair Lady, Camelot,* and part of *Jurassic Park.* In 2005 television shows in production on the lot included *ER, The West Wing,* and *Gilmore Girls.*

The two-and-a-half-hour Warner Bros. tour is a chance to go behind the scenes at a working studio. No two tours are the same because of production schedules; with a bit of luck, visitors will get to see a film in production or see a rehearsal or taping of a television sitcom or series. The twelve-passenger trams, led by a knowledgeable guide, go through the famous backlot of the 110-acre studio and visit some of the soundstages.

Warner Bros. Studios VIP Tour. *Photo courtesy Warner Bros. Studio VIP Tour*

The summer shooting schedule at the studio is usually very slow and not much actual production may be under way at that time; in any case, the summer is the busiest time for the tour, and reservations may be necessary several weeks in advance. The tour begins at the Visitor Center, inside Gate 4 at the corner of Hollywood Way and Olive Avenue.

Tickets are $39. Children younger than eight are not permitted. Parking is available at the Visitors Center, at 3400 Riverside Drive in Burbank. For information and reservations, call (818) 972–8687 or consult www.studio-tour.com or wbsf.warnerbros.com/home.html.

The tour is offered weekdays on the hour from 8:30 A.M. to 4:30 P.M.; in the summer, trams leave every half hour. The studio is closed on holidays and weekends. Reservations are required; they are accepted by telephone several weeks in advance. A longer deluxe tour, including lunch and more facilities, costs $125.

Photography (but not video cameras) is permitted on the backlot—the famous outdoor sets—but not allowed at the soundstages.

You are invited into the small theater by the recorded voice of announcer Gary Owens, welcoming you to "beautiful downtown Burbank." The short film—updated regularly—is an entertaining collage of some of Warner Bros. most famous stars and some of the best-loved punch lines from classic films. You'll see James Cagney, Henry Fonda, Clint Eastwood, Bette Davis, Ronald Reagan, Jodie Foster, and many others at work and play. Strung together are Michelle Pfeiffer's Catwoman "meow"; a very young Mickey Rooney as Puck in *A Midsummer Night's Dream* declaring "What fools these mortals be"; Jack Nicholson's "Here's Johnny!"; a brief conversation between Tom Hanks and Meg Ryan from *You've Got Mail*; and Bugs Bunny's "What's up, doc?" Among the favorite lines is the one delivered by a doe-eyed Bette Davis: "I'd like to kiss you, but I just washed my hair." The biggest laughs come from an assemblage of out-takes and flubs by famous stars.

■ THE WARNER BROS. STORY

Warner Bros. Studios is among the oldest motion-picture centers to be continuously occupied by the same company. Warner films have earned more than one hundred major Academy Awards, including six Best Picture Oscars for the films *The Life of Emile Zola* (1937), *Casablanca* (1943), *My Fair Lady* (1964), *Chariots of Fire* (1981), *Driving Miss Daisy* (1989), and *Unforgiven* (1992).

The studio was originally built for First National Pictures on farmland purchased from Dr. David Burbank, a dentist and rancher after whom the city of Burbank was named. The Warner brothers acquired the property in 1929, two years after they had revolutionized movies with their release of the first "talkie," Al Jolson's *The Jazz Singer.* Soon they were turning out movies at a feverish pace—eighty-six features in 1929 alone.

By the late 1930s Warner Bros. had built nine new soundstages (all of which are still in use today) with Darryl F. Zanuck as head of production and Busby Berkeley bringing his musical extravaganzas to theaters.

The studio also developed its own zany brand of animation at a rundown Hollywood annex somewhat affectionately known as "Termite Terrace," and after 1940 at the main studio. From the drawing boards of Tex Avery, Chuck Jones, and Friz Freleng sprang such classic and enduring characters as Bugs Bunny, Daffy Duck, Yosemite Sam, Sylvester and Tweety, the Road Runner, and Pepé le Pew. All voices for the original characters were performed by Mel Blanc.

The 1940s saw the studio add three more soundstages and many more classic titles, including *Yankee Doodle Dandy* and *The Treasure of the Sierra Madre.*

During the 1950s Warner became the first studio to switch part of its operation to television. At first Jack Warner tried to fight the advent of television with the major film hits *A Streetcar Named Desire, A Star Is Born,* and *Mr. Roberts.* But by the 1950s Warner had become the most successful major producer of series television in Hollywood, creating shows that included *Maverick, The Lawman, 77 Sunset Strip, Cheyenne,* and *Hawaiian Eye.*

The studio was purchased by the Kinney National conglomerate in 1969, and the whole company became known as Warner Communications, Inc. In 1972 Warner Bros. and Columbia Pictures joined forces to create a single production facility named The Burbank Studios. The studio now was like a small city with its own fire department, mail service, parks, bank, and bicycle shop. (In 1990 Sony purchased Columbia Pictures and moved the company off the Burbank Studios property.)

In 1980 Warner Bros. purchased the Samuel Goldwyn Studios in Hollywood,

Used Props

Warner Bros. claims the largest collection of antiques west of the Mississippi. During the Depression years of the 1920s and 1930s, Warner Bros. sent its art directors to Europe to buy up antiques for its production needs.

renaming it Warner Hollywood Studios. In 1988 the company acquired Lorimar Products and moved it to the Burbank lot. Finally, in 1989, Time-Life merged with Warner Bros., creating Time Warner Inc., one of the largest and most powerful media companies in the world. Time Warner has subsequently become part of AOL.

■ EXTERIOR SETS

Midwestern Street. Welcome to Smalltown, USA, complete with village green, gazebo, and town square. The residential section was built in 1941 for *King's Row* with Ronald Reagan, and the storefront section was constructed in 1945 for *Saratoga Trunk* with Gary Cooper and Ingrid Bergman. Later the set was used for television series including *The Dukes of Hazzard, Growing Pains,* and *Sisters.*

The street still includes the gazebo where Robert Preston declared there was trouble in River City in *Music Man.* And Paul Newman was arrested nearby for cutting down parking meters in *Cool Hand Luke.* Scenes from *Contact* with Jodie Foster and *Conspiracy Theory* with Mel Gibson were shot here. For many visitors, there's this: The street was used in the final episode of *Seinfeld.* Yada yada yada.

New York Street. Around the corner from the mid-west set is New York, used in many famous scenes. The New York of the 1920s was seen in *The Great Race* and in *The FBI Story* with Jimmy Stewart. On the road was the courthouse used in the 1960s *Batman* television series. It was also decked out in neon for the futuristic main drag of *Blade Runner* and later for scenes in *Batman Returns.* Robin Williams and Billy Crystal annoyed each other in *Father's Day* here.

Hennesy Street. Designed by Dale Hennesy for *Annie,* it was transformed into Kansas of the 1930s for *City Heat* and was also seen in *Dick Tracy, Pee-wee's Big Adventure,* and the television series *Scarecrow and Mrs. King.*

Nearby to Hennesy Street is the exterior of the emergency room entrance to the county hospital of *ER.* Overhead is a simulated stretch of elevated train tracks.

Laramie Street. This stretch of road and sagebrush was built in 1941 for westerns and served as the location for some of the best-loved films of all time, including *High Noon* with Gary Cooper. A very different kind of classic, Mel Brooks's *Blazing Saddles,* was also shot there. Television series that used Laramie included *Bonanza* in its last five years, the original *Maverick* series, *F Troop, Kung Fu,* and *Little House on the Prairie.*

The buildings on the western set are constructed at ⅞ scale, allowing filmmakers to exaggerate the height of cowboy actors; camera operators have to shoot from a low angle anyway to avoid filming power lines and skyscrapers located just outside the Warner Bros. lot.

1930s Set. Built in 1938 for *Angels with Dirty Faces* with James Cagney and Humphrey Bogart, the area has appeared in a long string of gangster movies and stories never envisioned at the time. For example, it was used as Gotham City for the *Batman* movies; in *Batman Forever,* it was where Robin stole the Batmobile and took it for a spin through the street. It has also served as Metropolis for *Superman* movies, as Atlanta for the TV series *The Client,* and as Chicago for *Sisters* and *ER.*

The set is made up almost entirely of facades; only a few structures have any interior spaces. With some special set dressing, the same streets stood in for Tokyo in *Karate Kid Part II,* and as Havana in *The Mambo Kings.*

Kings Row. Used for the Ronald Reagan classic of the same name, it also was featured in *Rebel Without a Cause.* On the same street you'll find the home of Marion the Librarian from *The Music Man,* the *Gremlins* house, the heart of Hazzard County, and the place where Elvira, the Mistress of the Dark, filmed some of her high-camp scenes. The area also played a part in *Grumpier Old Men* with Walter Matthau and Jack Lemmon.

The Jungle. The forested area was created in 1930 and was the home of *Tarzan.* It also served as Sherwood Forest for Errol Flynn as *Robin Hood* and for parts of *Camelot* and *Finian's Rainbow.* Scenes from the *Fantasy Island* television show were shot there, and a small pond in the jungle was Walton Pond in *The Waltons.* More recently the jungle was Vietnam in the television series *China Beach;* it was also used in films *Hot Shots Part Deux,* and *Six Days, Seven Nights* with Harrison Ford.

And a moment of high drama from the *ER* series was also shot in the small pond; it was here that actor George Clooney struggled to pull a small boy out of a drainage pipe while floodwaters raged all around him.

Costume Warehouse. The huge Costume Warehouse on the backlot is an occasional stop of the tram tour, depending on shooting schedules on the lot. The building includes no less than 8 miles of hanging rack space and 3½ miles of shoes. One section holds enough wedding gowns to open a bridal shop. There are aisles of straw boaters and fedoras, Roman gladiator outfits, and maternity and fat pads.

There's a small museum at the warehouse that on one visit included part of the *Batman Forever* wardrobe. The producers of that film spent $6 million on costumes; a great deal of that money went for latex-rubber suits worn by Batman and Robin; examples of the expensive duds were on display.

■ INDOOR SOUNDSTAGES

Warner Bros. has thirty-seven soundstages, which is the largest collection in Hollywood. Thirty-two are on its lot and five others are down the street. Most were built in the 1930s. Warner Brothers built its first new soundstage since 1945 on the lot; its first major feature was *Space Cowboys* with Clint Eastwood. Most of the stages do not have dressing rooms; movable trailers are parked outside many of the buildings.

The operating rooms for *ER* are within Stage 11. Next-door, Stage 10, was home to *Family Matters* for many years. Nearby is the Little Brown Schoolhouse, used by school-aged children involved in productions on the lot; state law requires young actors to attend four hours of school per day.

Stage 16. The tallest full-time soundstage in the motion picture industry, it was raised to its present height of 98 feet in the 1930s by William Randolph Hearst, who had moved his production company to the lot in hopes of creating pictures for girlfriend Marion Davies.

Stage 16 was later used for films that included *My Fair Lady, Camelot, Key*

Largo, Gremlins 2, and *Batman Returns.* Also known as the "lake stage," it can hold an entire "sea" of water, as seen in *The Old Man and the Sea* and *PT 109.* Steven Spielberg installed a waterfall for a scene shot at the stage for Universal's *Jurassic Park.*

A glass-and-chrome office building was constructed within for the rise and fall and rise of Michael Douglas and the rise and fall of Demi Moore in *Disclosure.* Scenes for a revived *Wild, Wild West* were done there as well.

Stage 19. The home of the spectacular dancing scenes from *Yankee Doodle Dandy,* it was also used in *The Story of West Point* with James Cagney, *Gypsy,* and a number of Doris Day musicals including *Calamity Jane.*

Stage 4. Used to shoot the popular television sitcom *Murphy Brown,* it was where Bette Davis filmed *Now, Voyager.* The stage was also home to the musical *Mame* with Lucille Ball, and was transformed into the fifth floor of the *Washington Post* for *All the President's Men.*

Stage 9. This stage once held the entire set of Rick's Café Americain for *Casablanca.* It was also used for the famous egg-eating scene in *Cool Hand Luke* and served for ten years as home to the television comedy *Night Court.*

Stage 8. Used for various television series, this stage also housed memorable scenes from *Who's Afraid of Virginia Woolf?* with Richard Burton and Elizabeth Taylor.

Stage 24. The long-time home of *Friends,* which despite its name was not very accommodating to visitors. Before the show's run ended, tickets to tapings were among the most difficult to obtain in Hollywood.

PARAMOUNT STUDIOS

This historic movie studio—where classics like *The Godfather,* the Bob Hope and Bing Crosby Road pictures, many of Elvis Presley's films, and hundreds more were filmed—is now mostly used for television production. The Paramount empire includes the holdings of the former Desilu Production Studio, formed by Lucille Ball and Desi Arnaz, and RKO-Pathé (home of many of the Fred Astaire–Ginger Rogers films).

A fascinating two-hour tour of the studio, at 5555 Melrose Avenue in Hollywood, is offered weekdays at 10:00 A.M., 11:00 A.M., 1:00 P.M., and 2:00 P.M. Tickets are $35. Call (323) 956–1777 for information and to make a reservation.

There's a reproduction of the famed Paramount Gate on Melrose Avenue; the real thing is a block east. Hollywood superstition still calls for young would-be stars to hug the wrought-iron gate, stare at the Hollywood sign in the distance, and declare the famous line from *Sunset Boulevard,* which was filmed on the lot: "I'm ready for my close-up, Mr. DeMille." Atop a soundstage at Melrose and Gower you can see the remains of the famous RKO globe and transmitter tower.

Classic films made at the studios include *The Ten Commandments;* the parting of the Red Sea took place in a parking lot. The same temporary ocean was used for many of the naval battle scenes for the 1982 miniseries *The Winds of War.*

Recent films and television shows that used the studio include *Happy Days, The Brady Bunch,* and *Stuart Little.* The bridge for *Star Trek's Enterprise* was located there; nearby is the *Forrest Gump* park bench.

The tour changes based on the current shooting schedule. On a recent tour we entered the *Nip/Tuck* set and on an eighty-five-degree May afternoon saw winter scenes for a Christmas television movie being shot on the New York backlot.

Visitors can try to obtain tickets to be in the audience for television tapings. TV series are usually shot on Tuesday and Friday with audiences, but additional action can be scheduled for any day. *Entertainment Tonight* is usually in production daily, while talk shows, including Dr. Phil, are usually taped in clusters, with several episodes shot on one day.

OTHER FILM STUDIOS (NOT OPEN TO PUBLIC)

Burbank Studios (Warner Bros. and Columbia)
4000 Warner Boulevard, Burbank. "Gower Gulch" is named after the would-be actors who would gather outside the gates in hope of gaining a job in one of the many classic silent westerns shot there in the 1920s. The original Columbia lot is now known as Sunset-Gower Studios and is used primarily for productions by ABC Television.

Culver Studios
9336 West Washington Boulevard, Culver City. Among various owners was Cecil B. DeMille. It later became RKO-Pathé. *King Kong* was filmed here; the studio's white mansion on Washington Boulevard was used for some of the scenes in *Gone with the Wind.* Today the studio is used mostly for television productions.

Hollywood Center Studios
1040 North Las Palmas Avenue, Hollywood. At one time the home of Harold Lloyd's production company, it was used by Howard Hughes for his 1927 silent movie *Hell's Angels* featuring the debut of Jean Harlow. Shirley Temple made her debut here as well, and the first episodes of *I Love Lucy* were made here in 1951. More recently, it was the location of Francis Ford Coppola's Zoetrope Studios. It now rents out its facilities to production companies.

KCET Studio
4401 Sunset Boulevard, Hollywood. Public television station KCET's studio was the former home of Monogram Pictures and Allied Artists. Monogram made famous low-budget films, including the Charlie Chan detective series and the Bowery Boys. For information, call (323) 953–5289.

Lorimar Telepictures
3300 Riverside Drive, Suite 405, Burbank. The one-time Metro-Goldwyn-Mayer studios, former home of Clark Gable, Greta Garbo, Katharine Hepburn, the Marx Brothers, and dozens of other icons of the day.

Raleigh Studios

650 North Bronson Avenue, Hollywood. Mary Pickford and Douglas Fairbanks made their films here in the 1920s and 1930s. They went on to use this location to form United Artists. Films made here include *Mark of Zorro, Hopalong Cassidy, Guys and Dolls,* and *The Best Years of Our Lives.* It was also the home of television's original *Superman* series.

20th Century–Fox Film Corporation

10201 West Pico Boulevard, Los Angeles. The much-reduced Fox Studio still includes major sets, such as the New York City set employed in numerous films including *Hello, Dolly!* It has also been used as an all-purpose downtown in many other films; you can see part of the set from the street. Films made at the lot include *The Sound of Music, Butch Cassidy and the Sundance Kid,* and the original *Planet of the Apes.*

TELEVISION STUDIOS

There are three principal ways to obtain tickets to see a television taping or live broadcast: connections, planning, or luck. Connections with someone in the industry may work at any time. Planning a few months ahead of time may give you tickets for specific shows; the very lucky may be able to walk into a show on the day of taping.

Audience Associates/TV Tickets

7471 Melrose Avenue, #10. Tickets to ABC, CBS, Disney, Fox, KTLA, NBC, Paramount, Sony, and Universal productions. Up to ten free tickets per request; call at least one day in advance but not earlier than one month before the date of your visit. Often has tickets for *The Tonight Show* and game shows. For information, call (323) 653–4105 or consult www.tvtix.com.

Audiences Unlimited

100 Universal City Plaza, Building 153, Universal City, 91608. (818) 753–3483. An agency that supplies audiences for more than fifty network shows produced at studios in Hollywood, Burbank, Culver City, and at Universal Studios Hollywood. Call to check on scheduled shows; send a self-addressed, stamped envelope for up to six free tickets. Allow several weeks for delivery. To order by phone up to sixty days in advance, call (818) 753–3470 or consult www.tvtickets.com.

Audiences Unlimited also operates a same-day ticket booth at Universal CityWalk and within the gates of Universal Studios Hollywood.

KTLA-TV

5800 Sunset Boulevard, Hollywood. Independent and Warner Bros. productions. The original home of Warner Bros. Studios. Al Jolson made the first "talkie," *The Jazz Singer,* here in 1927. Tickets available through Audiences Unlimited and Audience Associates.

NBC Television Network

3000 West Alameda Avenue, Burbank. (818) 840–4444 or (818) 840–3537. The studio offers seventy-minute guided tours of some of its stages and production facilities, including the home of *The Tonight Show* and a soap opera set. Tours depart at regular intervals weekdays from 9:00 A.M. to 3:00 P.M. Closed Easter, Thanksgiving, Christmas Day, and New Year's Day. Admission: adults, $7.50; children (5–12), $4.00. For tours, call (818) 840–3537 or consult www.studio audiences.com/tvstudios/nbcburbank.asp.

Studio Audiences

For a listing of a wide variety of available television tapings, consult the Web site for this company at www.studioaudiences.com.

The Tonight Show

Jay Leno took over the mantle as the King of Burbank when he took the helm of *The Tonight Show*. For much of the year he tapes his nightly talk and entertainment show from his custom-designed studio there.

If you want to be in the audience for taping of *The Tonight Show,* you can try for tickets at the NBC kiosk on Universal's CityWalk on the day of the show. (The booth may also have tickets for other shows.) You can call (818) 840–3537 for a recorded announcement of the taping schedule and upcoming guests.

Or if you have a few weeks' advance notice, send your request by mail to NBC Tickets, 3000 West Alameda Avenue, Burbank, CA 91523; include the day or days you hope to see a show and the number of tickets you need along with a self-addressed, stamped envelope.

Taping takes place about 5:00 P.M. Monday through Friday; with tickets in hand, you must be in line by 4:00 P.M.—even earlier if there is a particularly popular guest booked that night. Like it or not, the studio gives out more tickets than there are seats; on a typical day thirty to fifty people are turned away.

There is no parking lot for the studio, but early arrivals should find spaces around the corner at a location you could find only near Hollywood: Bob Hope Drive, across from Johnny Carson Park.

The slow and disorganized waiting line is annoying, but you might want to keep your eye out for strolling members of the crew looking for audience members to use in skits; on the night of one of my visits they were planting questions for "Iron Jay," Leno's dim-witted weight-lifter alter ego. You may also be offered tickets to the taping of sitcoms while you wait. The only way to avoid standing in line is to pull whatever strings you can to obtain invited VIP tickets; these tickets guarantee entrance to the show but not necessarily the best seats in the house.

TV Time

A one-hour television show requires about eight long days to shoot; filming takes place only on weekdays. Half-hour sitcoms take four or five days for each episode.

Visitors on the tour sometimes get to see rehearsals for shows. Tour guides can sometimes arrange for tickets to television tapings on the day of your visit. Most regular series go on "hiatus" from mid-spring through mid-summer, resuming production in July and August.

The Tonight Show studio seats just 320; there are only thirty seats on the "floor" of the studio. Lucky guests here are usually personally greeted by the host at the start of the show. The show is recorded straight through; in television terms that means it is "live on tape."

Sitcoms

You can obtain tickets to view the taping of many of the major sitcoms; the more popular shows may have a limited number of available tickets. Attending a taping is a lot of fun, and a great way to get up close and somewhat personal with television stars. The soundstages are quite small, seating only a few hundred guests in bleachers that extend along the several sets of a typical show.

Be aware, though, that volunteering to be part of the audience represents a huge investment in time—sometimes as much as six hours for the taping of twenty-two minutes' worth of usable scenes. The time is taken up with parking, a shuttle bus transfer to the studio, several layers of security, and the slow process of taping which includes multiple takes.

On a recent visit, we obtained seats for *Everybody Loves Raymond*. We gathered in Burbank at 1:30 P.M. and were seated in the studio about an hour later. The day began with the showing of a recent, not-yet-broadcast episode to get us in the mood. Then we were greeted by star Ray Romano and the rest of the cast. For the next four hours—with a bit of entertainment by a comedian and a free slice of pizza—we watched the crew film each scene several times. Along the way we watched the actors and writers make changes to the script between each take, honing the words to get the best reaction from the audience. I'm glad we saw *Raymond* when we did: The show ended production in 2005, its studio due to house a new show.

PART VIII
SPORTING ACTIVITIES

CHAPTER FIFTEEN

BEACHES, WATER PARKS, PARKS, AND ZOOS

STROLLING THE MAKE-BELIEVE STREETS of the Disneyland Resort, Knott's Berry Farm, Universal Studios Hollywood, or the concrete canyons of Los Angeles, it is sometimes hard to remember that you are within swimming distance of the Pacific Ocean and some of the most famous beaches on the West Coast.

There are dozens of swimming, surfing, and sunbathing strands along the 75-mile coastline from above Malibu to Newport Beach.

LOS ANGELES AREA BEACHES

Los Angeles County Beaches and Harbors Information Center. (310) 305–9545. www.beaches.co.la.ca.us/BandH/Main.htm.

■ NORTHERN SECTION

The beaches between Point Mugu and Malibu are among the least crowded in Southern California and offer excellent swimming, surfing, water sports, and fishing. There are public campsites at **Leo Carrillo** and **Point Mugu State Parks;** there are also some spectacular hiking trails that lead into the foothills.

Leo Carrillo State Park. 36000 Pacific Coast Highway, Malibu. There's something for everybody at this 1,600-acre beach named for actor Leo Carrillo (best known as Pancho on the television series *The Cisco Kid*). It's a fine swimming, surfing, and snorkeling beach (including a "clothing optional" section); there's also a nature trail that leads to tide pools and rock formations, and Sequit Point, which contains sea caves and a natural tunnel. (818) 880–0350 or (805) 488–5223. www.parks.ca.gov/default.asp?page_id=616.

Zuma Beach. 30000 Pacific Coast Highway, Malibu. Like wow, man: a handsome beach carpeted with valley girls and surfer dudes. The surf can get rough. At the paved side of the beach are playgrounds, showers, restrooms, and

LOS ANGELES AREA BEACHES

concession stands. beaches.co.la.ca.us/BandH/Beaches/Zuma.htm.

Point Dume. 7103 Westward Road, Malibu. South of Zuma and a little less known, it is still an excellent swimming and surfing site. From November to May the Point Dume headland is a prime vantage point to observe migrating California gray whales just offshore. beaches.co.la.ca.us/BandH/Beaches/PtDume.htm.

Malibu Surfrider Beach. 23200 Pacific Coast Highway, Malibu. This is the one you're thinking of, the one you've seen in the *Gidget* movies, the surfing competitions, and your dreams of hanging ten. There's nearly a mile of beach alongside the hulking Malibu Pier. There's also a marine preserve and a nature center. beaches.co.la.ca.us/BandH/Beaches/Malibu.htm.

■ CENTRAL SECTION

Las Tunas Beach. 19444 Pacific Coast Highway, Malibu. Below Malibu toward Santa Monica. A small beach with an offshore reef popular for diving and fishing. beaches.co.la.ca.us/BandH/Beaches/LasTunas.htm.

Topanga Beach. 18700 Pacific Coast Highway, Malibu. Another mile-long sandy beach between Topanga Creek at the end of Topanga Canyon Road, popular for surfing and swimming. beaches.co.la.ca.us/BandH/Beaches/Topanga.htm.

Will Rogers Beach. 16000 Pacific Coast Highway, Los Angeles. Donated to the state by the famous author and commentator, this 3-mile beach offers moderate surf, a playground, and gymnastics equipment. (310) 578–0478. beaches.co.la.ca.us/BandH/Beaches/WillRogers.htm.

Santa Monica Beach. Pacific Coast Highway at Colorado Boulevard, Santa Monica. A broad, attractive beach that has relatively gentle surf, it flanks the Santa Monica Pier, which includes a turn-of-the-twentieth-century carousel, arcades, restaurants, and gift shops. The pier is also used for fishing. (310) 578–0478. www.santamonicapier.org.

Venice Beach. 1531 Ocean Front Walk, Venice. The beach is quite nice, but the real attraction here is the **Venice Boardwalk,** the world capital of West Coast weird. The boardwalk is lined with food stands and shops; the roadway is populated with street performers and in-line skaters, and in and among the palm trees is the famous outdoor gym, **Muscle Beach.** You can rent roller skates or bicycles and join the circus. (310) 578–0478. www.venicebeach.com or beaches.co.la.ca.us/BandH/Beaches/Venice.htm.

■ SOUTHERN SECTION

Dockweiler Beach. 8255 Vista del Mar Boulevard, Playa del Rey. This is not the beach of your dreams, but it is a very lively local favorite for some reason. It

Santa Monica Pier

An out-to-sea amusement place that includes a Philadelphia Toboggan Company carousel built in 1922 and maintained and restored to its original splendor. The march of the hand-carved horses is accompanied by the incomparable sounds of an antique Wurlitzer organ. The pier also features some other more modern kiddie rides. (310) 458–8900. www.santamonicapier.org.

lies in the approach path of LAX and is alongside a sewage treatment plant and an oil refinery. There's a beach for swimming and surfing, a playground, and a bicycle trail. (310) 379–8471. beaches.co.la.ca.us/BandH/Beaches/Dockweiler.htm.

Manhattan Beach. Highland and Manhattan Boulevards. A fishing, swimming, surfing, and snorkeling beach with 2 miles of broad beachfront. There are more than one hundred volleyball courts. At the back of the beach is the Strand, a concrete promenade crowded with skaters, skateboarders, and joggers. (310) 379–8471. beaches.co.la.ca.us/BandH/Beaches/Manhattan.htm.

Nearby is **Sand Dune Park.** Thirty-third Street at Bell Avenue, Manhattan Beach. The park is just what it sounds like: a colossal, steep sand dune that kids can climb, slide on, and carry home in their bathing suits. There's also a playground and picnic area. Run by the Manhattan Beach Parks and Recreation Department. Open daily. Admission: free. (310) 802–5409. www.ci.manhattan_beach.ca.us/parksrec/facilities/sand_dune_park.

Hermosa Beach. Hermosa Avenue and 33rd Street, Hermosa Beach. A relatively quiet mile-long beach with a fishing pier and concession stands. beaches .co.la.ca.us/BandH/Beaches/Hermosa.htm.

Redondo Beach. Esplanade at Knobhill Avenue, Redondo Beach. A wide beach extending from the Redondo Pier with restaurants, gift shops, and concession stands. Excursion and fishing boats depart from the pier. (310) 379–8471. beaches.co.la.ca.us/BandH/Beaches/Redondo.htm.

Torrance Beach. 387 Paseo de la Playa, Torrance. A popular diving, surfing, and swimming beach with facilities, including a bathhouse and playground. beaches.co.la.ca.us/BandH/Beaches/Torrance.htm.

Malaga Cove. Paseo del Mar at Via Arroyo, Palos Verdes. A gazebo on the bluffs gives a great view of the cove; a path leads to the beach. (310) 379–8471.

Abalone Cove. 5755 Palos Verdes Drive South. On the Portuguese Bend of the Palos Verdes Peninsula with a view of Catalina Island. No lifeguards. (310) 379–8471. www.palosverdes.com/rpv/recreationparks/AbaloneCoveShoreline.

Point Fermin Lighthouse. 807 Paseo Del Mar, San Pedro. The lighthouse, built in 1874, sits on the bluff with a view of Catalina Island; trails descend to the beach below. There's a playground and a small amphitheater. www.sanpedrochamber .com/champint/ptfmlths.htm.

Cabrillo Beach. 3270 Steven M. White Drive, San Pedro. A generally calm waterfront with a playground and snack bar. Nearby is the Cabrillo Marine Museum. beaches.co.la.ca.us/BandH/Beaches/Cabrillo.htm.

LONG BEACH AREA

The 7-mile **Long Beach City Beach** is within the harbor breakwater and therefore generally offers calm water. The Belmont Pier offers fishing locations. East of Long Beach City Beach, the Alamitos Bay Peninsula reaches almost a mile into Alamitos Bay with calm waters on the bay side and surf on the ocean side. (562) 570–6555.

ORANGE COUNTY

Newport City Beach is another picture-perfect Southern California beach. There's a famous sand castle contest each summer. The Dory Fleet returns each morning to sell its catch on the west side of Newport Pier. (949) 722–1611.

LOS ANGELES AREA PARKS

Griffith Park is the true backlot of Los Angeles and Hollywood, some 4,100 acres of mostly undeveloped hilly land in the eastern Santa Monica Mountains. The park ranges from 384 to 1,625 feet above sea level and includes semiarid foothills and heavily forested valleys.

The park includes hiking trails, picnic areas, the first-class Griffith Observatory and Planetarium, the Los Angeles Zoo, a railroad and transit museum, the SR-2 simulator ride, a western heritage museum, and the Greek Theatre (an outdoor amphitheater).

The park is regularly used by Hollywood filmmakers for location shooting, with some of the most famous scenes including parts of *Rebel Without a Cause* and *King Kong*. A wilderness area that includes a former rock quarry was the location of the Batcave in the television and film versions of *Batman*.

When weather conditions are right—which in Los Angeles, unfortunately, is not very often—it is well worth the short trip up the hill to the park to see the view of the city below. Take appropriate big-city precautions if you make a visit to the park at night.

See Chapter 13 for more details on cultural activities.

Arriving by car, you can use any of eight entrances: Commonwealth Avenue, Ferndell Drive, Forest Lawn Drive, Riverside Drive, North Vermont Avenue, Interstate 5 (Griffith Park Drive or Zoo Drive exits), and Highway 134 (Victory Boulevard exit). MTA buses 96 and 97 connect downtown to the park.

The park is open from 6:00 A.M. to 10:00 P.M. daily; horseback and hiking trails and mountain roads close at sunset. The speed limit within the park is 25 miles per hour and is strictly enforced. (323) 913–4147. The City of Los Angeles Department of Recreation and Parks maintains a Web site about Griffith Park at www.laparks.org/grifmet/griffith.htm.

REGIONAL PARKS

California Department of Parks and Recreation. For information on state parks, call (818) 880–0350 or consult www.parks.ca.gov.

National Park Service. For information, call (818) 597–9192. For MISTIX Campground Reservations, call (800) 365–2267.

U.S. Forest Service. Angeles National Forest. (626) 574–5200. www.fs.fed.us. National Forest Recreation reservations: (877) 444–6777.

Angeles National Forest. If Griffith Park is the backlot of Los Angeles, then the Angeles National Forest is the outback. It's a gigantic preserve—some 695,000 acres—that sits like a shield over north Los Angeles, incorporating within it the San Gabriel Mountains.

The forest has nearly 600 miles of hiking and horse trails, nearly 200 miles of fishing streams, 400 miles of off-road trails, and sixty-four campgrounds. Several lakes are available for swimming, fishing, and boating. The park rangers offer a variety of programs in the summer.

Entrances to the park include Highway 2 from Pasadena, which becomes the Angeles Crest Highway that traverses most of the park from west to east; Highway 39, which enters from near Azusa and proceeds north to Crystal Lake; Big Tujunga Canyon Road from Sunland; and Mount Baldy Road from Glendora. (626) 574–5200 or (626) 335–1251. www.r5.fs.fed.us/angeles.

For further information, you can also call one of the visitors centers at the park:

■ **Chantry Flat Visitors Center.** Open weekends only from mid-November through mid-May. (818) 355–0712.

■ **Chilao Visitors Center.** (626) 796–5541.

■ **Crystal Lake Visitors Center.** (626) 910–2848.

Ernest E. Debs Park. Part of Arroyo Seco Canyon, this is an interesting piece of near-wilderness in northeastern Los Angeles. The 300-acre park includes a fishing lake, hiking trails, and picnic areas. Enter the park off Monterey Road, north of Huntington Drive. (213) 847–3989. www.laparks.org/dos/forest/pdf/ernestEDebspk.pdf.

Henninger Flats Museum. A small environmental museum on a fire road in the foothills of the San Gabriel Mountains near Altadena. (626) 794–0675.

Kenneth Hahn State Recreation Area. The park includes an Olympic Forest planted with trees and shrubs representing each of the nations that competed in the 1984 Olympics in Los Angeles. Recreational facilities include playgrounds, picnic areas, lake fishing, and hiking trails. Located on the western edge of Los Angeles, at 4100 South La Cienega Boulevard between Rodeo Road and Stocker Street. (323) 298–3660. www.parks.ca.gov/default.asp?page_id=21767.

San Gabriel Canyon Entrance Station. At the northern end of the mountains that lie east of Los Angeles is a range of peaks, many more than 9,000 feet tall; the biggest is Mount San Antonio, better known as Mount Baldy. For information about the San Gabriel Canyon, call (626) 969–1012. To contact the **Mount Baldy Visitors Center,** call (909) 982–2829.

Santa Monica Mountains National Recreation Area. A spectacular seaside preserve stretching 55 miles from Santa Monica to Point Mugu and including favorite beaches such as Leo Carrillo State Beach, Zuma Beach, Point Dume, and Malibu Surfrider Beach. (805) 370–2301.

The **J. Paul Getty Museum** is also within the park. *See the section on beaches in Chapter 15 and the chapter on museums for more details.*

Many miles of hiking and walking trails are marked; there are some 500 miles of trails in the park. For information stop by the Visitors Center off U.S. Highway 101 at 401 West Hillcrest Drive, Thousand Oaks. Open Monday to Friday from 8:00 A.M. to 5:00 P.M., Saturday, Sunday, and holidays from 9:00 A.M. to 5:00 P.M. Closed Christmas, New Year's, and Thanksgiving. (805) 370–2329. www.nps.gov/samo.

Satwiwa Native American Indian Cultural Center. Via Goleta Road, Newbury Park, within the Santa Monica Mountains National Recreation Area. Open Saturday and Sunday from 10:00 A.M. to 5:00 P.M. (805) 375–1930. www .nps.gov/samo/fos.

Will Rogers State Historic Park. 1501 Will Rogers State Park Road. The famous humorist and former cowboy's home and 187-acre estate were given to the public following his death in a plane crash in 1935. The home includes remembrances of Rogers's career and life; his private polo field is used for weekend games, and visitors are welcome. The park is open daily from 8:00 A.M. to sunset; tours are conducted from 10:30 A.M. to 3:30 P.M. every hour on the half-hour. Admission: free. Parking, $6.00. (310) 454–8212. www.parks.ca.gov/?page_id=626.

HISTORIC RANCHES

Paramount Ranch. Cornell Road, Agoura. Not quite the real thing . . . this 760-acre ranch was once used by Paramount Pictures to film some of its classic westerns; it was later used for early television horse operas. Among the stars who giddyapped around here were Bob Hope, Gary Cooper, and Claudette Colbert. The ranch was also recast as colonial Massachusetts for the film, *The Maid of Salem*, and China in *The Adventures of Marco Polo*. The remains of a false-front Western town from the TV years still stand, and there are hiking and nature programs available. The town was used for six years as the home of *Dr. Quinn, Medicine Woman*.

Nearby is the Peter Strauss Ranch, at 30000 Mulholland Highway, Agoura. Originally developed as a lakeside mansion for an early automotive pioneer and later as a sylvan resort, it was later owned by the actor whose name is now attached to it. There are hiking and nature trails and infrequent theatrical presentations and concerts at an outdoor amphitheater. (805) 370–2301 for Paramount Ranch and Peter Strauss Ranch. www.nps.gov/samo/maps/para.htm or www .nps.gov/samo/maps/peter.htm.

William S. Hart Park. 24151 North San Fernando Avenue, Newhall. The cowboy world of former western film star William S. Hart, about an hour north of Los Angeles and near the Six Flags California theme park.

The collection includes saddles and gear, weapons, and artifacts. The 250-acre ranch is home to farm animals and a herd of buffalo; the animals were a gift to the public by Walt Disney. The Spanish Colonial Revival–style mansion contains original furnishings, a collection of western art, Native American artifacts, and mementos of early Hollywood.

William S. Hart was born in Newburgh, New York, in 1864 and began an acting career in his twenties; at the age of forty-nine, Hart came west to Hollywood to start his movie career. During the next eleven years, he made more than sixty-five silent films, the last being *Tumbleweeds* in 1925. He lived at the ranch nearly twenty years until his death in 1946; in his will, Hart gave his Horseshoe Ranch to the County of Los Angeles.

The park is open daily; tours of the house are offered from mid-September to mid-June on Wednesday to Friday from 10:00 A.M. to 1:00 P.M. with the last tour at 12:30 P.M., and Saturday and Sunday from 11:00 A.M. to 4:00 P.M., with the last tour at 3:30 P.M. In the summer, tours are offered Wednesday to Sunday from 11:00 A.M. to 4:00 P.M., with the last tour at 3:30 P.M. Admission: free. (661) 259–0844, park; (661) 254–4584, museum. www.hartmuseum.org. On weekends you can visit the adjacent Saugus train station, restored to turn-of-the-twentieth-century realism. For information, call (661) 254–1275.

ZOOS AND ANIMAL PRESERVES

Los Angeles Zoo. 5333 Zoo Drive, Griffith Park, near the junction of the Golden State (I–5) and Ventura (Highway 134) freeways.

The zoo includes more than 1,200 rare and exotic animals from around the world, along with a magnificent set of botanical gardens. It is divided into geographical continents; a safari shuttle transports visitors from area to area for an extra charge of $3.50 for adults, $1.00 for seniors, and $1.50 for children 2–12.

An exciting area at the zoo is **Chimpanzees of the Mahale Mountains,** named after a thriving wild troop in Tanzania. It is the first phase of the zoo's planned Great Ape Forest; the second phase, the Red Ape Rain Forest, opened in mid-2000 and showcases orangutans.

When the Los Angeles Zoo opened in 1966 it was the third zoo to serve the city. The privately run Selig Zoo opened downtown in 1885. It was supplanted by the Griffith Park Zoo—largely a collection of former circus animals—in 1912. By 1956 the citizens of Los Angeles realized their city had outgrown the small zoo and passed a bond measure to help build a new one.

Open daily from 10:00 A.M. to 5:00 P.M.; closed Christmas Day. Admission: adults, $9.00; seniors (65 and older), $6.00; children (2–12), $4.00. Strollers and wheelchairs are available for rent. The Safari Shuttle transports visitors from area to area for an extra charge of $4.00 for adults, $1.50 for seniors, and $2.00 for children 2–12. (323) 644–4200. www.lazoo.org.

America's Teaching Zoo at Moorpark College. Moorpark College, Campus Road, Moorpark. A small collection of exotic animals. Open Saturday and Sunday, 11:00 A.M. to 5:00 P.M. Show times are noon, 1:00 P.M., 2:00 P.M., and 3:00 P.M. Carnivore feeding time is 4:00 P.M. Admission: adults, $5.00; children (2–12), $4.00. (805) 378–1441. www.moorparkcollege.edu/neatm.

W. K. Kellogg Arabian Horse Farm. California State Polytechnic University, 3801 West Temple Avenue, Pomona. Purebred Arabian horses on display daily; shows presented first Sunday of each month from October to June. Admission:

adults, $5.00; seniors and children (6–17), $3.00. (909) 869–2224. www.csu
pomona.edu/~equine/Kellogg.htm.

Santa Ana Zoo. Prentice Park, 1801 East Chestnut Avenue, Santa Ana. Smaller
mammals and birds, plus a children's zoo with petting section and playground.
The Zoofari Express train operates from Friday to Sunday on a track around a
section of the original children's zoo.

Open daily, weather permitting, from 10:00 A.M. to 5:00 P.M. Admission:
adults, $5.00; seniors and children (3–12), $3.00. (714) 836–4000. www.santaana
zoo.org.

ARBORETUMS

Descanso Gardens. 1418 Descanso Drive at Verdugo Boulevard, La Cañada
Flintridge. A wonderland of camellias, roses, azaleas, clivias, irises, lilies, and
other flowers and plants. Camellias are in blossom during the winter, from
October to March; lilacs are at their best in April; and roses and other glories
own the summer months.

Guided tours by tram are offered Tuesday to Sunday at 1:00, 2:00, and 3:00
P.M. The gardens are open every day except Christmas from 9:00 A.M. to 4:30 P.M.
Admission: adults, $6.00; seniors and students, $4.00; and children (5–12),
$1.50. Guided tour by tram, $2.00 all tickets. Enchanted Railroad (weekends),
$2.00 all tickets. (818) 952–4401. www.descanso.com.

The Arboretum of Los Angeles County. 301 North Baldwin Avenue near
Colorado Boulevard, Arcadia. More than 30,000 plants from around the world
outdoors and in greenhouses on the historic Rancho Santa Anita. Also on the
127-acre grounds are a former Santa Fe Railroad depot from Santa Anita, replicas of Indian homes, and a historic Queen Anne cottage.

Baldwin Lake, hidden within a stand of huge palm trees, was the setting for
many of the original Tarzan movies. At the far side of the lake is a restored
adobe, dating from 1839.

Guided tram tours are conducted on Wednesday at 11:00 A.M. Open daily 9:00
A.M. to 4:30 P.M. except Christmas. Admission: adults, $6.00; seniors and students,
$4.00; children (5–12), $1.50. Tram tickets, $2.00. Admission free on third
Tuesday of the month. (626) 821–3222. www.arboretum.org.

WATER PARKS

Raging Waters. In San Dimas where Interstate 10, Interstate 210, and
Highway 57 meet, about twenty-five minutes from Disneyland and thirty min-
utes from downtown Los Angeles. The largest water theme park west of the
Mississippi, there are two dozen rides and slides, including the Volcano
FantaSea, a smoking volcano with water slides descending to a blue lagoon.
Other attractions include a raft ride, a river ride, and a wave pool.

Another thrill: High Extreme, a 600-foot head-first plunge. A recent addition was The Wedge, a sort of half-funnel, four stories high. A three-person tube drops to the bottom, rises again, and drops once more.

Open weekends from mid-April to Memorial Day, daily from about June 1 to mid-September, and weekends from mid-September to the end of that month. Admission: $27.99; seniors (55 and older), $17.99; junior ticket (children less than 48 inches tall), $16.99; children (2 and younger), free. Parking $7.00. (909) 802–2200. www.ragingwaters.com.

Wild Rivers. 8800 Irvine Center Drive, Laguna Hills, off Interstate 405 at the Irvine Center Drive exit. An artificial mountain of water slides and tube rides, plus the Thunder Cove wave pool and the Explorer's Island play area for children. Open daily from 10:00 a.m. to 8:00 p.m. from mid-June to early September; from 11:00 a.m. to 5:00 p.m. weekends and holidays from mid-May to early June and in mid-September until early October. Admission: $26.98; children (less than 48 inches tall), $17.98; evening admission, after 4:00 p.m., $14.00. Parking $6.00. (949) 768–9453. www.wildrivers.com.

Six Flags Hurricane Harbor. *See the section about Six Flags Magic Mountain in Chapter 9.*

Soak City U.S.A. *See the section about Knott's Berry Farm in Chapter 8.*

CHAPTER SIXTEEN

SPORTING NEWS

MAJOR LEAGUE BASEBALL

The Los Angeles Angels of Anaheim and the Los Angeles Dodgers play major league baseball in a regular season that runs from April to early October.

■ LOS ANGELES ANGELS OF ANAHEIM

The boys of summer patrol the outfield at Angel Stadium of Anaheim, about 2 miles east of Disneyland Park off Katella Avenue. The Angels are strong competitors in the American League's western division; the regular season runs from April through late September.

The team was owned by the Walt Disney Company from 1996 to mid-2003, when it was sold to Phoenix businessman Arte Moreno. During the Disney years, the company spent more than $80 million to convert Edison Field to a modernized "retro" baseball park, including asymmetrical outfield dimensions with a family zone in left field, a gushing geyser and a rock garden in left center, and a view of the famous Angels A sign over the short right field porch. Every Angels home run and victory is saluted with fireworks.

In the stands it's a laid-back California scene. A gourmet restaurant behind home plate has tables in places that would be prime real estate at most other parks. There are usually plenty of seats available, especially early in the season. All of the views are unobstructed and the stadium is steeply raked, making all seats relatively close to the field.

To the displeasure of local politicians, the team renamed itself as the Los Angeles Angels of Anaheim for the 2005 season. Same team, same stadium, new logo.

Angel Stadium is located at 2000 East Gene Autry Way in Anaheim, about ten minutes from Disneyland. For information, call (714) 634–2000 or consult http://losangeles.angels.mlb.com. For tickets, call (888) 796–4256. Tickets range from about $9.00 to $45.00. Premium seating in the Diamond Club costs $75.00.

■ LOS ANGELES DODGERS

Dodger Stadium, 1000 Elysian Park Avenue, Los Angeles.

The Dodgers have played in Chavez Ravine for more than forty years. The stadium offers a handsome view of downtown Los Angeles to the south, and the San Gabriel Mountains to the north and east. The field has real grass and a view of the sky; the team averages one rainout every two years.

Depending on traffic, it takes at least forty minutes to drive the 29 miles from Disneyland to Dodger Stadium. The 56,000-seat stadium has parking for 16,000 automobiles on twenty-one terraced lots adjacent to the same elevations as the six different seating levels. For tickets, call (323) 224–1448 or consult http://los angeles.dodgers.mlb.com. Tickets range from about $6.00 to $125.00 with hard-to-obtain dugout seats going for as much as $400.00.

COLLEGE BASEBALL

■ UCLA–UNIVERSITY OF CALIFORNIA, LOS ANGELES

Bruins home games are played at UCLA's Jackie Robinson Stadium on Constitution Avenue in Los Angeles, from late January through June. Tickets are adults, $6.00; youth (16 and younger), $4.00. For information, call (310) 825–2101 or consult http://uclabruins.fansonly.com/sports/m-basebl.

■ USC–UNIVERSITY OF SOUTHERN CALIFORNIA

USC Trojans home baseball games are played at Dedeaux Field on campus. Call the ticket office at (213) 740–4672 or consult http://usctrojans.fansonly.com/sports/m-basebl/usc-m-basebl-body.html.

PROFESSIONAL BASKETBALL

The Los Angeles Clippers and the Los Angeles Lakers alternate possession of the Staples Center in downtown for National Basketball Association games. They play each other about four times a year, as well.

The Staples Center is located in downtown, near the intersection of the Interstate 10 (Santa Monica) and the Interstate 110 (Harbor) freeways, at the corner of Eleventh and Figueroa Streets, adjacent to the Los Angeles Convention Center.

For information, consult the individual teams or www.staplescenter.com.

■ LOS ANGELES CLIPPERS

The Los Angeles Clippers began in 1970 as the Buffalo Braves, one of three expansion franchises to join the National Basketball Association that year along with the Portland Trail Blazers and the Cleveland Cavaliers, as the league dealt with the challenge of the upstart American Basketball Association. The franchise later moved from Buffalo to San Diego and then to Los Angeles, changing its name from the Braves to the Clippers.

To be charitable, the Clippers have not been one of the leading lights of the league in its more than three decades of existence, finishing with a .500 or greater record only half a dozen times. Through 2004, they had not retired a single star player's uniform number. For information, call (213) 745–0400 or consult www.nba.com/clippers. Tickets range from about $10 to $285. For tickets, call Ticketmaster at (213) 480–3232 or consult www.ticketmaster.com.

■ LOS ANGELES LAKERS
The other hoopsters at the Staples Center have a much more storied history. Born as the Minneapolis Lakers in 1948, they moved to lakeless Los Angeles in 1960. They won their fifteenth NBA title in the 2002 season, and the uniform numbers of seven of their players are retired: Wilt Chamberlain, Elgin Baylor, Gail Goodrich, Magic Johnson, Kareem Abdul-Jabbar, James Worthy, and Jerry West. In 2005 the team's stars included the troubled Kobe Bryant; the era of Shaquille O'Neal ended the season before. Tickets range from a reasonable $10 (if you can find them) to as much as $1,900 for floor seats for games against the best teams in the league; lesser opponents command just $250 or so for the best seats. For information, consult www.nba.com/lakers. For tickets, call Ticketmaster at (213) 480–3232 or consult www.ticketmaster.com.

COLLEGE BASKETBALL

■ UCLA BASKETBALL
Pauley Pavilion, UCLA Campus, Westwood. Tickets range from about $10 to $35. For tickets, call (310) 825–2101 or consult http://uclabruins.fansonly.com/sports/m-baskbl.

■ USC BASKETBALL
Sports Arena, 3939 South Figueroa Street, Los Angeles. Tickets range from about $25 to $35. For tickets, call (213) 740–4672 or consult http://usctrojans.fansonly.com/sports/m-baskbl/usc-m-baskbl-body.html.

COLLEGE FOOTBALL

■ ROSE BOWL FOOTBALL GAME
The big football game traditionally pits the best of the Pacific Coast Conference against the best of the Big Ten Conference on New Year's weekend. (The famed Rose Bowl Parade is held on New Year's Day.) Tickets are hard to come by and usually sell out well in advance. For information, call (626) 449–4100 or consult www.tournamentofroses.com.

■ UCLA BRUINS

The Rose Bowl, 1001 Rose Bowl Drive, Pasadena. Tickets range from about $12 to $32. For tickets, call (626) 577–3100 or consult http://uclabruins.fansonly .com/sports/m-footbl.

■ USC TROJANS

LA Coliseum, 3911 South Figueroa Street, Los Angeles. Tickets range from about $15 to $35. For tickets, call (213) 740–4672 or consult http://usctrojans .fansonly.com/sports/m-footbl/usc-m-footbl-body.html.

HORSE RACING

■ HOLLYWOOD PARK

1050 South Prairie Avenue, Inglewood. Thoroughbred racing April to July and November to December; harness racing August to October. For information, call (310) 419–1500 or consult www.hollywoodpark.com.

■ LOS ALAMITOS

4961 Katella Avenue, Los Alamitos. Quarter-horse, Arabian, thoroughbred, paint, and Appaloosa racing year-round Thursday to Sunday. For information, call (714) 820–2800 or consult www.losalamitos.com/laqhr.

■ SANTA ANITA

285 West Huntington Drive, Arcadia. Thoroughbred racing at one of the country's most famous tracks. Morning workouts open daily from 5:00 to 10:00 A.M. during racing season, which is December to April and October to November. For information, call (626) 574–7223 or consult www.santaanita.com. Admission, $5.00; clubhouse, $8.50; Turf Club, $15.00.

PROFESSIONAL HOCKEY

■ ANAHEIM MIGHTY DUCKS

Arrowhead Pond of Anaheim, 2695 East Katella Avenue, Anaheim. NHL hockey. Not your basic hockey club, the team is owned by Disney; rumors of a sale have been common for several years. The Ducks had their best season ever in the 2002–2003 season, winning forty games and gaining a place in the play-offs where they were the surprise team; the Ducks ended up taking the New Jersey Devils to the seventh game of the Stanley Cup Finals in 2003. Then the 2004–2005 season was canceled because of a labor dispute. The season runs October to April. Tickets range from about $15 to $190. For information, call (714) 704–2701 or consult www.mightyducks.com. For tickets, call Ticketmaster at (714) 740–2000.

■ LOS ANGELES KINGS

Staples Center, Eleventh and Figueroa Streets. NHL hockey. Tickets range from about $25 to $350. For tickets, call Ticketmaster at (714) 740–2000 or consult www.lakings.com.

ICE SKATING

■ CULVER ICE ARENA

4545 Sepulveda Boulevard, Culver City. For information, call (310) 398–5718 or consult www.culvericearena.com.

■ PASADENA ICE SKATING CENTER

310 East Green Street, Pasadena. For information, call (626) 578–0801 or consult www.skatepasadena.com.

ROLLER SKATING

■ MOONLIGHT ROLLERWAY SKATING RINK

5110 San Fernando Road, Glendale. For information, call (818) 241–3630.

SKIING

Los Angeles's local ski region lies mostly due east in and around **Big Bear City** and **Big Bear Lake** in the San Bernardino National Forest. The resorts are about a hundred miles from Los Angeles, about a two-hour drive on I–10 and State Highway 18.

■ BEAR MOUNTAIN

Big Bear Lake. Vertical drop 1,665 feet. Longest run, 2½ miles. Nine chairlifts, including two high-speed quads, plus three surface tows. For general information, call (909) 866–5766; for reservations, call (909) 866–5841. Snow report: (800) 232–7686, www.bigbearmountainresorts.com. Lodging: (909) 866–5877 or (909) 866–4601.

■ MOUNT BALDY

San Bernardino. The biggest vertical drop in Southern California, at 2,100 feet. Located about 45 miles from Los Angeles. Four chairlifts. For information, call (909) 981–3344 or consult www.mtbaldy.com.

■ MOUNTAIN HIGH

Wrightwood. First opened in 1937. Vertical drop 1,600 feet. Ten chairlifts and two tows. For information, call (888) 754–7878 or consult www.mthigh.com.

■ SNOW SUMMIT

Big Bear Lake area. Vertical drop 1,200 feet. Eleven chairlifts. Longest run, 1¼ miles. For information, call (909) 866–5766; for reservations, call (909) 866–5841. Snow report: (800) 232–7686 or www.bigbearmountainresorts.com. Lodging: (909) 878–3000.

■ SNOW VALLEY

Big Bear Lake area. Thirteen chairlifts. Longest run, 1¼ miles. Vertical drop 1,030 feet. For information, call (909) 867–2751 or consult www.snow-valley.com. Lodging: (909) 878–3000.

PART IX

TOURING AROUND SOUTHERN CALIFORNIA

CHAPTER SEVENTEEN

DOWNTOWN LOS ANGELES

WALT DISNEY CONCERT HALL AUDITORIUM

The new jewel of the Los Angeles cultural scene, and a shining expansion of the Disney name into downtown, is the Walt Disney Concert Hall Auditorium. Designed by prominent architect Frank Gehry, the 2,265-seat theater is the home of the Los Angeles Philharmonic and the Los Angeles Master Chorale, as well as some of the world's premier ensembles and orchestras.

Members of the audience surround the orchestra platform; a 6,125-pipe organ occupies a central position between the seating blocks at the rear of the stage. Other design highlights of the main auditorium include hardwood walls and a ceiling made of Douglas fir. A 36-foot-high rear window and eight sky-lights allow natural light to enhance daytime concerts.

The auditorium seats are upholstered in a colorful floral pattern designed by Gehry, who named the pattern after Walt Disney's wife, Lillian. The pattern is in three basic color palettes of green, purple, and orange, and the fabric design was computer-assigned to the seats to create the effect of wildflowers scattered throughout the interior of the hall.

The structure also encompasses two outdoor amphitheaters, including the W.M. Keck Foundation Children's Amphitheater for children's programming and a second outdoor performing space. At the southwest corner of the Walt Disney Concert Hall complex is the Roy and Edna Disney/CalArts Theater (REDCAT), a 250-seat multiuse theater performance space, and a 3,000-foot art gallery owned, operated, and programmed by California Institute of the Arts.

The curved exterior is clad in stainless-steel panels. Each letter of the hall's name is perforated into the stainless steel that flanks the front stairway and is backlit after dark.

CHINATOWN–EL PUEBLO–LITTLE TOKYO AREA

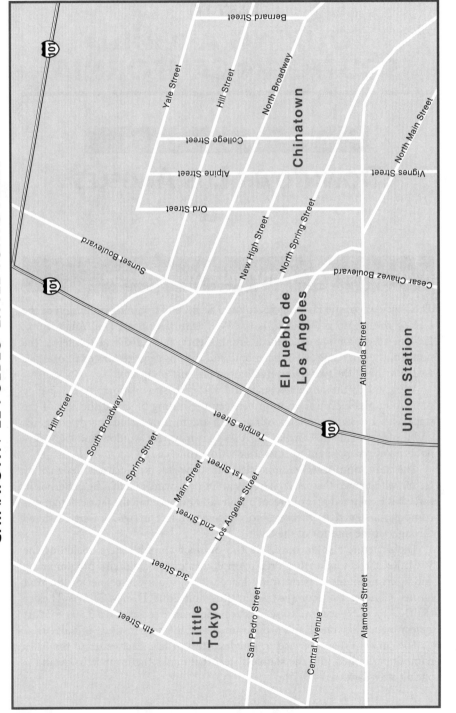

An expansive public garden wraps around the western and southern sides of the concert hall and is accessible to visitors from two public stairways. Travertine walkways lead visitors through a colorful garden featuring six types of trees, more than thirty varieties of shrubs and perennials, and ornamental grasses, allowing the garden to flower year-round.

Five levels of lobby spaces are bathed in natural light and punctuated by tree-like columns clad in Douglas fir. A main feature of the entrance lobby is the sweeping Mancini staircase that takes arriving visitors to the hall's garden level.

Patina, a full-service restaurant, is open on concert and nonconcert evenings. The Concert Hall Cafe also is open to the public daily for lunch and dinner, and for preconcert and intermission refreshments.

For information on performances, consult www.musiccenter.org/wdch. The box office for the Los Angeles Philharmonic can be reached at (323) 850–2000.

EL PUEBLO DE LOS ANGELES HISTORIC MONUMENT

El Pueblo was a group of mud huts established in 1781 by eleven families from Mexico. Today, a forty-four-acre park is the home of the city's first church, firehouse, theater, and other restored buildings from the original settlement of Los Angeles.

There's a visitors center in the 1887 Sepulveda House on Main Street. Other notable structures include the Garnier buildings used by Chinese immigrants at

El Pueblo de Los Angeles. *Photo by Jeff Hyman,* © *Corel Corporation*

the turn of the twentieth century. Free guided walking tours are offered Tuesday to Saturday at 10:00 A.M., 11:00 A.M., and noon.

El Pueblo is located within the area of Main Street, Sunset Boulevard, Macy Street, Alameda Street, and Arcadia Street. For information, call (213) 628–3562 or consult www.ci.la.ca.us/ELP.

Nearby to El Pueblo is **Olvera Street,** one of the oldest commercial streets of Los Angeles. Street vendors and colorful shops line the street between Alameda and North Main Streets. South of Olvera is **The Plaza,** once the center of the pueblo, and now the location of festivals and celebrations, including Cinco de Mayo.

Avila Adobe, at 10 Olvera Street, is the oldest remaining home in Los Angeles. It was built in 1818 by Francisco Avila, who was mayor of the pueblo at the time. The ravages of time and earthquakes have been repaired and the restored adobe is furnished with period artifacts. Free guided walking tours are offered Wednesday to Saturday at 10:00 A.M., 11:00 A.M., and noon. For information, call (213) 628–1274 or consult www.ci.la.ca.vs/ELP/avila.htm.

The **Old Plaza Firehouse** at 134 Paseo de la Plaza dates from 1884 as Los Angeles's first fire station. Restored as a museum of old firefighting equipment, the firehouse is open daily except Monday.

El Mercado at 3425 East First Street is a three-story indoor Mexican market, including a supermarket, restaurants, and stores.

Among the interesting restaurants along Olvera Street is **La Golondrina,** located within the Pelanconi House. The restaurant, whose name means "The Swallow," was Los Angeles's first brick edifice, dating back to 1850. Strolling mariachi musicians entertain guests.

CHINATOWN

Near El Pueblo and historic Union Station, Chinatown is bordered by Alpine, Spring, and Yale Streets and Bamboo Lane. Most of the shops and restaurants can be found on streets off Gin Ling Way, the "Street of the Golden Palace."

Chinese labor helped open California to the world and helped build Los Angeles. The Chinese did not, at first, share in the success of the Golden State. Laborers cut an early wagon road through the mountains near Newhall, worked on the mines of the Comstock in Nevada, and dug the difficult San Fernando tunnel that brought the Southern Pacific to Los Angeles in 1876. Most of the Chinese chose—or were forced—to live in a small area located close to Olvera Street. Living conditions were marginal, and anti-Chinese prejudice included what has become known as the Chinese Massacre of 1871, when nineteen men and boys were killed.

The Chinese influence continued as Chinese immigrants became fishermen, cooks, and servants and established farms that provided most of the vegetables sold in Los Angeles.

The old Chinatown was torn down in the 1930s to make way for the construction of Union Station. The new Chinatown, off North Broadway, opened in

1939 with businesses ready to serve the several thousand residents and with an eye on tourism. Shopping is a major pastime, and most stores are open in the evening. For authentic Chinese markets and restaurants, North Spring Street is worth a visit. There is also a Chinese cinema. About 10,000 people reside in Chinatown today.

Although small in comparison to Chinatown in San Francisco, the Los Angeles version is just as lively and colorful, especially in February. During the celebration of the Chinese New Year, traditional parades take to the streets and the sounds of music and firecrackers fill the air as dragons wind their way along.

The main entrance to Chinatown is through the ornamental **Gin Ling Way** pagoda gate at 900 North Broadway near College Street. Facing the gate is a statue of Dr. Sun Yat-sen, who led the overthrow of the Manchu dynasty in 1911 and is regarded as the founder of

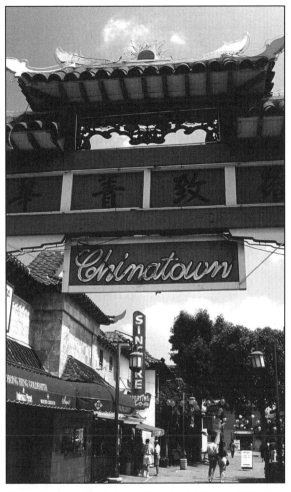

The gateway to Chinatown. *Photo by Jeff Hyman, © Corel Corporation*

the Republic of China. As you walk through the area, look at the roofs and upper structures of many of the buildings for images of animals and fish, considered good luck talismans.

Guided walking tours of the district are offered by the Chinese Historical Society of Southern California; for more information, call (323) 222–0856. The Los Angeles Old Chinatown Merchants Association maintains a Web site with information about the area, at www.chinatownla.com.

Over the years new waves of Asian immigrants have added to the mix. You'll find cuisine from China, Taiwan, Hong Kong, Vietnam, and more. Several tightly jammed shopping arcades transport you thousands of miles once you are through their gates. On Broadway you will find **Dynasty Center, Chinatown Plaza,** and **Saigon Plaza.**

Wing On Tong, at 701 North Spring Street, is a Chinese herb store that dates back nearly a century, and little has changed over time.

Farther down the street is the **Capitol Milling Company** at 1231 North Spring Street. Originally established in 1855 as the Eagle Mills, it was one of the earliest flour mills in California; it was also one of the original seven telephone subscribers to the Los Angeles Telephone Company in 1881. It continues as a commercial mill.

Philippe the Original, at 100 North Alameda Street, is one of those only-in-Los Angeles places, a delicatessen established by a French cook in 1908, which moved to Chinatown in 1948. According to the official legend, chef Philippe Mathieu accidentally dropped a sandwich into the roasting pan filled with juice still hot from the oven; the customer, a policeman, ate the sandwich anyway, and brought back friends for more "French Dip" sandwiches. For more information, consult www.philippes.com.

Mandarin Plaza at 970 North Broadway includes several dozen restaurants and stores. Near the intersection of North Broadway and Bernard Street is Association Row, home of many family and fraternal associations set up by Chinese immigrants.

F. See On Company at 940 Chungking Court is a renowned gallery for the sale of Asian art.

Those with a literary bent may want to visit the Chinatown Branch of the **Los Angeles Public Library** at 639 North Hill Street. Its collections include materials on Chinese, Vietnamese, and Spanish cultures. For information, consult www.lapl.org/branches/63.html.

LITTLE TOKYO

Bordered by First, Alameda, Third, and Los Angeles Streets, Little Tokyo is the cultural and commercial center for Japanese-Americans of the Los Angeles region. This is the largest Japanese community outside of Japan, with a population of more than 100,000. Older enterprises can be found in the many small shops and restaurants; newer development includes several large shopping malls, including the spectacular Yaohan Plaza at Alameda and Third Streets. Yaohan includes a sprawling supermarket of Japanese foods and a branch of the Japanese toy store Hello Kitty.

At Weller Court at Weller and Second Streets is another grouping of interesting stores; the central mall includes a monument to Japanese-American astronaut Ellison Onizuka, one of the victims of the *Challenger* disaster.

The **Japanese American Cultural and Community Center** at 244 San Pedro Street offers information on cultural events and festivals in Nisei Week in August, which celebrates American-born citizens of Japanese extraction. The center offers traditional Kabuki theater performances and the Doizaki Gallery of Art. For information, call (213) 628–2725 or consult www.jaccc.org.

The **Little Tokyo Business Association** offers guided tours during the week. For information and reservations, call (213) 628–2725.

The skyline of downtown Los Angeles. *Photo by Jeff Hyman, © Corel Corporation*

The **Higashi Hongwangi Temple,** at 8505 East Third Street, is an authentic Buddhist temple with a spectacular golden altar.

The **Japanese Village Plaza,** on First and Second Streets between San Pedro and Central, includes Japanese food stores, Japanese and Korean restaurants, and other unusual outlets.

The **Little Tokyo branch of the Los Angeles Public Library,** at 244 South Alameda Street, includes a large collection of Japanese-language books and research materials. For information, call (213) 612–0525 or consult www.lapl .org/branches/64.html.

LOS ANGELES FARMERS MARKET

The Farmers Market of Los Angeles is a bit of heaven for anyone who eats. Begun in the 1930s when farmers gathered in a field at what was then the edge of town, the market grew to include restaurants, food stands, art galleries, and shops. The stands sell items from all around the world. Market stands include cheese, poultry, meats, breads, ice cream, fruits, vegetables, and health food.

One after another are restaurants from Mexican to Chinese to Japanese to

American. On one Sunday morning visit, I had some New Orleans gumbo and corn bread washed down with fresh limeade and topped off with a sinful slice of pie.

You'll also find some spectacular fruit and vegetable stands, although there are not as many as there used to be. Some interesting crafts and gift shops are located across the parking lot.

The market is located at 6333 West Third Street off Fairfax between downtown Los Angeles and Hollywood. Three free hours of parking are allowed at the lot. The market is open daily except for major holidays from 9:00 A.M. to 9:00 P.M. Monday to Friday, from 9:00 A.M. to 8:00 P.M. Saturday, and from 10:00 A.M. to 7:00 P.M. Sunday. For information, call (323) 933–9211 or consult www .farmersmarketla.com.

CITY HALL

As Sergeant Joe Friday used to say as he drove past this place each week on his *Dragnet* beat: "Just the facts, ma'am." A mixed message of a building, unlike almost any other City Hall we know, it has a pyramid at its top with an observation deck on the twenty-seventh floor, and a domed rotunda at the base.

The building, located at 200 North Spring Street, has been a star in motion pictures from the moment it was completed in 1928; at that time Lon Chaney starred there in *While the City Sleeps*. Perhaps its most famous setting was in *War*

Los Angeles City Hall. *Photo by Jeff Hyman,* © *Corel Corporation*

of the Worlds in 1953; an 8-inch model of the building was destroyed with explosives in one of the major scenes.

City Hall was police headquarters for ten seasons of *Dragnet;* it was transformed to the Daily Planet in the *Superman* television series. *Kojak* and *Cagney and Lacey* used the building as a stand-in for New York City. Other cameos include scenes in *The Rockford Files, Matlock, Hill Street Blues,* and *LA Law.*

The building was restored and retrofitted in recent years to withstand earthquake damage.

KOREATOWN

Olympic Boulevard between Crenshaw Boulevard and Vermont Avenue. Another fascinating, far-flung outpost of an ancient Asian culture. Korean restaurants, grocery stores, and shops, as well as the Korean Cultural Center on Wilshire Boulevard at La Brea Avenue with a performance space, gallery, and library. For information on the center, call (323) 936–7141 or consult www.kccla .org.

WATTS TOWERS

A world-renowned example of primitive art and a landmark of the Watts area, Watts Towers were built by hand during a thirty-year period from the 1930s through the 1960s by Sabatino Rodia, an Italian tile setter. The towers are made of steel rods decorated with pieces of tile, dishes, and bottles, as well as bedframes, and other objects, including thousands of seashells. The towers are located at 1765 East 107th Street in Watts. For information, call (213) 847–4646.

The **Watts Towers Art Center** at 1727 East 107th Street, Watts, offers displays of art, poetry readings, and special exhibits that explore and celebrate the area's African-American culture. It is open for tours Friday, Saturday, and Sunday. Admission: adults (18 and older), $5.00, seniors and children (13–17), $3.00. The gallery is open Tuesday to Saturday from 10:00 A.M. to 4:00 P.M. and on Sunday from noon to 4:00 P.M. For information, call (213) 847–4646.

LOS ANGELES CENTRAL LIBRARY

A Los Angeles landmark from the moment of its completion in 1926, the library was reborn and expanded in 1993 from the ashes of a disastrous fire seven years earlier. It is now the third largest library in the country. It sits beneath a somewhat fanciful colored-tile pyramid tower. The library, located at Fifth and Hope Streets, is open Monday to Thursday from 10:00 A.M. to 8:00 P.M.; Friday and Saturday from 10:00 A.M. to 6:00 P.M.; and Sunday from 1:00 to 5:00 P.M. Guided tours are available daily. For information, call (213) 228–7168 or consult www .lapl.org/central.

HISTORIC WALKING TOURS

The Los Angeles Conservancy offers one- and two-hour walking tours on Saturday of historic neighborhoods and commercial areas, including the theater district, Union Station, and Pershing Square. Different tours are offered each day; tickets cost $10. Advance reservations are required. For information and reservations, call (213) 623–2489 or consult www.laconservancy.org.

BONNIE BRAE STREET

The 800 and 1000 blocks of South Bonnie Brae Street, near MacArthur Park, are beautifully preserved Victorian residences dating from the 1890s. They are regular locations for film shoots.

BROADWAY THEATER DISTRICT

Los Angeles's original theater district, cleverly named as Broadway, stretches from Third to Ninth Streets in downtown. The oldest of the legitimate theaters date to about 1910, and the first movie palaces opened in the 1920s.

Most of the movie houses have gone to seed, or at least to new roles as neighborhood homes to second- and third-rate films, but the exteriors and interiors remain interesting. Among the tired gems are the Art Deco Doremus Building at Ninth Street; the Cameo Theater at 528 Broadway, built in 1910 as a nickelodeon; and the Million Dollar Theater at 307 Broadway, built in 1918 by impresarios Sid and D. J. Grauman, of Chinese Theatre fame.

LOS ANGELES FLOWER MARKET

The wholesale market for florists and decorators, at 754 Wall Street, opens in the middle of the night for commercial clients. The public can enter Monday, Wednesday, and Friday after 8:00 A.M., and Tuesday, Thursday, and Saturday after 6:00 A.M. Admission is $2.00 during the week and $1.00 on Saturday. Get there early to browse and buy from the spectacular leftovers. For information, call (213) 622–1966 or consult www.laflowerdistrict.com.

CHAPTER EIGHTEEN

LOS ANGELES EAST

BEVERLY HILLS

From its very humble beginnings as a lima bean farm, Beverly Hills has grown to become a place where a different kind of bean is counted; the local sport is the barely disguised pursuit and display of wealth. How many other places do you know where the ZIP code (90210) can identify a television series, a line of clothing, and a way of life?

The small town (less than 6 square miles) lies within the City of Los Angeles but is an independent entity fiercely protected by its mostly upscale residents. Developed in 1906, the town was named after Beverly, Massachusetts; many of the early stars of Hollywood moved there, and the area became the center of attention in 1921 when Mary Pickford and Douglas Fairbanks built their famous mansion Pickfair in Beverly Hills.

Today many of the homes of the glitterati are hidden in the hills above the Hills, in the canyons above Sunset Boulevard, and behind massive hedges and imposing fences. You can see the hangers-on of the lifestyles of the rich and famous: trendy and overpriced restaurants, trendy and overpriced clothing and jewelry stores, theatrical agents, production companies, stockbrokers, and more. The main street of all of this excess is Rodeo Drive, a short connector that runs between Wilshire Boulevard and Santa Monica Boulevard.

Other famous structures include the **Beverly Hills Hotel** at 9641 Sunset Boulevard, built in 1912. There is a pink Mission-style main building as well as twenty-one bungalows on twelve lush acres. Howard Hughes rented Number 3 for years at a time; many other legends of Hollywood have made the cottages their temporary homes. For information, call (310) 276–2251 or consult www .thebeverlyhillshotel.com.

HOLLYWOOD

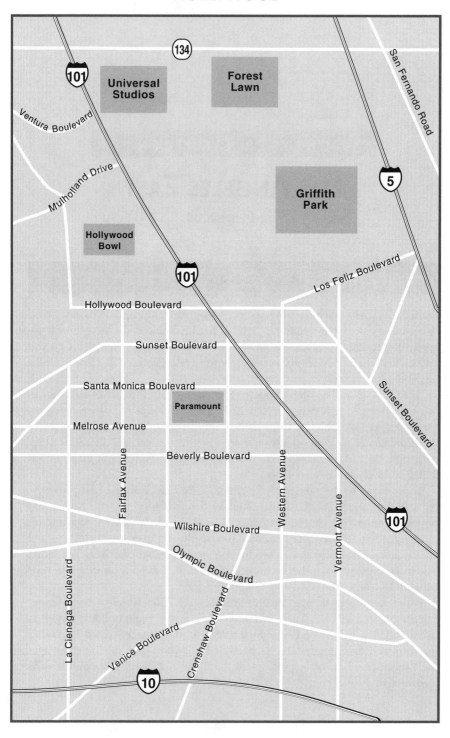

BURBANK

Beautiful downtown Burbank, which is neither downtown nor especially beautiful, is not quite Hollywood, but it is nevertheless the vital heart of the modern television and movie industry. It was built around the sprawling Warner Bros. Studios, where stars including James Cagney, Humphrey Bogart, Lauren Bacall, and others made many of their most famous films.

Today, major operations include Warner Bros., the Disney Studios at 500 South Buena Vista Street, and the NBC production facilities at 3000 Alameda Avenue. *You can read about tours of the Warner Bros. Studio in Chapter 14.*

HOLLYWOOD

Hooray for Hollywood, a state of mind as much as a place.

The area was first developed in the 1880s; the wife of the developer named the area Hollywood after an all-but-forgotten place of the same name near Chicago. Hollywood, California, began as a quiet fruit-farming community; things began to change soon after an early silent picture was filmed on a ranch there in 1906. The landscape and weather were perfect for tableau films, including Westerns, and the infant moviemaking industry moved from its mostly East Coast origins to Hollywood.

The famed Hollywood sign that looms over much of the area, by the way, dates to 1923 when it was built to publicize a housing development named Hollywoodland. The "land" is gone, but the 50-foot-high, 450-foot-long advertisement remains.

By the 1940s nearly the entire American film industry was located in Hollywood. In the years that have followed, the rising price of real estate has resulted in relocation of large portions of the business a bit farther outside of Hollywood proper.

A&M Records. Located in the former Chaplin Movie Studios at 1416 North La Brea Avenue and operated since 1966 as one of the premier recording studios, A&M was founded by musicians Herb Alpert and Jerry Moss. Chaplin's footprints are immortalized in front of Stage 3.

Capitol Records Tower. An unusual circular office building, at 1750 Vine Street, it was likened by some to a stack of records when it was built in 1956; perhaps, in this modern day, it would be thought of as a pile of CDs. A rooftop light flashes "Hollywood" in Morse code.

Capitol Records has purchased land just north of its building and announced plans to build a museum to house memorabilia from recording artists such as the Beatles, Frank Sinatra, Nat King Cole, and other Capitol stars.

Crossroads of the World. Called the world's first modern shopping center, it dates from 1936 and is now used for offices. The architecture is a very strange mélange of French Provincial, Tudor, Italian, Moorish, and Californian styles, with an ocean liner as a centerpiece. The Crossroads, located at 6671 Sunset

Boulevard, was used as the site of Demi Moore's office in the film *Indecent Proposal* and as Danny DeVito's seedy office in *L.A. Confidential.* A version of the center can be seen at the Disney–MGM Studios theme park at Walt Disney World in Orlando.

Egyptian Theater. Another creation of Sid Grauman, it was built in 1922 as the first of Hollywood's grand movie houses. A Middle Eastern predecessor to the Chinese Theatre, it was beautifully restored and reopened in late 1998 as the home and offices of the American Cinematheque film showcase. The 616-seat theater is used for presentations of film classics, lectures, and occasional celebrity movie premieres.

The theater is at 6712 Hollywood Boulevard. For information, call (323) 466–3456 or consult www.americancinematheque.com/egyptian/egypt.htm.

El Capitan Theatre. Built as a legitimate theater in 1922, it was converted in 1942 to become a showcase for Paramount films. Orson Welles's *Citizen Kane* opened here in 1939. Beautifully restored by the Disney Company, the theater specializes in Disney and Touchstone films, sometimes premiering movies a few weeks before general release.

When it was converted for movie use in the 1940s the opera boxes were removed; but in 1991 the boxes were returned and the spectacular gold-leaf ceiling was restored. The screen lies behind no fewer than three curtains, which open one after another to musical fanfare. Thoroughly modern touches include a THX sound system.

For special events, including premieres and some retrospective shows, the films are accompanied by short stage shows that feature special appearances, singing ushers, dancers, and Disney characters.

The El Capitan is located at 6838 Hollywood Boulevard, across the street from Mann's Chinese Theatre. For information on the theater, tickets, and scheduled events, call (323) 467–9545 or consult www.elcapitantickets.com.

Frederick's of Hollywood Lingerie Museum. There's less to see here than at almost any other museum we've visited, and there's a lot of it. A private collection of flashy garments includes personal belongings of Madonna (of course), Cher, Judy Garland, Mae West, the (er) Pointer Sisters, Zsa Zsa Gabor, Cybill Shepherd . . . and Milton Berle. The museum, at 6608 Hollywood Boulevard, is open Monday through Saturday from 10:00 A.M. to 9:00 P.M. and Sunday from 11:00 A.M. to 6:00 P.M. Admission is free. For information, call (323) 466–8506.

Guinness World Records Museum. The world's biggest, loudest, most impressive . . . well, you get the idea. Records are presented with replicas, videos, and multimedia displays. Open from 10:00 A.M. to midnight and until 1:00 A.M. on Friday and Saturday. Admission: adults, $10.95; seniors, $8.50; children (6–12), $6.95. Combination tickets with the Hollywood Wax Museum are also available. The museum is located at 6764 Hollywood Boulevard. For information, call (213) 463–6433.

Hollywood Wax Museum. Your basic tourist attraction, set in wax, with a celebrity focus. The museum is located at 6767 Hollywood Boulevard. For information, call (213) 462–5991 or consult www.hollywoodwax.com.

Hollywood Entertainment Museum. Located in the heart of Tinseltown, the museum offers an impressive collection of filmmaking artifacts, scripts, props, and more. Among the highlights: the bridge of the Starship Enterprise and the set of *Cheers*.

The central gallery of the museum, home of the permanent collection, is presided over by the 15-foot statue Goddess of Entertainment. Among the treasures of the collection is a fascinating miniature model of Hollywood, made in 1936. You'll also see a display of makeup, masks, and special-effects devices. The famed Max Factor museum of makeup closed in 1997, and many of its treasures were given or loaned to the Hollywood Entertainment Museum for display there.

Call to find out about changing exhibitions of film and television artifacts and special events. Admission: adults, $12.00; seniors (60 and older), $10.00; students with ID and children (5–12), $5.00. Parking $2.00. Open daily in summer from 10:00 A.M. to 6:00 P.M. and in winter from 11:00 A.M. to 6:00 P.M. Closed Wednesday from Labor Day to Memorial Day.

The museum is located at 7021 Hollywood Boulevard. For information, call (213) 465–7900 or consult www.hollywoodmuseum.com.

Hollywood High School. The alma mater of stars including Carol Burnett, James Garner, Rick and David Nelson, Stefanie Powers, John Ritter, Jason Robards, Mickey Rooney . . . and Judy Garland. A small museum of memorabilia from former students can be visited by advance appointment.

The famous ice cream shop where star Lana Turner was discovered was located across the street from the school at 1500 North Highland Avenue; despite Hollywood legends, it was not Schwab's Drugstore, which was located at 8024 Sunset Boulevard. In any case, both of the soda fountains have been torn down.

The school is located at 1521 North Highland Avenue. For information, call (323) 461–3891 or consult www.lausd.k12.ca.us/Hollywood_HS.

Hollywood Walk of Fame. Hollywood Boulevard between Gower and Sycamore Streets, and Vine Street between Sunset Boulevard and Yucca Street. Nearly 2,000 stars of the silver screen, early radio, and (lately) the television screen are memorialized with star-shaped plaques in the sidewalk.

The Walk was removed when work began on the Red Line subway, which runs from downtown Los Angeles to Hollywood; the stars were put back in place and shined to new luster in 1998.

Kodak Theatre. The new home of the Academy Award presentations offers guided behind-the-scenes tours. The thirty-minute tour includes a visit to the George Eastman VIP Room, the site of most postshow celebrity parties, and a stroll down the Winner's Walk where Oscar winners meet the press.

Tours are generally offered daily from 10:30 A.M. to 2:30 P.M., subject to change because of special events. Admission: adults, $15; seniors (65 and older) and children (3–12) $10. No photography is permitted.

The Kodak Theatre, at 6801 Hollywood Boulevard near Highland Avenue, is near Mann's Chinese Theatre. For information, call (323) 308–6300 or consult www.kodaktheatre.com.

Mann's Chinese Theatre. During the years the theater has been as much of an attraction as the great films that have debuted and played there. It was designed as a fanciful version of a Chinese temple inside and out.

Sid Grauman built the theater in 1927, and his name is noted in many of the early handprints and signatures in the concrete outside. The theater is in the heart of Hollywood at 6925 Hollywood Boulevard. For film schedules, call (323) 464–6266 or consult mann.moviefone.com/services/graumanmain.adp.

Ozzie and Harriet House. A must-see for those of a certain age. This was the actual home of the Nelson family, and it was used as the model for the house occupied by the family in their TV series. The home, at 1822 Camino Palmero Drive, is now a private residence and not open to visitors but it can be seen from the road.

GLENDALE

Just above Hollywood in the shadow of the San Gabriels, this old settlement is best known for its proximity to a very quiet neighborhood: the **Forest Lawn Memorial Park.** This 300-acre final resting place (they're positively ghoulish about their desire that it not be called a cemetery) resembles more a rolling green religious theme park. There are several famous church replicas, including the Wee Church o' the Heather and the Church of the Recessional. Displays include huge murals of Jesus and a mural of the signing of the Declaration of Independence accompanied by patriotic music. Residents of the necropolis and the nearby Forest Lawn Hills Memorial Park include Clark Gable and Carole Lombard, Stan Laurel, Buster Keaton, and Liberace.

Forest Lawn is free to the public. Visitors can enter a museum on the property and view some of the spectacular artwork, including the *Paradise Doors,* made from a cast of Lorenzo Ghiberti's original Gothic masterpiece; *Bronco Buster,* an original bronze by Frederic Remington; a mosaic rendering of John Trumbull's *Signing of the Declaration of Independence;* a full-size re-creation of Michelangelo's *David;* and a large collection of coins mentioned in the Bible.

Visitors are welcome every day from 8:00 A.M. to 6:00 P.M. The Forest Lawn Museum and Museum Store (really!) is open daily from 10:00 A.M. to 5:00 P.M. For information, call (800) 204–3131 or consult www.forestlawn.com.

CENTURY CITY

Century City is mostly famous for what it once was—the formal sprawling backlot of **20th Century–Fox** and, before that, the ranch of cowboy actor Tom Mix.

Just a small part of 20th Century–Fox remains, at 10201 Pico Boulevard. The studio is not open to the public, but you can drive by the formal gates to catch a glimpse of the huge New York set used in *Hello, Dolly!* and many other classic films.

The backlot was mostly sold off in 1961 and became an almost-instant city of office buildings, restaurants, shops, and condominiums mostly catering to the entertainment industry.

PASADENA

The end of the trail for numerous parties of settlers from Indiana in the 1880s, the city became a winter playground for the East Coast wealthy; many of their fabulous mansions can still be seen along Orange Grove Avenue. The name Pasadena means "crown of the valley" in the language of the Chippewa Indians.

Today Pasadena has a population of more than 132,000 and includes some of the best museums in the West, including the **Norton Simon Museum of Art** and the **California Institute of Technology,** which includes the NASA Jet Propulsion Laboratory. Pasadena is most famous, of course, for the Rose Bowl football game and the Tournament of Roses Parade that precedes it each New Year's Day. For information about Pasadena, consult www.ci.pasadena.ca.us.

ANGELES NATIONAL FOREST

On top of Old Baldy (known on the maps as Mount San Antonio), the view from 10,064 feet is unsurpassed. The huge wilderness area also includes lowland deserts and verdant meadows.

If you're not up to using the hundreds of miles of hiking trails, campsites, ski trails, and downhill slopes, you can take a spectacular 64-mile drive from one side of the forest to another along Highway 2 from La Cañada off Interstate 210 near Pasadena. The road threads its way among many of the larger peaks with views of Crystal Lake and Old Baldy; the road connects to Highway 138 southbound to San Bernardino on the other side of the forest. For information on facilities, call (626) 574–5200 or consult www.r5.fs.fed.us/angeles.

ANAHEIM

German immigrants took "ana" from the nearby Santa Ana River and "heim," meaning home, and named their remote village in 1857. They also brought cuttings from the Rhine and made Anaheim California's first important winemaking region and, before long, the leading wine area of the country. A blight some thirty years later wiped out the grape crops, and growers switched to oranges.

Industry and the discovery of oil changed the economy again. The opening of Disneyland in 1955 changed the nature of the area once more, and now tourism is one of the leading industries. For information about Anaheim, consult www.anaheimoc.org.

For details about Disneyland and Knott's Berry Farm, see Chapters 4 and 8.

ONTARIO

Graber Olive House. Free tours of one of California's leading olive processing companies, located at 315 East Fourth Street in Ontario, are offered weekdays and Saturday from 9:00 A.M. to 5:30 P.M., and on Sunday from 9:30 A.M. to 6:00 P.M. C. C. Graber established his olive farm and packaging facility in 1894. For information, call (909) 983–1761 or (800) 996–5483, or consult www.graber olives.com.

BARSTOW

Calico Ghost Town. Step back into California's mining past to a restored boomtown of the 1880s. The Calico Mountains included some of the richest silver finds of the West; for example, the Maggie Mine, which is part of today's ghost town. Most of the buildings in the park are real; there is also a museum with artifacts from the mining past.

The town was restored by Walter Knott, the founder of Knott's Berry Farm in Buena Park. Knott had worked in the mining camp near the end of its use. Today the ghost town is run by San Bernardino County as a park.

Special events include the Calico Hullabaloo, held on Palm Sunday weekend and featuring "horseshoe pitchin', stew cookin', and tobacco spittin'" competitions. Calico Days, held on the Columbus Day weekend, includes a Wild West parade, gunfights, games, and other events. The Heritage Festival on Thanksgiving weekend includes Old West and Indian art and sculpture.

Located on Ghost Town Road, off Interstate 15, 10 miles northeast of Barstow, Calico is open daily from 9:00 A.M. to 5:00 P.M., except Christmas. Admission: adults, $6.00; children (6–15), $3.00. For information, call (760) 254–2122 or consult www.calicotown.com.

SAN BERNARDINO

Big Bear Lake. A recreation area in the San Bernardino Mountains, about 100 miles east of Los Angeles. Summer activities include swimming and boating (rentals available) in Meadow Park, hiking, and camping. In the winter, there are several downhill ski areas and numerous cross-country trails. For information about Big Bear Ranger Station, call (909) 866–3437. For information about resorts in the area, call (800) 424–4232 or consult www.bigbearinfo.com. To get to Big Bear Lake, take Interstate 10 to San Bernardino, to State Highway 18 into the mountains.

Drivers can explore the Holcomb Valley—location of some of the sites of the 1860–75 Gold Rush—on a three-hour tour north of the lake. Maps and descriptions are available at the Ranger Station.

From Memorial Day through the end of October, visitors can take a ninety-minute tour of Big Bear Lake aboard the *Sierra Belle*, a small replica of a riverboat which departs several times a day from Pine Knot Landing in Big Bear Lake. Tickets in 2005 were adults, $12.00; seniors (ages 52 and older), $9.50; and children (4–12), $6.00. For information, call (909) 866–2628 or consult www.pine knotlanding.com.

RIVERSIDE

March Field Air Museum. From antique flying machines to the U-2 spy plane and the modern F-14, this museum at March Air Force Base, Van Buren Boulevard is open daily from 10:00 A.M. to 4:00 P.M. Admission: adults, $7.00; children, $3.00. For information, call (909) 697–6602 or consult www.march field.org.

Orange Empire Railway Museum. A sprawling museum of old railroad, trolley, construction, and maintenance cars from in and around Southern California is in the landmark 1893 terminal in Perris. On the weekends several trains or trolleys (still decked out in their original colors and advertising placards) cruise about on the museum's tracks.

Located at 2201 South A Street in Perris, the collection is open daily from 9:00 A.M. to 5:00 P.M. Closed Thanksgiving and Christmas. Trains and trolleys operate weekends and holidays from 11:00 A.M. to 5:00 P.M. Admission: free to museum except during special events; all-day train pass, adults, $8.00; children (5–11), $6.00.

For information, call (909) 657–2605 or consult www.oerm.org.

UCR California Museum of Photography. A collection of photographs and equipment from the dawn of art through modern day, at a museum operated by the University of California, Riverside. Open Tuesday to Sunday from noon to 5:00 P.M. Admission: $1.00 for the general public. 3824 Main Street, Riverside. For information, call (951) 784–3686 or consult www.cmp.ucr.edu.

PALM SPRINGS

Palm Springs is a thriving, even booming, oasis in the desert, a fascinating mix of desert heat and desolation, lush greenery, splendid spas, and snow-capped mountaintops.

Palm Springs is at the western edge of the Coachella Valley, about 107 miles southeast of Los Angeles. The city itself is only 487 feet above sea level, but it is all but surrounded by mountains, including 10,831-foot Mount San Jacinto; the Palm Springs Aerial Tramway climbs the mountain to the 8,516-foot level, sometimes taking visitors from summer heat to winter cross-country skiing and hiking conditions at the top.

Palm Springs averages 354 days of sunshine and fewer than 5½ inches of rain per year. The "high season" of Palm Springs runs from January to May; there is still plenty to do in the summer months, but the heat in the desert can be brutal. However, don't overlook the desert as the site of some spectacular and unusual vistas, wildlife, and vegetation.

Palm Springs Regional Airport is a mile from downtown. Los Angeles International Airport is two hours away by car.

There are more than 140 hotels in Palm Springs, ranging from modest bungalow courts to European-style bed-and-breakfasts to full-service luxury resorts and spas. You can call the Palm Springs Visitor Information Center at (800) 347–7746 for details on hotels and to make reservations or consult www .palm-springs.org.

There are four gambling casinos in and around Palm Springs, each operated by an Indian tribe. You won't find the flash of Las Vegas here, but you will have the chance to lose your paycheck at blackjack, pai gow, poker, other table games, slot machines, and sports books.

The **Spa Hotel & Casino,** operated by the Agua Caliente Band of Cahuilla Indians, is located in Palm Springs at 140 North Indian Drive. For information, call (760) 325–1461.

Casino Morongo, operated by the Morongo Band of Mission Indians, is about seventeen minutes west of Palm Springs off the Cabazon Apache Trail exit of I–10. For information, call (800) 252–4499 or consult www.casinomorongo .com.

Fantasy Springs Casino, operated by the Cabazon Band of Mission Indians, is located near Indio off I–10. For information, call (760) 342–5000 or consult www.cabazonindians.com/fantasysprings.html.

Trump 29 Casino, operated by the Twenty-Nine Palms Band of Mission Indians, is in Coachella off I–10. For information, call (760) 775–5566 or consult www.trump29.com.

Indian Canyons. Just minutes from downtown, Andreas, Murray, and Palm Canyons shelter North America's largest natural fan palm oases. There is also a trading post, hiking and horse trails, and picnic areas. The region is part of the domain of the Agua Caliente Band of Cahuilla Indians.

Palm Canyon, 15 miles long, is home to several thousand *Washingtonia filifera* palms that stand in striking contrast to the barren desert and rock formations. A trading post operated by the Cahuillas sells art and artifacts.

In 1876 the Agua Caliente Indians were deeded in trust some 32,000 acres to be used as their homeland; today, some 6,700 acres lie within the city limits of Palm Springs. What was once considered worthless desert, today is among the most valuable real estate in the country.

Open daily from 8:00 A.M. to 5:00 P.M. in fall and winter, and until 6:00 P.M. in spring and summer. Admission: adults, $6.00; seniors (62 and older), $4.50; children (6–12), $2.00. For information, call (760) 325–3400 or consult www .indian-canyons.com.

Desert Adventures. Guided tours to the natural and historic wonders of Palm Springs, Indian Canyons, Joshua Tree, and the Santa Rosa Mountains. Other offerings include off-road Jeep safaris, agriculture tours, and earthquake fault tours.

I took a tour of Indian Canyons in one of the company's signature red Jeeps; the canyons are just a few miles outside of Palm Springs but a world away. Among the stops was a lush desert oasis; alongside it was an ancient grinding rock used by families of Indians for generations. The streams are overflows of entrapment areas in mountains; these aquifers of ancient rainfall provide all the drinking water for the Palm Springs area. (Imported Colorado River water is used for irrigation purposes in the valley.)

Back out on the desert floor we were introduced to plants such as the poisonous jimsonweed, often called thorn apple, a hallucinogenic member of the nightshade family, sometimes used in some religious and personal experimentation; and the yrba senta plant, used as a poultice and mouthwash and smelling very much like Juicy Fruit gum.

And then there were the jumping cholla (pronounced choy-ah), which are especially nasty plants whose heads seem to fly off when a human or animal passes nearby. The barbs swell and push themselves as much as half an inch into the body. Very patient gourmets cook the cholla flowers for as long as fifteen hours for an artichokelike flavor.

The desert is also home to sheep, goats, deer, 30-inch-long chuckwalla lizards, scorpions, tarantulas, black widows, and recluse spiders.

Rates run from about $69 to $129 per person for scheduled tours. For information, call (760) 324–5337 or consult www.red-jeep.com.

Living Desert. A 1,200-acre desert interpretive center featuring exotic birds and animals, nature trails, botanical gardens, and a visitors center that has geological exhibits.

It's a stroll in the Coachella Valley desert, among coyotes, bighorn sheep, oryx, zebras, cheetahs, and meerkats. There are some interesting displays about the local ecology. Open from 9:00 A.M. to 5:00 P.M. daily September to mid-June; call for summer hours. Admission: adults, $10.50; seniors (62 and older), $9.50; children (3–12), $6.50. For information, call (760) 346–5694 or consult www.living desert.org.

Palm Springs Desert Museum. Collection of classic western American and contemporary California art, as well as natural science exhibitions and a full schedule of performing arts in the 450-seat Annenberg Theater.

The unusual collection includes an active seismograph charting current earth movement in the area, several dinosaur skeletons, a collection of intricate Apache baskets, a set of paintings by Frederic Remington, portraits by actor William Holden, and sculptures by western actor George Montgomery.

The museum is open Tuesday, Wednesday, Friday, and Saturday from 10:00 A.M. to 5:00 P.M., Thursday from noon to 8:00 P.M., and Sunday from noon to 5:00 P.M. Closed Monday. Adults, $7.50; children (6–17), $3.50; seniors (62 and older), $6.50. Free to the public every Thursday from 4:00 to 8:00 P.M. For information, call (760) 325–7186 or consult www.psmuseum.org.

Moorten Botanical Garden. Nature trails in a setting of 2,000 varieties of giant cacti, trees, birds, succulents, and flowers. Located at 1701 South Palm Canyon Drive, the garden is open Monday, Tuesday, Thursday, Friday, and Saturday from 9:00 A.M. to 4:30 P.M. and Sunday from 10:00 A.M. to 4:00 P.M. Closed Wednesday. Admission: adults, $2.50; children (5–15), $1.00. For information, call (760) 327–6555.

Knott's Soak City Palm Springs. A twenty-one-acre water playground—formerly **Oasis Waterpark**—with eighteen waterslides and other attractions, including body- and board-surfing, and an inner-tube ride. Located at 1500 South Gene Autry Trail, the water park is open from mid-March to late October. Admission: adults, $25.95; children (3–11), $14.95; after 3:00 P.M., adults, $15.95, and children, $11.95. For information, call (760) 327–0499 or consult www.soak cityusa.com.

Windmill Tours. They're one of the great unnatural wonders of the world—thousands of whirling windmills in the valley just north of Palm Springs along I–10. The operation claims the mantle as the world's most efficient power-producing wind farm. And they're open to the public for ninety-minute tours that go out to the farm and into the machinery. Tours are offered daily at 9:00 and 11:00 A.M. and 2:00 P.M. Admission: adults, $23; students, $15; children (6–12), $10. For information, call (760) 320–1365 or consult www.windmill tours.com.

Palm Springs Air Museum. One of the world's largest collections of World War II aircraft, many of which are still in flying condition. The museum, in a mordern building and hangars, sits alongside one of the runways at the Palm Springs Regional Airport. On most weekends, one or another of the lumbering bombers or fragile-looking fighters takes to the air.

The museum's collection includes a working B-17 Flying Fortress, and a P38 long-range fighter bomber named *Joltin' Josie.* You'll also find some unusual automobiles, including a three-headlamp 1948 Tucker and a 1930 Pierce Arrow. On the day of my visit, a B-25 bomber was offering tours to members and paying guests; its throaty engines echoed throughout the valley as it made low-altitude passes over the airport.

The museum, located at Palm Springs Regional Airport, 745 North Gene Autry Trail, is open daily 10:00 A.M. to 5:00 P.M. Admission: adults, $10.00; children (6–17), $5.00, seniors (65 and older) and military personnel, $8.50. For information, call (760) 778–6262 or consult www.air-museum.org.

Palm Springs Aerial Tramway. A spectacular climb more than a mile up the side of Mount San Jacinto in an eighty-passenger tram. The view from the cool top of the tram extends across the San Jacinto Valley; on a clear day you can see as far as the Salton Sea, nearly 50 miles away, created in 1905 as the result of a flood on the Colorado River diversion channel. A trail from the top of the tram leads 6 miles to the peak of Mount San Jacinto. During the winter you can rent sleds and saucers for use on a snow hill.

The base station for the tram is at 2,463 feet, and the mountain station tops out at 8,516 feet, where the temperature averages forty degrees cooler than the base. The tram travels about 12,800 feet in total over the fourteen-minute ride. There's a gift shop, cafeteria, and cocktail lounge at the top, too. You can watch a video about the making of the tram, and you can plant yourself on a mule for a twenty-minute tour on a trail. From the top, you can see the San Andreas Fault as it snakes through the valley about 8 miles away. The Nordic Ski Center is open November 15 to April 15, snow conditions permitting.

The attraction, located on Tramway Road, Palm Springs, off Highway 111, is open weekdays from 10:00 A.M. to 9:15 P.M.; weekends from 8:00 A.M. The last car up is at 8:00 P.M., and the last car down is at 9:45 P.M. The tram usually closes for maintenance for about a week in August; call for details. Admission: adults, $21; seniors, $19; children (3–12), $14. The tram also offers a Ride 'n' Dine ticket at the end of the day that includes a meal for adults, $30; children, $19.

For information, call (760) 325–1391 or consult www.pstramway.com.

Palm Springs Follies. If you happen to find yourself in Palm Springs in winter or spring, put aside dreams of Broadway and Hollywood and head for the Follies, a somewhat modernized vaudeville show with a vintage twist that has become a local favorite since it was revived in the Historic Plaza Theatre.

You'll find singers, tap dancers, comedians, magicians, trained dogs, and a flashy chorus line with an age restriction: Dancers must be older than sixty.

The Follies usually run from early November through the end of May, with breaks around Christmas. Tickets range from about $40 to $90. For information, call (760) 327–0225 or consult www.palmspringsfollies.com.

Joshua Tree National Monument. Off Highway 62, at Twenty-Nine Palms and Joshua Tree (another gate can be found at Cottonwood Springs, 25 miles east of Indio off I–10).

The stark beauty of the Colorado Desert in the valleys and the high Mojave Desert is within an easy drive from Los Angeles or Orange County. The two deserts come together at the Joshua Tree National Monument, which draws its name from the many Joshua trees found there. (Joshua trees are actually giant desert lilies that can reach 40 feet or more.) They were given their names by Mormon immigrants who thought the plants resembled the biblical prophet Joshua with upraised arms.

You can take your car on an 18-mile exploration on Geology Road, which goes to many of the park's more interesting areas. Hiking trails reach to Twenty-Nine Palms Oasis and other destinations. For information, call (760) 367–5500 or consult www.joshua.tree.national-park.com.

CHAPTER NINETEEN

ALONG THE COAST TO LONG BEACH, THE *QUEEN MARY,* AND CATALINA ISLAND

LONG BEACH

The long beach was a strip of sand used as a trading area between Indians of the mainland and those who came across from Catalina Island in canoes.

Outsiders built up the area after the turn of the twentieth century when Henry Huntington's Pacific Railroad arrived. When oil was discovered at Signal Hill in 1921 the population nearly doubled to 100,000. Today's economy is built on shipping and tourism, including the ocean liner *Queen Mary,* which is moored in the harbor. Fort MacArthur in San Pedro is an important military installation. The Long Beach Grand Prix is held in the city each spring.

Long Beach features two restored parks that are worth an afternoon stroll. Both are open Wednesday to Sunday afternoon and are free. A beach within the harbor is a popular spot for swimming, water skiing, and other water sports.

Downtown Long Beach is an attractive waterside city; at night, though, some areas of town are a lot less attractive. Use good judgment in making plans for explorations beyond the aquarium, *Queen Mary,* and other tourist areas.

For information about Long Beach, call (562) 436–3645 or (800) 452–7829 or consult www.visitlongbeach.com.

El Dorado Park Archery Range, site of the 1984 Olympic competition, is open to visitors and competitors. Call (562) 924–2880 or consult www.longbeach.gov/park/facilities/parks/el_dorado_regional_park.asp.

Farmers' Market. Among area markets are Huntington Park on Wednesdays; Long Beach East on Thursdays; Long Beach Downtown on Fridays; Cerritos on Saturdays; and Long Beach Southeast at Alamitos Bay Marina on Sunday. For information and hours, call (562) 436–4259 or consult www.harborareafarmers markets.org.

Rancho Los Alamitos. 6400 East Bixby Hill Road. A ranch house from the early nineteenth century with period furnishings and half a dozen agricultural buildings, including a working blacksmith's shop. Admission: free. Call (562) 431–3541 or consult http://longbeach.gov/park/facilities/rancho_los_alamitos_historic_site.asp.

Rancho Los Cerritos. 4600 Virginia Road. Includes a Spanish-style adobe, dating from the mid-nineteenth century, and surrounding gardens. Call (562) 570–1755 or consult www.rancholoscerritos.org/visitor.html.

LONG BEACH AQUARIUM OF THE PACIFIC

Skin divers equipped with microphones serve as underwater tour guides at the Long Beach Aquarium. With one million gallons of Pacific Ocean water in twenty-one exhibition tanks and twenty-six smaller tanks, the aquarium's three permanent exhibits offer visitors a virtual journey along the Pacific Rim from temperate Southern California and Baja to the more frigid waters of the Bering Sea and Kuril Islands, and on to the spectacular paradise of a Micronesian barrier reef. The collection includes more than 550 different Pacific marine species.

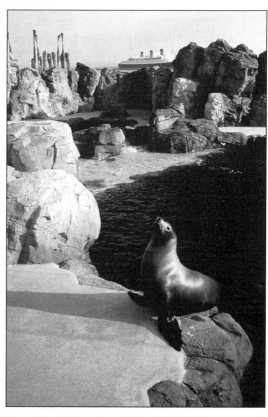

Shaped like an ocean wave, the building is the anchor of the Queensway Bay project in downtown Long Beach, across the bay from the *Queen Mary.*

Highlights of the exhibit include close encounters with the seals and sea lions of Santa Catalina Island, the leopard sharks and barracuda of Predator Place, and the sea turtles and other creatures of Baja and the Sea of Cortez. The Northern Pacific exhibit includes sea otters; puffins and other diving birds; and giant spider crabs, octopuses, and sea

Long Beach Aquarium of the Pacific. *Photo courtesy of AOCVCB* stars. The largest tank is devoted to the Tropical Pacific, including the dazzling Palauan living coral lagoon and the barrier reef of Micronesia.

The Long Beach Aquarium of the Pacific is located at 200 South Shoreline Drive, Queensway Bay, off the Aquarium Way exit of Interstate 710. Admission: adults, $18.95; seniors (60 and older), $16.95; children (3–11), $10.95. Behind-the-scenes tour and admission: adults, $29.95; seniors (60 and older), $28.95; children (7–11), $22.95. Parking $6.00. Open daily from 9:00 A.M. to 6:00 P.M. For information, call (562) 590–3100 or consult www.aquariumofpacific.org.

▊MUST-SEE▊ THE *QUEEN MARY*

The *Queen Mary* is a most unusual floating museum and an unusual place to spend the night, a well-preserved relic of the grand era of transatlantic ocean liners. Tours of the vessel take visitors from the keel to the upper decks with stops at the engine room, luxury staterooms, spectacular dining rooms, and the bridge.

The self-guided tour gives access to the many public rooms of the ship, as well as the engine room and the upper deck, including the bridge. The behind-the-scenes tour adds visits to the first-class salon and dining room, a luxury stateroom, the boiler rooms, and more; it is worth the extra charge.

Moored alongside the liner is the retired Russian submarine *Scorpion,* also open for tours.

The *Queen Mary* is an easy twenty- to thirty-minute drive from Anaheim, although traffic jams during L.A.'s rush hours—which sometimes seem to extend all day—can double the commute. You will see the big ship as you drive alongside the harbor across from the City of Long Beach.

The *Queen Mary* and the Foxtrot submarine are open daily from 10:00 A.M., closing at 5:00 P.M. Friday through Sunday and half an hour earlier the rest of the week. For information, call (562) 435–3511 or consult www.queenmary.com.

At her height the *Queen Mary* was the queen of the Atlantic, a floating palace of elegance, grace, and power. At her creation, she was unlike anything ever seen on the sea, a combination of engineering, craftsmanship, and artistry.

The *Queen Mary* began life as the glamorous solution to a difficult problem facing Cunard, the leading steamship company of its time. Cunard had lost many of its best vessels during World War I and faced competition unlike anything it had seen before. The company decided to create two ships that would be bigger and faster than any ocean liner in existence, two ships that would do the work of three.

Designing the plans for the ships took two years, with revolutionary solutions in hull shape, propeller design, and power plant. Each of the four steam turbines generated 40,000 horsepower, making the ship the fastest ever made.

If the *Queen Mary* were in service today, she would still be one of the fastest ships afloat, capable of a top speed of up to thirty-six knots, equivalent to about forty miles per hour. The speed came at some expense, though; at full cruising speed, the *Queen Mary* got 13 feet per gallon of fuel.

Queen Mary Tickets

Prices were in effect in 2005 and are subject to change.

	ADULT	CHILD (5–11)	SENIOR
GENERAL ADMISSION PASSPORT	$23.00	$12.00	$20.00
Behind-the-Scenes Guided Tour (plus admission passport)	$5.00	$3.00	—
ADVENTURE PASSPORT (general admission plus *Scorpion*)	$31.00	$20.00	$28.00
SCORPION SUBMARINE	$10.00	$9.00	$9.00

Parking: $8.00

When completed the *Queen Mary* was a bit more than 1,019 feet in length, with the showcase Promenade Deck stretching 724 feet; there were twelve decks in all. The hull's draft was nearly 40 feet, and the ship weighed 81,237 gross tons with hull plates from 8 to 30 feet in length and up to 1¼ inches thick. The hull was held together with more than ten million rivets; there were more than 2,000 portholes.

The ship's rudder weighed 140 tons. There were two 18-foot-tall anchors at the bow, each weighing sixteen tons; the 900-foot anchor chain added forty-five tons, with each 2-foot-long link weighing 224 pounds. The *Queen Mary* could hold 1,957 passengers, plus 1,174 officers and crew members.

Air conditioning was a new art at the time the ship was constructed, and only three rooms on the *Queen Mary* were cooled: the first-class dining room, the ballroom, and the ship's kennel.

Finally, in 1934, Cunard was ready to launch the greatest, most luxurious ocean liner ever built. Queen Mary herself pressed the launch button to release her floating namesake into the River Clyde. It took two more years to outfit her as a passenger vessel.

In May 1936 with her three massive, one-ton steam whistles blasting, the *Queen Mary* embarked on her maiden voyage to New York with nearly 2,000 passengers and a crew of almost 1,200 aboard. She received a spectacular greeting as she steamed up the Hudson River, including an airborne drop of thousands of white carnations.

In 1939 a round-trip first-class ticket sold for about $2,000, which was a lot of money back then; third-class passage was a pricey $500.

Dining aboard the *Queen Mary* was an event. All 800 first-class passengers could be served at once in the largest room ever built within a ship. The wine cellar on board contained more than 15,000 bottles, rivaling the finest restaurants in Europe.

The ship's engines were improved in 1938, allowing her to cross the Atlantic in just under four days, a world record that she held for fourteen years.

By the summer of 1939 the *Queen Mary* was an unqualified success. In

Queen Mary at her pier in Long Beach. *Photo by Corey Sandler*

September of that same year her first career was abruptly halted when Great Britain was drawn into war with Germany. The *Queen Mary* was conscripted into the war effort for use as a troop carrier.

Camouflaged with gray paint and capable of evading warships and even out-maneuvering torpedoes, the *Queen Mary* became known as the Gray Ghost. Berths were stacked up to six high, with troops sleeping in shifts during the five-day crossing. Sleeping accommodations were set up in drawing rooms, in lounges, and even within drained swimming pools. Five double-barreled cannons were installed, and 20-mm guns lined the upper decks; four sets of antiaircraft rocket launchers were installed. The guns, though, were never fired in anger.

On one memorable voyage, some 16,000 troops and crew were shoehorned into every corner of the vessel. No ship before or since has carried so many. Special assignments included transporting British prime minister Winston Churchill three times to conferences. Churchill approved the D-day invasion plans aboard the ship. During the course of the war, Adolf Hitler put a $250,000 bounty on the ship and offered Germany's highest military honor to the captain who could sink her.

By the end of her war service the *Queen Mary* had carried more than 800,000 troops, had traveled more than 600,000 miles, and had played a part in every major Allied campaign of World War II. She was also used to carry German and Italian prisoners of war to camps in North America.

At the end of the war the *Queen Mary* was fitted out as a floating hospital with surgical and intensive-care units to bring home the wounded. She later carried many returning troops and their war brides.

Regular passenger service resumed on July 31, 1947. After completing 1,001 crossings of the Atlantic, the *Queen Mary* retired from regular passenger service on September 19, 1967; she made one "Last Great Cruise" from October 31 to December 9, 1967, pulling into port for the last time at Long Beach. The RMS Foundation, which took over operation of the *Queen Mary* in 1993, signed a new twenty-year lease in 1996, and the ship was added to the National Register of Historic Places, so the Queen may have found her retirement home.

Among the interesting stops on the guided tour is the first-class lounge, an extraordinary room paneled with rare woods collected from around the world— some are from species no longer available.

On the wall of the first-class dining room is a huge mural showing the North Atlantic from England to the United States. Two tracks, occupied by small glass ships, mark the progress of the *Queen Mary* and her sister ship the *Queen Elizabeth;* at the peak of Cunard's history, the two ships crossed the Atlantic weekly on opposite schedules, passing in midocean.

■ A *TITANIC* COMPARISON

The *Queen Mary* was longer, wider, taller, and faster than the *Titanic.* And as her current owners point out with a straight face, the *Queen Mary* made 1,001 transatlantic crossings while the *Titanic* made, well, half a crossing.

Here are some of the statistics on the two ships:

	Queen Mary	*Titanic*
Length	1,019 feet	883 feet
Breadth	118 feet	93 feet
Height	181 feet	175 feet
Tonnage	81,237 gross tons	46,329 gross tons
Decks	12	8
Cruising speed	28.5 knots	21 knots

■ ART OF THE *QUEEN MARY*

Among the sometimes overlooked treasures of the *Queen Mary* are her works of art. Many of the original art pieces, including the huge murals and decorations of the principal public rooms, many smaller works of art, and decorative items are located throughout the ship in areas where the public does not usually visit.

In 1995 the ship opened a permanent exhibition of some of the art pieces in her own gallery on the *Queen Mary*'s Promenade Deck, immediately forward of the Queen's Salon.

Featured in the gallery are Dame Laura Knight's *The Mills Circus* from one of the first-class private dining rooms; S. Nicholson Babb's *Jupiter and Europa,* and Gilbert Bayes's *The Sea King's Daughter,* both bronze figure groups borrowed from the corner niches of the Queen's Salon. Kenneth Shoesmith's *Madonna of the Atlantic,* originally the altar piece for the Roman Catholic chapel, and Walter and Donald Gilbert's bronze doors, which originally adorned side entrances of the first-class restaurant, are also included.

■ RESTAURANTS AT THE *QUEEN MARY*

Sir Winston's. The *Queen Mary*'s most elegant restaurant offers a spectacular view of the coastline from the upper deck, with dinner served from 5:30 to 10:00 P.M. Specialties in the range of $18 to $36 include Swordfish Filet Nicoise and Beef Phylo Sir Winston's. For reservations, call (562) 435–3511.

Chelsea. A seafood eatery with a view of the sea. Specialties in the range of $14 to $24 include Lobster Pappardelle (rainbow pappardelle pasta with lobster tail and spinach in roasted bell pepper sauce) and Seafood Phylo. Open Wednesday to Sunday from 5:30 to 10:00 P.M. For reservations, call (562) 435–3511.

Promenade Cafe. Open for breakfast, lunch, and dinner, from 6:30 A.M. to 10:00 P.M. Specialties priced from about $8.00 to $20.00 include chicken linguine and blackened halibut. Salads and pasta dishes are also available.

Sunday Champagne Brunch in the Grand Salon. A buffet featuring food from around the globe with more than fifty entrees, including a special island for children. The Grand Salon is the former first-class dining room of the ship. Served from 9:30 A.M. until 2:00 P.M. Adults, $35; children (4–11), $12. For reservations, call (562) 499–1606.

Observation Bar. Evening entertainment, cocktails, and dancing in the original first-class bar, an Art Deco masterpiece. Open nightly.

■ THE HOTEL *QUEEN MARY*

The Hotel *Queen Mary* today offers 365 first-class cabins for rent at rates as low as $109 per night for a standard inside cabin without a porthole to $660 per night for a royalty suite. Guests who stay overnight can stroll the promenade deck, visit restaurants, and explore many of the self-guided tour areas of the ship. We stayed aboard the ship on a recent visit, using nearby Long Beach Airport as a convenient point of departure for an early morning flight. We marveled at the echoes of history in the public rooms, the hallways, and our small cabin.

One of the rooms is the Duke of Edinburgh Room, a luxury suite that was occupied by the Duke and Duchess of Windsor, Winston Churchill, and comic actors Laurel and Hardy, among others.

LONG BEACH CRUISE TERMINAL

Carnival Cruise Lines' new cruise-ship terminal opened alongside the *Queen Mary* in Long Beach in 2003. The single berth in San Pedro Bay is large enough to accommodate vessels as large as of one of the line's mammoth 102,000-ton "Destiny" class ships. Nearby is a parking garage with spaces for more than 1,450 vehicles.

The terminal will be used by many of the company's ships. In September of 2004, the line's 2,052-passenger *Paradise* began offering three- and four-day cruises to Baja, Mexico, from Long Beach. The shorter trips visit Ensenada, Mexico, while the four-day itinerary also adds a stop at Catalina Island.

Carnival is also the parent company for Costa Cruises, Cunard Line, Holland

America Line, Princess Cruises, Seabourn, and Windstar, and vessels from those fleets may also call at Long Beach.

Debarkation for passengers returning to Long Beach after a voyage takes place within a portion of the dome at the *Queen Mary*. Originally constructed in 1983 to house Howard Hughes's gigantic *Spruce Goose* seaplane, the dome is the world's largest clear-span dome. The structure closed in 1992 when the plane was given to a museum in Oregon.

The facility has been used as a motion-picture soundstage; it was home of the Batcave in *Batman Forever,* and was used in *Stargate, The Cable Guy,* and *The Haunting.*

NEWPORT BEACH

Orange County Museum of Art. 850 San Clemente Drive, Newport Harbor. Contemporary paintings, sculpture, and photography. Open from 11:00 A.M. to 5:00 P.M.; closed Monday, major holidays, and between major exhibitions. Adults, $7.00; seniors and students, $5.00. For information, call (949) 759–1122 or consult www.ocma.net.

Newport Harbor Cruise. 400 Main Street, Newport Harbor. Harbor cruises from the Balboa Pavilion. Open daily except Christmas. Tickets $7.00 to $10.00. For information, call (949) 673–0240 or consult www.funzoneboats.com.

BALBOA ISLAND

Balboa Island in Newport Harbor is an old-style amusement zone that includes the Balboa Pavilion, built in 1905 and restored to its former glory. Nearby is a Ferris wheel, bumper cars, arcade games, and fast-food stands.

A ferry costing 25 cents per pedestrian runs from the end of Palm Street on the Balboa Peninsula, twenty-four hours a day in the summer and all day for the rest of the year.

From Balboa Island you can take harbor cruises, including one on board a replica of a Mississippi River riverboat, or a more traditional boat. For information, call (949) 673–5245 or (949) 673–0240. For information on the island, consult www.balboa-island.com.

CATALINA ISLAND

About 27 miles off the coast and a world away, Catalina Island was a pirate and smuggler's outpost after its discovery in 1542 by Juan Rodríguez Cabrillo. The original occupants of the island were Gabrieleno Indians, who were wiped out by various later arrivals, including Russian seal hunters. The island was bought and sold by several wealthy Californians until it came into the hands of the

Wrigley (as in chewing gum) family. William Wrigley Jr. built the famous circular casino in 1929, and the modern era of the island as a tourist destination began.

Current residents of the island include a herd of free-running buffalo. The original animals were brought over to the island for the filming of a Hollywood movie, *The Vanishing American*; the beasts have flourished ever since.

You can travel to the island by ferry (about one to two hours) or by small plane (a twenty-minute hop). The 8-mile-wide, 21-mile-long island offers spectacular beaches. The principal settlement on the island is Avalon, which includes the famous casino; another port is located at Two Harbors. Nearly all of the island is owned by the Santa Catalina Island Conservancy and will be preserved as forever wild.

Cars may not be brought to the island, but bicycles and golf carts can be rented in Avalon. For information about Catalina Island, consult www.catalina.com.

■ ATTRACTIONS ON CATALINA ISLAND

Visitors come here to hike, ride horses, scuba dive, play golf, sportfish, or explore the Mediterranean charm of Avalon, which is home to numerous shops, hotels, restaurants, and cafes.

The **Avalon Casino,** constructed at a cost of $2 million at a time when a dollar was worth, well, a dollar, houses a charming ballroom still used for big-band concerts; an art gallery; and the Catalina Island Museum, where fossils, Native American artifacts, and natural history exhibits are on display. The museum is open daily, from 10:30 A.M. to 4:00 P.M.

Beyond Avalon, Catalina's 42,000-acre interior is a designated nature preserve with unique plants and animals. Developed campsites, cabins, and primitive camping areas are available.

There are numerous services, including tours and taxi (by land and sea) on the island. An intriguing attraction is the **Starlight** and **Emerald** semi-submersible vessels. Not quite submarines, they are tour boats with a basement. Passengers sit in a cabin beneath the sea level with a panoramic view of the waters and marine life around Catalina Island. Admission: adults, $33.25; seniors, $30.00; children, $16.75. Tickets are available at Discovery Tours outlets on the island.

■ BOAT SERVICE TO CATALINA

Catalina Express. San Pedro, Long Beach, and Dana Point to Avalon. San Pedro to Two Harbors. Round-trip tickets: adults, $49.00 to $51.00; children (2–11), $37.50 to $39.00. For information, call (800) 481–3470 or consult www .catalinaexpress.com.

Catalina Passenger Service. Fast catamaran ferry service on the 500-passenger *Catalina Flyer* from Balboa Pavilion in Newport Beach, about a seventy-five-minute trip. Round-trip tickets $44. For information, call (949) 673–5245 or consult www.catalinainfo.com.

■ AIRLINE SERVICE

Island Express Helicopter Service. Fifteen-minute flights from Long Beach and San Pedro Ferry Terminals to Catalina. Round-trip tickets are $140. (310) 510–2525 or (800) 228–2566. www.islandexpress.com.

Island Hopper Catalina Airlines. San Diego to Avalon. (858) 279–4595.

■ HOTELS ON CATALINA

Hotels and standard accommodations on Catalina generally range from about $50 to $200 per night with more expensive luxury rooms and condos also available. Fans of the Old West might want to consider staying at the Zane Grey Pueblo Hotel, the 1926 "pueblo" home of author Zane Grey. Because Catalina is an island, it is generally very important that you have a reservation.

Write to the Catalina Chamber of Commerce, P.O. Box 217, Avalon, CA 90704, for a copy of the visitor's guide, or call the Visitors Information Bureau at (310) 510–1520 for accommodation information.

■ CAMPING ON CATALINA

For hiking and biking permits, call the Catalina Island Conservancy office in Avalon at (310) 510–2595. Reservations by mail, fax, or Internet. Consult www.catalina.com.

You can also obtain information and reservations for camping through the Santa Catalina Company at (888) 510–7979 or by consulting www.scico.com.

Hermit Gulch Campground. Avalon. Nearby to Wrigley Memorial and Botanical Garden and hiking trails; about 1.5 miles up Avalon Canyon. For information, call (800) 322–3434 or consult www.scico.com/camping/camp_hermit_gulch.html.

Two Harbors Campground. Seaside camping. Tents and camping gear available for rent. For reservations, call (310) 510–2800 or (800) 322–3434 or consult www.scico.com/camping/camp_two_harbors.html.

Little Harbor is southeast of Two Harbors, in a protected cove with a sandy beach 17 miles from Avalon, and 7 miles from Two Harbors; it is very popular with youth groups. For information, call (310) 510–2800 or (800) 322–3434 or consult www.scico.com/camping/camp_little_harbor.html.

Parsons Landing is a remote site on the northwest shore accessible by a 7-mile trail from Two Harbors or by boat. For information or reservations, call (310) 510–2800 or (800) 322–3434 or consult www.scico.com/camping/camp_parsons.html.

Blackjack is in a grove of pine trees on 1,600-foot Blackjack Mountain in the center of the island, a 10-mile hike to Avalon or Two Harbors. For reservations, call (310) 510–2800 or (800) 322–3434 or consult www.scico.com/camping/camp_blackjack.html.

Ten undeveloped coves on the coastline, accessible only by boat, include **Frog Rock Cove, Willow Cove, Italian Gardens, Goat Harbor, Gibraltar Point Beach, Lava Wall Beach, Paradise Cove, Rippers Cove, Starlight Beach,** and **East Starlight Beach.** For information, consult www.campingcatalinaisland.com.

MISSION SAN JUAN CAPISTRANO

The Mission at San Juan Capistrano is a place of quiet beauty, as old and redolent of history as any place in California. The mission was founded by Father Junipero Serra, a Spanish Franciscan priest, on November 1, 1776—four months after the Declaration of Independence of the original thirteen colonies on the other side of the still-wild American continent. It was the seventh in a chain of twenty-one California missions.

Constructed of adobe (mud and straw), many of the early missions have fallen apart; San Juan Capistrano and several others were restored around 1900. Today the Mission San Juan Capistrano's chapel is the oldest building in California still in use. Fund-raising for a $20 million restoration project is now under way.

The native Americans who greeted Father Serra were the Acagchemem, a peaceful tribe; the Spanish renamed them the Juaneno. Some descendants of the Juaneno work at the mission today.

In 1821 the newly independent Mexican government took over California and forced the Spanish padres to leave; the mission was sold and the Indians evicted. After the Americans were victorious in the Mexican-American war in 1850, California came under dominion of the United States. In 1865 President Lincoln gave some of the California missions back to the church.

On the grounds of the mission is the remains of an old stone church, which was destroyed by an earthquake in 1812, an event that killed forty Indians who were in the church at the time. You'll be able to visit a number of rooms of the mission, restored as a museum. There's also a display about Native Americans, an archaeological field office, and even an homage to the swallows.

Today the place may be best known for the celebration of the miraculous return of thousands of swallows to the mission each March 19, on St. Joseph's Day. (Of course, some also come on March 18 and March 20, but there's no party for them.) The locals have a parade and other events on March 19; by the way, the sparrows traditionally pack their bags and fly south on October 23.

Those square-tailed cliff swallows traditionally come to southern California in March to nest; they return to their homes in Argentina, 6,000 miles away, in October. The oldest recordings of the migration of the swallows date to the late 1700s; however, there is evidence that the birds had been regular visitors well before then, nesting in the silt stone cliffs near the ocean.

To their credit the modern-day keepers of the mission do not make the claim that the swallows magically reappear on exactly March 19. A few "scouts" often arrive ahead of time. The arrival date of the main flock may vary from year to year because northward migration is affected by the weather's influence on available insect food as the birds travel. They move northward when the temperature warms up to about forty-eight degrees.

The mission is open daily from 8:30 A.M. to 5:00 P.M., except for Thanksgiving, Christmas, New Year's Day, and Good Friday afternoon. Admission: adults, $6.00; seniors, $5.00; children (3–12), $4.00. For information, call (949) 248–2049 or consult www.missionsjc.com.

CHAPTER TWENTY

WESTERN BEACH COMMUNITIES FROM SANTA BARBARA TO MALIBU AND SANTA MONICA

SANTA BARBARA

Located 92 miles north of Los Angeles, Santa Barbara is one of the oldest settlements in California. In 1542 explorer Juan Cabrillo entered the channel and claimed the region for Spain. He was greeted by the true discoverers of the area, the Chumash Indians, who lived in small villages along the Santa Barbara coast and the Channel Islands.

Sixty years later three Spanish frigates under the command of Sebastian Vizcaíno arrived in the channel after surviving a fierce ocean storm. A Carmelite friar on board one of the ships named the area after that day's saint, Barbara. It wasn't until 1782, though—after the birth of the United States on the other side of the continent—that Spain established a permanent presence in the area led by Father Junipero Serra, Captain Jose Ortega, and Governor Felipe de Neve.

The Spanish governed the area until 1822 when California became a territory of Mexico; in 1846 Santa Barbara was taken for the United States by Colonel John Fremont.

Santa Barbara was one of the leading film capitals of the world when the American Film Company opened its Flying A Studio around 1910 in what is now downtown. The studio made more than 1,200 silent pictures, mostly westerns, over a ten-year period before moviemaking's center moved south to Los Angeles.

Santa Barbara Airport, 8 miles north of downtown, is served by America West, American Eagle, Delta Connection, and United Airlines. For information on the airport, call (805) 967–7111 or consult www.flysba.com.

Arlington Theatre. Home to Santa Barbara's performing arts center, it was built in the 1930s as a grand motion picture palace. It includes a Spanish village in the lobby and a curved ceiling painted with stars. The facility is located at 1317 State Street. For information, call (805) 963–4408.

Botanic Garden. A public garden devoted to the display and study of California's native flora. Five miles of trails pass through re-creations of the deserts, the Sierra Nevadas, and the offshore islands. Open daily from 9:00 A.M. to 5:00 P.M. from spring through fall; in the winter open until 4:00 P.M. weekdays and until 5:00 P.M. weekends. Guided tours weekdays at 2:00 P.M., weekends at 11:00 A.M. and 2:00 P.M. The garden is located at 1212 Mission Canyon Road. Admission: adults, $7.00; seniors (60 and older), $5.00; students and teens (13–17), $4.00; children (5–12), $1.00. For information, call (805) 682–4726 or consult www.sbbg.org/index.cfm?.

Carriage Museum. An unusual collection of horse-drawn carts and carriages used by pioneers and early settlers. The vehicles include stagecoaches, buggies, firefighting equipment, and an antique hearse. Some of the carriages take to the streets of Santa Barbara each August during the Old Spanish Days parade. Located at 129 Castillo Street, the museum is open daily from 9:00 A.M. to 3:00 P.M.; on Sunday, the exhibit is open from 2:00 to 4:00 P.M.; closed Saturday. Admission: free, but donations are accepted. For information, call (805) 962–2353 or consult www.sbceo.k12.ca.us/~crane/carriage.

El Paseo. Within the area of State, De la Guerra, and Anacapa Streets, a historic Spanish-style shopping arcade was built around a 1920s residence. The arcade includes specialty shops, art galleries, and restaurants. For information, consult www.santabarbara.com/community/shopping/el_paseo.

El Presidio de Santa Barbara State Historic Park. Founded in 1782, the Presidio includes part of the original Presidio Real, the last Spanish military outpost in California. Among the restored buildings are the Presidio Chapel, the Padre's and Commandant's Quarters, and El Cuartel, the guard's house. El Cuartel, built in 1788, is the oldest building in Santa Barbara and the second oldest in California. Located at 123 East Canon Perdido Street. For information and hours, call (805) 965–0093 or consult www.parks.ca.gov/default.asp?page_id=608.

Mission Santa Barbara. Established in 1786 by Spanish Franciscans, it was the tenth of the California missions. The buildings were severely damaged in earthquakes in 1812 and again in 1925 but have been rebuilt. The mission continues as a Roman Catholic parish church and is open to the public for self-guided tours that include a museum, gardens, and the chapel. Located at 2201 Laguna Street, the mission is open daily from 9:00 A.M. to 5:00 P.M. Admission: adults, $4.00; free to children younger than 12. For information, call (805) 682–4149 or consult www.sbmission.org.

Santa Barbara County Courthouse. A stunning Spanish-Moorish building completed in 1929, it is worth a visit for a peek at its ornate interior and to make a climb up the 80-foot clock tower for a panoramic view of the city. An information booth is located in the lobby near the main archway. The booth is open from 8:30 A.M. to 4:30 P.M. weekdays and from 10:00 A.M. to 4:30 P.M. on weekends. Free docent tours are conducted at 2:00 P.M. daily except Sunday. Additional tours are conducted at 10:30 A.M. on Monday, Tuesday, and Friday. For information, call (805) 962–6464. The courthouse is located on Anacapa Street, between Anapamu and Figueroa Streets. Admission: free.

Santa Barbara Historical Museum. A broad collection of regional history, including artifacts, books, maps, and photographs from the Spanish exploration, the Wild West, and the settlement of California. Nearby the museum are two nineteenth-century adobes, including the Casa de Covarrubias at 715 Santa Barbara Street, built in 1817. Located at 136 East de la Guerra Street, the musuem is open Tuesday through Saturday from 10:00 A.M. to 5:00 P.M. and Sunday from noon to 5:00 P.M. Donations accepted. For information, call (508) 966–1601 or consult www.santabarbaramuseum.com.

MALIBU

The Chumash Indians called this place by a word meaning "where the mountains meet the sea." Taken first by the Spanish, Malibu was then bought by a Frenchman named Leon Victor Prudhomme, who sold off the land at 10 cents per acre in 1857. Today, of course, the land is worth hundreds of thousands or even more per acre.

The view of the beach is blocked in many areas by private homes. Malibu Surfrider State Beach is reserved for wave riders, but it's worth a peek for any visitors. For information, consult www.malibu.org.

SANTA MONICA

Portuguese explorer Juan Rodríguez Cabrillo discovered the broad bay that today runs from about Malibu to Redondo Beach in 1542 as part of a journey that included the first European visits to the Santa Barbara Islands and San Diego.

First named "Bay of Smokes" because of the rising smoke from Indian campfires in the area, it was later renamed as Santa Monica to honor the mother of fourth-century Saint Augustine.

The town became an important area in the 1870s with the arrival of a railroad line from Los Angeles; developers sold off small lots for beach cottages. With the growth of Hollywood, many movie stars built homes there. For information, consult www.santamonica.com.

The famous **Santa Monica Pier** (which includes the carousel used in the movie *The Sting*) is worth a visit, as are the many shopping and dining areas. For information, consult www.santamonicapier.org.

VENICE

Developer Abbott Kinney dreamed of a spectacular town in 1904 near the growing community of Santa Monica. It was to be an American re-creation of Venice.

He built a system of canals, spectacular beach pavilions, a huge amusement park, and other facilities, and the resort enjoyed a brief success before economic problems and competition from other communities brought it into decline.

In the 1950s Venice became a center of the beatnik culture. Today a few of the original canals and some of the buildings remain, and it has become a fashionable area once again. It is well known for its large artists' colony, and the boardwalk is one of the world capitals of weirdness. For information, consult www.venicebeach.com.

MARINA DEL REY

A large man-made harbor usually jammed with thousands of pleasure boats. Tours of the harbor and rental boats are available. **Fisherman's Village** in Marina del Rey, at 13755 Fiji Way, is a replica of a New England town with shops and restaurants, open daily. For information, call (310) 823–5411 or consult www.marinadelrey.com.

REDONDO BEACH

Railroad magnate Henry Huntington added to his fortune by selling lots next to the new railroad system. California's first serious surfers discovered the beach about 1907, and their descendants still rise early to catch the best waves. Today the area has a spectacular marina at King Harbor.

Redondo Beach is a local center for whale-, porpoise-, and seal-watching in King Harbor from December to April. California gray whales migrate south each year from the Arctic Circle to the warm-water lagoons of Baja California, Mexico. For information, consult www.visitredondo.com.

Redondo Beach Pier is a favorite dining, shopping, and amusement spot and a popular sport-fishing pier for visitors, located at the west end of Torrance Boulevard. For information, call (310) 374–2171 or (310) 374–3481.

Seaside Lagoon, at Harbor Drive and Portofino Way, has a heated saltwater pool, a beach, and volleyball courts. For information, call (310) 318–0681.

HEARST CASTLE, SAN SIMEON

William Randolph Hearst built his ultimate monument on a hilltop in the Santa Lucia Mountains overlooking the Pacific Ocean. An army of craftsmen labored for nearly twenty-eight years on the castle and guest cottages with 165 rooms and 127 acres of gardens, pools, and terraces. Inside the buildings is a jaw-dropping collection of Spanish and Italian antiques. Hearst Castle, now a state historical monument, is in San Simeon, about midway between Los Angeles and San Francisco, a six-hour drive from either city.

There are four daytime tours, each lasting just under two hours; all include the spectacular Neptune outdoor and the Roman indoor pools. Tour 1 includes the Casa Grande main house and the Casa del Sol guest cottage. The upper floors of Casa Grande are included in Tour 2. Guests on Tour 3 visit the Casa del Monte guest cottage and the north wing of Casa Grande. Tour 4, offered April through October, includes the Hidden Terrace and the exterior gardens and grounds as well as the Casa del Mar, the largest and most elaborate of the guest cottages, overlooking the Pacific Ocean.

The evening tour, offered in the spring and fall, includes docents in period dress appearing as Hearst's guests and domestic staff and a tour of Casa Grande, Casa del Mar, and the pools and gardens by night.

The Hearst San Simeon State Historical Monument, which includes Hearst Castle, is open for tours daily except Thanksgiving, Christmas, and New Year's Day. Reservations are recommended for tours. In peak season, from May 15 through September 15, tickets are $24 for adults and $12 for children (6–17). For the remainder of the year, adult tickets are $20 and child tickets $10. Year-round evening tours cost $30 for adults and $15 for children. Call (800) 444–4445 to purchase tickets or consult www.hearstcastle.org.

CHAPTER TWENTY-ONE

ORANGE COUNTY ATTRACTIONS

MOVIELAND WAX MUSEUM

The perfect stars: handsome, well-dressed, and completely amenable to any pose, role, or setting. They won't sign autographs, though: They're made of wax.

Movieland is the home of more than 400 wax likenesses that have been seen by millions during the past three decades. The museum is exclusively dedicated to the entertainment industry and surrounds the wax figures with re-creations of famous movie sets.

Movieland Wax Museum. *Photo courtesy of AOCVCB*

Here are some things we saw on a visit:

■ Elizabeth Taylor as Queen of the Nile in *Cleopatra*. The wax figure was sculpted from a mask of Taylor, and the gown is an exact copy from the movie.

■ A scene from the remake of *Perry Mason*, with defense attorney Raymond Burr grilling O. J. Simpson on the witness stand.

■ Abbott and Costello in baseball uniforms performing their famous "Who's on First?" routine.

■ John Wayne in a scene from the film *Hondo*, with costar Lassie.

■ A Chamber of Horrors including scenes from *The Exorcist*, *Psycho*, and *Friday the 13th*.

A full tour of the museum can take two hours. The museum, located at 7711 Beach

Boulevard in Buena Park, one block north of Knott's Berry Farm off the Santa Ana (Interstate 5) and (U.S. Highway 91) Freeways, is open every day of the year.

Tickets: adults, $12.95; children (4–11), $6.95; Combination tickets are also available with Ripley's Believe It or Not! Museum: adults, $16.90; children, $9.75. For information, call (714) 522–1155 or consult www.movielandwaxmuseum .com.

RIPLEY'S BELIEVE IT OR NOT! MUSEUM

Here are some of the things we saw:
- A dead bird in a glass container that was killed by a golf ball in flight at the Coombe and Hill Golf Club in New York in 1920.
- A lifelike statue of the Lighthouse Man of Chungking, China, who once guided American military dignitaries through the streets by the light of a 7-inch candle inserted into a hole in the top of his head.
- Something to inspire every American homemaker: a large drawing made up entirely from lint, and a version of *The Last Supper* made from 280 slices of carefully toasted white bread.
- A man who smoked through his eyes, and a talented chap who could inflate a balloon through his ear.

Robert L. Ripley was born in 1893 in Santa Rosa, California. He began his newspaper career at the age of sixteen. On December 19, 1918, while working as a sports cartoonist at the *New York Globe* and at a loss for an idea, Ripley gathered together a few sports oddities that happened to be on his desk, made them into a cartoon, and captioned them "Believe It or Not."

The museum is located at 7850 Beach Boulevard in Buena Park, just north of Knott's Berry Farm and across the street from its sister museum, the Movieland Wax Museum. Admission: adults, $8.95; children (4–11), $5.25. Combination tickets are also available with Movieland. For information, call (714) 522–1152 or consult www.ripleysbuenapark.com.

MEDIEVAL TIMES

An eleventh-century medieval banquet, complete with jousting knights, fair damsels in distress, and horseback entertainment. A typical menu includes soup, whole roasted chicken, spare ribs, herb-basted potatoes, and beer or soft drinks. They didn't use silverware back then, so neither will guests today. There are more than 1,100 seats, often filled with raucous visitors.

The theater is located at 7662 Beach Boulevard in Buena Park, across from Movieland Wax Museum and up the road from Knott's Berry Farm. Performances nightly. Admission: adult, $47.94; children (12 and younger), $33.95. Look for discounts in flyers and online. For information, call (714) 523–4740 or (888) 935–6878 or consult www.medievaltimes.com.

PART X

SAN DIEGO ATTRACTIONS

CHAPTER TWENTY-TWO

SAN DIEGO: SEAWORLD AND SAN DIEGO ZOO

THERE'S A LOT TO LIKE in San Diego: This sunny outpost near California's border with Mexico has more than a little bit of everything. There's beach and sand along the Pacific Ocean, the sprawling Anza-Borrego Desert to the east, and just a short drive outside of downtown is heavily wooded alpine country where the mountain peaks are often dusted with snow in winter.

In addition to its natural wonders, San Diego boasts of two world-class attractions: SeaWorld California and the San Diego Zoo.

SEAWORLD CALIFORNIA

SeaWorld likes to quote the African environmentalist Baba Dioum: "For in the end, we will conserve only what we love, we will love only what we understand, and we will understand only what we are taught."

SeaWorld California is a 166-acre marine life and entertainment park on San Diego's Mission Bay, 100 miles south of Anaheim and about a two-hour drive from the Disneyland area.

Opening and closing times vary by season. Hours are extended during holiday periods and summer nights from mid-June through Labor Day. Call (800) 380–3203 or (619) 226–3901 for current hours or consult www.seaworld.com.

From north or south, exit Interstate 5 at SeaWorld Drive. From the east, exit Interstate 8, to I–5 north to SeaWorld Drive west.

■ AROUND SEAWORLD

The fairly recent addition of R. L. Stine's *Haunted Lighthouse* is a spooky, twenty-two-minute adventure film that combines 3-D visual technology with special theatrical effects for an exciting "4-D" experience. Based on an original story by

SeaWorld Tickets

Prices were in effect in 2005 and are subject to change. Admission includes all shows, exhibits, and attractions except SeaWorld's Skytower and Mission Bay Skyride.

	ADULT	CHILD (ages 3 to 9)	CHILD (younger than age 3)
ONE-DAY TICKET	$46.95	$37.95	Free
DELUXE ADMISSION Two days, plus behind-the-scenes tour	$54.95	$44.95	Free
TWO-DAY ADVENTURE PASS Two consecutive days	$50.95	$41.95	Free
SOUTHERN CALIFORNIA VALUE PASS One entry to both SeaWorld San Diego and Universal Studios Hollywood for up to fourteen consecutive days.	$83.00	$63.00	Free
SOUTHERN CALIFORNIA ATTRACTIONS CITY PASS One entry each to SeaWorld, San Diego Zoo, Knott's Berry Farm, and Three-Day Disneyland Resort Park Hopper	$166.00	$127.00	Free

Parking: Cars $7.00, RVs $9.00

the popular *Goosebumps* author, the film stars veteran actors Christopher Lloyd, Lea Thompson, and "Weird Al" Yankovic, and was directed by Joe Dante, who also made *Gremlins*.

The story tells of two children vacationing with their family at a beach who meet a salty sailor who spins a tale of a haunted lighthouse. The adventure begins when a mysterious young boy leads the disbelieving children to the lighthouse.

The high-tech presentation uses four digital projectors; guests wear special glasses to allow 3-D visual effects to pop off the screen. Surround-sound speakers are built into the seats, which also include tactile and sensory effects in the seat backs and frames.

The creators of the film researched more than sixty lighthouses in North America in the quest for a filming location. In the end the qualities of multiple lighthouses were combined, and a lighthouse set was built on a soundstage in Culver City, California. Beach scenes were filmed at Point Dume State Preserve's Zuma Beach in California.

The hallmark ***Shamu Adventure,*** narrated by TV personality and animal expert Jack Hanna, highlights spectacular natural behaviors of killer whales, starring Shamu, Baby Shamu, and Namu. An interactive Web page dedicated to the show is at www.shamu.com.

At **Shamu Close Up,** guests can interact with killer whales. Depending on

SeaWorld California San Diego. *Photo courtesy of AOCVCB*

special activities, visitors may be able to experiment with hand and sound sig-nals for the whales, and watch training and feeding activities. A 70-foot-long acrylic wall allows guests to view the whales from beneath the surface of the water.

Manatee Rescue is the only place in the country outside of Florida displaying the endangered West Indian manatee. Several rescued and rehabilitated animals live within the containment, which has a large glass viewing port.

Sea lions and river otters are among the creatures in *Fools with Tools* at the Sea Lion and Otter Stadium.

The **Cirque de la Mer** show, presented in the summer season, is a strange journey to the mythical island of Amphibia where a variety of colorful amphib-ians—a hybrid of sea creatures and humans—possess superabilities, which they display in whimsical acrobatlike moves. Actors move across the water in a strange craft they call a *zorb*.

One of the hottest attractions at the park is a very cool place: **Wild Arctic,** a trip to the top of the world. Visitors board *White Thunder,* a jet helicopter sim-ulator that soars over the frozen landscape, offering breathtaking views of rocky glaciers and snowy ice floes; the craft barely escapes an avalanche by zooming into a narrow ice cave. We eventually land safely at Base Station Wild Arctic at the heart of the frozen North Pole.

We see the tools of the researchers who labor in the wreck of a 150-year-old exploration ship, the remnants of a failed expedition to find the Northwest

Passage. Part of the hull, upside down in the ice, forms a pool in the ice floes where beluga whales swim and play.

In another area, majestic walruses can be observed moving their snouts along the floor of the pool, using their vibrissae (whiskers) to search for food, and hauling it out onto ice floes using their powerful tusks. Behind a wall of ice is a stunning view of polar bears swimming below the surface of the water.

Rocky Point Preserve visitors get a true appreciation of the beauty of bottle-nosed dolphins and Alaska sea otters in their natural environment in this two-part attraction. Alaska sea otters, survivors of the 1989 Prince William Sound oil spill, are displayed in the natural rocky habitat. The dolphin habitat also includes a sophisticated wave pool.

Shipwreck Rapids takes castaways on a wet and wild journey in nine-passenger tubes through raging rapids; roaring waterfalls; a near-collision with a ship's propeller; and a dark, forbidding tunnel through the interior of a mysterious ship's engine room.

Shark Encounter presents the world's largest display of these fascinating animals. A submerged viewing tube allows SeaWorld guests to enter the sharks' habitat, a 700,000-gallon tank.

At **Forbidden Reef,** California moray eels and bat rays are displayed in one of SeaWorld's most popular displays. Visitors can touch and feed the graceful rays and enjoy underwater viewing of hundreds of moray eels.

The majority of SeaWorld's nearly 400 penguins live in the twenty-five-degree indoor display of **Penguin Encounter.** Featured nearby are auklets, puffins, and murres, the penguin's Northern Hemisphere cousins. An outdoor area houses Magellanic penguins, a temperate-zone species.

The **California Tide Pool** re-creates one of the ocean's richest environments, an intertidal zone. Guests are invited to roll up their sleeves and touch starfish and view sea urchins, sea cucumbers, California moray eels, spiny lobsters, and a variety of fishes.

The **Marine Aquarium** displays hundreds of fish and marine invertebrates from oceans throughout the world. Marine species as exotic as the lionfish and chambered nautilus live in re-creations of their natural habitats. Fish from freshwater habitats in Africa, Asia, and the Amazon River Basin are at the Freshwater Aquarium. The archerfish, capable of downing insects perched on branches overhead using bullets of water, is among the species on exhibit.

Shamu's **Happy Harbor** is a two-acre dream world for children of all ages, but especially adventuresome youngsters. Happy Harbor is like any other playground, although much more so. There are more than twenty places to explore, crawl, slide, jump, bounce, climb, and get wet.

The **Skytower** is a 320-foot-tall structure offering a panoramic view of San Diego's Mission Bay, skyline, foothills, bays, beaches, and the Pacific Ocean in a fifty-seven-seat cabin. Enclosed gondola cars ascend to a height of 100 feet on a ½-mile, round-trip journey over Mission Bay at the Skyride.

SAN DIEGO ZOO

To call the San Diego Zoo a "zoo" is sort of like calling Disneyland an "amusement park."

The unique animal collection, set within a one-hundred-acre tropical garden, includes 4,000 animals of 800 species from the standard favorites—lions, tigers, bears, elephants, giraffes, gorillas, and hippos—to the rare and exotic, including giant pandas from China, cuddly koalas from Australia, tree kangaroos from New Guinea, fierce Komodo dragons from Indonesia, and a collection of exotic Asian hornbills. There's also the Polar Bear Plunge, a refrigerated pool for bears and reindeer.

The best way to begin a visit is to take the forty-minute guided tour bus through miles of winding roads, down the canyons and up the mesas. Another option is the Kangaroo Bus Tour that follows the same bus route but allows visitors to hop on and off at nine stops. Finally, there is the Skyfari aerial tramway across the treetops over the Reptile House, Hippo Beach, Monkey Mesa, the Scripps Flight Aviary, and Gorilla Tropics.

The San Diego Zoo is located north of downtown in Balboa Park. Open daily from 9:00 A.M. to 4:00 P.M., until 9:00 P.M. in summer months. Admission: adults, $21.00; children, $14.00. Deluxe admission with bus tour and Skyfari aerial tram: adults, $32.00; children, $19.75. Two-park ticket (zoo and wild animal park within five days): adults, $54.45; children, $33.55. (619) 234–3153. www.sandiegozoo.org.

SAN DIEGO WILD ANIMAL PARK

In Escondido, 32 miles northeast of San Diego, the San Diego Wild Animal Park is a sprawling wildlife preserve that allows visitors to view herds of exotic animals as they might have been seen in their native Asia and Africa. On an 1,800-acre piece of land (about twenty times larger than its parent, the San Diego Zoo), more than 3,500 animals from 250 species roam.

The park includes the largest crash of rhinos in any zoo, as well as California condors, Przewalski's wild horses, lowland gorillas, Arabian oryx and addaxes from the Middle East, and herds of antelopes and gazelles.

The **Heart of Africa** is a walk through thirty acres of a re-created African wilderness with habitats from dense forests to grassy savannas and water holes. Guests walk near animals, including okapis, cheetahs, rhinos, giant elands, colobus monkeys, wattled cranes, warthogs, hornbills, and flamingos.

The Wgasa Bush Line Railway is a 5-mile, fifty-minute excursion into the bush.

Also popular are **Photo Caravan Tours,** truck rides into the heart of the large-animal enclosures. Caravans range in price from about $95 to $130 per person, depending on the length of the tour. Reservations are required; call (619) 718–3000.

The San Diego Wild Animal Park is located at 15500 San Pasqual Valley Road in Escondido, and is open every day. Winter hours are from 9:00 A.M. to 4:00 P.M.; in the summer, the park is open later in the day, depending on the hour of sunset. Admission, including Wgasa Bush Line Railway and all shows and exhibits: adults, $28.50; children (3–11), $17.50; children (2 and younger), free. Two-park ticket (San Diego Zoo and Wild Animal Park general admission to use within five days from day of purchase): adults, $54.45; children, $33.55. Parking is $6.00 per vehicle.

For information, call (760) 747–8702 or consult www.sandiegozoo.org/wap/visitor_info.html.

INDEX

ABOUT THE AUTHOR

Corey Sandler is a former newsman and editor for the Associated Press, Gannett Newspapers, Ziff-Davis Publishing, and IDG. He has written more than 160 books on travel, video games, and computers; his titles have been translated into French, Spanish, German, Italian, Portuguese, Polish, Bulgarian, Hebrew, and Chinese. When he's not traveling, he hides out with his wife and two children on Nantucket, 30 miles off the coast of Massachusetts.

Autry National Center

The Autry National Center pays homage to the American West—from its Native American roots to its pioneering past and the romance created by Hollywood. Whether it's the art of Frederic Remington or N.C. Wyeth, the tools and clothing of many cultures, or the costumes and props of film and TV, the whole family will enjoy this captivating exploration of the West's legacy.

TWO-FOR-ONE ADMISSION AT EITHER CAMPUS—

Museum of the American West in Griffith Park

or Southwest Museum of the American Indian on Mt. Washington

Autry National Center
4700 Western Heritage Way
Los Angeles, CA 90027-1462
www.autrynationalcenter.org • (323) 667-2000

Coupon valid during regular business hours and must be presented at time of purchase.

Cannot be combined with any other coupon or offer. Limit one coupon per customer.

Expires December 31, 2006.

The Getty Center

1200 Getty Center Dr.
Los Angeles, CA 90049
310-440-7300
www.getty.edu
www.getty.edu/museum

Experience art in a whole new way. Make a day of it at this gleaming, travertine icon on a hill overlooking the Pacific. Enjoy some of the world's finest collections of Classic to Pre-Renaissance art while taking in the views and the gardens.

Coupon valid during regular business hours and must be presented at time of purchase. Cannot be combined with any other coupon or offer. Limit one coupon per customer. Expires December 31, 2006.

10% discount in any museum store at the Getty Center